ACCOUNTANT'S DESK HANDBOOK

ACCOUNTANT'S DESK HANDBOOK

ALBERT P. AMEISS, PH.D.
Associate Professor of Accounting,
University of Missouri, St. Louis

NICHOLAS A. KARGAS, M.S., CPA
Assistant Professor and Chairman,
Department of Accounting,
Millikin University, Illinois

Prentice-Hall, Inc.   Englewood Cliffs, New Jersey

Prentice-Hall International, Inc., *London*
Prentice-Hall of Australia, Pty. Ltd., *Sydney*
Prentice-Hall of Canada, Ltd., *Toronto*
Prentice-Hall of India Private Ltd., *New Delhi*
Prentice-Hall of Japan, Inc., *Tokyo*
Prentice-Hall of Southeast Asia Pte. Ltd., *Singapore*
Whitehall Books, Ltd., Wellington., *New Zealand*

Third Printing . . . . . January, 1978

Library of Congress Cataloging in Publication Data

Ameiss, Albert P
    Accountant's desk handbook.

    Includes index.
    1. Accounting. 2. Financial statements.
I. Kargas, Nicholas,   joint author.
II. Title.
HF5635.A474   657   76-23101
ISBN 0-13-001396-X

Printed in the United States of America

A Word from the Authors

The *Accountant's Desk Handbook* is a comprehensive reference guide that provides prompt access to the latest in accounting theory and procedure for today's busy practitioner, financial manager and business executive.

The pace at which the field has expanded and continues to fine tune in response to the needs of today's financial environment has been such that someone whose last formal educational exposure was pre-1970 might find his/her education hopelessly out-of-date by today's standards.

That accounts for the first two reasons why this book was written.

1. It is a one-stop sourcebook that will, on demand, fill virtually any prominent voids in one's accounting knowledge.

2. It will add timely dimensions to one's professional competence in an ever-changing field that's rapidly flexing to absorb the benefits and impact of the opinion papers of the American Institute of CPAs, the position papers of the Financial Accounting and Cost Accounting Standards Boards, as well as government and quasi-government regulatory requirements.

But it does not stop there. The need for a one-stop sourcebook extends across the full spectrum of the business community making it nearly impossible to function effectively without being at least conversant with the trends, techniques and generally accepted accounting principles currently being employed in business operations. Therefore, the book will concretely flesh out the reader's knowledge in many key areas such as:

- financial accounting and methods of disclosure
- important aspects of internal reporting to aid in management decision-making, planning and control
- SEC regulations pertaining to the form and content of reports filed with the Commission
- impact of the Robinson Patman Act in management's pricing policies
- accounting regulations of the ICC and its uniform system of accounts and required reports
- Department of Labor legislation concerning labor-management reporting plus pension plan disclosure under ERISA

5

- Cost Accounting Standards Board requirements established for guidance in defense contract accounting and disclosure
- municipality accounting
- options available to management of firms in distress conditions
- accounting procedures for accomplishing a change-over from the individual proprietorship to partnership
- effective use of computer technology in a business environment
- justifying a management information system on a cost versus benefits basis
- guidelines influencing the work of the independent auditor
- objectives of audit procedures
- audit tests expected in assessing the system of internal control
- guidelines on organizing and developing audit workpapers
- requirements for audit reports and special reports such as cash basis accounting systems, nonprofit organizations and engagements where the standard short form is not applicable
- using profit performance monitors in a decentralized business atmosphere to maintain control and keep profits max-effective
- corporate application of tax accounting techniques and recommendations for improved external reporting

Throughout, a continued effort has been made to buttress pronouncements, theory, and practice with factual illustrations drawn from a cross-representative sphere of business experience and generously contributed outside sources to make otherwise staid principles easier to understand, digest, and apply to everyday business situations.

ALBERT P. AMEISS, **Ph.D.**

NICHOLAS A. KARGAS, **M.S., CPA**

Acknowledgments

The authors gratefully acknowledge advice, and helpful suggestions from a large number of professional accountants, educators, governmental representatives and accounting publishers which contributed to the development of this book. Although impossible to identify here, they have the sincere appreciation of the authors.

The contributions of the following individuals merit special recognition. Dean Emery Turner, University of Missouri—St. Louis, provided continuous encouragement throughout the years of preparation which this book required and very helpful advice with respect to the subject of quantitative accounting. Professor Schuchardt, also of the School of Business Administration, contributed importantly to the structure of the chapters on Managerial Accounting and Municipal Accounting. Providing the legal viewpoint in regard to effective tax planning and disclosure were Professor Joseph Giljum, of the same university and a practicing attorney and certified public accountant, and Mr. Lyle Pettit, Partner with Peat, Marwick, Mitchell & Co., St. Louis. The late Professor Norbert Terre assisted with a critical analysis of the chapters on financial accounting and disclosure.

Mr. Ray Kleinberg, Director of Corporate Accounting and Assistant Controller McDonnell Douglas Corporation, provided critical insights and constructive advice in connection with job order costing and management information systems. Mr. C. Walker Hutchison, Consultant in automated accounting systems, was particularly helpful in connection with the chapters involving the installation of major computer systems. With regard to government agencies, Mr. R.E. Hagen, Chief of the Section of Accounting of the Interstate Commerce Commission, assisted materially with information of the latest changes to the Commission's System of Accounts and their application.

The American Institute of Certified Public Accountants, the American Accounting Association, the National Association of Accountants and a long list of accounting publishers were most generous in granting permission to quote from their respective publications.

TABLE OF CONTENTS

Introduction to Financial Accounting disclosure formats and contents for external reporting • Use of the multiple-step and single-step types of income statements • Presentation of prior period adjustments with regard to the reporting of earnings per share, both primary and fully diluted • Accounting for future losses with respect to pronouncements of the Financial Accounting Standards Board • Presentation of optional balance sheet formats • Proper use of explanatory footnotes for optimal disclosure • Statement of Changes in Financial Position • Reports of earnings by products or corporate segments • Price-level Accounting • Consolidated statements of earnings, position report, and changes in financial position • Cost versus equity methods of accounting for investments in subsidiaries • Pooling and Purchase methods • Foreign subsidiary accounting with respect to consolidation with United States parent companies • Translation of foreign currencies • Reserves applicable to foreign operations.

Internally oriented accounting emphasizing planning, organizing, directing, staffing, and controlling as prime functions of management • Emphasis on futuristic accounting and forecasting • Relationship of Managerial Accounting to Financial and Cost Accounting • Characteristics of a Managerial Accounting system and techniques for use in decision-making • Behavior of fixed versus variable costs • Cost and investment centers to facilitate responsibility accounting and reporting • Importance of the contribution margin in the development of pricing strategies by marketing management.

Introduction to an in-depth analysis of balance sheet accounts—in the order of liquidity • Accounting pronouncements and corporate application with respect to current assets and liabilities • Short-term investments, accounts and notes receivable, contract accounts receivable, and inventories realizable within the operating cycle • Illusory inventory profits leading to the application of the last-in, first-out method of costing • Valuation of work-in-process inventories • Exclusion of deferred charges from current assets • Items properly includable under current liabilities • Estimates involved in the determination of current liabilities • Interest on payables and receivables • Exercise of right of set-off • Recording of dividends payable in cash, script, or in kind • Accounting for current liabilities involving the future • Provisions for possible future obligations and contingencies.

Continuing the analysis of balance items, long-term accounts and notes receivable are discussed in terms of existing pronouncements and current corporate practice • Use of creditor equity as a short cut to internal expansion • External expansion techniques through long-term investments, affecting business combinations • Bases of valuation of fixed assets • Control procedures for fixed asset accounting • Recording entries and details of subsidiary records suggested for property records • Questions of capitalization of major expenditures and improvements • Appreciation of fixed assets • Recovery of asset values through charges to operations including optional methods of depreciation, cost depletion, amortization and retirements • Deferred items not properly includable under current assets • Analysis of pension costs including past service • Handling of differences between cost of investments and equity in assets acquired • Timing differences in recording deferred income taxes • Valuation and presentation of long-term debt • Lease Accounting • Convertible debt • Contingencies and related appropriations of retained earnings.

Conclusion of the analysis of balance-sheet accounts • Composition of stockholders equity • Liquidation preference of preferred stock • Control procedures suggested for the maintenance of capital stock accounts • Capital in excess of par value • Treasury common stock • Stock dividends and split-ups • Control procedures with respect to items included in retained earnings • Listing of items to be excluded • Corporate readjustments and the dating of retained earnings • Use of a clearance account in effecting quasi-reorganizations • Distinctions between appropriations of retained earnings and estimated liabilities • Handling of common stock equivalents and dual presentation in the income statement showing primary and fully-diluted earnings per share • Treasury stock presentation in the balance sheet • Role of common stock in a growth-oriented firm.

• Acts of bankruptcy under the National Bankruptcy Act • Different approaches available in determining whether or not to liquidate a company • Quasi-reorganization as an alternative to bankruptcy • Accounting statements and procedures used by an administrator in discharging his responsibilities, assigned by court, in operating an insolvent firm • Accounting practice regarding the elimination of accumulated deficits • Reporting involved, including the Statement of Affairs, Realization and Liquidation, and the summary report—the executor's Charge and Discharge Statement.

Chapter Ten:
Securities and Exchange Commission and Special Regulatory Accounting Topics — 197

Constraints to corporate decision-making in the form of federal regulation • Accounting under the influence of regulatory commissions • The Securities and Exchange Commission • Form and content of registration statements and reporting under the Acts of 1933 and 1934 • Power of the Commission to determine accepted accounting principles under such legislation • Holding Company Act of 1935 • Investment Company Act of 1940 • The Commission's use of Regulation S-X and Accounting Series Releases • Management's responsibility for statements filed with the Commission • Reporting requirements, including Form 10-K, annual report to be certified by independent auditors, Form 10-Q, interim unaudited quarterly financial statements, and Form 8-K, monthly report required upon the acquisition of subsidiaries, or investments of comparable materiality • Legislation of other regulatory bodies having an impact on managerial decision-making • The Robinson-Patman Act, including allowances made for cost differences in serving customers with respect to price-fixing • The Interstate Commerce Commission's Uniform System of Accounts, and records prescribed by the Commission • Labor Department Legislation, including Labor-Management Reporting, Disclosure Act amended in 1965, labor organization information reports, Welfare and Pension Plan Disclosure Act, amended in 1962, outlining the responsibilities of plan administrators, and the Employee Retirement Income Security Act of 1974, containing broad new provisions for the private pension system • Federal Reserve System's Regulations covering various aspects of Securities Credit transactions • Cost Accounting Standards Board requirements, under Congressional authority, to introduce uniformity in procedures and disclosure to be followed by defense contractors.

Chapter Eleven:
Job Order Costing — 225

An internally oriented tool tailored to management's manufacturing needs for cost accumulation by discrete jobs within contracts • Relationship of general ledger and factory ledger accounts facilitating the use of decentralized accounting for manufacturing and delegation of authority for cost control to factory management • Comparison of budgeted costs with actuals by cost centers and programs for responsibility accounting

• Analysis of costs to assist in decision-making in typical questions of manufacturing management • Illustrated job cost ledgers and the maintenance of cost accumulation systems • Description of overhead accounts facilitating job costing by the use of overhead pools in such departments as engineering, manufacturing, procurement, and administration • Earnings determination by jobs under the cost completion method.

Another accounting speciality tailored to manufacturing management's needs where mass production of like units is involved • Methods of costing demonstrated include the weighted-average, modified first-in, first-out method, and the combination of the latter with standard costs • Discussion for bases for overhead distribution and the use of the step-down method of allocation of service department costs to production cost centers • Departmental process cost accounting and reporting illustrated, including the recognition of normal and abnormal spoilage and appropriate journal entries and disclosure of abnormal spoilage on the income statement.

Conclusion of coverage of specialized accounting procedures and techniques primarily for the benefit of manufacturing management's control efforts • References to the use of standard costs in both job costing and process costing systems were made in Chapters Eleven and Twelve, respectively, to serve as a basis for comparison • A typical standard cost system is illustrated, showing all required journal entries to enter actual and standard costs on the books, along with resulting variances for materials, labor, and overhead • Income statement presentation under standard costing systems—for both direct and absorption costing bases • Official pronouncement with respect to the inclusion of fixed overhead in inventory valuation.

Is the potential of the computer in facilitating management's functions and attaining its objectives realized only if top management insists on it? • Planning and scheduling steps in computer system installations to maximize overall corporate return on the software and hardware investment • Importance of obtaining total corporate requirements for planning the computer's workload by specific applications • Nature of the

systems and design efforts • Control techniques illustrated for meeting
installation target dates and individual system and programming
assignments • Billing methods to charge departmental users for services
performed, including allocated developmental costs • Typical system
description and write-up illustrated including input and output records,
processing and report formats.

Conclusion of Part II emphasizing management's responsibility to maximize
the return on the corporate investment in the total computer expenditure:
installation, systems development and operation • Importance of
justifying all applications developed and all programs using machine
time through effective control procedures and peer review • Adequate
top management time demanded to insure that overall corporate objectives
are determined and incorporated into management information systems
• Timely computer reporting to meet management's requirements serving
the basic functions of planning, organizing, staffing, directing and
controlling • Master information system comprising management planning,
sales order processing, materials planning and control, production
scheduling and dispatching and financial control • Flow chart of the
inputs, processing, and outputs of divisional manufacturing information
system.

The need for professional ethics and auditing standards • Obligations
under the Code of Ethics • Rules of Conduct and Numbered Interpretations
regarding independence, integrity, and objectivity • Competence and
technical standards • Relations with the client and colleagues • Other
responsibilities and practices • The auditor's opinion and generally accepted
auditing standards • General standards • Standards of field work
• Standards of reporting.

Objectives of audit procedures • Preliminary planning and the client
• Staff arrangements • Preparatory procedures • The audit program
• Interim and year-end audit procedures • Statistical sampling and
judgmental sampling • Selecting the sample size • Sampling plans and
interpreting the sampling results • Electronic data processing systems
and internal control • Other audit considerations in electronic data
processing systems • Illustrations of engagement letter format, basic
audit program, statistical sampling information sheet.

• Cash and working capital budgets • Illustration of a cash forecast
• Accepted methods of justifying capital expenditures, including the
payback method, return on investment, and discounted cash flow approach
• Program budgeting and program management • Importance of
organizational structure for successful project management, including the
breakdown of project cost responsibilities by management levels
• Accounting system components of program management, including
fund encumbrance, cost accumulation, cost accounting, and cost
reallocation • Evaluation of financial information systems for program
management.

Chapter Twenty-Three:
Effective Tax Planning and Management—Relevant
Pronouncements — 441

Impact of federal income tax expense on management's planning function
• Some relevant tax methods and elections • Doctrine of constructive
receipt • Accrual method, cash basis, hybrid methods, net worth,
installment sales, percentage of completion and completed contract
accounting methods • Emphasis on corporate tax policy disclosure
• Timing versus permanent tax differences • Illustration of income tax
disclosure on the income statement, statement of changes in financial
position, and presentation of provisions for temporary tax deferrals
• Official pronouncements regarding undistributed earnings of subsidiaries,
timing differences, the investment tax credit, and interim financial
reporting—provision for income taxes • Securities and Exchange
Commission Accounting Series Releases providing for improved disclosure
of income tax expense, presentation of prepaid expenses and deferred
charges and credits.

Chapter Twenty-Four:
Tax Accounting Management and Disclosure — 463

Importance of tax planning, management, and disclosure in accordance
with pronouncements in Chapter Twenty-three • Use of tax check-off
list and questionnaire in corporate tax review • Need for effective
communications in tax planning between client and public accountant
• Suggested tax accounting techniques for control • Application of tax
accounting principles • Disclosure of reasons for differences in the
company's effective tax rate from the statutory rate • Illustration of
disclosure in explanatory footnotes to financial statements, including
use of investment tax credit under the "flow-through" method
• Recommendations for improved income tax disclosure in the financial
statements and explanatory footnotes • A look to the future with respect
to the impact of Accounting Principles Board Opinions, Financial
Accounting Standards Board pronouncements, and governmental rulings
on financial disclosure with respect to tax accounting.

PART I

Applying Accounting Principles to Provide Full Disclosure — for External and Internal Reporting

1

Streamlined Methods in Financial Statement Presentation

The application of essential accounting principles to major types of financial and managerial reporting is emphasized in Part I. Both external and internal reporting requirements, representing the outputs of the accounting system, are identified in the first two chapters. To develop this financial disclosure, a foundation is built in Chapters 3, 4, and 5, respectively. These deal with current and noncurrent assets and liabilities and culminate with the equity accounts. Concentration is on accepted accounting principles and procedures that are recommended in recording transactions and in effectively disclosing financial information for the decision making needs of both investors and top management.

Such financial reports include conventional balance sheet and income statements; a summary of changes in financial position; price-level reporting; consolidated financial statements for entities under common control; budgetary reporting (responsibility accounting) for internal control and recommended budgetary forecasts for possible inclusion in annual corporate reports; reporting standards to be applied for foreign currency translation according to the Financial Accounting Standards Board; and, reports of earnings by product lines. These items are discussed in Part I.

ALL-PURPOSE FINANCIAL STATEMENTS

Formats for Income Statement Presentation

Two formats for income statement presentation are generally accepted—the "multiple-step" and the "single-step." A major difference between them is that the multiple-step approach indicates a number of captions and balances, including gross profit, income from operations, and net income before other items of income and expense or before federal income taxes. The single-step approach usually groups all revenues and all costs as illustrated in Figure 1-1.

As the principal financial statement, the income statement attempts to match all revenue earned during a reporting period with all costs incurred in so doing. Options exist with respect to the form of income statement which different managements prefer. The operations statement matches only those items of revenue and cost that apply to the business in which the firm is primarily engaged, effectively forcing all other costs incurred to be charged directly to retained earnings.

In the "all-inclusive" income statement, no costs are excluded for the period under review with the sole exception of *prior period adjustments.* This is in accordance with Accounting Principles Board Opinion No. 9,. "Extraordinary Items." These are non-recurring major costs that are charged against the period in which incurred and are discussed in the following paragraphs.

"Prior Period Adjustments" Distinguished From "Extraordinary Items"

Prior period adjustments are defined as items of material significance that can be traced to specific accounting periods, prior to that of the current year. Examples include substantial settlements of income taxes of prior years, contract renegotiation proceedings with respect to defense contracts, settlements of law suits, and claims from a prior period.

By contrast, *extraordinary items* are defined in APB Opinion No. 9 as those significantly different from the firm's usual costs of doing business.[1] Usual costs under this definition include *recurring, ordinary* gains or losses such as foreign exchange fluctuations of a normal nature, write-offs of receivables, and other common gains or losses, regardless of materiality.[2]

Examples of extraordinary charges are illustrated in Figure 1-1, described as "Provision for anticipated losses on divestments, net of income taxes," appearing after the caption, "Earnings before extraordinary charge." Both primary and fully diluted earnings per share (discussed next) are shown as income before and after such extraordinary charges.

Consolidated Statement of Earnings

Year Ended September 30 19XX

Net Sales	**$1,746,110,483**
Costs, Expenses and Other Charges:	
Cost of products sold	1,400,550,110
Depreciation	29,887,622
Administrative, research, distribution and general expenses. .	184,158,190
Interest	21,585,141
Earnings before income taxes and extraordinary charge . .	109,929,420
Federal, foreign and state income taxes	
including provision for deferred income taxes of	
$2,400,000 in 19X1 and $2,200,000 in 19X0	54,200,000
Earnings before Extraordinary Charge	55,729,420
Extraordinary charge—	
Provision for anticipated losses on divestments,	
net of income taxes of $4,700,000	4,800,000
Earnings for the Year	$ 50,929,420
Primary earnings per common share—	
Earnings before extraordinary charge	$1.72
Earnings for the year	$1.57
Fully diluted earnings per common share—	
Earnings before extraordinary charge	$1.63
Earnings for the year	$1.49

Figure 1-1

Consolidated Statement of Earnings Invested in the Business

Year Ended September 30 19XX

Earnings Invested in the Business **at Beginning of Year**	$ 311,727,713
Earnings for the year	50,929,420
	362,657;133
Cash dividends declared:	
Common stock	22,134,948
Preferred stock	1,373,263
	23,508,211
Earnings Invested in the Business at End of Year	$ 339,148,922

Figure 1-1 *(continued)*

Source: Ralston Purina Company Annual Report, 1971, St. Louis, Mo., p. 38.

Earnings Per Share—Primary and Fully Diluted

The term *common stock equivalents* is used in APB Opinion No. 15 to define securities *other than* common stock that should be treated *as common* in the presentation of primary earnings per share. Prior to the release of APB Opinion No. 9, the disclosure of earnings per share data in *any* form was rare. This Opinion was modified by APB Opinion No. 15, to the effect that earnings per share should be shown for earnings, both *before* and *after* extraordinary items as is done in Figure 1-1.

"Primary versus Fully Diluted" Earnings Per Share

Where a complex capital structure is involved, including potentially dilutive convertible securities, options, warrants, or other rights with respect to earnings per common share, a dual presentation is recommended on the face of the income statement. Included will be: (1) the primary earnings per share for outstanding common stock and common stock equivalents having a dilutive effect, and, (2) a "pro forma" showing reflecting the maximum dilution if all contingent issuances of common stock actually occurred in what is called a "fully diluted earnings per share."[3] Further details on earnings per share are contained in Chapter 5 which includes an analysis of net worth accounts.

In Figure 1-1, "Primary earnings per common share" are shown, followed by "Fully diluted earnings per common share," and both calculations are prepared for "Earnings before extraordinary charge" and afterward, in what is termed, "Earnings for the year."

About Future Developments

In a Discussion Memorandum, the Financial Accounting Standards Board (FASB) disclosed a project for comment, discussion, and public hearing which would lead to the creation of a financial accounting standard on "Accounting for Future Losses."[4] In this project, types of losses are considered at length as examples for the evaluation and development of criteria for future self-insured losses, future losses from expropriations by foreign governments, and future catastrophe losses of property and casualty insurance companies. Presently some companies are accruing these specific types of losses while others are charging them to expense in the period in which incurred. The objective of this Discussion Memorandum is to list and discuss the above types of accounting issues that must be resolved if a financial accounting standard is to be issued on the accounting for future losses.[5]

Accounting Changes—Effects on Earnings Per Share

In the interest of consistency, application of accounting principles once adopted should not be changed in accounting for similar transactions. Accounting treatment is recommended in APB Opinion No. 20, however, to effect four different types of corrections that are necessary to *past years'* operations because of: (1) the original use of incorrect accounting principles or procedures, or invalid estimates; (2) the need for later revision of estimates that were not in error when used, but were found incorrect when new facts were discovered; (3) the change from one *accepted* accounting principle to another, requiring adjustments to restate the accounts for the current period on the basis of what they would have been had the newly-adopted principle been in effect from the beginning; and, (4) changes in the make-up of the accounting entity making necessary the restatement of prior periods' operating results for the new entity.[6] In addition, earnings per share amounts, primary and fully diluted, should be shown on the restated pro forma income statement.[7]

Balance Sheet Formats

The conventional balance sheet or position statement form is a statement form that lists assets in the order of liquidity. This approach emphasizes the firm's working capital position and the extent of its short-term solvency. The fixed assets and long-term liabilities usually follow. Deferred items of cost and income, respectively, are reported next. The equities' interests conclude with a presentation of the elements comprising stockholders' equity. Although commonly accepted, this format varies with specific industries.

For example, regulated utilities in the United States report properties *first* and therefore use a reverse order of liquidity as illustrated in Figure 1-2, applying to Union Electric Company of Missouri. The source of such assets is shown first on the right-hand side of the balance sheet headed, "Capitalization." There follows "Long-term debt" and finally, "Current Liabilities."

Figure 1-2 illustrates the components of the firm's capitalization, both in the form of capital stock and retained earnings and also in long-term debt. Included in the stockholders' equity are the common stock less reacquired or treasury stock, and installments received on common stock subscriptions. Preferred stock and premium on the sale of preferred stock are shown as one figure accompanied by an explanatory footnote. Finally, capital surplus, or paid-in capital, is indicated as being principally the result of premium on common stock. This is detailed by footnote, as is retained earnings, completing the stockholders' equity section.

Another accepted balance sheet form is the financial position format which presents current assets less current liabilities, to arrive at working capital. Added to this figure is the total of all other assets. The total of long-term liabilities is subtracted, resulting in total stockholders' equity.

Use of Footnotes in Financial Statements

The disclosure of certain essential items of information in the form of footnotes is an integral part of the financial statement but should not be considered as a substitute for disclosure of accounting treatments in the body of the statement.

Footnotes provide the reader with a more complete understanding of the financial statement, including information as to: (1) the bases on which assets are stated; (2) the principles of consolidation; (3) commitments of an unusual nature such as compensation and stock option plans; (4) changes in application of accounting principles; and, (5) as indicated in conjunction with Figure 1-2, the composition of capital surplus, retained earnings, long-term debt and other balance sheet items requiring detailed explanation.

Retained Earnings

Retained earnings statements are reconciliations of retained earnings at the beginning and end of the period involved. In addition, a statement of changes in paid-in capital or capital surplus may be given or a footnote may disclose the particulars of additions and deletions during the period under review.

Figure 1-1 illustrates a "consolidated statement of earnings invested in the business" showing the balance in this account at both the beginning and end of the year. Illustrating the "clean surplus" philosophy, only the year's earnings are credited and dividends are charged against retained earnings. APB Opinion No. 9 recommends the charging of prior period items to retained earnings as noted above.

SPECIAL AND SUPPLEMENTARY STATEMENTS

Certain supplementary statements to the primary financial statements include: (1) the statement of sources and applications of funds, or the statement of changes in financial position described in APB Opinion No. 19;[8] (2) reports of earnings by product line; and, (3) comparisons of *conventional* statements with statements revised to give effect to price-level changes. These statements are described in detail below.

(1) Statement of Changes in Financial Position

In APB Opinion No. 19, the Board recommended that the above statement be required to supplement the financial statements with information that the income statement and balance sheet do not provide about the flow of funds and changes in financial position during each period.[9] This supplementary statement applies to all profit-oriented business entities. Certain guidelines are to be followed. Working capital or cash provided by operations for the period should be disclosed separately from that generated by extraordinary items.[10]

CONSOLIDATED BALANCE SHEET

December 31,
19XX

(Thousands of dollars)

Assets

UTILITY PROPERTIES, at original cost:

Electric	$1,777,641
Gas	35,822
Steam	9,600
Other	5,351
	1,828,414
Less accumulated depreciation	398,362
Utility properties, net	1,430,052

INVESTMENTS, at cost:

Capital stock of Electric Energy, Inc.	2,480
Other investments	964
Total investments	3,444

CURRENT ASSETS:

Cash	5,512
Deposits for payment of interest, and other deposits	4,373
Accounts receivable (less reserve for doubtful accounts of $245,002 and $307,852, at respective dates)	30,200
Unbilled revenue	14,341
Materials and supplies, including construction materials at average cost	16,265
Prepayments and other assets	848
Total current assets	71,539
	$1,505,035

Figure 1-2

Source: Union Electric Company 1971 Annual Report, pp. 16, 17

Union Electric Company and Subsidiaries

December 31,
19XX

(Thousands of dollars)

Capital and Liabilities

CAPITALIZATION:

Capital stock and surplus—
    Common stock, $5 par value, authorized 35,000,000, outstanding
      29,046,291 and 29,042,752 shares, at respective dates (excluding
      42,990 shares at par value in treasury); 411,969 and 517,360 shares
      reserved for issuance to employees (at $20.82 per share) pursuant

to an installment purchase plan	$ 145,231
Installments from employees on common stock subscriptions	3,850
Capital surplus, principally premium on common stock	
(see accompanying statement)	126,817
Retained earnings (see accompanying statement)	154,811
	430,709
Preferred stock, including premium of $1,570,755	
(see accompanying statement)	184,655
Total capital stock and surplus	615,364
Long-term debt (see accompanying statement)	748,000
Total capitalization	1,363,364
UNAMORTIZED PREMIUM, LESS EXPENSE, ON DEBT	3,056
CONTRIBUTIONS BY CUSTOMERS FOR CONSTRUCTION	
OF PROPERTY	6,722
ACCUMULATED DEFERRED TAXES ON INCOME	18,706

CURRENT LIABILITIES:

Accounts and wages payable	23,361
Bank loans and commercial paper	45,700
Taxes accrued	16,789
Other current liabilities	27,337
Total current liabilities	113,187
	$1,505,035

Figure 1-2 (continued)

A consolidated statement of changes in financial position is illustrated in Figure 1-3. Beginning with net income, items are added back which are neither sources nor applications of working capital under the heading "Charges to Income not involving working capital." The result is described as "working capital provided by operations." There should follow the working capital provided by extraordinary items and other sources of working capital. Total disbursements of working capital should then be deducted, resulting in a final item in the statement representing the net change in working capital.

CONSOLIDATED STATEMENT OF CHANGES IN FINANCIAL POSITION

	19XX
Financial resources were provided by:	
Operations—	
Net income for the year	$ 71,638,000
Charges to income not involving working capital—	
Depreciation	34,948,000
Deferred income taxes	6,829,000
Deferred investment tax credit	713,000
Other, net	804,000
Working capital provided by operations	114,932,000
Sale of common stock under option plans	3,763,000
Fair market value of common stock issued in exchange for real estate	3,881,000
	122,576,000
Financial resources were used for:	
Capital expenditures	73,214,000
Investment properties	2,208,000
Cash dividends paid	23,784,000
Reduction in long-term debt	11,509,000
Increased investment in unconsolidated subsidiaries, excluding transfer of land in the amount of $1,689,000 and $2,309,000, respectively	4,536,000
Other, net	93,000
	115,344,000
Increase in working capital	$ 7,232,000

Figure 1-3

Analysis of Changes in Working Capital

Increase (decrease) in current assets:

Cash	$	5,803,000
Marketable securities		2,333,000
Accounts and notes receivable		2,021,000
Inventories		(5,953,000)
		4,204,000

Decrease (increase) in current liabilities:

Accounts payable		3,863,000
Accrued salaries and wages		(951,000)
Accrued taxes, other than income taxes		(9,603,000)
Estimated federal and state income taxes		7,293,000
Other current liabilities		2,426,000
		3,028,000
Increase in working capital	$	7,232,000

Figure 1-3 *(continued)*

Source: Anheuser-Busch, Incorporated. Annual Report, 1971, St. Louis, Mo., p. 17

(2) Reports of Earnings by Products or Product Lines

Figure 1-4 shows the desirability of disclosure of revenues and profits by separable industry segments of a firm as urged of diversified companies in APB Statement No. 2, "Disclosure of Supplemental Financial Information by Diversified Companies."[11]

Information showing the profitability of major product lines, particularly over a period of years is of interest to investors, stockholders, financial analysts and, of course, internal management. A five-year period is used in Figure 1-4. A "percentage-type" pie chart is used to show profit from four major product lines: international 13%, agricultural 39%, restaurant 10%, and consumer products 38%.

Analysis of both production and distribution costs by products or product lines is required. In Figure 1-4, "earnings by business groups" result from a distribution of *all* costs, except "unallocated corporate expenses," to the four major business segments named.

Conglomerate Reporting of Earnings by Product Classes

SEC Releases No. 4922 and No. 8397, issued September 4, 1968, contained proposals that registrant companies state, for each of the past

Sales by Business Groups

(Dollars in millions)

Agricultural $1027.5

Restaurant $191.2

International $553.6

Consumer $661.3

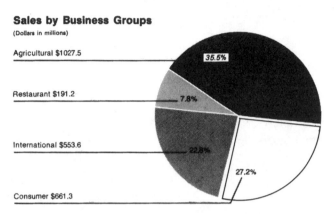

5 YEAR SALES COMPARISON BY BUSINESS GROUPS

| | Year Ended September 30 | | | |
	x3	x2	x1	x0
Agricultural	$1,027.5	$ 753.5	$ 753.8	$ 732.8
Consumer	661.3	474.9	394.8	321.9
International	553.6	400.5	332.0	293.3
Restaurant	191.2	145.2	111.1	69.2
Continuing Operations	2,433.6	1,774.1	1,591.7	1,417.2
Discontinued Operations		59.3	154.4	149.8
Total Sales	$2,433.6	$1,833.4	$1,746.1	$1,567.0

AGRICULTURAL	CONSUMER	INTERNATIONAL	RESTAURANT
ANIMAL & POULTRY FEEDS, POULTRY PRODUCTS, SOYBEAN PROCESSING AND RELATED OPERATIONS.	PET FOODS, SEA FOODS, CEREALS, RY KRISP, SOY PROTEIN AND OTHER PRODUCTS.	ANIMAL & POULTRY FEEDS, POULTRY PRODUCTS, PET FOODS AND OTHER RELATED OPERATIONS (INCLUDES CANADA).	JACK IN THE BOX RESTAURANTS AND SPECIALTY DINNER HOUSES.

Earnings by Business Groups

(Dollars in millions)

Agricultural $69.0

Restaurant $22.7

International $25.1

Consumer $77.5

5 YEAR EARNINGS COMPARISON BY BUSINESS GROUPS

| | Year Ended September 30 | | | |
	x3	x2	x1	x0
Agricultural	$ 69.0	$ 45.0	$ 63.2	$ 68.5
Consumer	77.5	73.9	60.4	47.0
International	25.1	23.7	18.8	18.0
Restaurant	22.7	19.0	13.5	12.2
Earnings Before Items Below	194.3	161.6	155.9	145.7
Discontinued Operations		(6.5)	(13.4)	(1.8)
Unallocated Corporate Expenses[1]	(22.5)	(13.3)	(11.0)	(12.1)
Interest Expense	(25.0)	(21.6)	(21.6)	(15.6)
Earnings Before Income Taxes[2]	$146.8	$120.2	$109.9	$116.2

Figure 1-4

Source: Ralston Purina Company Annual Report 1973, p. 29

five years, the approximate percentage of sales and the contribution to net income attributable to any class of products that contributed 10% or more to total sales and operating revenues, or to income before extraordinary items and income taxes, during either of the last two fiscal years.

(3) Price-Level Financial Statements

There are two procedures that give effect to price changes on a continuing basis. Of these, *Common-dollar accounting* deals *exclusively* with general price-level changes. It adjusts for *changes in the size of the measuring unit* used in accounting, namely, the dollars of each period's transactions varying in purchasing power during inflationary or deflationary periods. A restatement of the period's transactions is involved, using as the measuring unit, dollars of uniform general purchasing power.[12]

A second approach to price-level accounting is that of *Current cost reporting,* which modifies the matching concept of accounting by *changing the timing* of recognition of income without changing the total amounts involved.[13]

APB Statement No. 3, issued in June 1969, expressed the belief that general price-level information was not required for fair presentation of basic financial statements. General price-level statements may be used, however, to present useful information not available from basic historical-dollar statements but should be presented only as informative supplements to the basic financial statements, namely the balance sheet and income statement.[14]

Consolidations

Volumes have been written on the subject of consolidation accounting. But, since this is a pragmatic, "how-to-do-it" type text, coverage concentrates on firms faced with consolidation problems and their approaches to practical solutions.

Figures 1-1, 1-2, and 1-3 illustrate a Consolidated Statement of Earnings, Consolidated Balance Sheet, and Consolidated Statement of Changes in Financial Position. The Principles of Consolidation underlying the preparation of such statements are based on guidelines contained in Accounting Research Bulletin No. 51, "Consolidated Financial Statements," and APB Opinion No. 16, entitled "Business Combinations."

Control Still Essential

Both the American Institute of Certified Public Accountants and the Securities and Exchange Commission consider the element of control an absolute requirement for consolidation. According to Accounting Research Bulletin No. 51, the usual condition for a controlling financial interest is ownership of a majority voting interest, meaning direct or indirect control of over 50% of the outstanding voting shares of another company. However, control can be exercised by other means.

In Rule 4.02 of Regulation S-X, the Securities and Exchange Commission recognized that consolidated financial statements are the primary statements necessary for fair presentation. The Commission indicated that the registrant shall follow principles of inclusion or exclusion that clearly exhibit the financial condition and results of operations of the registrant and its subsidiaries.

Reasons Accepted for Non-Consolidation

In practice, certain reasons are accepted for non-consolidation of subsidiaries. These include major differences from the parent company in operations, in dates for closing the books, and lack of effective control by the parent company. However, the continuing trend toward corporate diversification and the increase in conglomerates, discussed in the next section, suggest the importance of Accounting Research and Terminology Bulletin No. 51. The latter suggests that "even though a group of companies is heterogeneous in character, it may be better to make a full consolidation than to present a large number of separate statements."[15]

Requirement for a Statement of "Principles of Consolidation"

An example of accounting practice in the United States is a General Motors Corporation Annual Report in which the principles of consolidation followed by the company are contained in a note to the financial statements to include *all subsidiary companies,* domestic and foreign, engaged in the relatively comparable operations of manufacturing or wholesale marketing. A separate schedule was shown for foreign operations outside the United States and Canada but included in the consolidated financial statements.[16]

A general reserve applicable to foreign operations was established by General Motors, to absorb extraordinary losses such as those arising from discontinuing operations in foreign countries either voluntarily or because of conditions beyond the corporation's control. Investments in subsidiary companies not consolidated because of operations unlike the parent's consisted of General Motors Acceptance Corporation and Subsidiaries. Exclusions from consolidation therefore were limited to finance and insurance companies only—activities wholly outside those of the company's primary business.

Another approach of a United States corporation to consolidate the operations of *both* domestic and foreign subsidiary companies is that of the International Business Machines Corporation.[17] A separate schedule was shown for consolidated foreign operations, indicating the net assets employed in such operations, and a comparison of gross income and net earnings compared with those of the previous year.

Cost versus Equity Method of Accounting
for Investments in Subsidiaries

In APB Opinion No. 18, the Accounting Principle Board defined the above methods of carrying investments in subsidiaries on the books of the parent companies.

Under the *cost method,* the parent company (investor) records investment in the stock of the subsidiary at cost. Income is recorded on the parent's books from this investment only when dividends are received. Therefore, the net accumulated earnings of the subsidiary subsequent to the date of investment are recognized by the parent only when and to the extent that they are distributed by the subsidiary. By the same token, dividends received in excess of the subsidiary's earnings when acquired are considered a return of investment to the parent.

Under the *equity method,* the acquiring company (the new parent) records an investment in the stock of the subsidiary at cost, but adjusts the amount of that investment each accounting period to recognize the parent's share of the earnings or losses of the subsidiary after the date of acquisition. The amount of this change in the subsidiary's equity is included in the net income of the parent.

Dividends received from the subsidiary reduce the carrying amount of the investment in contrast to treatment under the cost method in which such dividends represent the parent's only credit to income from the subsidiary. A series of operating losses of the subsidiary may indicate that a decrease in value of the investment has occurred, according to APB Opinion No. 18, which is not temporary and should be recognized on the parent's books even though the decrease exceeds what would otherwise be recognized under the equity method.[18]

The equity method was used in carrying the parent's investment in subsidiaries with respect to the consolidated statements shown in Figures 1-1 (Ralston-Purina) and 1-3 (Anheuser-Busch), but the cost method was used by Union Electric Company (Figure 1-2).

CONSOLIDATIONS, CONGLOMERATES, AND MULTINATIONAL ENTERPRISES

Three events of the past decade were identified by Fisch and Mellman that stress the growing importance of business combinations. These are: (1) the great merger movement; (2) the dominant trend toward conglomeration; and, (3) the growth of international business which has not only increased the complexity of intercorporate relationships, but also the problems of accounting for investments in affiliated companies.[19]

Background information contained in APB Opinion No. 16 cited such major developments in describing two methods of accounting for business combinations, namely the pooling and purchase methods.

Most business combinations before World War II were classified either as a "merger," according to APB Opinion No. 16, that is, the acquisition of one company by another, or as a "consolidation," the formation of a new corporation. Both types of combinations generally followed traditional principles of accounting for the acquisition of assets or issuance of shares of stock.[20]

After World War II the legal form of the combination was emphasized less than that of a "continuance of the former ownership or a new ownership."[21] New ownership was accounted for as a purchase; continuing ownership was accounted for as a pooling of interests according to APB Opinion No. 16. Carrying forward the stockholders' equity and including retained earnings of the companies involved became a vital part of the pooling of interest method.

The purchase and pooling of interests methods differ markedly in the amounts ascribed to assets and liabilities at the time of combination and income reported for the combined enterprise, as indicated below.

Purchase Method

Under this method an acquiring corporation records acquired assets at cost, less liabilities assumed from the selling corporation. Any difference between the cost of the acquired company and the fair market values of tangible and identifiable assets less liabilities is recorded as a debit or credit differential. Other terms used for such differences are goodwill and negative goodwill.

Pooling of Interests Method

The pooling of interests method accounts for a merging or uniting of the ownership of two or more companies without changing such ownership interests. The exchange of equity securities permits this marriage to be accomplished without the disbursing of cash or other resources and with the stockholders' interests continuing as before. The assets and liabilities of both companies are carried forward to the new corporation at prior book values, with certain exceptions described below.

The Accounting Principles Board concluded that both the purchase method and the pooling of interests method are acceptable in accounting for business combinations, but not as alternatives. Particular circumstances dictate the use of one or the other in specific transactions. For example, as observed above, the *pooling of interests* method of accounting applies only to combinations effected by an exchange of stock, not those involving cash, other assets, or liabilities.

The *purchase* method of accounting applies to combinations effected by paying cash, distributing other assets, or incurring liabilities, according to APB Opinion No. 16. Under the pooling of interests method, an exchange of stock to effect a business combination is really a transaction between the combining *stockholder groups* and not a sale of a corporate entity. Therefore, a new basis of accountability for the assets of the combined corporations is not justified under pooling.[22]

Differences in accounting treatment under the two methods are the following:

Under the Purchase Method

(a) Assets and liabilities of the acquired firm are reported by the purchaser at cost at date of acquisition—the price paid for the acquired company representing the *fair market value* at that date;

(b) Individual assets acquired are reported at individual fair market values at date of acquisition and liabilities at present "debt" value;

(c) The excess of the total purchase cost over the book value of assets acquired (less the liabilities assumed) is reported as a debit differential or goodwill from acquisition, subsequently amortized as a charge to income, or allocated to the subsidiary's assets to bring them up to their fair market value. Any excess may be amortized as goodwill over a period not to exceed 40 years.

If a credit differential resulted, the excess of book value over the cost of the subsidiary is used to reduce the latter's asset values all the way to zero, if necessary, and the remainder amortized as deferred income over not more than 40 years.

Under the Pooling Method

(a) Assets and liabilities of the joining companies are reported at previously existing *book values* of each. Adjustments may be made to reflect consistent applications of accounting principles. However, fair market values at the time of the combination are *not* substituted for book values as is the case under the purchase method;

(b) Goodwill (or differential of any kind) does *not* result from the combination as would be the case under the purchase method; and,

(c) Retained earnings of the combining companies are simply added to determine the retained earnings balance of the combined companies at date of acquisition.

Conglomerate Reporting of Earnings by Product Classes

SEC Releases No. 4922 and No. 8397, issued September 4, 1968, contained proposals that registrant companies state, for each of the past five years, the approximate amount of percentage of sales and the contribution to net income attributable to any class of products which contributed 10% or more to total sales and operating revenues, or to income before extraordinary items and income taxes, during either of the last two fiscal years.

Non-Consolidation Due to Differing Accounting Principles

As noted earlier, a pronouncement on consolidation, stipulated one reason for non-consolidation of subsidiaries to be material conflict in the accounting principles followed by the subsidiary and the parent. In a survey made by one of the authors of this text, a number of United States companies reported that they consolidated the operating results of foreign subsidiaries notwithstanding major differences in the accounting principles followed by such subsidiaries. Such techniques are illustrated below.

Consolidation Policies with Respect to Foreign Subsidiary Operations

Foreign subsidiary reporting usually facilitates the parent's consolidation procedures. To aid these procedures, the subsidiary (1) provides data that when consolidated with the parent's financial information *will* result in financial statements prepared in accordance with the latter's generally accepted accounting principles; (2) conforms to the subsidiary's local governmental financial reporting requirements; and (3) permits the most advantageous tax administration in the subsidiary's country.[23]

As to the techniques followed in consolidations, financial statements of foreign subsidiaries of United States companies are generally prepared in accordance with the latter's accounting principles and no *real* difficulty in reconciling the parent's statements with official governmental reporting requirements of other countries appears evident. Adjustments can be made in preparing consolidated financial statements so that if local rules require that tax calculations be based on the *actual* books, such special treatment is given in consolidation.

Decentralization Approach to Foreign Subsidiaries

A decentralized managerial approach to foreign subsidiary accounting procedures and disclosure was reported by Standard Oil of New Jersey, under which the foreign subsidiary's financial statements were certified by public accountants who were familiar with local regulations and requirements in that country as well as with the general accounting practices of the parent company. As a result, financial statements received from more than 200 Exxon (previously Standard Oil of N.J.) affiliates were consolidated by the parent with only a few minor adjustments applied in consolidation. Comparable decentralization was found on the part of other large multinational enterprises.[24]

Mobil Oil Corporation reported the use of an International Chart of Accounts, distributed to all Mobil subsidiaries, which is of assistance to the foreign subsidiaries in preparing their financial reports for consolidation purposes and includes sections that:

(a) Define the various balance sheet and income statement accounts that are recommended for each subsidiary's use;

(b) Outline and explain the format in which the balance sheet and income statements should be submitted;

(c) Describe the procedures to be followed for the consolidation of accounts; and,

(d) Establish the principles to be used for the conversion of foreign currency amounts into U.S. dollars.[25]

Since Mobil is incorporated in the United States, consolidated financial reports must conform with the generally accepted accounting principles of the United States. However, the foreign subsidiaries may not necessarily follow these same procedures in their local currency recording and reporting and may follow local accounting customs.

Principles of Consolidation—Domestic and Foreign Subsidiaries

The financial statements of Ralston Purina (Figure 1-1) were supported by a statement of consolidation policy. The accounts of the company and its majority-owned subsidiaries were consolidated. Minority interests in earnings of certain subsidiaries, the company's share of the net earnings of unconsolidated 20% to 50%-owned companies, and foreign exchange losses were indicated as immaterial and included in administrative, research, distribution and general expenses. Note that the accounts of the foreign subsidiaries were translated at current exchange rates, except for properties and related depreciation, which were translated at rates prevailing at dates of acquisition.[26]

General Motors reported on "Significant Accounting Policies" in a footnote to its annual consolidated financial statement. Included were descriptions of its *principles of consolidation, translation of foreign currencies,* and *general reserve applicable to foreign operations.* Excerpts follow:

PRINCIPLES OF CONSOLIDATION

The consolidated financial statements include the accounts of the Corporation and all domestic and foreign subsidiaries which are engaged principally in manufacturing or wholesale marketing of General Motors products. General Motors' share of earnings or losses of nonconsolidated subsidiaries and of associates in which at least 20% of the voting securities is owned is generally included in consolidated income under the equity method of accounting. Intercompany items and transactions between companies included in the consolidation are eliminated and unrealized intercompany profits on sales, to nonconsolidated subsidiaries and to associates, the investments in which are accounted for by the equity method, are deferred.

TRANSLATION OF FOREIGN CURRENCIES

Real estate, plants and equipment, accumulated depreciation and obsolescence and the provision for depreciation and obsolescence are translated into United States dollars at exchange rates in effect at the dates the related assets were acquired. Other assets and liabilities, deferred credits and reserves are translated at exchange rates in effect at the date of the balance sheet; other items of income and expense are translated at average exchange rates for the months in which the transactions occurred. Accumulated unrealized net loss from translation of foreign currency accounts of any foreign subsidiary is charged to income and accumulated unrealized net gain is deferred.

GENERAL RESERVE APPLICABLE TO FOREIGN OPERATIONS

The general reserve applicable to foreign operations . . . is available to absorb extraordinary losses, such as losses from discontinuing foreign operations in any locality, either voluntarily or because of conditions beyond the Corporation's control. There has been no change in this reserve since its establishment.[27]

A minimum of 20% of voting stock served as the criterion for consolidation of General Motors subsidiaries that were accounted for on the equity basis. A reserve was made available for extraordinary losses and emergencies resulting from loss of control of foreign subsidiaries. This reserve is deducted from "Net Assets Attributable to Operations Outside the United States and Canada" in Note 12, "Foreign Operations" reproduced as Figure 1-5. In addition, "Undistributed earnings of nonconsolidated subsidiaries and associates" are added back to net income as a source of funds in that company's "Statement of Changes in Consolidated Financial Position," Figure 1-6. Conversely the presentation of such funds generated from foreign operations is matched under the "Application of Funds" by the "Investments in nonconsolidated subsidiaries and associates."

Note 12. FOREIGN OPERATIONS

Net assets, sales and income attributable to operations outside the United States and Canada, included in the consolidated financial statements, are summarized in the following table. Net sales include sales to United States and Canadian operations. Net income includes provisions for deferred income taxes on unremitted earnings of such foreign operations and other consolidation adjustments and, includes earnings (loss) attributable to the major overseas manufacturing subsidiaries, as follows: Adam Opel AG, $97 million; General Motors-Holden's Pty. Limited, $20 million; and Vauxhall Motors Limited, ($9 million).

Net Assets Attributable to Operation Outside the United States and Canada

	Western Europe	United Kingdom, Australia, New Zealand and South Africa	Other, Principally Mexico and South America	December 31, 19X2 Total	December 31, 19X1 Total
			(In Millions)		
Assets:					
Total current assets	$ 766	$ 648	$376	$1,790	$1,479
Property—net	526	360	195	1,081	1,075
Other assets	24	17	105	146	109
Total assets	1,316	1,025	676	3,017	2,663
Liabilities:					
Bank borrowings and notes payable	68	142	62	272	380
Other current liabilities	376	258	134	768	614
Total current liabilities	444	400	196	1,040	994
Long-term debt of subsidiaries	362	65	117	544	366
Other liabilities and reserves	143	70	18	231	206
Total liabilities	949	535	331	1,815	1,566
Balance	$ 367	$ 490	$345	1,202	1,097
Less General Reserve Applicable to Foreign Operations				142	142
Net Assets Attributable to Operations Outside the United States and Canada				$1,060	$ 955
Net Sales Attributable to Operations Outside the United States and Canada				$4,741	$4,112
Net Income Attributable to Operations Outside the United States and Canada				$ 169	$ 103

Figure 1-5

Source: General Motors Corporation Annual Report for 1972, p. 34

GENERAL MOTORS CORPORATION and Consolidated Subsidiaries

STATEMENT OF CHANGES IN CONSOLIDATED FINANCIAL POSITION

for the years ended December 31, 19X2 and 19X1

	Year 19X2	Year 19X1
Source of Funds		
Net income	$2,162,806,765	$1,935,709,493
Depreciation and obsolescence of real estate, plants and equipment .	912,432,511	873,102,334
Amortization of special tools	874,221,875	917,566,408
Undistributed earnings of nonconsolidated subsidiaries and associates, deferred income taxes, etc.—net	(98,357,457)	(164,609,583)
Total current operations	3,851,103,694	3,561,768,652
Disposals and retirements of property	57,171,936	57,382,512
Increase in long-term debt	175,259,397	334,394,340
Proceeds from sale of newly issued common stock	706,164	922,090
Total	4,084,241,191	3,954,467,594
Application of Funds		
Dividends paid to stockholders	1,285,994,571	985,371,948
Expenditures for real estate, plants and equipment	940,037,584	1,012,968,050
Expenditures for special tools	898,542,491	630,702,160
Investments in nonconsolidated subsidiaries and associates	9,786,630	47,514,676
Other—net	(84,507,720)	15,114,436
Total	3,049,853,556	2,691,671,270
Increase in working capital during the year	1,034,387,297	1,262,796,324
Working capital at beginning of the year	4,530,387,297	3,267,590,973
Working capital at end of the year	$5,564,774,932	$4,530,387,297
Increase (Decrease) in Working Capital by Element		
Cash, government securities and time deposits.	($ 395,185,967)	$2,911,682,479
Accounts and notes receivable	81,988,467	998,547,666
Inventories	208,594,182	(123,491,324)
Prepaid expenses	106,417,795	221,673,259
Accounts, drafts and loans payable	(263,513,545)	(546,417,302)
United States, foreign and other income taxes payable	975,507,081	(1,522,071,177)
Other taxes, payrolls and sundry accrued items	320,579,622	(677,127,277)
Increase in working capital during the year	$1,034,387,635	$1,262,796,324

Certain amounts for 19X1 have been reclassified to reflect comparability with classifications for 19X2.

Figure 1-6

Source: General Motors Corporation Annual Report for 1972, p. 32.

By contrast with companies that consolidated subsidiaries owned by as little as 20% of the outstanding voting stock, Texaco reported companies in which its investment was *less* than 50% as nonsubsidiary companies. The latter were *not included* in the consolidated financial statements. These investments were carried at cost on the parent's books but the information was given in a footnote as to the parent's equity in such nonsubsidiary companies as follows:

> Texaco's equity in earnings of nonsubsidiary companies accounted for on the equity basis exceeded dividends received . . . by $80,869,000 . . . .
>
> Texaco's interest in the net earnings of other nonsubsidiary companies, which are carried at cost, approximated dividends received from such companies . . . . Equity in the underlying net assets of nonsubsidiary companies carried at cost exceeded the carrying value of the investment in such companies by approximately $1,000,000.
>
> At December 31, 19___, investments in nonsubsidiary companies owned 50% or less consisted of $763,220,000 applicable to companies operating in the Eastern Hemisphere and $85,254,000 applicable to companies operating in the Western Hemisphere. [28]

There appears to be a definite trend in practice toward the consolidation of foreign subsidiaries, with the most frequently excluded subsidiaries being those located in countries with a history of recurring political and economic instability. Rule 4.02 of SEC Regulation S-X cautions in this respect that due consideration be given to the propriety of consolidating foreign subdiary operations which are carried on in terms of *restricted foreign currencies* with the operations of domestic that is, United States corporations.

Perhaps the spectacular growth of the multinational enterprises will lead to the development of more meaningful uniformity both domestically and between countries as far as accounting principles and financial disclosure are concerned. At present much remains to be desired in this respect as indicated in this Chapter. Accounting differences among countries will have to be reconciled, or accounting practices eliminated which are clearly improper when compared with the selected standard.

If this is accomplished, a global view of the multinational enterprise may become a reality in which domestic and foreign affiliates can be given identical treatment in consolidation and investors may enjoy meaningful uniformity in reporting.

REFERENCES

[1]American Institute of Certified Public Accountants, Opinions of the Accounting Principles Board (APB Opinion No. 9). "Reporting the Results of Operations." December 1966, par. 19.

[2]*Ibid.*, par. 21.

[3]American Institute of Certified Public Accountants, APB Opinion No. 15, "Earnings Per Share." par. 15.

[4]Financial Accounting Standards Board Discussion Memorandum, entitled, "Accounting for Future Losses." March 13, 1974.

[5]*Ibid.*

[6]American Institute of Certified Public Accountants, APB Opinion No. 20, "Accounting Changes." para. 7 thru 13.

[7]*Ibid.*, par. 26.

[8]American Institute of Certified Public Accountants, APB Opinion No. 19, "Reporting Changes in Financial Statements." par. 7.

[9]*Ibid.*, par. 12.

[10]*Ibid.*, par. 10.

[11]American Institute of Accountants, APB Statement No. 2, "Disclosure of Supplemental Financial Information by Diversified Companies." par. 11 & 12.

[12]Earl A. Spiller, Jr., *Financial Accounting,* 1971, pages 607-8. Reprinted with permission from Richard D. Irwin, Inc., Homewood, Ill.

[13]*Ibid.*

[14]American Institute of Accountants, ARS No. 3, "General Price-Level Statements." par. 25.

[15]American Institute of Accountants, ARB No. 51, "Consolidated Financial Statements," par. 3, *Accounting Research and Terminology Bulletins,* Final Edition, 1961.

[16]General Motors Corporation Annual Report 1970, page 36.

[17]IBM Annual Report 1970, page 27.

[18]American Institute of Certified Public Accountants, APB Opinion No. 13, "Equity Method for Investments in Common Stock." par. 6.

[19]Jack H. Fisch and Martin Mellman, "Accounting for Investments in Affiliated Companies," *The Journal of Accountancy.* November 1969, Vol. 128, No. 5, page 42.

[20]American Institute of Certified Public Accountants, APB Opinion No. 16, "Business Combinations." par. 9.

[21]American Institute of Certified Public Accountants, *Accounting Research and Terminology Bulletin,* Final Edition, 1961, American Institute of CPAs No. 40. par. 1.

[22]*Op. cit.,* American Institute of Certified Public Accountants, APB Opinion No. 16, par. 28.

[23]The Quaker Oats Company, letter of December 15, 1966, signed by R.A. Bowen.

[24]Exxon (previously Standard Oil Company, New Jersey) letter dated December 22, 1966, signed by the Controller.

[25]Mobil Oil Corporation, letter dated August 25, 1966, signed by C.E. Arthur.

[26]Ralston Purina Company Annual Report, page 32.

[27]General Motors Corporation Annual Report for 1972, page 33.

[28]Texaco Annual Report of 1971, Footnotes to the Financial Statements.

2 Managerial Accounting for Internal Reporting

This chapter describes managerial accounting and reporting and the cost and revenue concepts considered appropriate for effective internal accounting. The total accounting function is divided into (1) financial accounting, (2) cost accounting, and (3) managerial accounting, in order to differentiate and indicate interrelationships.

Description of Accounting for Management

The broad purpose of the overall accounting system of an organization is to provide quantitative or financial information to *both* internal (management) and external audiences. Bookkeeping and statistical records maintained by a business firm are merely compilations of data, converted through selection and organization of relevant data into accounting reports designed to serve the specific needs of particular report readers.

To meet the needs of different audiences, different techniques of accounting and reporting have been developed by the accounting profession. The first of these is financial accounting, a term frequently used to describe accounting reports designed primarily for external audiences, as discussed in Chapter 1. Reports intended primarily for internal use have been designated as "managerial" accounting.[1] The latter has evolved from the former.

In tracing the development of managerial accounting, the National Association of Accountants found that beginning as a technique for recording a proprietor's financial condition, modern *management accounting* began when the accountant undertook to measure gains and losses from operations to help management in appraising the *outcome of decisions.*[2] Keeping a historical record remains a basic accounting function, but much greater emphasis is now placed upon making such accumulated experience a more useful guide to decision-making which will affect financial results *in the future.*[3] Thus, while financial accounting concerns history, managerial accounting uses such history to focus primarily on the future.

Orientation to the Future

The overall objective of managerial accounting is to aid management in predicting, controlling or influencing the *future operations,* sales and profits of the business firm. In their attempt to plan their future, business managers have had to develop methods for predicting the course of future events, for determining what factors they could influence or control, and for developing planning and feed-back techniques for evaluating performance and appraising these plans and drawing up new ones.

A review of the literature indicates that authors who characterize "management" as choosing between alternatives, define managerial accounting broadly as accounting for decision-making.[4] Other authors subdivide this basic management function (decision-making) and describe internal accounting as an aid to management in (1) planning,[5] and (2) controlling. As they progress from the level of generalities to accounting reports and techniques for *specific purposes,* their opinions converge and they commonly include among these purposes (1) the planning and budgeting of current operations, (2) the budgetary control of current operations, and (3) specific short and long-term decision-making.

Scope of Managerial Accounting

Much has been written with respect to the future orientation of managerial accounting. In fact, an exposure draft has been released by the American Institute of Certified Public Accountants regarding standards for the preparation of financial forecasts, so that such projections could be made available to external users in the same way that they have been to internal management.[6]

Future costs and revenues are required for short (perhaps one year) planning periods and for long-range planning (usually three to five years). Information is needed as a base from which to project the future. Therefore, past information achieves some importance as a guide or springboard from which to plan future operations and the funding for that future scope of activity. The income statement, balance sheet, and cash flow statements suggest the immediate past performance with respect to the level of operations achieved, the working capital generated from such operations, and the financial position of the firm as of the date of preparation of the last balance sheet.

The scope of managerial accounting also includes all reports of a financial character useful to management in planning including: formal budgeting with emphasis on the master budget; the sales volume and all production and distribution costs for earning the projected profit, by products and segments of the business. In addition, controlling and directing are managerial accounting aspects that are served through responsibility reporting.

Relationship of Managerial Accounting to Financial Accounting

Failure to differentiate between the purposes of financial and managerial accounting tends to be confusing with regard to revenue-cost concepts and reporting format appropriate to each of these areas of accounting. This lack of differentiation may be due to the fact that neither of these accounting areas are mutually exclusive. They are related in that both utilize (to the extent that managerial accounting employs bookkeeping information) the same stock of basic accounting data and are at times served by the same cost accounting techniques. Generally, financial and managerial accounting differ in that each is primarily intended for a different audience.

Financial accounting emphasizes the concept of "stewardship"— capital managers reporting the results of their past performance to present and prospective capital contributors (owners and creditors), as noted in Chapter 1. While financial accounting is useful and necessary to an external audience, and also provides management with an *overall* "score-keeping" device,[7] it does not generally provide the *detail* needed by managers who seek to know and control the results of each phase of their operations.

Managerial accounting, on the other hand, places its main emphasis on future costs, revenues and performance—using past results as a basis for evaluating past performance and as one basis for projecting future revenue and expense. Also concerned with overall goals and overall performance, it provides detailed information about specific operating functions and *accountable individuals*. It usually embraces the concept of "responsibility accounting" (holding appropriate individuals accountable for performance), and provides detailed information comparing *actual* costs of specific responsibility centers (departments or cost centers) with a yardstick, that is, budgeted or standard costs. Cost control and relevant cost determination for specific decision-making purposes are also emphasized.

Relationship of Managerial Accounting to Cost Accounting

Authors who deal with accounting systems differ as to the limitations they place on what is embraced by "cost accounting." (Cost accounting is discussed in later chapters of this deskbook.) Cost determination of manufactured products for financial accounting reports appears to be included universally as one of the purposes of cost accounting. Many authors expand the role of cost accounting to include the determination of historic costs, classified in terms of cost centers, departments, products and major responsibility centers. These segregations permit the preparation of financial statements and budgetary control.

A strong relationship exists between managerial accounting and cost accounting. The former can be considered to be an outgrowth of cost accounting. One major difference between them is that cost accounting is concerned exclusively with the determination of the full cost of manufactured products (as opposed to purchased merchandise) for inventory costing purposes. Such costs of manufacture serve in the preparation of financial statements by providing a reasonable basis for dividing the total cost of production for a period between the cost of goods sold for the period and the value of the ending inventory.

Cost accounting provides a detailed system of dividing up the factory into functional processing centers and of collecting cost information from each center. The costs incurred by these production or cost centers and those assigned or allocated to them are also allocated to the products produced in each center. As the product moves from one processing center to the next, the cost of the work done on the product is accumulated. When the product is finished, the total accumulation of factory costs represents the "cost" of the product.

The scope of the discipline referred to as cost accounting was later expanded, and it incorporated some cost concepts and measurement techniques that *simultaneously* served both financial *and* managerial accounting needs. Examples of such dual purpose concepts were standard costs and direct costing. These are discussed at greater length in Chapter 13.

Direct (Variable) Costing

Direct costing was developed primarily to improve financial statements by re-defining inventoriable manufacturing costs. In this approach to product costs, only the variable costs of production are classified as product or inventoriable costs. The fixed portion of factory overhead costs appears on the income statement as a *period* expense. It is seen as the cost of having a given production capacity available during the period, a cost incurred whether or not management actually employs the capacity.

The variable costs, however, (raw material, direct labor and variable overhead costs) represent the *actual* costs associated with the use of plant capacity in the manufacturing of products, and are the only costs involved in producing products—using factory capacity rather than merely having it available. Therefore, only the variable costs should be inventoried as product costs under the concept of direct costing. This can affect the income statement of a manufacturer. By consistently charging off the total fixed cost portion of factory overhead on the income statement, direct costing overcomes the *apparent* distortion between sales volume and net income that can exist under absorption costing when differences exist between production and sales volume.

Direct costing serves practical managerial accounting needs. Specifically, in deciding between alternative uses of plant facilities, management is interested in information about the differential revenues and costs associated with these alternatives. Frequently, *but not always,* it is the variable costs that will be different, and therefore the only costs relevant to the decision. Examples of such decisions that are affected by variable costs are: to accept or reject a "special order" which must be priced below its "full" cost; to sell a product that is saleable after it is only partially processed or to process it further; and to make or buy a component part of a product.

In the light of these overlapping cost techniques, cost accounting can be defined as that branch of accounting concerned with various cost and work measurement techniques that provide quantitative financial information for either financial or managerial accounting purposes or both.

The Limitations of Managerial Accounting

In spite of its practical value, managerial accounting can never be more than an *aid* to management—it can never be a *substitute* for management or eliminate the need for management judgment. One reason for this is that such accounting places emphasis on the future, which can never be known with certainty. The factors that influence the future are dynamic, not static. Even statistical analysis and subjective probability concepts (which seek to quantify variables that cannot be measured objectively) while providing additional information can only narrow the range of uncertainty.

A second reason that managerial accounting cannot be a substitute is that accounting reports are limited to quantifiable information, and, as a result, do not provide information about those aspects of a particular problem or decision area that cannot be reduced to simple mathematical or financial terms.

In addition, the managerial accounting concepts and reporting techniques that have developed over time have been built largely upon the assumption that profit maximization is the overall objective of top management. The behavioral sciences have indicated that this classical view of the primary goal of a business organization is, at least an over-simplification, if not totally inaccurate. Some behavioralists feel that managerial accounting should no longer be oriented toward profit maximization, but should reflect more closely the various goals of the individual members of the firm and the overall objectives of the firm which are said to be organization survival.[8]

For the present, at least, the accountant continues to employ the classical assumption, in keeping with the limited role of accounting as merely a source of quantifiable financial information. At best, the accountant hopes to point out to management the economic costs associated with the selection of alternative courses of action. After receiving such information from the accountant, who occupies a *staff* position, it is the responsibility of *line* managers to determine the priority of the organization's goals and to select an appropriate course of action.

From a pragmatic point of view, in spite of its limitations, managerial accounting has proven useful to management. A contributing factor that has caused managerial accounting and related mathematical techniques to grow in importance is the communications problem that goes with the continued growth in size and complexity of business units. Accounting reports have proven to be effective means of communicating both the overall and detailed financial objectives of a firm, providing management with feedback that gives rise to control and performance evaluation. Therefore, while management accounting reports provide only limited information, they have been important typically in larger firms as a vehicle for planning and controlling operations.

The Essential Characteristics of a "Good" Managerial Accounting System

Frequently, discussions of reporting and reporting techniques move too quickly to the mechanics of practice employed in accumulating and summarizing data and in preparing reports. Without an understanding of the end purposes of management reports, and of the basic concepts that have been developed in harmony with such purposes, any discussion of practices may be premature or meaningless. A discussion of the basic concepts that underly managerial accounting precedes consideration of cost accounting practices and techniques developed in detail in Part II.

Accounting concepts applied in managerial accounting reports are those used in such functions as (1) pre-budget profit planning, (2) budgeting of current operations, (3) controlling operating costs and revenues—or evaluating the performance of individuals, and, (4) profitability measurement of products, product lines and/or business segments for purposes of decision-making in product-pricing based on contribution to fixed costs and profit, product or segment discontinuance, and other related aspects.

Such informational needs are discussed below under three major headings:

1. The Behavior of Costs
2. Management Control—Both Costs and Revenues
3. Responsibility Centers

The Behavior of Costs—Fixed Versus Variable

Information regarding cost-volume-profit relationships within a business organization can be a valuable aid to management in profit-planning, cost budgeting and control, and in decision-making where changes in volume are a factor. To serve these purposes, the operational costs are classified in terms of their behavior with volume changes. That is, costs that are not expected to change in *total* with fluctuations in the volume of activity are referred to as *fixed costs,* and those that do tend to vary with changes in volume are called *variable costs.*

Fixed Costs

All costs are subject to change over a sufficiently long period of time or with sufficiently large increases in volume. But a "fixed cost" in accounting terminology is one that remains constant in amount within a given period of time (the budget period) and in regard to a given range of activity (the "relevant range").[9]

Types of Fixed Costs

This general category of fixed costs has been divided further into (1) committed or sunk costs and (2) discretionary or managed or programmed costs. These classifications refer to the degree of short-run discretionary control that top management can exercise over fixed costs. Committed fixed costs are those that management cannot reduce, even in the short-run, without a reduction in present capacity and without a detrimental effect on the company's ability to meet its *long-run* sales-production objectives. In fact, these costs would continue to exist even if the volume of sales and production were temporarily reduced to zero.

The second category of fixed costs—the programmed or managed costs—are those that are generally more discretionary in nature and are decided upon by management at the start of the budget period. These are illustrated by training program costs, advertising, or research and development expenditures that can be eliminated at management's discretion.

Variable Costs

Costs that vary in *total* with the volume of productive activity attained are termed *variable costs,* increasing or decreasing with like changes in activity. As a result of this behavior, they are frequently referred to as *activity costs,* directly related to the actual employment of productive resources.

Two basic classifications of these costs are (1) pure variable costs, those that increase proportionately with increases in the volume, in sales or in productive work such as sales commissions, cost of goods sold, and shipping and delivery expense; and (2) semi-variable costs, those that change in total in the same *direction* as changes in volume but not *proportionately* thereto. Examples are curvilinear costs, that bear a curvilinear as opposed to a linear relationship to changes in activity volume and mixed costs which contain both fixed and variable cost elements. The semi-variable costs behave as variable costs by increasing and decreasing in the same *direction* as the volume of activity but differ in that a portion of such a cost is usually incurred even at zero volume of production. This fixed cost portion of a mixed cost represents the minimum cost of having a service factor available, as illustrated by maintenance and repair costs. These generally increase and decrease with production volume (typically curvilinearly); however, a certain minimum cost will be incurred for building and equipment maintenance even if the plant is shut down temporarily.

A final type of variable cost is the step-variable cost (or step cost) whose changes also are *not proportionate* to changes in volume. These cost factors cannot be acquired in units comparable in size to units of work or production. When the work load exceeds the capacity of the present staff, an additional *whole member* must be hired even though the increased work could be handled by a fraction of an employee, as illustrated by administrative costs of secretaries, clerical employees, and supervisors.

Uses of Cost Behavior Concepts

Even though the fine-line distinctions that characterize the sub-classifications given above may not be essential to internal accounting in every company, some distinction between costs that tend to change with volume and those that tend to remain constant is vital to many managerial accounting needs. To the extent that a company's cost structure contains a mixture of both fixed and variable costs, a general knowledge of the company's cost-volume-profit relationship is useful to management for:

1. *Profit planning* (or break-even analysis). Cost behavorial concepts allow management to estimate reasonably what costs "would be" at any level of activity within the capacity range.
2. *Formal budgeting.* This provides top management with information regarding "what costs should be" at a specified volume of

activity, thereby providing a device for preparing budgets and criteria for reviewing those budgets prepared at lower management levels.

3. *Cost control.* These cost elements permit flexible or adjustable budget cost control. A flexible budget is one based on the actual volume of work performed during the period, as opposed to the work load originally assumed in the planning budget. Such an adjustable budget allows management to compare the actual costs incurred during a period with the costs that should have been incurred in the light of the actual work load or volume.

4. *Decision-making.* Criteria are provided for decisions related to the expansion, contraction or elimination of corporate activities discussed below.

Management Control—Both Costs and Revenues

Internal accounting aids in the continuous function referred to as management control, "the process of assuring that resources are obtained and used effectively and efficiently in the accomplishment of company objectives."[10] Control refers to management's effort to influence the actions of individuals who are responsible for performing tasks, incurring costs and generating revenues. Planning and control are generally considered to be two phases of a single process in that planning refers to the way that management plans or wants people to perform, while control refers to the procedures employed to determine whether actual performance complies with these plans.

Accounting control, in its broadest sense, covers the establishment of overall company objectives, the determination of specific objectives of individuals within this framework, and the procedures—standards of performance and reporting techniques—used to determine whether actual performance has, in fact, complied with these predetermined goals and objectives.

Management control means influencing the performance of people, and generally requires the fixing of individual responsibility for the results of operations of specific departments or cost centers. This requirement has given rise to three interrelated accounting concepts—responsibility centers, controllable costs and revenues, and standards of performance.

Responsibility Centers

For purposes of both planning and control, the operations of a business should be broken down into its components (centers) where action is initiated and therefore is, at least to some degree, controllable.

A responsibility center is an organizational unit (function, department or division) headed by a single individual who has complete or substantial control over the activities of people or processes within the center, and therefore, has control over the results of their activity.[11] The manager or individual in charge of a responsibility center may be held accountable for expense incurrence only (expense or cost center); for revenue generation only (revenue center); for both revenues and expenses (profit center); or for a given rate of return on investment (investment center).

This single individual is, within the organizational structure, responsible for the performance of all persons who report to him or her. Top management represents the highest or ultimate responsibility center from the point of view of capital providers (owners and creditors). Within the organization, moving from the broadest to the narrowest in scope, are the investment centers, profit centers, the revenue centers and the expense (cost centers). The purpose of establishing responsibility centers is to pinpoint accountability thus aiding profit-planning by letting top management know who is responsible for favorable or unfavorable operating results by specific departments or responsibility cost centers.

Controllable Costs

Only those cost and revenue factors that are within the control of a responsibility center are relevant to measuring or controlling the performance of the individual in charge of that center. Ideally, the company's organizational structure should be such that all costs and revenues are controllable at some level within the organization, and that no costs or revenues be left unplanned or uncontrolled.[12]

Standards of Performance

In addition to dividing the organization into responsibility centers and establishing controllable costs and revenues, management control requires the recognition of "standards of performance." Management must determine "how good" or "how bad" actual performance has been if it is to exercise control. The problem confronting performance evaluation is one of finding a *standard,* or a basis of comparison that realistically indicates what performance should have been.

These standards may or may not be formalized into a budget or employed in a system of budgeting control. While a budget may be used as a standard, a formal budget is not a prerequisite to management control.

The establishment of responsibility centers and standards of performance and the development of a system for reporting actual current performance provide a basis for control. For cost control purposes, however, a budget provides a basis for comparison in situations where standard costs are not measurable. A standard unit cost[13] can be established only for those functions characterized by a repetitive activity and a measurable unit of work. A budget is not so limited but includes committed and programmed costs as well.

To the degree possible, the standard for cost control purposes should incorporate a unit concept (unit of activity) so that a flexible budget—one adjusted to the total throughput of productive activity—can be employed in the evaluation of performance.

Responsibility Accounting and Reporting

The process known as management control embraces the establishment of both overall and specific company objectives, the assignment of responsibility to individuals charged with the achievement of these objectives, and the development of procedures for reporting the actual performance of these responsibility centers in comparison with the standard in use. Therefore, the purpose of the control system, whatever its form, is to aid management in evaluating performance, to suggest whether or not corrective action is required, and to indicate where in the organization such effort is appropriate.

Importance of Business Segments in Decision-Making

An almost limitless scope of management decision-making makes it necessary to discuss only those decisions related to changes important to marketing and manufacturing management alike, such as changes in the sales mix with emphasis on pricing and production decisions, or the complete elimination of a product, territory, customer category, branch office or plant, or other business segment.

The term segment, in this context, refers to separable products and markets existing in multi-product companies with such an existence that each could be eliminated without discontinuance of all company operations. Therefore if an individual product in a multi-product firm can be discontinued or dropped from the product line and the company can continue to function, such a product can be said to be separable. Figure 2-1 illustrates the matching of product or territory costs with forecast sales.

This results in marginal income, after deducting variable expenses, and net contribution to profit after allocable fixed costs have been applied. "Common" fixed costs are not allocated to specific products or territories thus approximating direct costs only to such company segments, and resulting in information as to their respective profitability or contribution to profit. This is also shown percentage-wise in Figure 2-1.

Profit planning by segments refers to selecting among alternative uses of company resources to achieve a desired or "target" total profit. Profit-planning by segment requires that the profitability of each segment be measured or estimated so that the overall profitability of all feasible combinations or alternatives can be determined.

Relevant Cost and Revenue Concepts in Managerial Reporting

For purposes of selecting among alternative projects, accountants and economists commonly agree that the relevant economic factors are the "differential" costs and revenues involved. The only costs and revenues that need to be considered in making a selection among alternatives are those that will be different in one alternative as opposed to another. Those that remain the same regardless of the choice are irrelevant and are not pertinent to the decision at hand.

The costs and revenues that will be different, of course, vary with the nature of the alternatives being considered. For example, if the decision is in regard to expanding or contracting the use of present plant capacity, only the costs that vary with production (the activity costs) will be different and therefore are the only costs pertinent to the decision. On the other hand, the fixed costs are involved in decisions regarding adding to or reducing capacity.

Costs and revenues relevant to measuring segment profitability for decision-making purposes are the separable costs and revenues that have also been referred to as "escapable or avoidable." Conceptually, these *are the costs and revenues that would be eliminated if the segment in question were eliminated or dropped from the line.*

The Use of Separable Costs in Profit-Planning

The sole purpose of isolating the separable costs (and revenues) of a segment from the joint costs is to provide information for profit-planning by segment. Total profits can be derived from various segment combina-

Contribution by Products—First Quarter 19XX (*)

	Company Amount	Products Sigma Amount	Products Zeta Amount
Forecast sales	$400,000	$250,000	$150,000
Variable costs standard			
Of goods sold	220,000	130,000	90,000
Of marketing	20,000	12,500	7,500
Total variable	240,000	142,500	97,500
Marginal income	160,000	107,500	52,500
Direct fixed costs			
Production	50,000	35,000	15,000
Marketing	30,000	18,000	12,000
Total direct	80,000	53,000	27,000
Product contribution	80,000	$ 54,500	$ 25,500
Common fixed			
Production	20,000		
Marketing	24,000		
Administrative & general	11,000		
Total common	55,000		
Pre-tax income	$ 25,000		

Contribution by Sales Territories—First Quarter 19XX (*)

	Company Amount	Territories Eastern Amount	Territories Western Amount
Forecast sales			
Sigma	$250,000	$150,000	$100,000
Zeta	150,000	97,500	52,500
Total	400,000	247,500	152,500
Variable costs at standard			
Of goods sold	220,000	137,000	83,000
Of marketing	20,000	12,375	7,625
Total variable	240,000	149,375	90,625
Marginal income	160,000	98,125	61,875
Direct territory costs			
Advertising	12,000	7,000	5,000
District sales office	35,000	18,000	17,000
Travel	3,000	1,800	1,200
Total direct fixed	50,000	26,800	23,200
Territory contribution	110,000	$ 71,325	$ 38,675
Common fixed			
Production	70,000		
Marketing	4,000		
Administrative & general	11,000		
Total common	85,000		
Pre-tax income	$ 25,000		

Figure 2-1

Contribution By Sales Territory—First Quarter (**)

| | Company | | Sales Territories | | | | | |
| | | | Eastern | | Central | | Western | |
	Amount	%	Amount	%	Amount	%	Amount	%
Net Sales	$9,000,000	100	$4,000,000	100	$3,000,000	100	$2,000,000	100
Variable Cost of Sales								
Production	5,012,500	56	2,280,000	57	1,587,500	53	1,145,000	57
Marketing	450,000	5	200,000	5	150,000	5	100,000	5
Total Variable	5,462,500	61	2,480,000	62	1,737,500	58	1,245,000	62
Marginal Income	3,537,500	39	1,520,000	38	1,262,500	42	755,000	38
District Territory Costs								
Advertising and Promotion	680,000	7	272,000	7	220,000	7	88,000	4
District Sales Office	260,000	3	160,000	4	40,000	1	60,000	3
Travel and Entertainment	75,000	1	30,000	1	25,000	1	20,000	1
Total Direct	1,015,000	11	462,000	12	285,000	9	168,000	8
Territory Contribution	$2,522,500	28	$1,058,000	26	$ 977,500	33	$ 587,000	30
Common Fixed Costs								
Production	1,890,000	21						
Marketing	90,000	1						
General and Administrative	180,000	2						
Total Common	2,160,000	24						
Net Profit	$ 362,500	4						

Figure 2-1 (continued)

Source: National Association of Accountants, * "Responsibility Accounting for Management Control," EDO-3 p. 18, 19.
**EDO-1 p. 26. Integrated Management Accounting, National Association of Accountants, New York.

tions that might be presented in the form of a mathematical formula or model, capable of considering all such factors in each combination at the same time. This sophisticated tool is popular among accountants with management science exposure and consulting experience.

To illustrate: A straightforward financial model for a defense contractor will show inputs of both an external and internal nature along with the financial planning aspects required to project a balance sheet and income statement by the entire firm or a business segment, such as a division or subsidiary thereof. Goals in the form of such financial ratios as rate of return on investment (by entire firm or segments), cash flow, current ratios and planned dividends are usually incorporated into such planning.

The Importance of the Contribution Approach

The contribution approach to measuring segment profitability is considered one of the most useful in profit-planning. As indicated in Figure 2-1, this approach measures segment direct contribution to overall profit, ignoring joint costs as far as individual segments are concerned. The latter are viewed as a lump sum that must be recovered by the total contribution of all segments involved. The relative profitability of each segment is measured in terms of its contribution toward covering the joint costs and providing some profit. Such segment profitability is analogous to product contribution at the margin, that is, the excess of the product's revenue when compared with variable costs, resulting in its contribution to fixed costs and profit.

The joint costs are not allocated to segments on the grounds that (1) they are irrelevant to the selection of a combination because they will remain unchanged regardless of the combination selected, (2) the allocation of joint costs must, of necessity, be made on an arbitrary basis, and therefore cannot be meaningful for decision-making, and (3) the allocation actually may create the misleading impression that a segment is unprofitable and should be eliminated or curtailed when in fact it is making a substantial contribution to joint profits.

The concepts of fixed and variable costs play an important role in both segment and individual product profit-planning. Having ascertained the separable costs of a segment, and further classified them in terms of behavior with volume, management can determine what the profit contribution will be at any given volume of activity. This kind of information is essential to decisions regarding the expansion or contraction of activity of individual segments.

total amount shown in the statement, "Reporting Changes in Financial Position."[5]

Short-Term Investments

Figure 3-1 shows short-term investments carried at cost described as part of a continuing program to keep working capital invested and earning interest to the maximum extent possible, whether held for several months or only a few days.[6]

Sun Oil Company and
Consolidated Subsidiaries

Consolidated Statement of Financial Position
(Excerpt only)

Assets at December 31	19XX

Current Assets

Cash	$ 58,904,000
Short-Term Investments, at cost	34,218,000
Accounts and Notes Receivable	373,602,000
Crude Oil and Refined Products	173,543,000
Materials and Supplies	40,835,000
Work-in-Process	18,834,000
Total Current Assets	$699,936,000

Liabilities and Stockholders' Equity at December 31	19XX

Current Liabilities

Accounts Payable and Accrued Liabilities	$247,293,000
Notes and Bonds Payable	46,770,000
Taxes, other than Income Taxes	47,729,000
Income Taxes	73,272,000
Total Current Liabilities	$415,064,000

Figure 3-1

International Business Machine Corporation's "marketable securities" were reported at the lower of cost of market in its consolidated balance sheet.[7] In this connection, investments in securities (whether marketable or not) or advances that have been made for the purposes of control, affiliation, or other continuing business advantage are normally excluded from the current asset classification.

Accounts and Notes Receivable

In general, receivables should be reported net, after reduction by allowance accounts to cover anticipated collection losses. Receivables from officers, employees, or affiliated companies are shown separately from trade receivables.[8]

The net amount of receivables are shown in Figure 3-1 after the allowance for bad debts by customers and others under short-term credit extended in the company's normal course of business. Examples of amounts included are the retail charge account purchases, money that dealers owe for products delivered to their stations, and amounts owed on the company's sale of crude oil.

Contract Accounts Receivable

In long-term construction work, the contracts receivable account is used to record amounts due the company for work accomplished under contracts, usually supported by a breakdown by contracts or purchase orders in subsidiary ledgers. Fixed Price and Cost-Type billings are maintained separately and the receivables are divided into uncollected and unbillable categories. The latter are those on which documentation is lacking.

Billing procedures usually differ with respect to Fixed Price (FP) type contracts and Cost Plus Fixed Fee (CPFF) type contracts, as illustrated below.

FP Contract Billing Terms

Progress billings are frequently made as work progresses, typically based upon a 70% rate applied to allowable cost (direct and overhead) plus inventory, or 85% of direct labor and material cost plus inventory. In small businesses these rates are frequently raised to 75% and 90% respectively, after receipt of permission from the involved governmental agencies. Progress billing provisions (except in the case of small business concerns) have been made available when:

(a) There is a six month or longer cycle time from the incurrence of initial cost to the first delivery; or,
(b) The contract is for $1,000,000 or more.

Progress billing limitations, based on total allowable cost and inventory are typically written as follows: The lesser of (1) 70% of incurred allowable cost and inventory or (2) 70% of the undelivered price. For example, under a FP contract with 12% target earnings, the progress billing limitation would be $\frac{70}{112}$ or 62.5%.

CPFF Billings

Generally, CPFF billings are made in two breakdowns:

(1) Cost Billings
(2) Fee Billings

Normally, a 15% of fee holdback or $100,000, whichever is less, is applied on CPFF Contracts, and this is usually recovered about one year after delivery.

Net Delivery Billings

The difference between the price and progress billings made against delivered contract items may be calculated as follows: Price less progress billing liquidation = Net Delivery Billings.

Inventory Calculation

Any one of several assumptions as to the flow of cost factors is used in costing out inventory to production, such as first-in, first-out (FIFO); last-in, first-out (LIFO); specific identification; and, average cost. The major objective in selecting a method is to choose that which, under the particular circumstances, most clearly reflects periodic income under generally accepted accounting principles.

The valuation of inventories affects not only the working capital position of a company, but also its reported profits. FIFO operates on the assumption that inventories are sold in the order in which they are acquired, and, therefore, the cost of the earliest acquisition is charged to *cost of sales.* Conversely, ending inventory is that most recently acquired, valued at the latest unit costs.

Under LIFO, inventories are presumed used in the inverse order of their acquisition, that is, the cost of the *latest* acquisition is charged to Cost of Sales. The year-end inventory is reported at the *earliest* costs of acquisition.

Both FIFO and LIFO inventory valuation methods may be modified by using standard costs, job order costs, or process cost plans without affecting the basic FIFO or LIFO inventory valuation method.

The specific identification method is limited to inventories consisting of relatively few, but large cost items, as might be the case with dealers in large appliances. Average cost is used for inventories of a homogeneous nature where little fluctuation in cost normally exists. An illustration is given in the case of General Signal Corporation on page 73.

Dollar Value Method Under LIFO

LIFO may be accomplished simply under the dollar value method. The inventory valuation at the beginning of the year is compared with that at the end of the year, stated in dollars at the same price level. The size of the inventory is measured by the number of dollars even though some of the items in inventory have increased in physical quantity and others have decreased.[9] Only changes in the inventory pools are taken into account; increases and decreases in physical quantities of specific items are recognized as a component of the pool total.[10]

When adopting the dollar value method of calculating inventories under LIFO, consideration should be given to:

(1) Which inventories are to be placed on LIFO;
(2) The determination of the inventory pools to be measured in dollars, such as:
    (a) One broad pool consisting of all inventories of the company,
    (b) Separate pools for:
        1. Material, and
        2. Labor and overhead
    (c) A commodity pool
    (d) A departmental pool
    (e) A group of individual items of different sizes.[11]

A departure from the cost basis of pricing the inventory is required when the utility of the goods is no longer as great as cost.[12] The difference is recognized as a loss for the current period and the inventory is stated at a lower level designated as "market." A definite floor is indicated as far as market is concerned, as follows:

> As used in the phrase "lower of cost" or "market" the term "market" means current replacement cost (by purchase or by reproduction, as the case may be) except that:
>
> (1) Market should not exceed the net realizable value (i.e., estimated selling price in the ordinary course of business less reasonable predictable costs of completion and disposal); and,
>
> (2) Market should not be less than net realizable value reduced by an allowance for an approximately normal profit margin.[13]

Illusory Inventory Profits—The Case for LIFO

During periods of double-digit inflation the use of the FIFO method of inventory evaluation can create inventory profits by matching old inventory costs against current sales.[14] This leads to serious questions about the quality of reported earnings of companies using FIFO. Such illusory inventory profits are taxable—to the corporation as well as to its stockholders in the form of dividends. At a time of rising prices when a company needs an increasing cash flow to replenish its inventory, danger exists that its net cash flow will be reduced substantially by a tax pay-out caused in part by inventory profits under the FIFO method.[15]

"Inventory profit" is defined in SEC Accounting Series Release No. 151 as that resulting from the holding of inventories during a period of rising inventory costs, measured by the difference between the historical cost of an item and its replacement cost at the date of sale.[16] The Commission's Release urged registrants to identify and disclose such inventory profit that might be included in the firm's reported net income, along with a disclosure of the relationship of changes in costs and selling prices.[17]

Under inflationary conditions, LIFO offers the advantage of matching current costs with current sales prices, resulting in lower taxable income. If prices are adjusted to reflect increased inventory acquisition costs, illusory inventory profits can be prevented and the adverse effects on cash flow can be corrected as a result of lower income taxes. However, if elected for tax purposes, LIFO must also be used for financial reporting. Revenue Procedure No. 75-10 of the Internal Revenue Service permits taxpayers electing LIFO, re-electing LIFO, or extending an existing LIFO election to make certain disclosures of the effect of this procedure on income for the period in which the change was made.[18]

In addition, APB Opinion No. 20 requires a company changing to LIFO to disclose that fact in the year of change and the firm's rationale in changing from its previous method. Not only must reasons be cited as to why LIFO is preferable in determining inventory cost but disclosure must be given as to the effects of the change on income before extraordinary items and net income in that year and on the per share amounts both before and after extraordinary items.[19]

An example of compliance with both APB Opinion No. 20 and SEC Accounting Series Release No. 169 in summarizing operational changes resulting from a switch to LIFO is the following:

> In order not to overstate reported profits as a result of inflation during the year, the company changed its method of accounting for inventory from First-in, First-out to Last-in, First-out. This was necessary because of the rapid increase in prices in 19xx which caused inventories sold to be replaced at substantially higher prices. The effect of the change was to decrease reported earnings by $XXX,XXX, or $X.XX per share.[20]

Costing Methods Illustrated

Variations in inventory reporting are required for different types of industries, as described below. But one generalization is possible— inventories, whether raw materials or finished products, are normally priced at the lower of average cost or market. Ralston Purina Company, for instance, priced finished products of animal and poultry feeds, pet foods, and soy bean products generally at the market price of ingredients plus manufacturing costs.[21] Other finished products, principally sea foods and poultry products, were priced at production cost but not in excess of market.[22]

Other illustrations of inventory "cost" calculations follow:

First-In First-Out

TRW INC.[23]

Current Assets:

    Inventories—Note B $237,432,506

NOTE B: *Inventories*—Inventories are valued at the lower of cost (principally first-in, first-out) or market. The inventories at December 31, 19X4 and 19X5 were classified as follows:

	19X4	19X5
Finished Products and work in process	$166,515,102	$167,582,169
Raw Materials and supplies	70,917,404	63,601,629
Totals.	$237,432,506	$231,183,798

Average Cost

GENERAL SIGNAL CORPORATION[24]

Current Assets:

Inventories (Note 2):
Raw materials, purchased parts and work in process $23,113,453
Finished goods 17,045,292

NOTE 2: *Inventories*—Inventories at December 31, 19XX are stated at the lower of cost or market, cost being determined principally on the basis of average or standard costs; the cost of a minor portion of the inventories is determined on the last-in, first-out (LIFO) basis.

Last-in First-out

MOBIL OIL CORPORATION[25]

Current Assets:

Inventories:
Crude oil and products $643,920,000
Materials and supplies 68,317,000

From Financial Review
Inventories—Inventories are valued at cost, which was lower than their aggregate market value at December 31, 19XX. Substantially all domestic inventories of crude oil and petroleum products—repre-

senting about 36% of the worldwide total of all inventories at December 31, 19XX are valued under the last-in, first-out method. All other inventories are valued at average cost.

Standard Cost

CORNING GLASS WORKS[26]

Current Assets:

> Inventories (Note 3) $71,172,343

NOTE 3: *Inventories*—Inventories are valued at the lower of cost (current standard or actual cost) or market. At December 29, 19XX they consisted of: finished goods—$29,905,157; work in process—$21,398,829; raw materials and accessories—$12,390,327; and supplies and packing materials—$7,478,030.

Retail Method

W.T. GRANT COMPANY[27]

Current Assets:

> Merchandise inventories (including merchandise in transit) at the lower of cost or market determined principally by the retail inventory method $208,482,684

Production Cost

THE BABCOCK & WILSON COMPANY[28]

Current Assets:

> Inventories at lower of cost of market less advance payments on contracts:
> 19XX —$44,622,993; 19XX —$23,522,479) . . . $160,300,471

Notes to Financial Statements
NOTE 2 (in part): *Inventories*—The consolidated inventories at December 31, 19XX are summarized below:
> Raw materials and supplies . . . . $ 61,634,000

Work in process	134,534,000
Finished products	8,755,000
	$204,923,000
Less: Advance payments	44,623,000
	$160,300,000

Contracts in Process and Inventories

MCDONNELL-DOUGLAS CORPORATION[29]

Contracts in process and inventories include certain items to which the U.S. Government held title by reason of contract provisions.

Orders in process for commercial aircraft (including military versions) and certain other commercial products were stated on the basis of production costs incurred less the costs allocated to delivered items, reduced (where applicable) to realizable market after giving effect to the estimated costs to complete each order or contract.

Government contracts in process were primarily accounted for on a percentage-of-completion method wherein costs (including general and administrative expenses) and estimated earnings were deemed sales as the work was performed, and the amount stated for each contract represented the accumulated costs plus estimated earnings, less amounts billed to the customer.

Certain contracts contain incentive provisions which provide increased or decreased earnings based upon performance in relation to established targets. Incentives based upon cost performance were recorded currently, and other incentives when the amounts could reasonably be determined. As most work is performed under long-term contracts, adjustments of costs and earnings may be made during and after completion of the contracts; therefore, earnings recorded in the current year may include adjustments applicable to sales recorded in prior years.

Contracts in Process (Fixed Price)

This account is useful in recording the costs incurred and estimated accrued earnings applicable to undelivered items on Fixed Price Contracts, excluding progress payments made to subcontractors. Subsidiary accounts usually are used to control these costs by elements as follows:

(a) Accrued Earnings (described below);
(b) Labor charges to the contract or job;
(c) Material charges
(d) Direct charges
(e) Overhead—Actual
(f) Deliveries (Credit)

(a) Accrued Earnings

This account records the accumulated value of estimated earnings accrued on undelivered items in order to spread the earnings over the accounting periods involved.

Contracts in Process (Cost-Type)

This account contains all costs incurred on CPFF and other cost-type contracts, supported by subsidiary accounts for accumulated costs by elements of the following types:

(a) Labor
(b) Material
(c) Direct Charges
(d) Overhead—Actual
(e) Billed Costs

Prepaid Items

It is generally agreed that prepaid items are those items properly chargeable to future periods. But whether or not such items are included under *current assets* depends upon the specific nature of the item. Prepaid expenses such as interest, rents, taxes, insurance, current paid advertising service not yet received, and operating supplies *have* been included under current assets under the theory that if not paid in advance, they would require the use of *current assets* during the operating cycle.

In Figure 3-1, all prepaid and deferred charges are excluded from current assets. The asset group consists of payments and expenditures incurred that are carried forward to be charged against income in one or more future years. Included are insurance premiums, long-term debt expenses, rents, pension costs, and goodwill, that is, the excess of cost of investments over equities in net assets acquired.[30]

In contrast, Ralston Purina Company included "Prepaid expenses" under current assets. However, the asset labeled "excess of investment over book value of subsidiary assets acquired" was shown separately under "Investments and other assets."[31]

Deferred Charges Excluded From Current Assets

The most common types of deferred charges excluded from current assets are: (1) future income tax benefits; (2) financing charges; and, (3) organization expense. These are illustrated under the heading of "Deferred Charges and Other Assets" in Chapter 4.

Current Liabilities

The following balance sheet illustrations *include* under Current Liabilities obligations that have entered into the operating cycle, with respect to: (1) the acquisition of materials or supplies; (2) collections received in advance of the performance of services or delivery of finished products; (3) obligations arising from salaries, wages, commissions, rentals, royalties, income taxes, serial maturities of long-term debt; (4) obligations incurred by the corporation as an agent in collecting cash for later submission to the state or federal government; and, (5) accruals for incurred expenses that are not definite in amount as of the balance sheet date or are indefinite as to the identity of the payee. Accruals of both kinds are illustrated below.

Items excluded from current liabilities are obligations falling due later than one year after balance-sheet date or expected to be refunded or paid by funds segregated from general cash, or to be liquidated through long-term debts floated to provide increased working capital for long periods.

Current Liabilities Estimated as to Amounts

The reporting of liabilites where the identity of the debtor is known but the amount of liability is not known as of the balance sheet date is illustrated with respect to income taxes accrued and explained in the following footnote:

NOTE 5: *Federal Income Taxes*—The Company's Federal income tax returns for the period from June 1, 19XX to May 28, 19XX are currently under examination by the Internal Revenue Service. The amount of additional liability, if any, is not determinable. The deferred Federal income taxes result from the use of depreciation deductions for tax purposes which in the aggregate, have exceeded book depreciation.

The consolidated earnings for the year ended June 1, 19XX include the net earnings of the Bahamian subsidiary in the amount of $192,240. No provision has been made for Federal income tax on these earnings since management of the company intends to permanently invest the earnings of the subsidiary in the foreign operations. Had the earnings been returned to the United States, Federal income tax of approximately $96,000 would have been incurred.[32]

Current Liability Accruals in Which the Identity of the Debtor Is Unknown

A manufacturing company's annual report includes estimates such as the following: "Reserves for completion of contracts and product corrections and current portion of special reserves." A sample footnote describes this special reserve:

> The Company has estimated that implementation of policy changes will result in substantial costs and losses for (a) parts replacement, warranty costs, repossession losses and price allowances and (b) relocation and discontinuance of facilities and products.[33]

Accrued liabilities are shown in Figure 3-1 in the form of incurred obligations for which actual payment has not yet become due, illustrated by interest and payroll debts payable in the following year but applicable to operations of the current year.

Taxes reported as liabilities in Figure 3-1 include both domestic and foreign income tax liabilites, accrued obligations, such as sales, excise, and oil production taxes and taxes collected from employees and customers in the corporate capacity of collection agent for federal and state governmental authorities.

Customer Progress Payments

This account illustrates the liability to customers to provide services for which progress payment billings have been made on fixed price contracts or purchase orders. This account is typically found on the balance sheet of companies engaging in defense contracts or long-term construction contracts.

Interest on Payables and Receivables

APB Opinion No. 21 requires recording for notes payable or receivable when the face amount does not reasonably represent the present value of the consideration involved in an exchange. If a note is non-interest bearing or has a stated interest rate that is different from the rate of interest appropriate at the date of the transaction, the note is to be recorded at its present value.

Importance of APB Opinion No. 21

Both the sales price and profit to the seller and the purchase price or cost to the buyer can be misstated if APB Opinion No. 21 is not followed. Interest income or expense in subsequent periods can also be misstated. Payables referred to include secured and unsecured notes, debentures, bonds, mortgage notes, equipment obligations and some accounts payable.

When a note is issued for cash and no other right or privilege is exchanged, it is presumed to have a present value at issuance measured by the cash proceeds exchanged. But, if cash *and* other rights or privileges are exchanged for a note, the value of the *rights or privileges* should also be included in recording the liability by establishing a note discount or premium account. This is important because the *effective* interest rate may differ from the rate stated on the note. For example, a manufacturer may loan cash to a supplier that is to be repaid in five years with *no* stated interest. The reason for not charging interest may be to obtain a lower price from the supplier than the prevailing market price or to gain other concessions. The difference between the present value of the note and the cash loan to the supplier is regarded in APB Opinion No. 21 as an addition to the cost of the products purchased during the contract term, and should be amortized as interest income over the five year life of the note.

Such discount is *not* a liability separable from the note which gives rise to it, but should be reported in the balance sheet as a direct deduction from the face amount of the note, rather than as a deferred charge or deferred credit. The description of the note should include the effective interest rate; the amortization of discount should be reported in the income statement; and the costs of issuance should be shown in the balance sheet as a deferred charge according to APB Opinion No. 21.

Right of Setoff

The offset of any asset (current or otherwise) against a liability, such as taxes payable, is in violation of APB Opinion No. 10. The sole exception to this principle occurs where a purchase of securities represents an advance payment of income taxes, due in the relatively near future.

Dividends Payable in Cash

A current liability for cash dividends payable is recognized as of the declaration date, with a debit to retained earnings and a credit to cash dividends payable. This liability is cancelled when the dividend checks are released.

The corporate board of directors has the obligation to watch the firm's working capital position, and must be aware that the mere fact that a favorable balance exists in retained earnings does not mean that adequate cash is available for dividends.

Dividends Payable in Script

A corporation may issue script dividends—written *promises* to pay a sum certain in dollars at a specified future date. This keeps the firm's regular dividend payment record intact year after year even though the company is temporarily short of cash. Stockholders can hold such notes until maturity or sell in the interim if desired.

When the script dividend payable is declared, the retained earnings account is debited and the credit is entered to script dividends payable, until paid.

Dividends in Kind

If cash is not available, the board of directors may distribute property of other kinds as dividends called, "dividends in kind," such as securities of other companies. Retained earnings is debited and a credit is made to dividends payable in stock of the company involved. When the distribution is made, the dividend payable account is debited and the investment account credited, recording the removal of that asset from the books.

A corporation may distribute stock dividends if it has retained earnings. Stock dividends permit the corporation to retain, within the business, net assets produced by earnings while at the same time offering stockholders *some* evidence of growing equity, namely an increase in the number of shares held by *each* stockholder. The process of capitalizing retained earnings by debiting that account and crediting capital stock reduces the retained earnings balance and with it the temptation to stockholders to seek dividend payments at a time when cash is not available. For further treatment of this topic see Stockholder's Equity, Chapter 5.

Other Current Liabilities

In addition to the usual current liabilities already mentioned, loans on life insurance policies must be added. These loans are classified as current liabilities when by their terms or by management intent they are to be repaid within twelve months. The *pledging* of life insurance policies to secure a debt does not affect classification any more than does the *pledging* of receivables, inventories, real estate, or other assets used as collateral for short-term loans.

Management intent is paramount in account classification. When a loan on a life insurance policy is obtained from the insurance company with management's intent that it will *not* be paid but will be liquidated upon maturity of the policy, that loan should be excluded from current liabilities and placed under long-term liabilities.

By the same token the current liability classification is not intended to include contractual obligations falling due at an early date but intended by management to be refunded from *noncurrent* assets. Otherwise, working capital would be stated in error, that is, current liabilities would *not* be matched with current assets.

Liabilities Involving the Future—Warranties

For a certain period of time following a sale, a manufacturer may promise to assume all or part of the cost of replacing defective parts and performing necessary repairs on such products. These warranties or guarantees represent future costs to such manufacturers. Although indefinite as to amount, date and even customer identity, such warranties constitute a potential liability and should be shown as current liabilities. The amount is an estimate of costs to be incurred after sale and delivery to correct product defects under the warranty provision.

Alternatives in Recording Warranty Costs

Several methods of accounting are available for warranty costs. Under one method, the manufacturer follows a "cash" basis of accounting. Warranty costs are charged to expense in the period in which the manufacturer complies with the warranty. No liability is estimated or recorded for *future* costs arising from warranties, nor is the *period* in which the *sale* was made charged with costs of making good on outstanding warranties on such sales.

Under another method, warranty costs are *accrued* at the time of sale and estimated future warranty costs charged to the year of *sale.*

An alternative approach defers a certain percentage of the original sales price until some future time when actual costs are incurred or the warranty expires under the assumption that at the time of sale *two different things were really sold:* (1) the product and (2) service—the warranty.

Contingencies

Contingent liabilities represent *possible* future obligations in which the liability is not yet a fact and may never materialize, as is the case with law suits pending. An estimated liability (such as Federal Income Taxes), involves the existence of a liability certain in everything but amount.

Items appearing as liabilities that do not fall under the above liability types include reserves for self-insurance, reserves for repairs, reserves for price declines, and minority interests. Because of their presentation on balance sheets these items give the impression to readers that they are real liabilities; they are not. Reserves for self-insurance, for example, represent possible future losses which may never take place and do not result from past events.

Failure to pay past or current insurance premiums does not create an obligation to do so in future years as a self-insuror. The insurance risk may simply never materialize into a loss. The uninsured building may never burn! Reserves for major repairs may represent *future* outlays but should not be related to *past* transactions. However, if it is desired to debit retained earnings for such potential liabilities, an account labeled "Retained earnings appropriated for self-insurance" should be credited and shown with other retained earnings reserves.

The nature of current assets and current liabilities was analyzed for the purpose of encouraging more useful presentation in financial statements. The conventional definition of a strict, one-year interpretation of either current assets or liabilities is not recommended. Instead, emphasis should be placed on the operating cycle of the business to identify working capital inclusions. Financial statements of a *going* concern are prepared on the assumption that the company will continue in business and creditors tend to rely more upon the ability of debtors to pay their obligations out of the proceeds of *current* operations rather than from liquidation of assets.

REFERENCES

[1]Sun Oil Company, "Understanding Sun's Accounting Terms," 1970 Annual Report Addition, March 1971. Philadelphia, Pennsylvania.

[2]Accounting Research and Terminology Bulletins, Final Edition, 1961, American Institute of Certified Public Accountants, Inc., Principle C-1.

[3]APB Accounting Principles, Current Text, as of February 1, 1971, Vol. 1, AICPA, 1968, page 2021.07.

[4]*Ibid.,* page 2021.15

[5]APB Opinion No. 19, pp. 377-378, Copyright 1971, American Institute of Certified Public Accountants.

[6]*Op. cit.,* Sun Oil Company, "Understanding Sun's Accounting Terms," page 8.

[7]IBM Annual Report 1970, page 24.

[8]*Op. cit.,* Accounting Research and Terminology Bulletins, Final Edition 1961, Principle C-1.

[9]Uniform Accounting Manual for the Electrical Manufacturing Industry, Seventh Edition, amended 1960, published by the National Electrical Manufacturers Association, page 417-C.

[10]*Ibid.*

[11]*Ibid.*

[12]Accounting Research and Terminology Bulletins, Final Edition, 1961, American Institute of CPAs, page 30.

[13]*Ibid.,* page 31 Copyright (c) 1961 by the American Institute of Certified Public Accountants, Inc.

[14]"Getting the most out of LIFO," THE PRICE WATERHOUSE REVIEW, 1975 Volume 20 Number 1, C. Paul Jannis, New York, N.Y. page 8.

[15]*Ibid.,* page 10.

[16]Accounting Series Release No. 151, "Disclosure of Inventory Profits Reflected in Income in Periods of Rising Prices," Securities and Exchange Commission, Washington, D.C., January 3, 1974.

[17]*Ibid.*

[18]Revenue Procedure 75-10, Technical Information Release, Internal Revenue Service, Washington, D.C. January 23, 1975, Section 3.

[19]APB Opinion No. 20, American Institute of Certified Public Accountants.

[20]Accounting Series Release No. 169, "Financial Disclosure Problems Relating to the Adoption of the LIFO Inventory Method," Securities and Exchange Commission, Washington, D.C., January 23, 1975.

[21]*Op. cit.*, Ralston Purina Company and Subsidiaries Annual Report to the Stockholders for 1971, page 32.

[22]*Ibid.*

[23]"Accounting Trends and Techniques," 1969, 23rd edition, copyright © 1969 by the American Institute of Certified Public Accountants, Inc., page 41.

[24]*Ibid.*, page 41

[25]*Ibid.*, page 41

[26]*Ibid.*, page 42

[27]*Ibid.*, page 42

[28]*Ibid.*, page 42

[29]McDonnell-Douglas Corporation, 1970 Annual Report page 21.

[30]*Op. cit.*, "Understanding Sun's Accounting Terms," page 9 and 10.

[31]*Op. cit.*, Ralston Purina, page 32.

[32]*Op. cit.*, Accounting Trends and Techniques, page 87.

[33]*Ibid.*, page 84.

4 "Below the Line" Items — Noncurrent Assets and Liabilities

Long-term assets and liabilities are of concern to parties interested in the firm's long-term performance, the return on investment in such long-term assets, and the best use of this capability for internal expansion.

A Shortcut to Internal Expansion— The Use of Leverage

A frequent route to internal corporate expansion involves the use of long-term financing, assuming that the return from such borrowing exceeds its cost. This chapter demonstrates the use of cost/benefit analyses as a managerial tool in achieving such corporate growth objectives. So-called "below the line items" are the following noncurrent accounts: (1) long-term receivables; (2) investments; (3) properties—plants and equipment; (4) intangible assets—prepaid and deferred charges; (5) long-term debt; and, (6) minority interests.

Accounts and Notes Receivable (long-term)

One of the advantages of long-term leasing is that of achieving expansion in productive facilities by firms with relatively limited capital at their disposal. By applying the cost/benefit analysis test to such ventures, an expanding firm with a good track record as far as return on investment is concerned, may find its most economical approach to asset acquisition in long-term leasing such as described by Bank Building and Equipment Corporation in a footnote to its annual statements:

> In 19X1 and 19X2, the Company executed two twenty-five year leases with certain customers to finance their building construction. The transactions have been accounted for as sales. The lease receivables have been recorded exclusive of unearned interest of $600,000 in 19X1 and $645,000 in 19X2. Interest earned amounted to $45,000 in 19X1 and $47,000 in 19X2.

External Expansion Techniques—Investments in Affiliated and Unconsolidated Companies

Rapidly expanding companies may find *external* expansion preferable to internal growth techniques.[2] Acquisition of existing firms may involve less risk than a spin-off of corporate departments. The hope is that such new subsidiaries will be able to compete with established firms selling the same product line. A record of successful operations over a reasonable period means that a company has the organizational structure and managerial know-how that may make it an attractive target for a business combination with a would-be parent company, making external expansion feasible to the latter company.

Basis of Valuation

Corporate practice with respect to investments indicates two accepted approaches, namely, carrying the investment at equity or at cost. Under the latter method, the investor corporation does *not* maintain its investment account at the amount of its equity in a subsidiary, but keeps that account at cost. The proper use of the equity method in carrying investments in subsidiaries is described in a footnote as follows:

> The accompanying financial statements include the accounts of all subsidiaries other than wholly-owned finance and home-building companies. These finance and home-building companies are reported in the financial statements as investments carried on the *equity basis* and, accordingly, their earnings are included in income.[3]

The question of when to include or exclude a subsidiary from the consolidated financial statements for all entities under common control was considered in Chapter 1. Operations of subsidiaries in businesses unlike the parent's are not consolidated as illustrated in the exclusion of finance companies in the above case.

Other Investments and Other Assets

Investments in companies *other* than affiliates are typically shown under this caption, along with miscellaneous notes, bonds, sinking funds, self-insurance funds, deposits on lease holds, and other items that are *not* expected to be turned into cash within the current operating cycle.

Specific items of this nature, properly *excluded* from current assets are (1) cash accounts, restricted as to usage and designated for purposes other than current operations, such as the acquisition or construction of fixed assets; (2) cash segregated in compliance with the terms of contracts, such as a bond indenture; (3) receivables arising from unusual transactions, including loans or advances to affiliates, officers, or employees, that are *not* expected to be collected within the current operating cycle of the business; and, (4) cash surrender values of life insurance policies on corporate officers.

Illustrated Presentations of Noncurrent Assets

Practical examples of the presentation of such noncurrent assets include that of Phoenix Steel Corporation described in a footnote to the annual balance sheet as follows:[4]

Cash, Restricted funds in escrow $4,036,340

> NOTE 2: Cash, restricted funds in escrow—The restricted funds in escrow are held by the Trustee under the indenture securing the Industrial Revenue bonds. Such funds represent debt service reserves and retainages on construction cost as follows:

	December 31	
	19X1	19X2
Debt service reserves	$3,431,237	$3,371,249
Retainage for plant modern-		
ization program	605,103	615,886
	$4,036,340	$3,987.135

The Singer Company included "Prepaid and deferred expenses" (discussed later in this Chapter) under "Other Assets" as follows:

Other Assets:

Other assets at December 31, 19X1 and 19X2 were as follows:

	19X1	19X2
	(Amounts in Millions)	
Prepaid and deferred expenses	$55.5	$59.6
Mortgages and other	11.9	13.5
Intangibles, less amortization	17.3	17.4
Deposits	9.3	6.5
	$94.0	$97.0

Fixed Assets (Properties, Plants and Equipment)

Properties, plants and equipment used permanently in the business are properly recorded at original acquisition cost, less depreciation, cost depletion, or amortization, depending upon the nature of the asset. The net amount remaining after such write-offs represents original costs that have not yet been recovered through charges against income.

As to asset valuation, Accounting Principle C-2 of the Inventory of Generally Accepted Accounting Principles of the American Institute of Certified Public Accountants states that fixed assets should be carried at cost of acquisition or construction unless such costs are no longer meaningful. In this connection, costs of construction to be charged to the asset account include direct costs as well as overhead costs incurred, such as engineering, supervision, administration, interest and taxes.

A control procedure and catalogue of property units have been found useful in listing fixed assets by types, stating minimum dollar expenditures for properties to be capitalized, stipulating that lesser dollar amounts be expensed, and directing that items no longer in service be removed by a debit to the Allowance for Depreciation for that asset type. Fixed asset control procedures of a manufacturing company might include the following:

Cost Basis

Costs of fixed assets to be capitalized include sales taxes and freight and are to be recorded net of discounts.

Construction Completion

Facilities are usually capitalized when substantially complete and occupancy is started. Subsequent final additions to cost are capitalized as incurred and depreciation is taken.

Capitalization

On fixed assets other than construction of major facilities, capitalization occurs as the cost is incurred. Depreciation is begun the month following capitalization of the asset. If a factory order is set up for an installation, the asset is charged to the factory order and depreciation is begun as the factory order is completed and the asset capitalized.

The original acquisition of units of real estate or personal property is capitalized on the books at cost plus freight and installation except that such items costing $500 or less are considered as expense.

Disposition—Other Than by Sale

Disposition of an asset may be effected by means other than sale or conversion to cash; e.g., abandonment, etc. If this occurs, the transaction is recorded as follows:

A charge is made to depreciation expense and a credit to the appropriate accumulated depreciation account in the amount required to fully depreciate the asset.

The asset is written off against the then equal, accumulated depreciation account.

Detailed Subsidiary Records

These usually consist of periodical computer runs and manually-posted property record cards that show the following:

Acquisition date
Acquisition costs
Amount to be depreciated
Monthly depreciation
Depreciation to date

Appreciation of Fixed Assets

Accounting Research and Terminology Bulletin No. 43, Final Edition, 1961, American Institute of CPA's, Chapter 9, Section B, noted that while cost is the recognized basis for fixed asset valuation, write-ups to appraised values have been made in the past because of rapid rises in price levels. When appreciation is entered on the books, income is to be charged with depreciation computed on the written-up amounts so that a company cannot at the same time claim larger property valuations in its statement of assets and take depreciation on asset values existing *before* the write-up.

Major objections to reporting financial effects of price-level changes in the past have been related to two things: (1) the alleged limitations of price index numbers; and, (2) a fear that statements based on historical costs were to be abandoned.

With respect to the first objection, Statement No. 3 of the Accounting Principles Board included an evaluation of index numbers available. The conclusion was reached by the APB that an index of the *general* price level should be used, rather than an index of the price of a specific type of goods or service.

Both the gross national product implicit price deflator, issued quarterly by the Department of Commerce, and the consumer price index of the Department of Labor are acceptable. Because of differences in coverage and the system of weight used, the two indexes may change at different rates in the short run, but over the long run the indexes have changed at approximately the same rate.

With respect to the second objection, namely, the fear expressed by some that statements based on historical costs might be abandoned, paragraph 25 of APB Statement No. 3 appears to be an adequate answer. It states that general price-level information is recommended for presentation *in addition to* the basic historical-dollar financial statements, but never in lieu of them.

APB Opinion No. 6 stated that property, plant and equipment should *not* be written up by an entity that reflects appraisal market or current values that are above cost to the entity. But this statement can not apply to foreign operations in the event of serious deflation or currency devaluation.

No examples of financial statement presentations in annual reports were found that showed the effects of price-level changes as a supplement to the basic historical-dollar financial statements. However, reference was made to the effects of continuing inflation such as the following footnote:

EATON YALE & TOWNE, INC.[5]

To Our Shareholders (page 3)

Inflation was the major challenge to management in 19___. Some of the effects of inflation can be illustrated by the fact that our labor costs rose 5.5 percent while material costs increased six percent, for a total of $45,100,000. These increased costs could not be entirely offset by cost reduction or price increases in a faltering economy. To counteract price erosion and other inflationary pressures, we instituted rigid cost controls, consolidated operations and streamlined personnel requirements at all levels.

Recovery of Asset Value
Through Charges to Operations

Appropriate provisions or allowances should be made in order to charge operations with the investment in depreciable assets over the estimated life of all assets. The allowance for depreciation should be shown on the balance sheet as a deduction from fixed assets after the latter have been relieved for all dispositions.

What is required to make these charges is a systematic approach using one of the following methods of determining depreciation: (1) straight line; (2) decreasing charge; and, (3) increasing charge. The decreasing charge method has become important since the adoption of the Internal Revenue Code of 1954, resulting in frequent use of the sum-of-the-year's digits and double-declining balance methods.

The provisions of Accounting Research and Terminology Bulletin No. 44 (revised)[6], state that there may be situations in which the declining balance method is adopted for income tax purposes but other appropriate methods can be used for financial accounting purposes. In such cases, however, accounting recognition is to be given to deferred income taxes if the amounts involved are material, as discussed below under "Deferred Income Taxes."

Ralston Purina's footnote with a reference to production facilities on lease indicates that these facilities have been capitalized as plant and equipment. This is in accordance with accepted practice for long-term leases providing for purchase options, with the liability being credited as discussed later in this chapter under "Long-Term Debt."[7]

The following distinctions are suggested between terms frequently confused, namely, Depreciation, Depletion and Amortization, used in the write-off of asset values to operations.

Depreciation

Depreciation represents the decline in value of plant and equipment due to wear and tear of normal use and obsolescence, measured year by year through the charging of a portion of the asset's original cost against income.

Cost Depletion

The reduction in the value of an investment in producing oil and gas acreage illustrates the proper use of the term *depletion.* The investment may be debited for expenditures for mineral rights, including the purchase price and lease bonuses paid to land owners. Also, each year that part of the value of producing acreage that is lost or depleted as gas and oil are produced is charged to operations, reducing income received from the sale of the minerals extracted.[8]

Cost depletion is not to be confused with the mineral depletion allowance, calculated for Federal Income Tax purposes which relates to the extraction of natural resources. This deduction, used only in the calculation of taxes, is confined by statute to a stated percentage of income, and does not appear in the income statement.

Amortization

Amortization, an accounting technique similar to depreciation, charges off the cost of certain assets, usually intangible assets such as patents, copyrights, and goodwill against income over a period of years.

Retirements

The retirements account represents charges against income for the undepreciated value of facilities that are taken out of service, that is, retired, prior to the end of their estimated useful lives. For example, a productive unit with an expected life of 20 years, torn down and replaced after 15 years of service, has remaining 5 years of service value. This value is eliminated as a retirement charge at the time that the unit is dismantled.

All three of the above types of expense, that is, depreciation, depletion, and amortization represent an exhaustion of usefulness resulting in a systematic charge of fixed asset costs to operations.

**Prepaid and Deferred Charges—Not
Included Under Current Assets**

Deferred charges *excluded* from current assets include future income tax benefits, financing charges and organization expenses. Such deferred charges are properly eliminated from current assets and shown as a separate caption, usually as the last major category of assets on the balance sheet after properties, plants and equipment.

Pension Costs as Prepaid Items

According to APB Opinion No. 8, accounting for the cost of written and unwritten pension plans should not be discretionary, that is, should not fluctuate with earnings or the availability of funds or be effected by Federal Income Tax rates currently in effect. An accounting method should be followed that includes the actuarial cost method consistently applied from year to year, with accounting emphasis on the income statement rather than the balance sheet.

No portion of pension cost is to be charged against retained earnings. The annual charge to income must fall within a defined minimum-maximum range charged each year in a rational, systematic manner to income. The balance sheet should record the existence of any pension plan in effect and the following particulars, either in the financial statements or their notes:

1. An indication that such plans exist, identifying or describing the employee groups covered;
2. Details of the company's accounting and funding policies;
3. The amount provided for pension costs for the period under review;
4. The excess, if any, of the actuarially computed value of vested benefits over the total of the pension fund, and any balance sheet pension accruals, less prepayments or deferred charges; and,
5. Significant matters affecting comparability for all periods presented, such as changes in accounting methods (actuarial cost method, amortization of past and prior service cost, treatment of actuarial gains and losses, etc.), changes in circumstances (actuarial assumptions, etc.), or adoption or amendment of a plan.[9]

Compliance with such principles is illustrated by the American Zinc Company as explained in a footnote to the financial statements:

Note 3—Pension Plans:
   The company has non-contributory pension plans for substantially all of its employees. Total pension expense for the year was $854,000 which includes amortization of prior service cost over a forty-year period. It is the present intention to fund within the succeeding year only the minimum amount required to keep the plans actuarially sound and this amount is included in current liabilities.[10]

Excess of Cost of Investments Over
Equities in Net Assets Acquired

This deferred charge, sometimes referred to as a debit differential or simply as goodwill, usually represents the excess price paid for the net assets of subsidiary companies acquired over the book value of such companies at the date of acquisition. This excess is to be charged against income regularly over a period of years, not to exceed 40 according to APB Opinion No. 17. Such differential between the acquisition price and the book value of the subsidiary's net assets acquired may turn out to be of a debit *or* credit nature, frequently caused by failure to properly record *all* the assets or liabilities by the company being acquired. Such debit differential should be prorated to the subsidiary's identifiable assets and liabilities and any excess over their fair value constitutes the goodwill discussed above.[11] In the disposal of a credit differential, APB Opinion No. 16 calls for its allocation to noncurrent assets of the subsidiary (excluding long-term marketable securities) on the basis of fair market values. The excess after the assets are reduced to zero is to be shown as a deferred credit and amortized over 40 years.

The straight-line method of amortization is to be applied in the write-off of such intangible assets to benefiting periods, according to APB Opinion No. 17,[12] unless a company demonstrates that another systematic method is more appropriate. Financial statements are to disclose the method and period of amortization and in no event is the intangible asset written off in the period of acquisition.

Factors to be considered in estimating useful lives of such intangible assets include the legal or contractual provisions that limit the maximum useful life; provisions for renewal or extension that might alter a specified limit on useful life; and, the effects of obsolescence and other economic factors that can reduce such useful life. The period of amortization is not to exceed 40 years even though at the time of acquisition analysis of certain intangible assets may indicate indeterminate lives likely to exceed 40 years.[13]

An illustration of the write-off of intangibles, such as goodwill or debit differentials, is the following:

THE AMERICAN SHIP BUILDING COMPANY[14]

Cost in excess of net tangible assets of businesses acquired, less amortization (Note 3) $1,004,020

> NOTE 3: Acquisitions— . . . . . In April and May, 19___, the Company acquired, in separate transactions, all of the outstanding

stock of two other companies for a combined cash purchase price of $940,000. The excess of the respective purchase prices over the fair value of tangible assets acquired is being amortized to operations over a 40 year period.

Deferred Income Taxes

If a company takes the maximum depreciation allowed for tax purposes on an accelerated method but accounts for internal purposes on a straight line basis, a "timing" difference occurs between taxable income and business income that will be offset in later years when straight-line depreciation exceeds the fast write-off.

Timing differences reduce income taxes otherwise payable early in the asset's life, providing temporary tax relief. Higher taxes result later in the asset's life, however, attesting to the fact that such "timing differences" do *not* represent permanent differences between taxable and book income. Therefore, the resulting income figure for *tax purposes,* during any one year of the asset's life, affords an unrealistic view of the company's earnings and tends to be misleading if presented as the true income for such years. To give full disclosure, the income statement should show the amount of tax normally paid on the income reported using straight-line depreciation at the tax rates existing when the asset was acquired. Any difference betwen this tax estimate and the actual tax liability for the year is credited to the deferred income tax account.

For book purposes, the amount charged to tax expense remains constant year by year, resulting in stockholder reports consistently based on straight-line depreciation. But the deferred income tax account picks up the difference between this constant tax expense each year and the *actual liability* for taxes payable as it appears on the company's tax return for that year. Such practice is illustrated in Ralston Purina's footnote to its income statement, as follows:

> For income tax purposes depreciation is computed on accelerated bases where permitted. The excess tax depreciation taken over book depreciation has resulted in a tax deferral which has been included in income taxes charged against earnings and credited to deferred income taxes.[15]

Unamortized Debt Expense

Previously, the excess, or unamortized discount, that a firm pays to liquidate a debt over the actual cash proceeds received from the creditor was disposed of through several different methods as follows: (1) by a direct write-off to income of the year in which the debt is incurred; (2) by amortization over the remainder of the original life of the bond issue being retired; and, (3) by amortization over the life of the *new* bond issue, usually floated for the purpose of retiring an existing bond issue at a higher interest rate than that currently available.

To correct this situation, APB Opinion No. 6 was issued, stating that such discount should be treated uniformly as a part of the cost of the new debt and written off systematically over the life of that indebtedness. Each period's operations are to be charged and the amount of discount remaining carried forward on the next balance sheet as a direct deduction from long-term debt. As noted earlier, long-term payables have achieved importance because of the desire to use leverage in the form of both short and long-term financing.

One approach to effective use of a firm's resources is found in the use of leases discussed below, instead of the use of the firm's capital.

Long-Term Debt

Debt incurred upon which repayment is due more than one year after the balance sheet date is considered long-term. The question of valuation and presentation of such debt is treated in APB Opinion No. 21. Debt instruments, such as long-term notes payable given for properties, goods, or services, are to be recorded on the books at the note's cash value. This seems reasonably straight-forward. But at least three situations can arise to cause problems: (1) no interest rate may be stated on the instrument; (2) the rate, if stated, may be unreasonable in terms of the existing money market; or, (3) the face value of the note may be significantly different from the cash value of the property or the market value of the note itself.

APB Opinion No. 21 recommends that all future cash flows (principal and interest) be discounted, using an appropriate, realistic interest rate in order to find the present value of the note. This interest rate should reflect such variables as the credit position of the issuer, prevailing interest rates on the market for similar instruments, collateral, and other relevant factors involved.

The determination of the present value may result in either discount or premium being attributed to the issuance of the long-term note that is to be shown on the balance sheet as a deduction from or as an addition to, the face value of the note and disposed of to interest expense over the life of the note. Costs of issuance are to be reported in the balance sheet as deferred charges as noted earlier in this chapter.

Long-term obligations have been defined as those that consist of *present* obligations, arising out of *past* actions—transactions *not* payable within the operating cycle of the business or within approximately one year if more than one operating cycle occurs within that year.[16] Bonds payable, mortgage notes payable, long-term notes payable, lease obligations, pension obligations, and long-term contracts for the purchase of properties fall within this category. The balance sheet presentation is discussed below for such items.

Bonds Payable

Borrowing from the general public for long-term funds frequently takes the form of bonds when the amount of money required is too large for any *one* lender to supply.

In whatever form long-term debt is issued, it is usually accompanied with restrictions for the protection of the lenders in a "bond indenture" or agreement, often printed on or attached to the formal instrument that evidences the debt. Restrictions might include the dollar amounts authorized to be issued in such instruments, the interest rate at which issued, the due date or dates, the collateral or fixed assets securing the debt, the sinking fund provisions required to meet repayments of principal and interest as the due date arrives, working capital, or dividend restrictions imposed by the lenders on the borrowers along with limitations as far as the incurrence of additional debt is concerned.

When needed for a thorough understanding of the financial position and the results of operations of the company, such restrictions should be described in the company's financial statements, in the body of the statement or in a footnote thereto, as illustrated below from the McDonnell-Douglas Corporation's notes to its consolidated financial statements:

> Under a Revolving Credit Agreement with a group of sixteen banks, effective 1 December 19___, MDC can borrow through 31 December 19___ a maximum of $400,000,000 on unsecured notes of 90 days or less, with interest at ¼ of 1% above the prime rate through 30 June 19___, and ½ of 1% above the prime rate thereafter. The Agreement required MDC to maintain a minimum working capital and net worth, restricts indebtedness, and limits cash dividends and other stock payments to an aggregate of 50% of the net earnings subsequent to 31 December 19___.[17]

American Zinc Company included these explanatory excerpts as to its long-term debt and refunding loan agreement:

> The refunding loan agreement requires annual prepayments on the Guaranteed Notes on October 1 of each year in an amount equal to one-half of the excess of the cash flow from operations over a specified amount for the preceding fiscal year. A deficiency in any fiscal year from the amount specified is to be deducted from any subsequent excess before determining the amount of the required prepayment.
>
> The refunding loan agreement provides, among other things, that the company will maintain an excess over current liabilities of at least $7,000,000 through June 30, 19___ and $6,000,000 thereafter. The agreement further requires that cash dividends and stock redemptions shall not be made if, after giving effect thereto, the net worth of the company shall be less than $35,000,000. [18]

Mortgage Notes Payable

A promissory note falling under this caption differs from an ordinary promissory note (or debenture) because under this caption it is secured by a mortgage that pledges title to specific property for the loan.

Mortgages payable in full at a maturity date are shown as fixed liabilities on the balance sheet until the year of maturity when they are shown as current. If payable in installments, the current installments of the mortgage payable are shown as current liabilities and the balance due more than a year hence is reported as a fixed liability.

Both the straight-line method and effective interest method are considered acceptable for periodic amortization of discount and expense or premium on debt if not materially different, in accordance with APB Opinion No. 21.

Lease Accounting—Long-Term

Two accounting methods are generally used for the handling of leases as long-term indebtedness.

In the first approach, no asset or liability is recorded. But footnote disclosure is recommended in APB Opinion No. 5 showing the length and nature of the lease and annual rentals to be paid.

Details of such an executory type of lease agreement are disclosed in Ralston Purina's Annual Report in footnote form as follows:

> Various properties are occupied under non-cancellable long-term leases. Such leases expiring more than three years from September 30, 19___

provide for minimum annual rentals of approximately $6,526,000. Of this amount, $960,000 relates to leases expiring within five years, $1,592,000 to leases expiring after five but within ten years, $2,180,000 to leases expiring after ten but within fifteen years, and the balance of $1,794,000 to leases expiring after fifteen years.[19]

The second method treats the lease transaction as a financial transaction in which an asset is acquired and a long-term liability created. The asset account is called "Leased Assets" and the liability account is termed "Lease Obligations" in the amount of the future rental payments. These rental payments represent the present value of all the annual payments required. Since assets under lease have a limited useful and physical life, the capitalized value is to be amortized by charges to operations to an account called Amortization Expense—Leased Assets and a credit to Accumulated Amortization of Leased Assets over the *life* of the asset rather than the *term* of the leases.

This treatment is in accordance with APB Opinion No. 5, which states:

> When the lease is in substance an installment purchase of property, the property and related obligation should be included in the balance sheet as an asset and liability, respectively, at the discounted amount of the future lease rental payments.[20]

An example of this method in practice is found in a recent Annual Report of Burndy Corporation where the long-term liability is reported in the balance sheet and explanatory footnote as follows:

BURNDY CORPORATION[21]

Long-term Debt—Portion due after one year:

Long-term lease purchase obligations (Note 5) $565,100

NOTE 5: *Long-Term Lease/Purchase Obligations*—The long-term lease/purchase obligations represent the present value of annual rentals for land and manufacturing plant of $50,000 to 19X1 and a final payment of $415,000 in 19X2.

Pension Liability

A company may limit its legal obligation by specifying that pensions shall be payable only to the extent of the assets in the pension fund or in the sinking fund created for that purpose. Pension plans normally continue indefinitely, however, and legal curtailments of the company's liability are not normally invoked while the company continues in business. Therefore, APB Opinion No. 8 states that accounting for pension costs should *not* be discretionary as was noted also under "Pension Costs as Prepaid Items," earlier in this chapter.

The entire cost of benefit payments ultimately to be made should be charged against income subsequent to the adoption, or amendment of a plan, and no portion of such cost should be charged against retained earnings.

The difference between the amount charged against income and the amount paid is to be shown in the balance sheet as accrued or prepaid pension cost. But if the company has a legal obligation for pension costs in excess of amounts paid or accrued, this excess should be shown as both a deferred charge and a liability. Unfunded prior service cost does not usually constitute a liability that should be disclosed in the balance sheet.[22]

Contingencies and Related Reserves

Disclosures, mentioned above, such as long-term leases of an executory nature, and assets pledged as security for loans, though requiring explanatory footnotes, are not classified as contingencies under Accounting Research Terminology Bulletin No. 50 because they do not possess the same degree of uncertainty. A contingency in this context refers to an existing situation involving considerable uncertainty through a related *future* event which may result in a realized loss or a liability.

Disclosure of contingencies should be made in the financial statements or appended footnotes indicating the nature of the contingency, with an estimate of monetary loss anticipated or with reasons why an estimate cannot be given.

In this connection a word of caution may be in order. Contingency provisions and reserves are not to be created and misused as a means of arbitrarily reducing income or shifting income from one period to another.[23] A most important objective of income presentation is the avoidance of any practice that leads to income equalization.

If a provision for a reserve made against income, is not properly chargeable to current revenues, not only is net income for the period understated, but if the reserve is used to relieve later periods of charges applicable to them, the income of such periods is also incorrectly reported.

Reserves are improper if created:

(1) for general undetermined contingencies;
(2) for indefinite possible future losses, such as, losses on inventories not on hand or not contracted for;
(3) for the purpose of reducing inventories other than to a basis that is in accordance with generally accepted accounting principles;
(4) without regard to a specific loss, related to the operations of the current period; or
(5) in amounts not determined on the basis of reasonable estimates of costs or losses.[24]

If a reserve of this type is set up, Accounting Research and Terminology Bulletin No. 43 states that it should be created by an appropriation of retained earnings and no losses are to be charged to it. No part of it should be transferred to income or used to affect the determination of net income for any year. Restoration to retained earnings is to be made when such an appropriation is no longer considered necessary. As to balance sheet classification, it should be shown as a part of shareholder's equity.

An example of the creation of such an appropriation for a contingent liability of uncertain amount follows from the Annual Report of Union Electric Company of Missouri.

The Federal Power Commission licenses for the Osage and Taum Sauk hydroelectric (operated since 1931 and 1963, respectively) require that after the first twenty years of operation certain percentages of project earnings in excess of specified rates of return be credited to amortization reserves.

In a 1971 case not involving the Company the Commission asserted a general policy for the determination of such amortization reserves. That case is now the subject of review by the United States Court of Appeals. Based on the principles set forth in that case a preliminary estimate indicates that the Company would be required to credit, as of December 31, 1971, approximately $2,000,000 to an amortization reserve for the Osage project, representing provisions applicable to the period from 1951. The Company is unable to determine the ultimate outcome of the matter at this time.[25]

Deferred Credits

Income received or recorded before it is earned, and income taxes payable in years *beyond* the present are included under the deferred credits caption.

An illustration of the use of the deferred credit account applies to the recognition of income for tax purposes upon completion of long-term contracts as described by Bank Building Corporation in a footnote to an annual report:

> For income tax purposes, income from construction contracts is recognized on the *completed contract basis.* Deferred income taxes have been provided for this and certain other differences between taxable income and income reported in the financial statements.[26]

In addition, negative goodwill or the credit differential also constitute deferred credits. As described in this chapter, these represent the excess of an acquired firm's book value over the acquiring firm's purchase price.

Minority Interests

Under the equity method of accounting for investments in controlled subsidiaries, the parent company reflects in its investment account that percentage of the subsidiary's net worth that it owns. The balance is shown under "minority interests." In an annual report, the account "Minority Interest in consolidated subsidiaries" is shown by American Brands, Inc,[27] following the "Deferred Income Taxes and other deferred credits" on the parent's consolidated balance sheet. The consolidated balance sheet portrays the assets and liabilities of the entire entity as a single entity even though minority interests exist. This follows the accounting position that each group of shareholders, including the minority interests, has a fractional interest in the *undivided* net assets of the subsidiary, rather than a fractional equity in any *specific* assets or liabilities.[28]

In conclusion the principle of "leverage," using a creditor's money to supplement the stockholder's investment and achieve economies of scale, finds a good tool in long-term debt as previously discussed. Such debt can become a permanent means of financing in order to increase earnings available to stockholders beyond the amount of capital that they can raise.

When a larger rate of return is earned on such borrowed funds than has to be paid as interest or debt service, the excess represents income to the stockholders. In addition, long-term creditors, having no vote, do not pose a threat to corporate management. Therefore, control is not diluted through the influx of such creditor capital.

On the other hand, sophisticated lenders will hedge their loans with all restrictions considered necessary for protection as illustrated previously under "Bonds Payable." These relate to dividend declarations, amount of working capital balances to be maintained by the company at all times, issuance of additional debt instruments by the company and future fixed asset expenditures. Retained Earnings appropriations to assist in protecting working capital against stockholder pressure for dividend payments in the face of long-term obligations, are described in the next chapter entitled "Analysis of Stockholders Equity."

REFERENCES

[1]Bank Building and Equipment Corporation of America, "Notes to Consolidated Financial Statements," year ending October 31, 1971, page 23.

[2]For in-depth treatment of this concept in business combinations, see *Advanced Accounting,* Griffin, Williams, and Larson. (Ill., Richard D. Irwin, Inc.), 1971.

[3]Singer Company, Annual Report for the year 1971, page 22.

[4]"Accounting Trends and Techniques," Annual Survey of Accounting Practices Followed in 600 Stockholders' Reports, 25th Edition, American Institute of Certified Public Accountants, 1971, page 89.

[5]*Accounting Trends and Techniques, op. cit.,* page 49.

[6]American Institute of Accountants, APB Opinion No. 44 (revised), July 1958, Accounting Research and Terminology Bulletins, final edition, 1961 page 1-A, American Institute of CPAs.

[7]Ralston Purina Company, Annual Report, "Summary of Accounting Principles and Other Financial Data." 1971, page 33.

[8]"Understanding Sun's Accounting Terms," page 2.

[9]APB Opinion No. 8, Accounting for the Cost of Pension Plans, par. 16,17, and 49.

[10] American Zinc Company, Annual Report of 1970, page 18.

[11]Griffin, Williams and Larson, *Advanced Accounting,* Richard D. Irwin, 1971, page 287.

[12]APB Opinion No. 17, Intangible Assets, American Institute of Certified Public Accountants, August 1970, par. 26-30.

[13]*Ibid.*

[14]*Accounting Trends and Techniques, op. cit.,* page 91.

[15]Ralston Purina, *op. cit.,* page 33.

[16]Kieso, Mautz, and Mayer, *Intermediate Principles of Accounting,* Wiley and Sons, Inc., Copyright (c) 1969, page 449.

[17]McDonnell-Douglas Corporation, consolidated financial statements of 31 December 1970.

[18]American Zinc Company, 1970 Annual Report.

[19]Ralston Purina Company, Annual Report for 1971, page 33.

[20]APB Opinion No. 5, par. 9.

[21]*Accounting Trends and Techniques, op. cit.,* page 115.

[22]APB Opinion No. 8, *op.* cit.

[23]APB Opinion No. 43, Accounting Research and Terminology Bulletins, final edition page 41.

[24]*Ibid.,* page 41.

[25]Union Electric Company of Missouri, 1971 Annual Report, *op.* cit., page 19.

[26]Bank Building Corporation, *op, cit.,* page 23.

[27]*Accounting Trends and Techniques,* 27th Edition, American Institute of Certified Public Accountants, 1973, page 172.

[28]Griffin, Williams, and Larson, *Advanced Accounting, op. cit.,* page 214.

5   Analysis of Stockholders Equity

Equity, or the ownership interests of corporate shareholders, includes the following items: (1) the total stated values of preferred stock issued; (2) the total par value of common issued, or stated value of no-par common; (3) capital in excess of par or stated value; (4) earnings employed in the business or appropriated to meet significant corporate objectives; and, (5) treasury stock.

Preferred Stock

Preferred stock may be cumulative, in which case no common stock dividends can be declared and paid until all preferred dividends in arrears have been taken care of. The frequently used *convertible* characteristic of preferred stock means that each share of preferred can be converted into a stipulated number of common shares. "Common stock equivalents" and other varieties of convertibles to common are discussed later in this chapter.

In the event of the firm's dissolution, *preferred* stockholders have a preferential right to receive a stipulated amount for each share before the common stockholders receive any return of their capital as indicated below.

Liquidation Preference of Preferred Stock

Preferred stock may be issued that has a preference in involuntary liquidation considerably in excess of the par or stated value of the shares. The difference between this preference in liquidation and the par or stated value of the shares may be of major significance to the users of a firm's financial statements. APB Opinion No. 10 recommends that, in these cases, the liquidation preference of the stock be disclosed in the equity section of the balance sheet, either parenthetically or short-extended, rather than either on a per share basis or by disclosure in footnotes.

In addition, the financial statements should disclose the total per share amounts at which preferred stock may be called or which are subject to redemption, and the total and per share amounts of overdue, cumulative preferred stock dividends.

An example of preferred stock presentation in the balance sheet features cumulative preferred stock, no-par value, but with stated values for each of the issues outstanding, as follows:

Preferred stock, without par value (entitled
to cumulative dividends), authorized 3,000,000
shares—

Stated value of shares outstanding, $100 per share—	December 31 (Thousands)
$6.40 Series—300,000 shares	$ 30,000
$4.56 Series—200,000 shares	20,000
$4.50 Series—213,595 shares	21,359
$4.00 Series—150,000 shares	15,000
$3.70 Series— 40,000 shares	4,000
$3.50 Series—130,000 shares	13,000

Stated value of shares outstanding, $92.25 per share—	
$8.00 Series—350,000 shares	32,288

Stated value of shares outstanding, $97.50 per share—	
$8.00 Series—425,000 shares (issued in 19___)	41,437
Total	$177,084[1]

Entries Required to Maintain Capital Stock Accounts

The maintenance of capital stock accounts, namely, capital stock issued, capital in excess of par value, and common stock in treasury, is illustrated in Figure 5-1.

Illustrated Control Procedure—Maintenance
of Capital Stock Accounts

Capital Stock Issued—Common—(Capital Stock)
_____

This account reports the par value of all common stock shares ($_____
_____), owned by stockholders, in accordance with the
Corporate Charter filed with the Secretary of the State of _____.

Credits to this account may arise from the declaration of stock dividends,
issuance of stock under employee incentive plans, or sale of additional
authorized shares. This credit is limited to the par value of shares issued
and any excess is credited to CAPITAL IN EXCESS OF PAR VALUE.

Debits to this account arise from the cancellation and retirement of any
outstanding shares.

Capital in Excess of Par Value
_____

This account shows the balance of Capital Stock transactions over or
under the par value or cost of the shares issued.

Credits to this account are the result of tranfers from RETAINED
EARNINGS for the amount in excess of the par value of dividend shares
distributed. Credits also result from issuance of additional authorized
shares or disposition of treasury stock at a price in excess of the stock's
par value or cost.

Debits may occur upon corporate reorganization, or upon issuance of
Capital or Treasury Stock for consideration valued below the stock's par
value or cost.

Common Stock in Treasury
_____

This account records the cost of the company's common stock purchased
by it on the open market.

Credits may occur upon disposition of the stock through cancellation or if
given out as additional employee reimbursement.

Figure 5-1

The *authorized* total of common shares is frequently presented
below the issued and *outstanding* shares that have been legally issued for

cash or other consideration accepted by the board of directors or that have been issued through stock dividends and stock splits.

Outstanding stock excludes reacquired or treasury stock. Common stock held in treasury at cost, is often deducted on the balance sheet from the issued and outstanding common stock. The computation of earnings per share is based on the weighted average of shares outstanding during the period. In determining the number of shares outstanding, reacquired shares are normally excluded.

As a result of the growing use of complex securities and the complications that this produces in the computation of earnings per share, additional disclosure was urged in APB Opinion No. 15 to explain adequately the rights and privileges of the various kinds of securities outstanding. Information is to be included as to dividend and liquidation preferences, participation rights, call prices and call dates (with respect to preferred), conversion or exercise prices and pertinent dates, sinking fund requirements, and unusual voting rights.[2] Such complex capital structures are illustrated in the case of the Singer Company, whose capital stock situation is described next.

Shareholders Equity

The capital stock of the Singer Company is summarized below:

	December 31, 19XX		
	Shares Issued	Stated or par value	Liquidation preference
		(Amounts in Thousands)	
Convertible preferred stock, without par value;			
Authorized 3,500,000 shares:			
Series $3.50, authorized 2,110,000 shares	1,604,385	$ 20,857	$160,439
Series $1.50, authorized 452,571 shares	452,571	4,073	31,680
$12.50 Series A through C, authorized 100,000 shares . . .	71,557	7,156	35,779
	2,128,513	$ 32,086	$227,898

Common stock, par value $10 per
share; Authorized 25,000,000 shares   15,738,396 $157,384

Common stock issued includes treasury stock of 214,468 and 141,116 shares at December 31, 1971 and 1972, respectively, which is carried at cost.

> The Series $1.50 Class A voting preferred stock has a stated value of $9 per share and is *convertible* at the option of either the holders or the Company into .9 share of common stock on or after January 1, 1972. Holders are entitled to receive cumulative cash dividends at the rate of $1.50 per share per annum prior to payment of dividends on common stock. The stock is callable for redemption after December 31, 1974, in whole or in part, at a price of $70 per share.[3]

Preferences and rights of the preferred stock are shown in Singer's footnotes, including the fact that holders are entitled to cumulative cash dividends at rates shown for each class prior to the payment of dividends on common. In addition, the reader is informed that the stock is callable for redemption on dates indicated at a stated redemption price of $70.00 per share. In another footnote the total number of shares issued during the year is indicated along with the number of shares of common reserved for conversion of preferred and the exercise of stock options, the stock purchase plan and the executive incentive compensation plan.

Capital invested by the stockholders is seen as the corpus of the enterprise,[4] to be fully maintained and any impairment accounted for currently and cumulatively. Operating deficits or losses, dividend distributions in excess of earnings, or treasury stock acquisitions exemplify such impairments to capital.[5]

Stock Dividends and Split-Ups

The issuance by a corporation of its common shares to its common shareholders, called a stock dividend, may be done to give the shareholders a part of retained earnings without distribution of cash or other property. No change occurs in either corporate assets or in the shareholders' respective interests. However, Accounting Research and Terminology Bulletin No. 43, Final Edition, 1961, states that the corporation should account for the *stock dividends* by transferring retained earnings to common stock, achieving a permanent capitalization of such earnings in an amount equal to the fair value of the additional shares issued.

A stock split-up refers to the issuance of common shares to common shareholders to increase the number of outstanding corporate shares. The point at which the number of shares issued becomes large enough to influence the market price is usually 20% or 25%, representing a stock split-up, but this volume varies, depending on the number of previously outstanding shares.

A *stock split-up* does not require a transfer from retained earnings. The corporation's report to its shareholders as to the nature of the issuance, that is, the nature of management's intentions is a principal consideration in recording the stock distribution as a stock dividend or as a split-up.[6]

Capital in Excess of Par or Stated Value

An account called *capital in excess of par stated value* may be used to show the difference between the value of the preferred and common at *market* and their total *stated* or par values. An example of the utilization and changes in this account is presented in the last section of this chapter.

Earnings Employed in the Business

Cumulative profits retained in the company after payments of cash dividends and transfers to common stock for stock dividends, comprise the balance of the account termed "Retained Earnings" or "Earnings Retained for Growth," as shown in Figure 5-2. Also illustrated are typical journal entries, both debit and credit types, normally made to this account.

The retained earnings account can be reduced by cash and property dividends, stock dividends, treasury stock requirements, recapitalizations, absorptions of losses, or prior period adjustments. As a result, one author has called this account the "meeting place" of the balance sheet and income statement accounts, representing the net accumulated earnings to the corporation.[7]

An illustration of such items that properly find their way into retained earnings is the following:

RETAINED EARNINGS

This account contains the undistributed net corporate earnings to date. Debits to this account arise through entries for:

> Dividend declarations
> Previous years' material
>   adjustments (prior period
>   adjustments)
> Current year's net loss

Credits arise through transfer of the current year's net earnings to this account.

Figure 5-2

Items Excluded From Retained Earnings

Retained earnings are generated only from income through transactions with parties *outside* the company and never through *internal* activities. For example, earnings are not recognized in the construction of machinery "in-house" at a lower cost than the company would have to pay on the outside. The savings realized are *not* income to be included in retained earnings because they originated within the company.

By the same token, income cannot be recognized on transactions with a company's own stockholders involving treasury stock since the purchase and sale of treasury stock are simply contractions or expansions of the firm's own paid-in capital.

Entries Involving Retained Earnings

Retained earnings in its entirety must be *unrestricted* as to dividend distributions unless such distributions are clearly indicated in the financial statements or through appropriations of retained earnings.[8] Figure 5-2 illustrates specific entries made to retained earnings and appropriated retained earnings accounts.

Transfers of retained earnings to invested capital accounts can be made after formal corporate action has changed the composition of the equity capital.[9] In addition, accumulated deficits may be eliminated against invested capital accounts after stockholder approval, establishing a new base line of accountability.[10]

Full disclosure in the event of reorganization requires that all new retained earnings from that point in time are clearly segregated and dated. Procedures involved are discussed next.

Corporate Readjustments—Impact on Retained Earnings

A corporation may, without formal court proceedings of dissolution of the corporation, establish a new basis for accounting of assets and corporate capital through a quasi-reorganization or corporate readjustment, following approval by its stockholders.[11] The result may be to give the company a "fresh start" with respect to assets, legal capital, and retained earnings.

A corporation may sustain heavy losses over a period of time, resulting in a deficit in retained earnings and a related overstatement of the carrying value of certain assets. A restatement of assets and paid-in capital through a corporate readjustment may remove the deficit from the books.

Readjustment Procedures

A clearance account called "Clearance–Quasi-Reorganization", is normally used to accomplish the restatement of balance sheet accounts, after the amounts involved have been determined. Retained earnings should be charged to the full extent of the balance in that account.

A new retained earnings account may be established, dated to run from the effective date of readjustment. This dating must be disclosed in financial statements until such time as is no longer necessary, usually five to ten years following the reorganization. Full disclosure of the readjustment procedures followed and their effects should be reported on the financial statements of the period involved.

Such readjustments are particularly important to a corporation with little prospect of improving its operating results because of high depreciation or other *fixed* charges against income. By reducing the values of its assets and its legal capital to a more reasonable basis, the deficit is eliminated.

In regard to depreciation charges, if plant accounts are written down to a more realistic amount, the result is that depreciation charges in subsequent statements are less than depreciation charges deducted for income tax purposes. This "tax benefit" is received by the reorganized company during the remaining life of the related asset, meaning that higher depreciation charges are continued for tax purposes only, on the same basis as before the reorganization. For book purposes, the lower depreciation charges must be recorded, based on the new, adjusted asset valuations.[12]

Appropriated Retained Earnings

Several types of retained earnings appropriations are used in practice to accomplish certain objectives such as: (1) to observe legal restrictions on retained earnings required by the laws of the state of incorporation. (One of these is to protect the firm's creditors by requiring that the corporation maintain its legal capital intact at all times for the benefit of the creditors. If and when the corporation wishes to reacquire its own stock, this restriction can be recognized in the accounts by an appropriation of retained earnings); (2) to adhere to contractual restrictions on retained earnings required by contracts such as those involved in floating bonds, to insure redemption at date of maturity through appropriations of retained earnings thus making the latter unavailable for dividends in the amount appropriated; and (3) to provide appropriations by the firm's board of directors at its discretion for purposes such as possible inventory declines, self-insurance, plant expansion, or general contingencies.[13]

In the event of reacquisition of its own stock, a firm may accomplish the first objective of retained earnings appropriations (above). The capital impairment arising from treasury stock acquisition requires a debit to retained earnings and a credit to an appropriated account because by state law the creditors must be protected to the full extent of the legal capital of the corporation. If a portion of capital stock is removed by reacquisition, something, namely, retained earnings, has to be substituted in the amount of the cost of such treasury stock. When this stock is sold, the entry is reversed.

The second reason for appropriating retained earnings is illustrated in practice in floating a bond issue. A corporation may agree as a condition precedent to obtaining the bond proceeds that retained earnings be reduced and retained earnings appropriated be credited. This action is to prevent the dissipation of assets through dividend payments. In addition, the amount agreed upon during the full term of the bond issue can be segregated in a special fund to meet the retirement of the bonds as they mature. When the bond is paid off, the appropriated amounts are returned to a "free" status, that is, back to retained earnings.

The third named in this section is illustrated by retained earnings appropriations for modifications on customer's contracts on a warranty or guarantee basis and by appropriations to cover possible employee terminations in the event of contract cancellations.

A major reason that appropriations are set up at the discretion of the board for possible future losses is to prevent retained earnings from being used as a basis for dividends. Such an appropriation is never to be charged with a loss if and when it occurs. The actual loss is charged to the period in which it is discovered or definitely determined. Otherwise, the earnings of that period are bypassed, overstating the profit of that period by not charging it with *all* losses applicable to it. Earnings per share, discussed below, are likewise distorted through such improper use of retained earnings appropriations.

Distinction Between Appropriations of Retained Earnings, Estimated Liabilities and Valuation Accounts

Certain accounts can confuse readers of financial statements because some listings appear to overlap in function. For example, accounts termed *estimated liabilities* can be confused with retained earnings appropriated for possible losses of various kinds. The distinction becomes clear when an estimated liability is set up by a charge to an expense account and a credit is given to the estimated liability account. When the obligation arises and payments are made, the estimated liability account is charged and cash is credited. An example of the latter is the workmen's compensation estimated liability. Experience indicates that some charges will recur and the only unknown factor is the amount involved. These charges represent losses that really accrue.

Are "Savings" Realized When a Firm Acts as Self-insuror?

On the other hand, there are potential losses that may or may not happen such as fire losses to inventory or to properties for which the firm may choose to act as self-insuror. The decision to self-insure against these potential losses may be accompanied by an appropriation of retained earnings and by *no* charge to the period's income account. But such appropriated retained earnings accounts cannot be charged with any realized loss. If the fire occurs, the loss is charged to that period and the credit is to cash or to whatever account payable the firm wishes. Although it is not charged, the appropriated retained earnings account can be debited and retained earnings credited to absorb the realized fire loss that will reach the retained earnings flowing through the income account of the year of the fire.

An optional procedure is to credit appropriated retained earnings for insurance premiums that would be paid if the firm were not on a self-insurance basis, and charge it for transfers to retained earnings based upon losses actually sustained. The resulting balance in the appropriated account for fire loss will measure the savings accruing to the company as a result of the self-insurance plan.[14] In addition, the appropriation for fire loss may be funded so that cash or the equivalent will be available for property replacement.

One problem inherent in the use of appropriations of retained earnings is the inference to the reader of the firm's financial statements that *all* retained earnings not so earmarked are available for dividends. This is usually not the case and this can be made clear by a footnote. Restrictions of retained income are illustrated in an American Airlines footnote to its statements as follows:

> American's debt agreements limit the amount available for payments of cash dividends on common stock. Under the provisions of the most restrictive of these debt agreements approximately $68,700,000 of American's retained earnings of $238,599,000 was not restricted for payment of cash dividends at December 31, 19____.[15]

With respect to the distinction between the use of valuations accounts and retained earnings appropriations, valuation accounts are established by charges to current revenue to provide for such losses as inventory obsolescence or deterioration, and credits to inventory to reduce inventory to the lower of cost or market. Such losses must be actually recognized.

However, it may be desired by management to set up an appropriation of retained earnings for *possible future* inventory decline. If so, no losses realized in the future can be charged to this type of appropriation anymore than to any other retained earnings appropriation, nor should any part of it ever be transferred to income. A loss on inventories requires disclosure in the income statement of the period in which it is recognized.

Earnings Per Share—Primary versus Fully Diluted

The caption reading, *primary earnings per share* in most income statements consists of earnings attributable to outstanding common stock and common stock equivalents.[16] A second caption reads, *fully diluted earnings per share.* According to APB Opinion No. 15, items that should be disclosed on the income statement include: (1) earnings per share for all periods covered by the statement of income; (2) a summary of pertinent rights and privileges of various securities outstanding, including dividend and liquidation preferences, participation rights, call prices and dates, and voting rights; and, (3) an explanation in the income statement of the basis upon which primary and fully diluted earnings per share are calculated. The latter are defined in Figure 5-3 and illustrated in the presentation of the Singer Company's operation as follows:

> Primary earnings per share is calculated by dividing net income after deducting the preferred dividend payments on the Series $3.50 preferred stock by the weighted average number of shares of common stock and common stock equivalents outstanding during the year. Common stock equivalents are shares of common stock reserved for issuance upon conversion of Series $1.50 Class A and $12.50 Series A through G cumulative convertible preferred stocks and shares relating to common stock options, granted if the average market price exceeded the option price during the period.
>
> Fully diluted earnings per share is calculated by dividing net income by the weighted average number of shares of common stock and common stock equivalents outstanding during the year, with the additional assumption that the Series $3.50 preferred stock had been converted.[17]

Figure 5-3 gives definitions under APB Opinion No. 15 for common stock equivalents, options, dilution, dual presentation, and primary and fully diluted earnings per share.

APB Opinion No. 15

Common Stock: A stock that is subordinate to all other stocks of the issuer.

Common Stock Equivalent: A security that is not, in form, a common stock but that usually contains provisions to enable its holder to become a

Figure 5-3

stockholder and because of the terms or the circumstances under which it was issued, is in substance equivalent to common stock.[1]

Option:[1] The right to purchase shares of common stock in accordance with an agreement, upon payment of a specified amount.

Dilution: A reduction in earnings per share resulting from the assumption that convertible securities have been converted or that options and warrants have been exercised or that other shares have been issued upon the fulfillment of certain conditions.

Dual Presentation: The presentation with equal prominence of two types of earnings per share amounts on the face of the income statement—one is primary earnings per share; the other is fully diluted earnings per share.

Primary Earnings per Share: The amount of earnings attributable to each share of common stock outstanding, including common stock equivalents.

Fully Diluted Earnings per Share: The amount of current earnings per share reflecting the maximum dilution that would have resulted from conversions, exercises, and other contingent issuances that individually would have decreased earnings per share and in the aggregate would have had a dilutive effect.

[1]Thus, stock options, warrants, or comparable instruments may have a low cash yield or none at all but have definite value because of the privileges they confer to the holder to acquire common stock at pegged prices over a specific period of time. These are always to be regarded as common stock equivalents.

Figure 5-3 *(continued)*

Treasury Stock—both Common and Preferred

The most practiced presentation for common treasury stock is to subtract its cost from all preceding equity items to arrive at true stockholders' equity. These shares represent stock reacquired, held by the company, and carried at the cost of reacquisition, for various purposes discussed below. Another approach that is used in the case of preferred treasury stock is that of deducting the latter at par or stated value from preferred outstanding of the same class.[18]

General Motors Corporation reported the acquisition and composition of its treasury stock at the year's end suggesting the substantial use of reacquired stock for employee compensation and performance motivation as follows:

Common Stock in Treasury

During 19XX, the Corporation acquired for employee plans 2,529,501 shares of common stock for $176,795,035.

Common stock in treasury included (1) 660,119 shares ($52,348,955) held for installment deliveries of bonus awards related to prior years and contingent credits related to terminated stock options, (2) 373,253 shares ($29,955,964) available for contingent credits related to outstanding stock options and (3) 495,673 shares ($34,044,237), available for future bonus awards and contingent credits.[19]

General Electric Company held common treasury stock under the deferred incentive compensation plans recorded at *market value* at the time of allotment with the liability recorded under other liabilities. The company's remaining common treasury stock was carried at *cost.* Corporate objectives for these shares were for compliance with future requirements, including possible conversion of General Electric Overseas Capital Corporation convertible indebtedness.[20]

Retirement of preferred stock through the operation of a preferred stock sinking fund, created by earmarking 5% of annual net earnings for such funding, is described below in a footnote by O'Sullivan Corporation:

> Preferred Stock Sinking Fund—The certificate of incorporation provides that, each year, 5% of the annual net earnings shall be set aside as a fund and used, in the sole discretion of the Board of Directors, to purchase and/or redeem preferred stock. On December 31, 1972, the net accumulated requirements for this purpose totaled $49,821. The Directors are not required to purchase or redeem any preferred stock until this fund equals or exceeds $10,000. In February 1973, 2,555 shares of preferred stock, costing $47,903, were retired by the sinking fund.[21]

How Common Stock is Used in a Growth-Oriented Firm

An analysis of changes to summarize two years of transactions in common stock is demonstrated below. Stock splits are used in a growth-oriented corporation to conserve working capital for operating purposes, while paying modest dividends on common. Common is issued in return for real estate acquisitions and stock options used as supplementary executive compensation as follows:[22]

| | Common Stock | | Capital in Excess of Par Value |
	Shares	Amount	
Balance, December 31, 19X1	22,599,744	$22,600,000	$70,452,000
Stock options exercised—19X2	25,930	25,000	772,000
Balance, December 31, 19X2	22,625,674	22,625,000	71,224,000
2-for-1 stock split in form of a dividend . .	22,625,674	22,626,000	(22,626,000)
Shares issued in real estate acquisition . . .	78,000	78,000	3,803,000
Stock options exercised—19X3	187,036	187,000	3,576,000
Balance, December 31, 19X3	45,516,384	$45,516,000	$55,977,000

In summary, an analysis of corporate practice in this chapter indicates adherence to specific accounting principles: 1) The capital invested by stockholders as the corpus of the enterprise or corporate entity whose identity must be fully maintained;[23] 2) Any impairment of invested capital resulting from operating deficits, losses of any nature, dividend distributions in excess of earnings, and treasury stock purchases is to be accounted for both currently and cumulatively;[24] 3) Retained earnings are to be shown as the cumulative balance of periodic earnings less dividend distributions of whatever nature; 4) The entire balance is deemed to be unrestricted as to dividend distributions unless restrictions exist (as was illustrated with various examples of retained earnings appropriations); 5) In regard to retained earnings decreased by transfers to invested capital accounts, accumulated deficits are eliminated against invested capital accounts;[2 5] 6) The emphasis of ratios with respect to book value and earnings per share, both primary and fully diluted is important.

This chapter concludes the analysis of corporate balance sheet accounts and their usage in practice. The next chapter deals with Partnerships—their formation, dissolution, methods of dividing profits between partners and steps involved in transforming the partnership into a corporation.

REFERENCES

[1] Union Electric Company, 1971 Annual Report, page 18.

[2] APB Opinion No. 15.

[3] Singer, Annual Report, December 31, 1971, *op. cit.,* page 27.

[4] Accounting Research and Terminology Bulletin No. 43, Final Edition, (AICPA) 1961, Principle B-2, Appendix A.

[5] *Ibid.*

[6] Accounting Research and Terminology Bulletin No. 43, *op. cit.*

[7] *Intermediate Accounting,* Simons and Karrenbrock, Fourth Edition, South-Western Publishing Company, page 643.

[8] Accounting Research and Terminology Bulletin No. 43, *op. cit.*

[9] *Ibid.*

[10] *Ibid.*

[11] *Ibid.*

[12] Accounting Research and Terminology Bulletin No. 46, Final Edition (AICPA) 1961, "Discontinuance of Dating Earned Surplus."

[13] Karrenbrock, *op. cit.,* chapter 22, page 669-673.

[14] Karrenbrock, *op. cit.* chapter 22, page 675-677.

[15] American Airlines, Annual Report for 1971, page 16.

[16] Harry Simons and J.M. Smith, *Intermediate Accounting.* Fifth Edition, South-Western Publishing Co., 1972, page 789.

[17] Singer Company, *op. cit.,* page 23.

[18] *Accounting Trends & Techniques,* 27th Edition, 1973, American Institute of Certified Public Accountants, New York, page 201.

[19] General Motors Corporation, *op. cit.,* page 38.

[20] *Accounting Trends, op. cit.,* page 203.

[21] *Ibid.,* page 204.

[22] Anheuser-Busch, *op. cit.,* page 18.

[23] Accounting Research and Terminology Bulletin No. 43, *op. cit.,* Principle B-2.

[24] *Ibid.*

[25] *Ibid,* Principle B-5.

6   Partnerships – A Guide to Key Agreement Clauses, Entries, and Reporting

Characteristics

A partnership can be any group of persons bound together by a contractual relationship. The result is an individual entity as far as third parties are concerned that can own property, sue and be sued just as any individual can.

Partners act as *general* agents of this association with power to bind the partnership for their acts with third parties. If a *limited* partnership exists, one or more partners do *not* have power as general agents and this fact must be conveyed in all firm letterheads and other communications indicating the makeup of the partnership so that third parties are not misled.[1]

Comparison With Corporate Form

Unlimited liability is involved as far as general partners are concerned in contrast to corporate stockholders whose liability is limited to the cost of their fully paid stock. The limited partner's liability is comparable to such stockholders.

As to continuity, any change in the composition of the partnership because of death, new partners, etc., normally results in its termination.

---

[1]For information in greater depth as to partnership formation, maintenance of partners' accounts, the statement of changes in partners' capital accounts, and other intricacies of partnership accounting, the reader is referred to *Advanced Accounting,* Fourth Edition, Simons and Karrenbrock, South-Western Publishing Co., 1968, Chapter 1.

The corporation doesn't have a problem in the transfer of ownership interests nor in continuity of existence. Another difficulty encountered by the partnership is its trouble in raising large amounts of capital and going public; the corporation (once established profit-wise) can accomplish these objectives much easier.

The corporation usually pays more in the way of income taxes than the partnership. Stockholders are subject to double taxation—first on corporate profits and second on dividends paid to such stockholders. The partnership files an information return but does not pay taxes, operating in conduit fashion, whereby the partners report their distributive shares of the partnership income on their individual tax returns, whether or not distributed. Thus, the partner's share of partnership income becomes a part of his total income subject to tax.

Articles of Partnership—Items To Spell Out

Even though a partnership can be formed orally, the articles of partnership spell out the rights and duties of each partner including: (1) the agreed upon investments by each partner; (2) the values assigned to such investments; (3) the rights and powers of each partner; (4) the accounting period or fiscal year; (5) the profit and loss sharing ratio; and, (6) any special provisions required to reimburse partners for the recognition of differences between investment and service contributions. Other factors to be made clear in the agreement include withdrawals permitted or investments required by each partner *before* the effective beginning date and their treatment in the accounts. Any other factors that the partners want to include in the agreement, such as paying for life insurance on the partners for their beneficiaries' benefit or for the surviving partners, or special procedures for settlement of a partner's interest upon his withdrawal, etc., must be provided for.

Things to Watch

Each partner's interest in the firm's *capital* must be distinguished from his share in its *profits.* The former is in his capital account, consisting of his original investment, subsequent investments and withdrawals and his share of the firm's profit or losses to date. The agreed upon profit and loss sharing ratio determines each partner's capital growth. Partners can agree to any kind of sharing of profits and losses and in the *absence* of any express agreement the ratio is interpreted to be equal between the partners.

Another determinant of each partner's capital balance is the valuation of assets invested by them in lieu of cash. Subsequent sales of these assets in an amount other than the book figures result in profits or losses divided between partners in the profit and loss sharing ratio. These assets must be stated at their fair market values at date of investment and the capital accounts credited accordingly.

When the Business Entity Changes
To or From a Partnership

When it is desired to change from an individual proprietorship to a partnership or from a partnership to a corporation, the old books of the previous entity can be kept or new books opened. If new books are opened, entries are required, as shown in Figure 6-1, to close the old books and transfer the net assets to the new firm. Entries are made on the new books detailing the assets, liabilities, and capital balances taken over by the new entity.

Journal Entries Recording the Changeover from an
Individual Proprietorship to a Partnership

(1) Assume that old Proprietorship Books are to be used:

(a)

Allowance for Doubtful Accounts	$ 500	
Inventory	4,000	
Allowance for Depreciation, Furniture & Fixtures	3,000	
Goodwill	5,000	
Trade Accounts Receivable		$ 800
Furniture & Fixtures		2,000
Schmidt, Capital		9,700

Recording adjustments to old Proprietor's capital account pursuant to Articles of agreement signed to participate in Partnership with Brown:

(1) Specific receivables of $800 are not accepted and must be written off;

(2) An allowance of 5% is to be provided for doubtful accounts taken over by the new partnership, after aging the accounts;

(3) Furniture and fixtures are to be valued at fair market value ($20,000) less depreciation sustained to date of 50%; and,

(4) Goodwill to the old partner has been agreed to at $5,000.

Figure 6-1

(b)

Cash	$20,000	
Brown, Capital		$20,000

Recording cash investment of second partner, Brown.

(2) Assume that new books are to be opened for the partnership:

(a)

Cash	$ 5,000	
Trade Accounts Receivable	10,000	
Inventory	6,000	
Furniture and Fixtures	20,000	
Goodwill	5,000	
Allowance for Doubtful Accounts		$ 500
Allowance for Depreciation		10,000
Accounts Payable		7,000
Schmidt, Capital		28,500

Recording agreed-upon values of old Proprietorship accounts on new Partnership books pursuant to signed Articles of Agreement ((1)(a) above.)

(b)
(Same entry as (1)(b) above.)

Figure 6-1 *(continued)*

Conversion From a Sole Proprietorship

Matters that have to be agreed upon in converting from a sole proprietorship include the amounts at which each of the assets will be valued and goodwill to be allowed the old proprietorship in coming into the partnership.

Partners' accounts may include capital and drawing accounts and partners' receivable or payable accounts. Transactions to credit or charge the partner's capital account can be recorded right in the capital account but a cleaner audit trail results if a separate drawing account is opened. For example, it is easier to determine that the partners' drawings are staying in line with the original agreement if these are charged to a separate drawings account than if buried in each partner's capital account along with credits from investments and profit or loss pro rata distributions.

Keeping the Capital Accounts Clean

An important reason for using separate accounts is to improve account visibility, insuring that various provisions to properly reward the partners are complied with. For example, a permanent, minimum amount of investment by each partner may be stipulated and interest allowed on capital balances exceeding such required amounts. Conversely, interest may by agreement be charged on any capital account deficiencies. Thus, a credit balance shown in a drawing account would indicate that the partner had withdrawn less than the increases that took place in his interest in the business, whereas a debit balance would indicate that he had withdrawn more. But this is visible only if a separate account is opened for each partner's drawings and not buried in the partner's capital accounts.

When profits, losses, and withdrawals against profits are summarized in the drawing accounts and these accounts are left open, the latter accounts perform like retained earnings accounts in a corporation and the partner's capital accounts like corporate capital stock accounts.

Agreement Must be Specific Regarding Profit and Loss Sharing Ratio

Profits and losses can be divided equally in an arbitrary ratio—in the ratio of the partner's balances in their capital accounts (original, beginning, ending, or average balances), or interest can be allowed on partner's capitals. The balance can be divided on an arbitrary basis, or salaries or bonuses may be allowed for each partner's services and the balance divided on an agreed upon basis.

Points to Watch!

When the partnership agreement provides without qualification that interest is to be allowed on investment balances of each partner, interest must be on the bases stipulated, that is, on capital balances at the beginning or end of the period or on average balances. Even though the firm's operations result in a loss or if earnings are less than the allowable interest amount, the credit is legally required. After the entry for the interest as is called out in the articles of agreement, and a deficit occurs, it is transferred to the partner's drawing accounts in the P & L sharing ratio. See journal entry illustration in Figure 6-2.

Entries in the partner's drawing accounts should be limited to the regularly allowed drawings. Any excess should be charged directly to that partner's capital account. Additional investments during the period will be recorded as credits to the capital account. The result will be a clean balance in the capital accounts without the need for a great deal of analysis (because drawings are kept separate) before the average capital ratio distribution can be determined. In general, the partnership books should be kept in a way that makes it easiest to arrive at the distribution of profits based on whatever agreement the partners have.

Journal Entries Reflecting Partner's Profit and Loss
Sharing Ratio

Interest on Capitals

Assumption:

(1) Partnership Articles of Agreement state that interest of 8% shall be allowed on *average* balances in each partner's investment account; remaining profit to be shared equally:

(a)

Profit and Loss	$3,990	
Schmidt, Drawing		$2,310
Brown, Drawing		1,680

Crediting interest on partners' capital accounts as follows:

(1) Schmidt: Interest on $28,500 at 8% for 9 months:	$1,710
" " $30,000 at 8% for 3 months:	600
	$2,310

(2) Brown: Interest on $20,000 at 8% for 6 months:	$ 800
" " $22,000 at 8% for 6 months:	800
	$1,680

(3) Partnership earnings for the year were $1,300.

(b)

Schmidt, Drawing	$1,345	
Brown, Drawing	1,345	
Profit and Loss		$2,690

Charging the partners equally for the deficit for the year:

Figure 6-2

Partnership profit for the year: $1,300
Deduct interest on capitals: 3,990

Deficit divided equally, accord-
   to Partnership agreement: 2,690

Figure 6-2 *(continued)*

Interest on Partner's Loans or Advances

Interest charged to a partner on a loan *from* the partnership is recorded as *interest income* to the partnership. Conversely, interest paid to a partner on a loan to the partnership, as opposed to an addition to his capital account is an expense or cost of doing business to the partnership. The interest rate must be stated in the partnership agreement.

Salaries or Bonuses to Partners

Partnership articles may direct that a certain salary or bonus be paid to one partner and not to others. This may be based on the amount of contribution to the business. Such salaries must be paid even though the period's profit is inadequate or if a loss occurs! In the latter case, the period's loss is increased by the salary amount and the total carried to each partner's capital account in the P & L sharing ratio.

Intent of the Partners Must
be Reflected on the Books

The most important thing to reflect is the *intent* of the partners, stipulated in the partners' agreement. For example, a partner's bonus may be directed in the agreement to be in the form of a percentage of profits. If so, the agreement must be so drawn as to specify whether the percentage is to be applied to the firm's profits figure *before* or *after* deduction of the bonus. Otherwise, the original intent of all partners when going into business may not be properly recorded.

Watch the Base on Which
Bonuses are Calculated

When there are nonrecurring revenue or expense items, should these be excluded from the base on which the partners' bonuses are figured? Or should the bonus payment apply only to the actual profit from operations? Only the signed agreement can answer these questions. When both salaries and interest are allowed by the agreement, drawing accounts are credited for both allowances and any balance in P & L is divided in the P & L sharing ratio, as illustrated in Figure 6-3.

Journal Entries Illustrating Partners' Distribution through Bonuses, Salaries, and Interest

Assumption:

(1) Partnership Articles of Agreement state that:

(a) Interest credited per Figure 6-2;
(b) Bonus to be paid to Schmidt of 10% of Partnership profit *after* salaries, bonuses, and interest on capitals; and,
(c) Profit for the year of $20,000

(2) To determine amount of Schmidt's bonus:

$$X(\text{bonus}) = 10\% \ (\text{Profit} - \text{salaries} - \text{interest} - X)$$
$$X = 10\% \times (\$20{,}000 - \$5{,}000 - \$3{,}990 - X)$$
$$X = \$11{,}010 - .10X$$
$$1.1X = \$11{,}010$$
$$X = \$1{,}000$$

Figure 6-3

Reporting Partner's Distributions in the Earnings Statement

A full analysis of the distribution of earnings may be reported at the bottom of the income statement. Where salaries, interest, or bonuses are paid to partners, a schedule shows all particulars, that is, partnership income less all distributions and the balance left for final distribution.

Partners' expense accounts are closed at the end of the period, resulting in the amount of earnings distributable in the agreed profit and loss sharing ratio. Salaries and bonuses are listed with other expenses in arriving at such partnership net income or loss for the period.

Prior Period Adjustments

Corrections of prior period errors in a partnership require a search back to the year in which the error occurred to find out what the P & L sharing agreement was at that time, so that the capital accounts can be corrected accordingly. A comparison of what each partner should have received with what he did receive, based on the profit agreements for that period, must be made. Problems may arise in this connection. For example, should extraordinary items receive current recognition in this year's income statement (and distribution to the partners) or be included in the restatement of the prior fiscal period's income in which the error was discovered?

Sales of securities or other assets for gains or losses accrued over a number of years illustrate such extraordinary items. Failure to measure depreciation satisfactorily in prior periods may further complicate the issue. Answers to all such questions should be anticipated when the partnership agreement is drafted.

Statement of Changes in Partner's Capital Accounts

A third statement is required in addition to the partnership's balance sheet and income statement explaining changes in the partner's accounts in an accounting period. Starting with the capital accounts at the beginning of the period, each partner's capital contributions are added, withdrawals subtracted.

The period's distribution of profit or losses is applied, after giving effect to the salaries, bonuses, capital on investment balances and all prior period corrections described in this chapter. Ending capitals for each partner result thereby affording a clear audit trail for analyses as shown in Figure 6-4.

As a result, analysis is simplified, including the audit of the partnership books and the determination that the articles of partnership have been complied with in all particulars.

Statement of Changes in Partners' Capital Accounts

Assumptions: Same as used in Figure 6-3.

Schmidt and Brown, Partnership
Statement of Changes
For Year Ended _____

	Schmidt	Brown	Total
Beginning Capitals:	$28,500	$20,000	$48,500
Contribution during year:	1,500	2,000	3,500
	30,000	22,000	52,000

Figure 6-4

Distribution of year's income:	Schmidt	Brown	Total
Interest on capitals (Figure 6-2)	2,310	1,680	3,990
Salaries	5,000		5,000
Bonus (Figure 6-3)	1,000		1,000
Balance divided equally:	5,005	5,005	10,010
Total	13,315	6,685	20,000
Balance	43,315	28,685	72,000
Less partners' drawings:	5,000	4,000	9,000
Ending Capitals:	$38,315	$24,685	$63,000

Figure 6-4 *(continued)*

7 Practicalities of Municipal Accounting and Reporting

The same accounting functions of analyzing, recording, summarizing, and interpreting the financial transactions of an economic enterprise apply also to the activities and programs of the federal, state, and local levels of government and the public services provided in established geographical areas. Accounting procedures used to record such governmental operations constitute municipal accounting and are characterized by "stewardship reporting," because of a predominantly legal orientation.

Fund Accounting

In governmental accounting the primary accounting unit is referred to as a fund, representing an accounting entity featuring a self-balancing set of accounts for recording resources used in the operation, as well as related liabilities, allowances, and equities. Such groups of accounts are segregated for the purpose of carrying on specific operations in accordance with relevant regulations.[1]

Perhaps the unique features of fund accounting are that specific objectives are attributable to each fund and within each fund the set of accounts is self-balancing, with its own resources and related liabilities. Each governmental entity has many separate indentifiable activities, each of which can result in the creation of a separate fund, depending upon the size and operation of the city or other unit involved.

Specific funds that will be discussed are: (1) the *general fund;* (2) *special revenue fund;* (3) *rotating or revolving fund;* (4) *special assessment funds;* (5) *capital project funds;* (6) *debt service funds;* (7) *trust and agency funds;* and (8) other self-balancing groups of accounts, such as the *general fixed assets group* and the *general long-term debt group.*

The General Fund

All revenues and activities not recorded in a special fund are usually accounted for in the *general fund.* Therefore, most governmental operations are recorded in the general fund.

Sources of revenues for this fund include property taxes, licenses, fines, and penalties. Expenditures follow the typical municipality functions such as fire, police, sanitation, and administrative activities. Closely related to such functional classifications are those indicating the expenditure object, illustrated by wages, supplies, and many types of operating costs.

Budgetary Accounts Used in the General Fund

Before discussing the procedural detail involved in keeping the general fund ledger, an explanation follows with respect to budgetary accounting entries usually reflected in that fund. This is necessary because budgetary accounts are formally journalized in the general fund, using such accounts as the *"estimated revenues account"* and *"appropriations"* (or authorized expenditures).

Budgetary objectives of a municipality usually combine both planning and control. An estimate of anticipated revenues and expenditures for a given period comprises a planning budget. After approval by the appropriate legislative body, the budget becomes a relatively inflexible control device. Although in commercial accounting, budgets are frequently used for planning and control, the budgets are not usually recorded in the accounts. In governmental accounting, the authorized budget is formally recognized in special budgetary accounts, i.e., *estimated revenues* and *authorized expenditures* that constitute a formal record of the financial plan.

To distinguish between planned results (used in budgetary accounts) and the real world, so-called proprietary accounts are used to record actual transactions. The result is that *Revenues,* a proprietary account, can be compared in total with its corresponding budgetary account, *Estimated*

Revenues, to see how closely actual receipts approximated those planned for the period.

Encumbrance Accounting in the General Fund

The use of *encumbrances* is peculiar to governmental accounting. This technique restricts expenditure authority. In practice, purchase orders or other commitment documents, such as purchase requisitions, are recorded on the books of the general fund, thereby committing or encumbering such amounts. The balance represents this fund's estimated "free" or available budget for future expenditures. When the invoice is received, such encumbrance accounts are reversed and the actual amount of the liability is set up.

An account usually found in the general fund is that of *Appropriations,* a formal legislative authorization to the governmental unit of the stated dollar amount that it can spend for a specified purpose within a specified period of time. The appropriation is the legal spending authorization approved by the legislative body. Partial (usually quarterly) allocations of this annual appropriation, known as *Allotments* are made as a further effort to prevent overexpenditure by the municipality throughout the budget year.

The general fund requires entries recording the approval of the budget at the beginning of the year, by journalizing the budgetary accounts mentioned above. These are the estimated revenues and expenditures (appropriations) that operate as a control on actual expenditures for the period. A balancing account, called *Fund Balance,* represents the planned free revenues budgeted by the spending unit. Examples of such entries will follow.

Accounting Procedures in Practice

Flow Chart I conveys an overall view of the flow of municipality source documents into original books of entry, recording a fund's receipts and disbursements. Balance sheet and operating account titles used in municipalities in recording such transactions are illustrated below.

Transactions are then entered in the original books of entry shown in Flow Chart I, being summarized at the end of each period and posted to each ledger account in which there has been activity. This flow of the municipality's transactions from source documents through books of original entry into books of final entry—the ledgers of each fund—is traced in Flow Chart II.

FLOW CHART I

MUNICIPALITY'S FLOW OF DOCUMENTS ILLUSTRATED

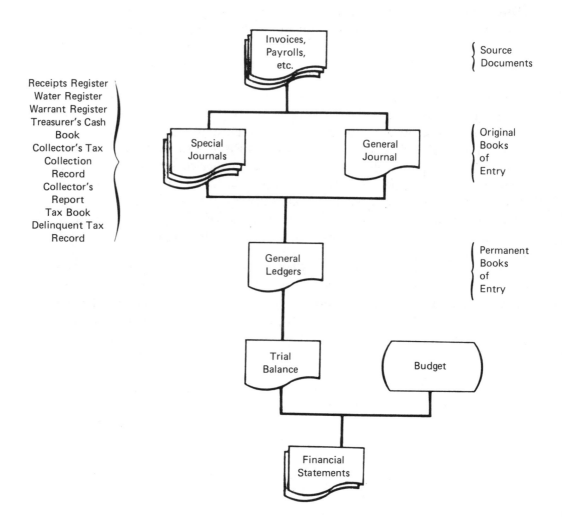

FLOW CHART II

ACCOUNTING FLOW BY FUND

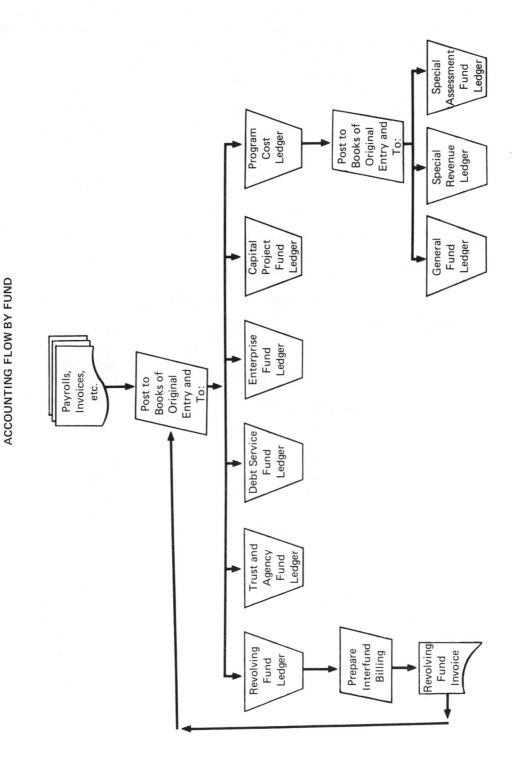

Entries necessary to open the books for the fiscal year, recurring entries, procedures at the end of each month, and entries to close the books at the end of the period are indicated below.

Typical Entries in the General Fund

Budgetary accounts, opened in the books of the general fund following approval of the budget for the fiscal year, are journalized in practice as follows:

ENTRY # 1

	Debit	Credit
Estimated Revenues	$ x--x	
Appropriations		$ x--x
Fund Balance		$ x--x

The recording of receivables required by the levy of taxes may be recorded as shown below:

ENTRY # 2

	Debit	Credit
Taxes Receivable	$ x--x	
Allowance for Un-collectible Accounts		$ x--x
Revenues		$ x--x

If any part of the tax levy becomes delinquent, it is transferred to Taxes Receivable—Delinquent and the allowance for uncollectible accounts also reclassified to show the delinquency. In contrast to the accrual basis of accounting followed in Entry #2, entries for other revenues, such as licenses and fees, are usually recorded on a cash basis.

The *encumbrance procedure* records future commitments as soon as a committing document is issued. The issuance of a purchase order, for example, usually results in an entry to earmark or encumber that amount of the municipality's appropriation for the fund involved, as illustrated on the next page.

ENTRY # 3

	Debit	Credit
Encumbrances	$ x--x	
Reserve for Encum-brances		$ x--x

The debit to encumbrances (by fund) in the amount of the liability incurred, records the amount encumbered or committed. The "free" or uncommitted balance is thus constantly available, but on an estimated basis because the source document involved—the purchase order—can be changed in amount.

When the invoice is received from the vendor for which this purchase order was issued, the liability becomes firm. At this time the encumbrance entry is reversed (in the exact amount set up in Entry #3) and replaced with the *actual* liability, as recorded in Entries #4 and #5:

ENTRY # 4

	Debit	Credit
Reserve for Encumbrances	$ x--x	
Encumbrances		$ x--x

ENTRY # 5

	Debit	Credit
Expenditure Accounts (by fund, program, etc.)	$ x--x	
Accounts Payable, etc.		$ x--x

Certain expenditures such as salaries, wages, bond interests, and other recurring expenditures are not encumbered (see Entry #6) because the amount is known, doesn't have to be estimated and, therefore, can be recorded as a firm commitment without the intermediate steps involving encumbrance accounts.

ENTRY # 6

	Debit	Credit
Salary Expense	$ x--x	
Salaries Payable		
(or cash)		$ x--x

The chart of accounts is usually designed to facilitate the accumulation of actual operating expenditures by funds, programs, and object of expenditure permitting comparison with the respective budgetary amounts. The computer's capabilities, offering multiple sorts of source data once captured, lend themselves admirably to this purpose. Properly programmed, the computer can produce printouts by *fund* (to show the amount of free budget remaining) as well as by *program* (for purposes of managerial control discussed later in this chapter).

Closing Sequence

Both budgetary and operating accounts are closed at the end of the municipality's accounting period and the difference transferred to the *fund balance* account. Journal Entries #7 and #8 show in skeleton form the closing entries in which the month's estimated revenues exceed actual revenues, and appropriations exceed the total of actual expenditures and encumbrances.

ENTRY # 7

	Debit	Credit
Revenues	$ x--x	
Fund Balance	$ x--x	
Estimated Revenues		$ x--x

ENTRY # 8

	Debit	Credit
Appropriations	$ x--x	
Expenditures		$ x--x
Encumbrances		$ x--x
Fund Balance		$ x--x

Entries #7 and #8 facilitate an analysis of the fund balance. All budgetary and actual accounts, identified in earlier entries, have now been closed to fund balance—with one exception—the *reserve for encumbrances!* This account cannot be closed because it represents commitments made but not yet finalized by delivery of the items involved and receipt of an invoice. As a result, this account is often reclassified at the beginning of the following year to *Reserve for Encumbrances—Prior Year* and charged in the new year when the goods or services involved are received and invoiced.

Since the "unencumbered" portion of each year's appropriation usually lapses at the end of that fiscal year, the authority to expend funds from that year's appropriations in the following year must be contained in the reserve for encumbrances account. This account is normally included with fund balance in the presentation of total equities of that particular fund at the end of the fiscal period.

The financial statements required for the general fund usually include a balance sheet, a statement analyzing the changes in fund balance, a comparison of actual revenues with estimated revenues, and finally, a statement comparing appropriations with expenditures and encumbrances. These are illustrated under "Financial Reporting for Municipalities," page 151.

Special Revenue Funds

Revenues from specific taxes or other special sources for the financing of specific activities are accounted for under *special revenue funds.* Such activities may include the maintenance of public parks or schools, often administered by special boards or commissions.

Such funds are accounted for as separate entities and monies authorized by the creating authority cannot be used for other purposes. In some cases, the operation of a special revenue fund is controlled by the general budget of the governmental unit, requiring both budgetary and proprietary accounts as described above under "Budgetary Accounts Used in the General Fund."

Revolving Funds

Services performed by one department primarily for the benefit of other municipality departments are often accounted for through *revolving funds.* These internally-oriented services should be distinguished from services for the general public, which are typically accounted for in *Enterprise Funds.*

Revolving funds may be established initially by advances from the general fund, by the sale of bonds, or by contributions. This fund operates much as would a commercial, private business offering the sale of services, except that the target is a break-even operation rather than a profit-making one as in industry.

No need normally exists for budgetary control in such a fund because total expenditures are limited to the amounts that "customers," that is, other departments of the same municipality, are authorized to spend for the revolving fund's services. The latter are illustrated by the municipality's garage or fleet operation, requiring fixed assets that are recorded as such in the revolving fund and depreciated over their useful lives. Such depreciation expense as well as all other costs of operation is used to price services rendered to benefiting departments. The financial statements include a balance sheet and statement of operations for each such revolving fund.

Special Assessment Funds

To finance permanent improvements, *Special Assessment Funds* are used. These assessments are usually local in nature and usually financed from general revenues or through the issuance of general obligation bonds. Each special assessment project requires its own accounting records, usually involving budgetary and proprietary accounts, appropriations, and encumbrance procedures.

Upon creation of the fund, an account, such as *improvements authorized* is debited and appropriations credited. When assessments against specific beneficiaries are levied, a receivables account is debited and improvements authorized is credited. Upon completion of the project, an entry is usually made in the *general fixed assets fund* discussed below, debiting the specific asset accounts for the total cost of construction or acquisition of each with an offsetting credit to an investment account in that fund.

Capital Project Funds (Bonds Funds)

Many capital projects are financed by a variety of sources in addition to bond issues, creating the need for the *capital projects fund,* which accounts for the receipt and expenditure of monies used to acquire major, long-term capital additions and improvements. After such a project is officially authorized, a receivable is debited and a corresponding appropriations account credited. Encumbrance procedures are followed for capital projects, comparable to those illustrated in the general fund account.

After construction of the project is completed, all costs involved are set up as assets, properly identified in the *general fixed asset group* of accounts (as described under special assessment fund) and the capital projects fund is closed. If it were necessary to float bonds to finance the project, such bonds are retired either from the debt service fund or from the general fund, as authorized originally, and are not recorded as liabilities of the capital projects fund.

Debt Service Funds

The payments of interest and principal on all long-term municipality debt, other than special assessment and revenue bonds, are functions of so-called *Debt Service Funds.*

To service long-term debt, monies are received and accounted for in the debt service fund as a credit to revenues. Budgetary accounts are involved to record the income estimated necessary to retire specific debts. Cash disbursements of such monies for interest, debt retirements, and other service costs are charged to expenditures in this fund and the appropriations account is credited.

Bonds are recorded as liabilities at maturity date in the debt service fund. The entry is a debit to "expenditures" and a credit to the bond liability account. Cash generated from investments of the debt service fund is used to pay such indebtedness. As noted above, certain funds, such as "special assessment funds," service their own debts and do not involve the debt service fund.

Trust and Agency Funds

Assets now owned but *held* by a governmental unit in the capacity of trustee or agent must be accounted for. Each trust fund must be set up as a separate account. Budgetary accounts are normally not required except for pension funds, but a distinction must be maintained at all times between principal and income if the trust fund is non-expendable.

Enterprise or Utility Funds

Self-supporting, utility-type funds, sometimes called *enterprise funds,* when operated by municipalities are accounted for using essentially the same accounts as those used by privately owned firms rendering similar services. All fixed assets are recorded and depreciated so that full costs are covered in billings to the general public.

Under the caption "Revolving Funds," services discussed were of an interdepartmental nature, involving services to various municipality departments by another department. In contrast, the utility funds concentrate on such activities as electricity, gas, or water utilities furnished to the public at large.

General Fixed Assets

All fixed assets of the municipality are grouped in one general category called the *general fixed assets fund,* with the exception of assets used in the enterprise, revolving and trust funds. Fixed assets in this fund are purchased from general revenues, from special assessments or from the proceeds of general obligation bonds, financed from capital projects funds.

Fixed assets are recorded at original cost or at appraised valuation, and the credit is entered to an investment account, indicating the funding source of that asset. Depreciation is not generally provided in the general fixed assets fund.

General Long-Term Debt

This group of accounts is used to accumulate the total outstanding bonded debt of the municipality as of the balance sheet date. It neither accounts for the proceeds from the sale nor payment of bonds, because the former function is handled through the capital projects fund, and the latter through the debt service fund.

Feedback providing information needed for the best possible allocation of the municipality's resources may emphasize *program* budgetary control without sacrificing the legally-required fund-oriented reporting system. The computer's contribution in the total effort is outlined in broad terms below.

The Impact of the Computer
on Municipality Accounting

The role of the computer in municipality accounting appears to be in approximate relationship to the size of the community served. Thus, communities under 20,000 or 25,000 population would not be expected to have their own stand-alone computer installations. However, within the next several years it appears a distinct possibility that shared systems and shared computer facilities will be put to good use by smaller, contiguous municipalities.

FLOW CHART III

FUND CONTROL—BUDGET PREPARATION

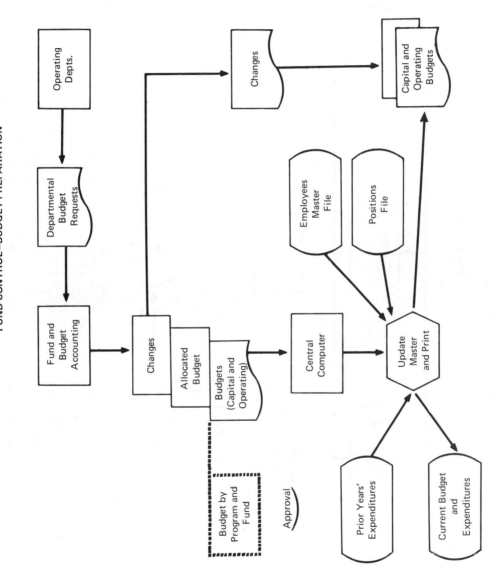

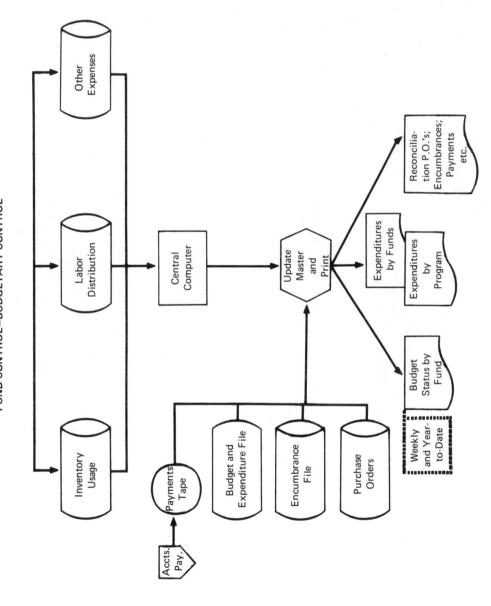

FLOW CHART IV

FUND CONTROL—BUDGETARY CONTROL

Flow Chart III suggests the operation of such automated systems for budget *preparation* purposes. A shared system can facilitate budget preparation on a program or departmental basis by cost center and line items as desired.

Flow Chart IV shows how budgetary *control* reports can be produced as outputs from the processing of material usage summaries, labor distribution, and other source documents. Both budgetary and actual information are shown in updating the data base. Appropriate records can be selected and a printout furnished to each of the municipalities according to their requirements, both content and time-wise, with proper protection for proprietary information.

Both stewardship and managerial reports are possible. Examples in Flow Chart IV include printouts showing monthly expenditures by funds and accounts within funds, or weekly fund status reports, comparing allotments and total expenditures resulting in the amount of "free budget" for each fund. Managerially-oriented reports are equally available by computer program. These printouts are discussed in greater detail under "Financial Reporting for Municipalities" which follows next.

Financial Reporting for Municipalities

Next consider the *outputs* of the system—the instruments of financial disclosure. Each of the funds described in preceding chapters are shown in Table I with an indication of the kinds of statements that their specific function normally requires. Thus, Table I indicates that all funds, with the exception of the General Long-Term Debt Fund, require a balance sheet. Notes (a), (b), and (c) to the table indicate special reporting features of certain funds such as the fact that the Enterprise or Utility Funds require a balance sheet presentation similar to commercial utilities offering the same services. For that reason, fixed assets and related long-term liabilities precede current assets and liabilities, respectively.

Of the major statements listed in Table I, the balance sheet has certain unique features—in comparison with industrial balance sheets—including the showing of reserve for encumbrances and fund balance accounts. Characteristics, similar to those seen in industrial statements, include the ranking of assets in liquidity order for funds other than utility funds, and liabilities in priority order. On the other hand fixed assets are usually not shown with related allowances for depreciation. The only funds that usually carry depreciation accounting are the special assessments fund and utility funds.

TABLE I

MUNICIPALITY REPORTING—FUND-ORIENTED

Types of Financial Disclosure
Suggested for Specific Funds

Function of Statement	General Fund	Special Revenue Funds	Revolving Funds (Working capital)	Special Assessment Fund	Capital Projects Fund (Bond Fund)	Debt Service Fund (Sinking Fund)	Trust and Agency Funds	Enterprise or Utility Funds	General Fixed Asset Group	General Long-Term Debt Fund
Balance Sheet	X	X	X	X	X	X	X	X (a)	X (b)	
Analysis of Changes in Fund Balance	X	X	X	X	X	X	X	X		
Comparison of Actual and Budgeted Revenues	X	X	X	X	X	X	X	X		
Comparison of Appropriations with Expenditures and Encumbrances	X	X	X	X	X	X	X	X		
Statement of Actual and Estimated Revenues, Expenditures, & Fund Balance	X	X		X	X	X (c)	X	X		
Comparison of Actual with Estimated Expenditures	X	X	X	X	X	X	X	X		
Budget Summary—Revenues—All Funds	X	X		X	X	X	X	X		
Budget Summary—Expenditures—All Funds	X	X	X	X	X	X	X	X		
Budget Status Report (Weekly/Monthly)	X	X	X	X	X	X				
Expenditures by Program (Monthly and Year-to-Date)	X	X		X	X	X	X			
Statement of Operations			X					X		
Statement of Cash Receipts and Disbursements				X	X	X	X			
Changes in General Fixed Assets by Source and Function									X	
Amounts of Bonds Payable by Dates and Related Requirements for Retirement										X

NOTES: (a) Fixed Assets and Long-Term Liabilities are listed before all others in their respective categories, which is usual practice with privately-owned utilities.

(b) Fixed Assets are shown by types and the source of funding indicated.

(c) Statement compares the fund's revenue with contribution requirements.

Another statement listed in Table I is the "Analysis of Changes in Fund Balance" which can be used for each fund, usually with the exception of the General Fixed Asset Group and the General Long-Term Debt Fund or as a summary statement for all funds of the municipality. Somewhat similar in form to the conventional statement of changes in retained earnings, the Fund Balance report shows additions and deletions from beginning balances to arrive at ending balances for each fund.

Reports for Budgetary Control

The analysis of changes in fund balances is usually an externally-oriented report but can be supplemented with a monthly report of internal value for the municipality's managers, entitled "Budget Status Report," illustrated in Figure 7-2. Described in greater detail below, this report shows object expenditures, such as personal services, operations, repairs and maintenance, and capital expenditures for each fund in comparison with its appropriations and the free balances of each fund at the end of the reporting period.

In Figure 7-1, a budgetary control report is illustrated with respect to municipality expenditures by funds. Actual expenditures and firm commitments, or encumbrances, are totalled and compared with the original, or adjusted budget, to pinpoint potential overruns. Details are included as to the objects of such expenditures, including personal services and contractual services by responsibility centers, such as City Council, City Manager, and the Municipal Court.

CITY OF BERKELEY[*]

General Fund

Statement of Expenditures
(and Comparison with Budget)

Year ended June 30, 19XX

	Budget		
	Original	Adjusted	Total
General Government:			
City Council:			
Personal services—salaries	$1,400.00	1,400.00	1,395.00

Figure 7-1

	Original	Budget Adjusted	Total
Contractual services:			
Travel and expense	3,000.00	3,000.00	5,942.99
Memberships	1,235.00	1,235.00	1,160.28
Consultant	3,000.00	5,561.83	5,561.83
	7,235.00	9,796.83	12,665.10
Total City Council	8,635.00	11,196.83	14,060.10
City Manager:			
Personal services—salaries	9,189.24	9,189.24	9,189.24
Contractual services:			
Printing and publishing	300.00	300.00	—
Equipment repair	100.00	100.00	125.69
Travel and expense	800.00	675.00	450.82
Memberships	150.00	150.00	15.00
Training	50.00	50.00	30.00
	1,400.00	1,275.00	621.51
Commodities:			
Supplies	75.00	75.00	84.82
Fuel	200.00	325.00	313.86
Lubricants	10.00	10.00	6.56
Books—publications	65.00	65.00	128.40
	350.00	475.00	533.64
Capital outlay—automobile	600.00	—	—
Total City Manager	11,539.24	10,939.24	10,344.39
Carried forward	20,174.24	22,136.07	24,404.49
Municipal Court:			
Personal services—salaries	2,820.00	2,820.00	2,820.00
Carried forward	$ 2,820.00	2,820.00	2,820.00

Figure 7-1 (continued)

(*) Source: City of Berkeley, Missouri. Annual Report for Fiscal Year, ended June 30, 1968.

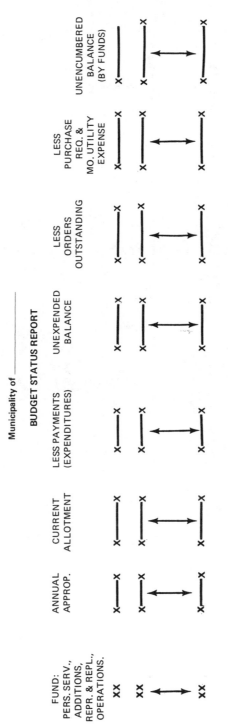

Figure 7-2

Source: "Cost Accounting—Its Role in a Hospital Information System," A.P. Ameiss and W.A. Thompson, *Management Adviser*, a Publication of the American Institute of Certified Public Accountants, Inc., copyright (c) 1971, (March-April, 1971, p. 33.)

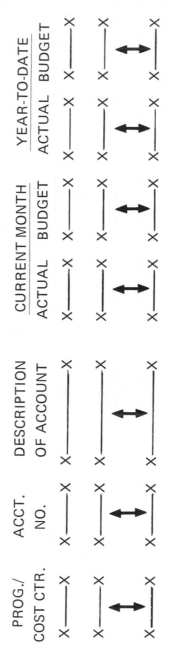
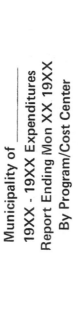

Figure 7-3

Source: "Cost Accounting—Its Role in a Hospital Information System," A.P. Ameiss and W.A. Thompson, *Management Adviser*, a Publication of the American Institute of Certified Public Accountants, Inc., Copyright (c) 1971, (March-April, 1971, p. 33.)

Figure 7-3 illustrates a budget status report prepared on a monthly or "as needed" basis which might be important in the last month or last weeks of the municipality's fiscal year. The annual appropriation for each object of expenditure (personal services, etc.,) is shown with the quarterly allotment, which represents the effective budget for that period. From the latter amount expenditures and encumbrances by object are subtracted resulting in the free balance figure.

When the fiscal year nears its completion, it is customary for the budget status report to be produced on a weekly or even daily basis (usually during June) so that current knowledge exists as to what is still available for that year. This report is vital if the entire appropriation for the year is to be used and over-expenditures avoided. As a result, many agencies of state and municipal governments use this report format as a *weekly* report throughout the year and on a daily basis, if necessary, in the waning weeks of the budget year.

Evaluation of Fund-Segmented Reporting by Municipalities

Critics have alleged that the necessity for stewardship reporting by funds has militated against the kind of progress in internal managerial reporting for municipalities that has been realized in commercial accounting. The charge has been made that the fund accounting concept should be seen for what it really is—a means or device for limiting resource applications to authorized purposes, not an irreducible principle of governmental accounting.[2]

If this view is taken, the premise can be supported that the accountability or stewardship function of municipal accounting can be discharged other than by means of the current formal and rigorous accounting processes used. Fund accounting does meet the municipality's need to segregate resources being collected and used for specified purposes, but this custodial emphasis is coupled with annual appropriation-expenditure periods and legal requirements that spending authorizations not be exceeded. As a result, it is alleged that what has resulted is a proliferation of funds, complex appropriation and encumbrance accounts, and legalistic reporting practices.

The major objection, from a reporting point of view, is that fund accounting is becoming archaic because governmental units are becoming larger and more complex, requiring an emphasis on more professional and less custodial management in governmental administration.[3] For example, managerial accounting, which has received a great deal of acceptance in commercial accounting, is virtually nonexistent in municipal accounting. Program budgeting, an application of managerial accounting, is virtually nonexistent in municipal accounting.

Effective planning for future programs and the control of current activities requires follow-up data and action which fund accounting cannot *directly* supply because such programs are usually supported from *several* sources or funds. While reports can be generated as *supplementary* data from fund accounting to provide costs by program or department, there appears to be no tendency to do so.

One barrier to managerial reporting is that the budgets are not currently in a format to accommodate such responsibility accounting. But a more basic reason may be that state law typically demands an accounting by source and use, as well as by object or service paid for in many cases, and therefore, the entire budgeting-accounting-reporting approach follows traditional fund accounting. Such reports satisfy typical *external* reporting requirements, but do little or nothing to reinforce the program responsibility-center approach to fiscal planning.

The Case for a Managerial Approach
to Municipal Accounting

Under the managerial concept of municipal accounting and reporting, the tables are turned with respect to the basic objectives described earlier in this chapter. Stewardship reporting by funds was considered the prime essential in municipal accounting and the entire system was structured to facilitate such *external,* legalistic disclosure.

By comparison, under the managerial approach, *internal* reporting is emphasized which treats planning and control information as basic. Stewardship reporting in this context is relegated to the rank of an important, but secondary, product.

The result is a new reporting focus in municipal accounting, requiring a redesigned accounting system. Expenditure account groupings must be expanded from the present objects (personal services, operations, repairs and replacements) to include program and cost center or department. Encumbrance accounting finds a replacement in the less formal commercial accounting approach of reporting of expenditures plus outstanding orders against budgeted amounts resulting in a favorable or unfavorable variance for appropriate corrective action by management.

Equally important is the abandonment, under such managerial

accounting, of separate accounting entities for every fund source. In lieu of traditional fund accounting, accountability for the use of resources in accordance with legal authorization is assured through a financial planning-budgetary reporting process and the use of special cash accounts. A comprehensive budgeting approach is claimed that recognizes imposed restrictions on the use of certain resources, but is not fragmented by separate accounting entries.[4]

Potential Role of the Computer

Figure 7-3 illustrates a budgetary control report resulting from the application of responsibility accounting to municipality operations. Since control is by programs rather than funds, such programs must be defined and budgeted while restrictions on resource usages are planned for. Expenditure accounts must be organized in the chart of accounts according to major departments and/or broad programs, as well as funds, and the source documents must indicate such data.

The emphasis in the managerial accounting system is on costs for internal, *program-oriented* purposes, but a *secondary* sort of the input documents is required by funds to permit the preparation of the traditional fund accountability reports illustrated earlier. Therefore, data relative to each expenditure transaction, as to program, fund, department, or cost center must be captured in the source document and included in the input unit. Such processing lends itself admirably to the use of punched cards and computer sorting and processing.

Under this system, fund accounting-type accountability continues to be provided by the balance sheet and no need exists to link the various revenue accounts directly with specific expenditures. Every restricted use receipt, every authorized expenditure is charged to a specific cash account. Accruals or deferrals are also coded to correspond to the related cash account which, therefore, provides interim accountability for legally restricted funds. In addition, year-end analyses outside the chart of accounts of cash transactions, can be contained in punched cards and provide data for the traditional revenue and expenditure reports by fund.

Shared Systems and Shared Facilities

In evaluating the cost effectiveness of using the computer for managerial reports of the kind described above, particularly in the case of municipalities with populations under 20,000 one would probably rule out the use of a stand-alone, third generation computer and the staffing costs that go with it. However, the emergence of "shared systems" may offer an attractive alternative to neighboring communities by permitting them to share the cost of programs containing instructions for the processing and printout of reports that satisfy the dual objectives of managerial (internal) control and fiduciary (external) accountability.

In addition, the use of "shared facilities" or other versions of rented time can be made available to each municipality. So-called "automation" companies and "service bureaus" are available to provide tailored or "packaged programs" for processing on the bureau's computer when periodic statements are desired.

REFERENCES

[1]National Committee on Governmental Accounting, Municipal Finance Officers Association of the United States and Canada, *Governmental Accounting, Auditing, and Financial Reporting* (Chicago, 1968), page 67.

[2]George C. Mead, "A Managerial Approach to Governmental Accounting", *The Journal of Accountancy*. March 1970, Vol. 129, No. 3, page 50.

[3]*Ibid.*

[4]*Ibid.*, page 51.

8   What Quantitative Accounting Offers Management

Certain mathematical and statistical techniques have been developed to help solve business problems and promote decision-making with respect to both qualitative and quantitative factors. Management decision models have been created that integrate and correlate related factors. Since mathematicians have been involved, it is natural that such models usually have been precise in mathematical formulations, but less than precise in their definitions of the business-oriented problems involved, the cost or revenue concepts used, and the qualification of these concepts.[1]

Nature of Mathematical Application in Accounting

The adaptation of applied mathematics to the managerial functions of planning and control have included replacement, queuing, and inventory control theories.[2] Other mathematical applications capable of assisting management in these functions include cost estimation, control charting, and the use of production labor estimation for budgeting purposes through such techniques as the learning curve. Multiple regression analysis represents another example, offering matrix approaches to process cost accounting and the secondary or "step-down" allocation of overhead from service to direct production cost centers.[3] The use of linear programming to minimize distribution costs may suggest the impression that cost and managerial accounting are the sole beneficiaries of quantitative or mathematical accounting.

But financial accounting applications also can benefit from mathematical techniques. For instance, the use of time series mathematics (compounding and discounting) is important with respect to problems relating to mortgages, sinking funds, pensions, and annuity and sinking fund methods of depreciation, and the use of matrix inversion in bonus and tax computation. The matrix approach also assists in preparing the statement of affairs and in eliminating intercompany profits in consolidated financial statements.[4]

Mathematical statistics have also been recommended for application to practical problems to help cope with the risks of uncertainty. One objective is to develop an optimum management strategy that would use the principle of the probability that a given set of conditions will occur a given number of times.[5] The use of probabilities and statistics can be important tools in managerial decision-making. For example, the development of the sales budget involves many probabilities: (1) amount of potential loss from overstocking; (2) amount of potential loss from being out of stock; and, (3) incremental costs of producing additional quantities of the finished product on an overtime or emergency basis to make up for such outages.[6] Assuming that the necessary data can be obtained, the above probabilities can be expressed mathematically and an optimum strategy developed, based on the probability that a given set of conditions will occur a given number of times. Hopefully the result, if used, will reduce management's margin of error.

Model-building applicable to business problems includes the so-called "business game," based on the game theory. The objective is to attain maximum profitability by choosing a formula or strategy from a number of alternatives, developed with the assistance of the computer. Two or more teams are competing for the same goal, attempting to work out the probable consequences (both favorable and unfavorable) of taking alternate courses of action and anticipating the competitors' strategy.[7] The mathematics of such complex situations requires a computer, as does the feedback of results to the various teams on a fairly rapid basis so that the game is not delayed.

How Does the Model Work?

The classical inventory control model is used in the determination of the most economic quantity for ordering or manufacturing inventory items. The theory underlying the economic order quantity is to determine that quantity that will minimize the total variable cost (TVC) associated with inventory—assumed to be a function of two costs: the cost of ordering; and the cost of carrying inventory. Given the annual requirement for an item, ordering costs, expressed in costs per order, will vary inversely with the average annual inventory. Conversely, the cost of carrying the inventory—warehousing, taxes, insurance, and capital invested—will tend to vary with the average annual inventory. The classical inventory formula is stated as follows:[8]

$$Q = \frac{2RO}{IC'} \text{ where:}$$

Q equals economic order quantity
R equals annual requirement in units
O equals ordering cost per order
C equals unit cost of the inventory item
I   equals cost of carrying the inventory expressed as a percentage of the dollar value of the average annual inventory

The point at which total variable cost is at a minimum should indicate the economic order quantity. The same use of probability statistics has been of assistance in adjusting break-even analysis to reflect conditions of risk and uncertainty and to establish the level of protective stock necessary to determine feasible inventory-control procedures.[9] Both probabilistic decision models and applications of Bayesian statistics have been used to make the judgments of decision-makers more precise in connection with the above types of decisions which operating management must make. However, probability and statistics are useful only when combined with a thorough examination of the firm's accounting records.[10] This combination requires the decision-maker to think more deeply about his available options, based on empirical data from past experience reported from the accounting records. The result should be a sounder basis for decision-making than the "educated guesses" or rule of thumb guides previously used by management.[11]

Financial Modeling for Top Management?

Is top management prepared to adapt to the more sophisticated types of analysis which mathematics and statistics and the mechanics of quantitative-analytical techniques are making available? The answer may be yes, only if such techniques are interpreted in terms that are readily understandable and if analysts are available to properly use and explain the advantage of such tools to chief executives and their vice-presidents. The creation of profit-planning groups, frequently headed by a certified public accountant who can communicate effectively with top management, suggests that the value of such techniques is being recognized in decision-making at that level. For example, the use of optimization by such groups of accountants, statisticians, and mathematicians, has been found useful in determining that combination of resources that will yield the highest return on capital employed.[12] This is a consideration of top management when the capital expenditures pertain to plant expansion or the right price to be paid for the acquisition of a subsidiary. Two fundamental approaches to this technique include the use of differential calculus and the other dynamic programming, of which linear programming is a special procedure, imposing restraints in the form of linear inequalities. Rather than burden this level of management with the intricacies of such techniques, emphasis should be placed on the utility of the method in enabling the decision-maker to select from alternatives that solution that appears optimal. Decisions involved may pertain to the optimal combination of products to maximize profits or the capital expenditure decision mentioned above, or distribution problems involving such variables as the determination of market areas for specific warehouses.[13]

Financial modeling has been used to describe the process of developing financial statements and ratios referring to future projections and based upon a defined set of assumptions and logical relationships.[14] To be useful tools to management such models must meet the critical test in terms of contributing to the achievement of corporate goals. While financial modeling cannot be used as a substitute for planning, it can be helpful in improving planning within an organization. Where the emphasis is on annual budgets, a model can be set up in monthly increments and adjusted to reflect monthly operating results and budget revisions.[15]

Such models can be helpful to management in meeting the demands of investors, and analysts; for sales forecasts and earnings projections. Figure 8-1 illustrates one of the first corporate forecasts included in an annual report in the United States. Released on the last day of the year being reported upon, it was necessary to estimate the operating results of the last two months, including net sales, operating costs, interest expense, provision for income taxes, and extraordinary items. The result is a three-fold comparison—the current year's performance compared with actuals of last year and forecast figures of next year, including earnings per share, both primary and fully-diluted, before and after extraordinary items.[16]

Fuqua Industries' 1972 preliminary annual report, statement of consolidated income *
[In thousands of dollars]

	Actual 1971	Estimated 1972	Forecast 1973
Net Sales and Revenues	$366,557	$430,000	$484,000
Operating Costs and Expenses	331,072	385,600	431,600
Interest Expense	8,006	8,700	10,000
Total Costs and Expenses	339,078	394,300	441,600
Operating Income Before Taxes	27,479	35,700	42,400
Provision for Income Taxes	13,477	17,700	21,000
Net Operating Income	14,002	18,000	21,400
Extraordinary Item	(3,500)*	—	—
Net Income	$ 10,502	$ 18,000	$ 21,400
Earnings Per Common and Common Equivalent Share (8,541,000 shares in 1971, 9,500,000 shares in 1972, and 10,000,000 shares† in 1973)			
Net Operating Income	$ 1.59	$ 1.85	$ 2.09†
Extraordinary Item	(.41)	—	—
Net Income	$ 1.18	$ 1.85	$ 2.09†
Earnings Per Common Share Assuming Full Dilution (9,731,000 shares in 1971, 9,870,000 shares in 1972, and 10,000,000 shares† in 1973)			
Net Operating Income	$ 1.44	$ 1.80	$ 2.09†
Extraordinary Item	(.36)	—	—
Net Income	$ 1.08	$ 1.80	$ 2.09†

*Loss on the sale of a business.
†Earnings-per-share forecast for 1973 does not include shares which may be issued in either stock dividends or in acquisitions.

Figure 8-1

Source: "Case of the Fuqua forecast." John K. Shank and John P. Calfee Jr., p. 44 *Harvard Business Review.* November-December 1973.

Although Figure 8-1 was developed without the assistance of an automated model, the procedures for developing the forecast sales and earnings lend themselves to such models. Internally generated budgets were received from all Fuqua divisions, prepared quarterly, and summarized without major adjustments to produce the overall forecast for the coming year. Each quarter updated forecasts are developed by each division, giving effect to changes in operations and economic conditions which come to light during that quarter. The similarity to automated models in this procedure lies in the periodic, formal reappraisal which is permitted, based on the business performance outlook in view of recent history.

Thus unanticipated sales expansion in particular markets can be matched with changes in production with reference to raw material requirements (the automated production module); or advertising and promotion programs; or changes in channels of distribution (the automated marketing module).[17] The usefulness of automated models and their simulation is emphasized in such situations as described above where updated reports, both actual and forecast, are desired on a quarterly basis with a minimum of time available before publication.

Such updated budgets lend themselves to financial modeling in the form of computer programs which can be useful in reducing the time required to prepare and revise the projections, thus reducing expensive time of accountants and budgeteers and improving the accuracy of the projections.[18]

Automated Financial Models

Most automated financial models use the same algebra found in accounting, namely addition, multiplication, division and the accounting equation that debits must equal credits. In addition, the models usually include logic routines for depreciation calculations, interest rates, discounting of cash flow, return-on investment calculations, and growth rates,[19] suggesting their potential for significant time savings. In addition, the once expensive computer programs for such purposes have given way to the development of packages and specialized programming languages that reduce substantially the time and cost of programming a financial modeling system. A model that previously took 20 man-weeks to write and test can be completed in as little as two man-weeks by an analyst skilled in use of the new packages or languages. As a result, the systems analyst can program the models he has designed thus eliminating the programmer from the cycle along with the problem of communications between systems analysts and programmers. The result has been the development of models that are more comprehensive in nature and adaptable to the needs of executives and planners who use them, permitting revisions more easily.[20]

In answer to management's "what if" questions, financial models can be of particular value in evaluating alternate plans and strategies. Because of short response time and low cost of analysis with models, management is inclined to ask more questions and receives as a result a better knowledge of the financial implications of price changes, product or division sales promotions, changes in product mix or changes in distribution methods.

Financial modeling has been used in operating management systems, serving as a part or module of a corporate model made up of a number of such modules. Figure 8-2 illustrates the nature of the input-output relationships for a divisional type of operation.[21] A number of modules may be consolidated to form group models with the input-output relationship shown in the middle section of the exhibit or consolidation can be carried further so that a model of the whole corporation is formed as in the lower part of the exhibit.[22] Using this model as a basic building block, together with the successive layers suggested in Figure 8-3, management can ask "what if" questions with respect to the effects of proposed price increases, cost changes, equipment acquisition and financing charges.[23]

Both revenue and cost flows involved in the input-output relationships are shown in Figure 8-3 in generalized form.[24] Here a large integrated operation includes a complex of subsidiaries and divisions consolidated in group models and a corporate model, with intercompany sales and purchases indicated between groups and divisions.[25]

On-line, Real-time, Decision-making Models

The modeling concept discussed above is illustrated in the simulation of the production model illustrated in Figure 8-4. Each module involves a basic process in the production flow from raw materials to finished products, simulating the costs incurred in: (1) conversion of ores to molten iron; (2) conversion of molten iron to steel ingots; (3) processing of ingots; and, (4) finishing the steel into various end products.[26]

By definition modeling is the process of taking tangible organizational interrelationships and translating them symbolically into a logic that is expressed by a set of algebraic equations.[27]

INPUT—OUTPUT RELATIONSHIPS (using three types of models—
internal to the division, group, and corporate consolidation models.)

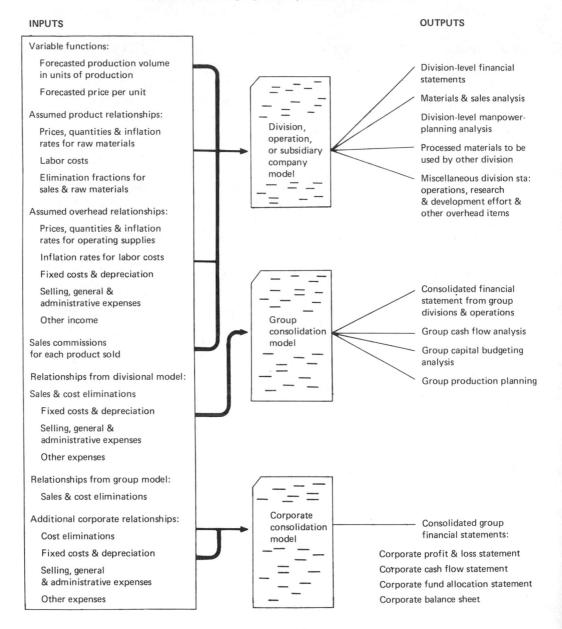

Figure 8-2

(a) Source: "Corporate models: on-line, real-time systems." James. B. Boulden and Elwood S. Buffa,
Harvard Business Review, July-August 1970, p. 76.

FLOWS OF SALES AND COSTS

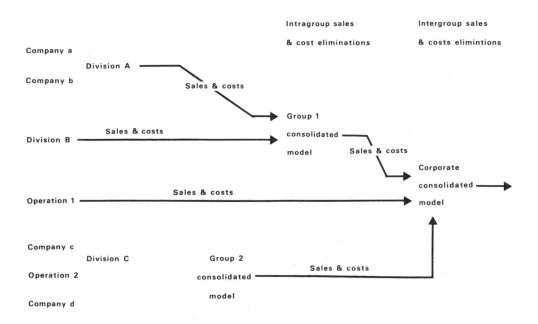

Figure 8-3

Illustrating the use of models to show both intragroup and intergroup sales and cost elimination in corporate consolidated model.

Source: "Corporate models; on-line, real-time systems" James B. Boulden and Elwood S. Buffa, *Harvard Business Review* , July-August, 1970, p. 77.

On-line and real-time are used in this context to mean the direct connection of the decision to a computer, giving almost instantaneous response to this user as well as others who share the computer.[28]

The "what if" questions which management can ask via such models include: "How much raw material is required to meet production forecasts; What are the cost effects of various hot metal-to-scrap ratios and the resulting yields under various assumptions of raw material costs; What are the capacity requirements for proposed levels of operation?"[29]

The end results of the system depicted in Figure 8-4 include the cash-flow statement, the balance sheet and the income statement for the steel division and for the corporation. The corporate model permits the consolidation of the divisional models into a corporate level income

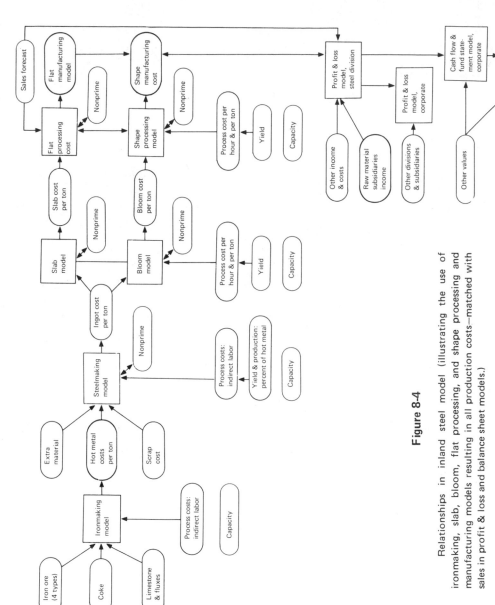

Figure 8-4

Relationships in inland steel model (illustrating the use of ironmaking, slab, bloom, flat processing, and shape processing and manufacturing models resulting in all production costs—matched with sales in profit & loss and balance sheet models.)

Source: "Corporate models: on-line, real-time systems" James B. Boulden and Elwood S. Buffa, *Harvard Business Review*, July–August 1970, p. 78.

statement and balance sheet. The result is a clear framework for communications between the company's operators and managers and a new basis for evaluating operating, policy, and other "what if" questions. Precious time is saved because such models are on-line, real-time to the computer processing unit, eliminating the tedious and time-consuming batch inputs, coding, and key punching effort required previously. Models of the nature described above permit managers to "talk" with them and the computers are shared by different managers, leading to the description of these systems as "interactive and time-sharing."[30] As a result, certain managers have been found willing and even anxious to use the computer and these models in their decision-making processes.[31]

Models for the Analysis of Potential Acquisitions
Prior to Merger

In many conglomerates, corporate planners make a routine assessment of potential acquisitions, developing screening data to assist them. Published historical data and personal assessment of market potential are used, and the development of a series of models to analyze target companies has been suggested as a means of creating a consistent, analytical framework.[32]

One corporate modeling system includes a module developed to undertake the valuation of a company and evaluate differing bids in a merger situation.[33] This merger analysis module uses a simplified model based on standard accounting rules to evaluate a target company's future worth. Planners valuing such companies are presented with five different methods from this module, some predominantly backward looking in assessing past performance, and others futuristic.

The results are in the form of five different valuations, resulting from the adoption of each set of assumptions and providing a range of values to assist management in selecting an appropriate figure as a basis for the bid for the target company or companies.[34] Equally important is the role of the model to produce defensive strategies in a defended bid in the hands of the target company, subject, of course, to the financial knowledge of the decision-makers using the model's output.[35] A merger analysis model can be used at each stage of negotiation in a competitive bid situation to make analyses. Also, a mixture of cash, stock, debentures, or other securities can be bid for a given proportion of the target company's shares through the modeling system and consolidated balance sheets automatically produced for any option analyzed.[36]

Planning, Evaluation, and Review Techniques (PERT)
in Quantitative Accounting

Although PERT is usually considered a control technique for monitoring the accomplishment of a specific program, it has been found useful in meeting recurring accounting responsibilities, such as the monthly closing application in Figure 8-5.[37] This application of PERT in job costing in the electronics industry expedites the monthly closing in a division and corporate environment where the latter's income statements include all divisional operating results each month. Extreme pressure is therefore exerted on each division to meet corporate management's reporting deadlines. Not only must all material, labor, and overhead cost be accumulated by jobs at the divisional level and sent to corporate accounting by the date set each month, but provision must be made for "bottlenecks" including computer breakdowns, manual tracking and correction of errors in cost accumulation, failure to receive closing data, or failure to balance cost ledger sheets.

The techniques illustrated in Figure 8-5 combine the use of PERT and CPM (the Critical Path Method) to detail all the activities required to close the books (from the date of cutoff for materials used, labor, and overhead charges from all overhead pools to all jobs worked on in the division) and to pinpoint those activities that take the longest time as a group to accomplish.[38] Each activity appears in Figure 8-5, along with the number of man-hours required for its completion. A number of different arrow paths are shown from start to finish and the total time required for each is the sum of the man-hours indicated for all tasks along that route. The critical path is the longest in terms of man-hours from start to finish, indicating the minimum overall time necessary to complete the closing. Only by careful attention to this path can the deadlines set by corporate management for the review of the statements be met.

Impact of Quantitative Accounting on Management

A number of reasons exist why quantitative accounting—in fact, management science as a discipline—has not had a more significant impact on operating management and industry as a whole. Grayson observes a difference in these two cultures—the university-situated or staff-management scientist and the operating executive. The latter usually operates by rough rules of thumb and intuition, frequently under heavy pressure to make decisions *now!* No time is available for the kind of mathematical analysis or research that the exponents of management science, sometimes called operations research, can usually afford.[39]

Reasons given for this gap between manager and management scientist follow and may explain in part the failure of quantitative accounting to receive greater acceptance in industry:[40]

1.) Resistance to change exists on the part of managers in particular and industry in general to the models and other techniques described in this chapter, requiring that they be educated or at least "sold" through well-planned presentations on the benefits these tools provide;

2.) Long response time is usually required by management scientists, who operate in a time frame that is slower than that of line managers and whose approach is usually a very thorough, methodical one even when the manager's time pressures dictate the advantage of a "quick and dirty" solution, and;

3.) The tendency for most management science exponents to use "simplifying assumptions" and strip away so much of a real problem confronting managers that the technically beautiful resolution may be completely useless to the line manager. Time constraints, data-availability questions, people problems, power structures and political pressures that make management the challenge of frequently "living by one's wits" are all excluded or simplified out of existence.

However, there is reason for optimism in believing that the use of mathematical and statistical techniques described in this chapter will find greater acceptance on the part of management, particularly in the function of planning. Answers are needed by top management in an ever-increasing number of problem areas, not the least of which is the pressure by the Securities and Exchange Commission and others in regard to the publication of sales and profit forecasts. Fuqua's example in this chapter shows how simulation models may be extremely important in the development of such forecasts and their periodic updating for public release. Due to the growing complexity of corporate structures, the use of models may become very helpful in determining what corporate acquisitions to make and what reimbursement to offer. In addition, by giving a free hand to the use of techniques described in this chapter the real utility of the computer as a top-management tool may be realized. But it can't be, as has been claimed, a case of "the tool (whether a technique or a computer) in search of a problem"[47] —it must be the right approach at the right time if operating management is to benefit in its important functions of planning and controlling.

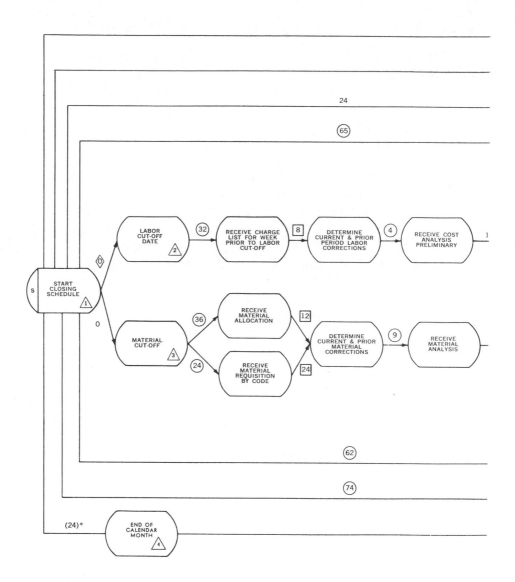

Figure 8-5

Source: "PERT For Monthly Financial Closing," by Albert P. Ameiss and Warren Thompson, pages 32, 33, 34, 35. Published by Management Advisor, Jan.-Feb., 1974. Copyright© 1974, American Institute of Certified Public Accountants, Inc.

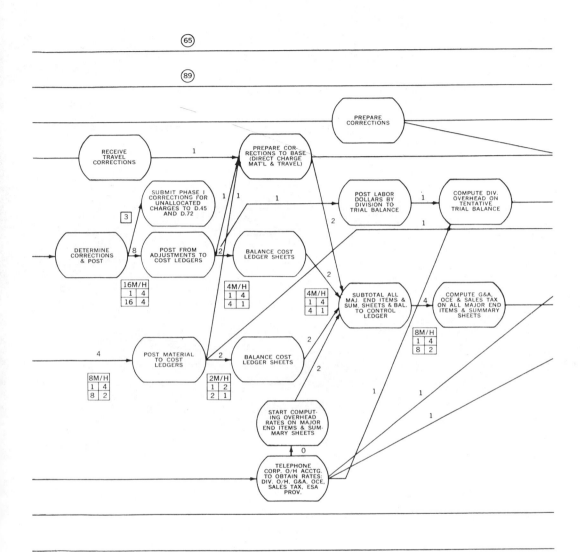

CLOSING SCHEDULE

Figure 8-5 *(continued)*

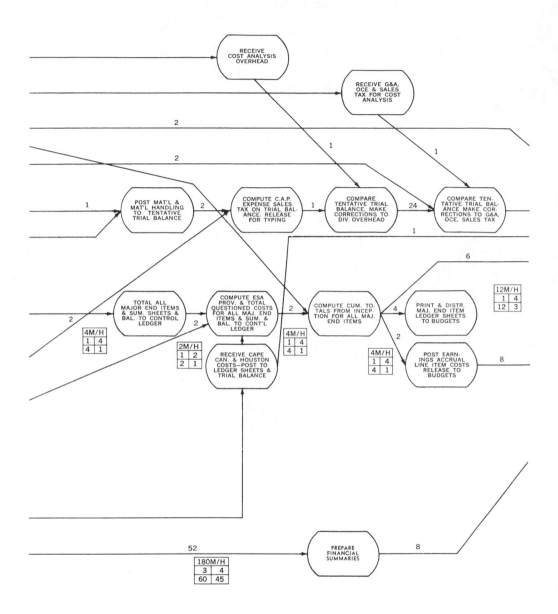

Figure 8-5 *(continued)*

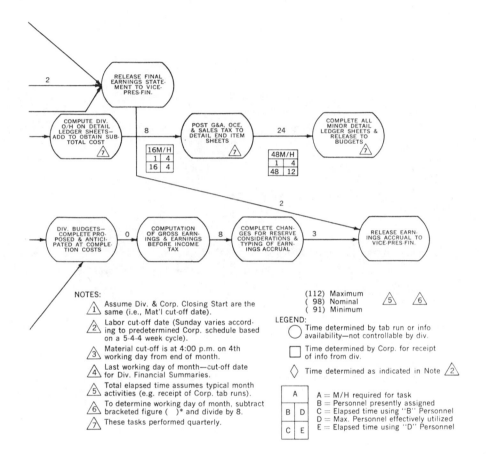

Figure 8-5 *(continued)*

REFERENCES

[1]Terrill, William A., and Patrick, Albert W., *Cost Accounting for Management.* Holt, Rinehart, and Winston, Inc., 1965, New York.

[2]A. Wayne Corcoran, *Mathematical Applications in Accounting.* Harcourt, Brace & World, Inc., 1968.

[3]*Ibid.*

[4]*Ibid.*

[5]"Accounting & The Computer." AICPA, 1966, New York, p. 217.

[6]*Ibid.*

[7]*Ibid.*

[8]Terrill, et.al, *op. cit.,* Figure 22-1.

[9]"Mathematical and Statistical Applications of Accounting." *The New York Certified Public Accountant.* Frederick Alan Provorny, July 1967, p. 530.

[10]*Ibid.,* p. 531.

[11]*Ibid.*

[12]*Ibid.,* p. 528.

[13]*Ibid.,* p. 520.

[14]Donald R. Smith, "What A Chief Executive Should Know About Financial Modeling." *Price Waterhouse & Co. Review.* 1973, p. 31.

[15]*Ibid.,* p. 33.

[16]John K. Shank and John B. Calfee, Jr., "Case of the Fuqua Forecast." *Harvard Business Review.* November-December 1973, p. 44.

[17]*Ibid.,* p. 42.

[18]Donald R. Smith, *op. cit.,* p. 32.

[19]*Ibid.,* p. 33.

[20]*Ibid.*

[21]James B. Boulden and Elwood S. Buffa, "Corporate Models: On-line, Real-time Systems." *Harvard Business Review.* July-August 1970, p. 73.

[22]*Ibid.*

[23]*Ibid.*

[24]*Ibid.*

[25]*Ibid.*

[26]*Ibid.,* p. 77, 78.

[27]*Ibid.,* p. 66.

[28]*Ibid.*

[29]*Ibid.,* p. 81.

[30]*Ibid.*

[31]*Ibid.*

[32]"Models, Mergers, and the Planning Gap." B.S. Dale, "Management Accounting" *Journal of the Institute of Cost and Management Accountants,* London, England, April 1974, p. 109.

[33]*Ibid.*

[34]*Ibid.*

[35]*Ibid.*

[36]*Ibid.*

[37]Albert P. Ameiss, Warren A. Thompson, "PERT for Monthly Financial Closing." *Management Adviser,* American Institute of Certified Public Accountants, January-February, 1974, pp. 30-36.

[38]*Ibid.,* p. 31.

[39]C. Jackson Grayson, Jr., "Management Science and Business Practice." *Harvard Business Review,* July-August, 1973, p. 41.

[40]*Ibid.*

[41]*Ibid.*

9 Ramifications of Fiduciary Accounting

Under the classification of Fiduciary Accounting, the following topics are discussed in the order shown:

(1) Acts of bankruptcy, protection afforded under the National Bankruptcy Act, and major accounting implications;

(2) Corporate liquidation effected through several different approaches;

(3) Quasi-reorganization as an alternative to bankruptcy and the kinds of accounting entries required to accommodate the reorganization procedures approved by the Board of Directors and stockholders;

(4) Accounting statements required in (1), (2), and (3) above; and,

(5) Accounting procedures and statements required in discharging the responsibility of the fiduciary, executor, or administrator of an estate, or of the trustee of an insolvent business.

Purpose of the National Bankruptcy Act

A financially embarrassed firm can initiate reorganization, or dissolution, or legal reorganization may be forced upon it by its creditors. The National Bankruptcy Act permits a firm, with stipulated exclusions by industries, to petition that it be adjudged a bankrupt. The purpose of the Act is to provide an equitable distribution of available assets to the bankrupt firm's creditors and to give the debtor a clean slate as far as future business ventures are concerned.

Certain acts of bankruptcy are stipulated in the Act that must have happened or been committed by the debtor within four months prior to the filing of the bankruptcy petition, whether done so by the debtor or his creditors. Among these are: any acts evidencing intent to defraud creditors, such as the concealment or transfer of assets to preferred creditors through such intent; the transfer while insolvent of assets to preferred creditors; the making of a general assignment for the benefit of creditors; or the admission in writing of inability to pay debts and the desire to be adjudged a bankrupt.[1]

Liquidation Accounting Characteristics

Four separate studies cited by Copeland indicate agreement on certain important ratios for predicting financial crises five years before failure actually occurred.[2] These include the ratios of: (1) cash flow to total debt; (2) net income to total assets; (3) total debt to total assets; (4) working capital to total assets; and (5) no-credit interval.

Accounting analysis is important in the case of a firm whose ratios indicate financial difficulty to determing whether the company should seek voluntary bankruptcy because of insolvency or other acts spelled out in the National Bankruptcy Act; seek a solution with its creditors; or, take other appropriate action.

In direct contrast to the traditional "going concern" concept of accounting, the liquidation valuation approach cannot accept assets at acquisition cost and their allocation to revenues over the economic life of the assets. Conversely, the accrual basis of accounting presumes a going concern and therefore cannot satisfy the needs of a balance sheet prepared to determine whether liquidation should be elected and the realization to creditors and owners that can be expected.

A *legal* statement of affairs (Figure 9-1)—not to be confused with the traditional *accounting* statement bearing the same name—must be presented with the petition in bankruptcy.[3] Information required includes many of the items contained in the accounts of the debtor and illustrated below. In addition to schedules detailing assets individually, liabilities, and pertinent items with reference to secured and unsecured debts, the identity of the firm's auditors, and descriptions of procedures followed, such as inventory-taking, are also required.

After the above information discloses all assets, it is necessary to assign values in liquidation—as opposed to the customary "going concern" valuations. A trustee is named who may be the receiver selected to administer the debtor's property pending the court's action on the bankruptcy petition. Assuming the petition is granted, the creditors usually meet and name the trustee who now manages the bankrupt's business. He must give a report of his stewardship to the parties involved—the court, creditors, and the bankrupt, supporting the validity of all claims paid, the amount of cash remaining, if any, and operating statements in adequate form for review by the court.[4]

Liquidating dividends paid to stockholders must be approved and notification furnished that these represent a return of capital rather than a regular dividend charged to retained earnings. Provisions of the corporate charter, the state laws, and income tax regulations may suggest liquidation through the purchase or reacquisition of capital stock from owners as a more advantageous approach for the latter. In some states, laws may restrict treasury stock activities of this kind in order to preserve a base of legal capital available to creditors under the limited liability corporate privilege.[5] Still another method of liquidation is the *spin off* whereby a segment of the corporation's operation is separately incorporated, with specific assets and liabilities inherent in its function. The capital stock of this subsidiary is then distributed to parent company stockholders.[6]

Superior Products, Inc.

Balance Sheet

May 15, 19XX[*]

Assets

Current assets:			
Cash		$ 1,750	
Notes receivable		15,000	
Accounts receivable	$35,000		
Less allowance for bad debts	3,500	31,500	
Accrued interest on notes receivable		300	
Inventories:			
Finished goods	$15,000		
Goods in process	22,000		
Raw materials	10,000		
Miscellaneous supplies	1,500	48,500	
Prepaid insurance		1,200	$ 98,250
Investments:			
Stock of Hanson Co. (500 shares)			40,000
Plant and equipment:			
Machinery and equipment	$55,000		
Less allowance for depr. on mach. and equip	15,000	$ 40,000	
Buildings	$50,000		
Less allowance for depreciation on buildings	5,000	45,000	
Land		35,000	120,000
Intangibles:			
Goodwill			20,000
Total assets			$278,250

Figure 9-1

Liabilities and Stockholders' Equity

Liabilities

Current liabilities:

Taxes payable	$ 600	
Wages payable	1,200	
Notes payable	55,000	
Accounts payable	102,000	
Accrued interest on notes payable	1,200	
Accrued interest on bonds	750	$160,750
Long-term debt:		
First mortgage bonds		50,000
Total liabilities		$210,750

Stockholders' Equity

Capital stock	$100,000	
Additional paid-in capital	12,000	
	$112,000	
Less deficit	44,500	
Total stockholders' equity		67,500
Total liabilities and stockholders' equity		$278,250

Figure 9-1 *(continued)*

Source: *Advanced Accounting, Comprehensive Volume,* Fourth Edition, Harry Simons and Wilbert E. Karrenbrock, South-Western Publishing Company, 1968, p. 645.

Quasi-Reorganization

Many firms do not go through the wringer in the sense of the bankruptcy proceedings discussed above. Although corporations may find a series of lean years and show losses in those years, retrenchment is effected in ingenious ways to avoid bankruptcy. Declining sales over a period of years will undoubtedly see an impact on the firm's relations with its bank, for example if the firm is unable to meet its seasonal loans and "get out of the bank" at least once a year. A simple review of the income statement and balance sheet indicates trends and danger signals discussed earlier in this chapter. Not only the bank, but creditors as well will recognize failure to take cash discounts and very definitely notice the accounts that are more than thirty days in arrears. Holders of notes and preferred stockholders will be quick to respond to any delinquencies in meeting such obligations.

Since a shortage in working capital is the most immediate problem in the case of such distressed firms, new financial arrangements have to be found with a cooperative bank. Frequently a bank will endeavor to assist an old established customer who experiences financial embarrassment by working out a joint arrangement with an acceptance firm and splitting the line of credit between them. For example, where a firm received the prime rate of interest on its seasonal loans from its banking connection of many years, totalling perhaps $500,000, the company may find that sustained losses on the income statement for several years will result in action by the bank terminating that arrangement. Where the relationship has been a long and fruitful one, many banks will seek to assure the customer of the same total for working capital, but will share the risk with another financial house. Perhaps the bank will take $250,000 at something more than the prime rate and locate the remaining $250,000 with an acceptance firm at the latter's interest rate, often twice that of the bank. Such arrangements will usually be hedged with protective measures as far as the interests of the lending institutions are concerned.

Steps by firms in the process of reorganization or quasi-reorganization may include the following:

(1) With approval of the board and stockholders, write off the deficit with a debit to capital stock, usually requiring action to reduce the par value of the stock; and

(2) Obtain approval of the creditors to accept equity in the firm in lieu of creditor claims, resulting in a reduction of the firm's liabilities, a credit to retained income to eliminate the deficit, and a pro-rate or total reduction of the previous stockholders' equity as the old creditors in effect become the new owners.[7]

After the deficiency in the retained earnings account has been eliminated through steps such as those listed previously, earnings developed thereafter may be dated to provide future investors or creditors with information to properly evaluate the firm's credit. Write-downs of assets to reflect current values and relieve future periods of excess depreciation or amortization charges should be shown as extraordinary charges in the year in which the entry is made, in accordance with provisions of APB Opinion No. 9.

Accounting Practice Regarding the Elimination of Accumulated Deficits

The Board of Directors of General Plywood Corporation approved a restatement of the capital accounts whereby the deficit was eliminated by a charge to paid-in capital.[8]

The practice of dating retained earnings, indicated above, and discussed in ARB No. 46 was not widely visible in a recent sample of corporate disclosure.[9]   Under the caption of shareholders' equity, one firm reported the dollar amount of its outstanding common stock, followed by additional paid-in capital, and retained earnings "since June 1, 19___."[10]

Accounting Statements Used in Liquidations and Reorganizations

The accounting statement of affairs shows *both* liquidating and balance sheet values in the same report. The result is that a comparison of the two sets of values is facilitated—book values versus values expected to be realized at liquidation date. In addition, the accountant is given the assurance that no unintentional omission of assets or liabilities has occurred. If such an omission has happened the book values, shown as the first column in the statement of affairs for both the asset and equity sides, will not balance.

A deficiency statement or account usually accompanies the statement of affairs to provide further detail. This control device explains the apparent paradox to creditors—that they cannot be paid in full notwithstanding the fact that the assets at ledger values exceed the liabilities.[11] The deficiency statement performs the balancing act of the statement of affairs, being debited for losses on realization of assets and credited for gains on realization of assets as well as losses to stockholders and creditors.

An Illustrated Statement of Affairs

The development of financial distress in the life of a firm is usually preceded by a number of warnings or storm signals which a trained observor might detect from the financial statements, particularly from the balance sheet. For this reason the latter is shown in Figure 9-1 as a logical starting place for the preparation of the accounting version of a statement of affairs.

Analyses of the working capital ratio and the acid test ratio, show symptoms of the firm's financial illness that are confirmed in the deficit of $44,500. Since balance sheet values are based on going-concern valuations, it is necessary to obtain estimated liquidation values in the event of a forced realization of the firm's assets. In addition, information is required as to any additional liabilities that might exist over and above those shown in the accounts and securities pledged or mortgages held by various creditors to secure specific obligations. In this example, appraisals of the company's assets indicate that forced realization of the assets will result in the following recoveries:[1][2]

Cash	$ 1,500
Notes receivable, $14,000 and accrued interest, $300	14,300
Accounts receivable	19,000
Finished Goods	14,000
Goods in process after completion (estimated costs to complete: materials, $2,000; additional labor, etc., $2,500)	25,000
Raw materials remaining after completion of goods in process	8,500
Miscellaneous supplies	500
Prepaid insurance	Nothing
Machinery and equipment	18,000
Buildings	
Land	50,000
Stock of Hanson Co. ($60 per share)	30,000
Bond redemption fund securities, $10,500, and accrued interest, $250	10,750
Goodwill	Nothing
Patents completely written off the books in past years but that have a realizable value	10,000

It is estimated that, in addition to the liabilities shown on the balance sheet, the following amounts will have to be paid:

Liquidation costs	$ 6,000
Notes receivable discounted that will probably be dishonored without possibility of recovery by the company	5,000
Probable judgments on damage suits pending	20,000

Obligations of the company are secured as follows:

Obligation	Security
Notes payable of $20,000 on which interest of $400 is accrued	300 shares of Hanson Co. stock
	Notes receivable
Accounts payable of $30,000	Land and buildings and bond
First mortgage bonds	redemption fund securities

The preparation of the statement of affairs can perhaps be seen best through the use of a building stone approach, culminating in the final or completed presentation in Figure 9-2.

Attention should be given first to the liabilities with highest priority. By law these are the liquidation costs required in preserving the bankrupt's estate, wages payable to employees not in excess of $600 to each earned within three months before filing date,[13] and taxes due to the United States, state governments or municipalities. Such *prior claim liabilities* will be the first subtracted from remaining free assets after secured liabilities have been taken care of, as shown in the lower left-hand side of Figure 9-2.

Succeeding steps in the preparation of the statement of affairs continue with the second caption under liabilities, "Fully secured creditors." The first mortgage bonds, plus accrued interest, are covered in full by the buildings that such bonds apparently financed. This amount of $50,750 is so indicated (deducted contra), directing the reader to the opposite side of the statement and the caption, "Assets pledged with fully secured creditors." Under the latter heading in Figure 9-2, the assets are listed at book values in the left-hand column, at $45,000 and $35,000 for buildings and land, respectively. The appraised value of these assets of $55,000 is entered in the "Appraised" column and is reduced by $50,750, representing the claims of fully secured creditors mentioned above. The balance is extended to the column "Estimated Amount Available" in the amount of $4,250.

A similar approach is followed with "Partly secured creditors" with notes payable and accounts payable, covered by assets of $18,000 (300 shares of Hanson Company stock at $60 per share) and $14,300 in notes receivable, respectively. The $20,000 notes payable, plus accrued interest of $400, exceed the appraised value of the 300 shares pledged by $2,400 which is extended to the far right-hand column labeled "Amounts Unsecured." The same treatment of partly secured accounts payable ($30,000) with notes receivable and accrued interest (totalling $14,300) results in the extension of the difference of $15,200 to the "Amounts Unsecured" column. Conversely, the showing of these pledged assets under "Assets pledged with partly secured creditors" results in an excess of such assets over the notes and accounts payable, which are partly secured, in the amount of $12,000 shown under "Free Assets" and which is extended to the column "Estimated Amount Available."

The statement is completed by listing all unsecured liabilities under the heading, "Unsecured creditors" and inserting all such amounts in the

**Superior Products, Inc.
Statement of Affairs
May 15, 1967**

Assets

Book Value	Assets	Appraised Value	Estimated Amount Available	Loss or (Gain) on Realization
$ 45,000	Assets pledged with fully secured creditors: Buildings	$ 55,000		$ 25,000
35,000	Land			
	Less claim, first mortgage bonds, and accrued interest (see contra)	50,750		
24,000	Total (deducted contra)		$ 4,250	
	Assets pledged with partly secured creditors: Hanson Co. stock, 300 shares (deducted contra)	$ 18,000		6,000
15,000	Notes receivable	$ 14,000		
300	Add accrued interest	300		
	Total (deducted contra)	$ 14,300		1,000
	Free assets:			
1,750	Cash	$ 1,750	1,750	
31,500	Accounts receivable	19,500	19,500	12,000
15,000	Finished goods	14,000	14,000	1,000
22,000	Goods in process Estimated value after completion $25,000			
	Less costs to complete: Raw materials $2,000 Labor, etc. 2,500 4,500	20,500	20,500	1,500
10,000	Raw materials Required to complete goods in process $ 2,000 Balance, estimated to realize 8,300	10,500	10,500	(500)
1,500	Miscellaneous supplies	500	500	1,000
1,200	Prepaid insurance	0		1,200
16,000	Hanson Co. stock (200 shares)	12,000	12,000	4,000
40,000	Machinery and equipment	18,000	18,000	22,000
0	Goodwill	0		20,000
20,000	Patents	10,000	10,000	(10,000)
				$ 84,200
	Estimated amount available		$111,000	
	Creditors with priority (see contra)		14,300	
	Estimated amount available to unsecured creditors (approximately 64¢ on the dollar)[1]		$ 96,700	
	Estimated deficiency to unsecured creditors		54,200	
$278,250			$150,900	

Liabilities and Stockholders' Equity

Book Value	Liabilities and Stockholders' Equity	Amount Unsecured
	Creditors with priority:	
$ 600	Estimated liquidation expenses	$12,500
	Taxes payable	600
1,200	Wages payable	1,200
	Total (deducted contra)	$14,300
	Fully secured creditors:	
50,000	First mortgage bonds	$50,000
750	Add accrued interest	750
	Total (deducted contra)	$50,750
	Partly secured creditors:	
20,000	Notes payable	$20,000
400	Add accrued interest	400
	Total	$20,400
	Less security: Hanson Co. stock (see contra)	18,000 $ 2,400
30,000	Accounts payable	$30,000
	Less security: notes receivable and accrued interest (see contra)	14,300 15,700
	Unsecured creditors:	
35,000	Notes payable	$35,000
800	Add accrued interest	800 35,800
72,000	Accounts payable	72,000
	Estimated liability on notes receivable discounted	5,000
	Estimated liability on damage suits pending	20,000
	Stockholders' equity:	
100,000	Capital stock	
12,000	Additional paid-in capital	
(44,500)	Deficit	
$278,250	Total unsecured liabilities	$150,900

[1]Estimated amount available, $96,700, divided by total unsecured liabilities, $150,900, equals estimated amount payable on claims, 64%, or 64 cents on the dollar.

Figure 9-2

unsecured amount column. All remaining "Free assets" are listed under that caption and the differences between book values and appraised values are extended to the "Estimated Amount Available" column. The result is shown in the lower left-hand column of Figure 9-2, where the remaining total of unsecured creditors, $150,900 is matched with the estimated amount remaining for such liabilities. The difference of $54,200 represents a deficiency equal to 64¢ on the dollar with respect to unsecured liabilities.

Based on this information, a decision can be made as to whether to proceed and liquidate the business or to attempt to continue operations under a trustee with the hope of a better return to the creditors and perhaps a return to solvency. If the latter course of action is selected, the operations of the trustee or receiver may be the subject of periodic *Statements of Realization and Liquidation* which are discussed next. An analogy is made between this report of the trustee's stewardship and that of the fiduciary of an estate in what is called the *Charge and Discharge Statement.*

The Statement of Realization and Liquidation

As suggested above, the function of the receiver in many cases is to operate in a profitable manner a business that has been showing losses, or to establish the fact that liquidation is inevitable. The trustee's recommendation may take the form of the statement of realization and liquidation which usually has the following captions:

ASSETS

Assets to be realized:
  Receivables
  Inventory
  Equipment (net of depreciation)

Assets Acquired:
  Receivables

Assets realized:
  Receivables

Assets not realized:
  Receivables
  Inventory
  Equipment (net)

LIABILITIES

Liabilities liquidated:
  Trade Accounts Payable

Liabilities not liquidated:
  Accounts Payable

Liabilities to be liquidated:
  Accounts Payable

Liabilities assumed:
  None

PROFIT OR LOSS FOR THE PERIOD

Charges:	Credits:
Purchases	Sales for cash
Expenses	Sales on account
Totals	Totals

Supporting the receiver's report would normally be a balance sheet, prepared in conventional manner on a going concern basis. Included are, of course, all the accounts including cash and stockholders' equity accounts that are excluded in the statement of realization and liquidation. However, the profit shown in supplementary form to the statement of realization and liquidation would be credited to retained earnings and perhaps explained in detail in an accompanying income statement in a format such as the following:

_____ Co.

Income Statement

For Period Ended _____

	Book Value	Proceeds	Loss or (Gain)
Loss and gain on liquidation:			
Receivables			
Inventory			
Net gains over losses			
Depreciation on equipment			
Other costs			
Net income for the period			

At this point the receiver may be relieved of his fiduciary relationship, turning over the assets not realized, cash, liabilities not liquidated, and any new liabilities incurred in his period of operation, as directed by the court.

The receiver's responsibility in following directions of the court— assuming the management of the distressed company, accounting for his stewardship at intervals specified, and ultimately being discharged of this responsibility—are comparable in many ways with that of the executor of an estate and his fiduciary relationships discussed below.

Statement of Accountability—Fiduciary of an Estate

The executor or administrator normally assumes the management of an estate which, however, may not include the assumption of the estate's liabilities. One difference between the responsibilities of the trustee of a firm under bankruptcy proceedings and the administrator of an estate is that the latter must distinguish in his accounts between the principal or corpus of the estate and its income. Separate reporting of each is necessary in many cases in order for the administrator to observe the directions of the will of the deceased, if such a will existed, or to follow the directions of the court if it assumed that responsibility.

The executor's report of his management of the estate may take the form of the *Charge and Discharge Statement* discussed next.

Summary Report—Executor's Charge and Discharge Statement

The format of the executor's summary report follows, which is submitted to the court of appropriate jurisdiction.

Estate of _____
A. Smith, Executor
Charge and Discharge Statement
For the period _____ to _____

As to Principal

I Charge myself with:		
Assets taken over (Schedule A)	$xxx,xxx	
Assets discovered (Schedule B)	xxx,xxx	
Gain on realization	xx,xxx	$xxx,xxx
I credit myself with:		
Funeral and administrative expenses	$ x,xxx	
Debts of decedent paid	x,xxx	
Legacies paid (Schedule C)	xx,xxx	
Loss on realization	xxx	$xxx,xxx
Balance as to principal		$xxx,xxx

As to Income

I charge myself with:	
Income for period (Statement attached)	$ xx,xxx

I credit myself with:

Expenses chargeable to Income	$ xx,xxx	
Distributions to beneficiaries from Income (Schedule D)	xx,xxx	xx,xxx

Balance as to Income $ x,xxx

In each schedule identified, details are contained supporting the summary amount shown in the charge and discharge statement.[14]

In this section reference has been made to the fiduciary as the "executor," assuming that the decedent left a valid will and named an individual in that will to be his executor. It is beyond the scope of this chapter to discuss the various state laws with respect to the disposition of the estate laws of descent controlling the disposition of real property where no will is found and laws of distribution regulate the disposition of personal property. In such a case, where no will exists, the fiduciary is selected by the court and known as an administrator.[15] The same formats for reporting, illustrated above, are recommended for the administrator as for the executor.

In addition the decedent's will may direct that property contained in his estate be placed in trust, whereby title passes to a trustee who manages it for persons named.[16] A trustee has whatever authority is specifically delegated to him by the trust instrument and is charged with exercising the care of a prudent manager. He is subject to removal from this function by a court of competent jurisdiction, under the Uniform Trusts Act, for due cause and upon notice to the beneficiaries.[17] Again the distinction between principal and income must be maintained and the reporting instrument can be the charge and discharge statement, with modifications based on the specific functions to be reported on by the trustee.

Whether his responsibility relates to the liquidation or management of a "sick" firm, a quasi-reorganization (in which case no formal fiduciary may be named—the function is performed by someone, usually the chief operating officer) or an estate or trust. The fiduciary is delegated specific authority to perform stated acts as the agent of the court or the decedent, where a will was left, and is required to give an account of his stewardship at intervals specified, using appropriate and meaningful reports, such as recommended in this chapter.

REFERENCES

[1]*Advanced Accounting.* Ronald Copeland, D. Larry Crumbley, Joseph F. Wojdak. Holt, Rinehart and Winston, Inc., 1971, p. 363.

[2]*Ibid.,* p. 369.

[3]*Ibid.,* p. 367.

[4]*Ibid.,* p. 364.

[5]*Ibid.,* p. 371.

[6]*Ibid.,* p. 372.

[7]*Ibid.,* p. 373.

[8]General Plywood Corporation, "Consolidated Statement of Stockholders' Equity," *Accounting Trends & Techniques,* Twenty-Seventh Edition 1973, American Institute of Certified Public Accountants, page 309.

[9]*Ibid.,* p. 190.

[10]*Ibid.*

[11]*How to Solve Accounting Problems.* Hammond & Smith, Prentice-Hall, p. 113.

[12]*Advanced Accounting. Comprehensive Volume,* Fourth Edition, Harry Simons and Wilbert E. Karrenbrock, published by South-Western Publishing Company, 1968, p. 645.

[13]*Advanced Accounting.* Charles H. Griffin, Thomas H. Williams and Glen A. Welsch, 1966, p. 658. Reprinted with permission from Richard D. Irwin, Inc., Homewood, Ill.

[14]For a discussion in greater detail, see *Advanced Accounting,* Griffin et. al, pp. 674-681.

[15]*Ibid.,* p. 695.

[16]*Ibid.,* p. 700.

[17]*Ibid.,* p. 701.

10 Securities and Exchange Commission and Special Regulatory Accounting Topics

The accounting topics discussed in this chapter relate to control under various federal agencies. They are as follows:

(1) The Securities and Exchange Regulations, with particular reference to the form and content of registration statements and periodic reports;

(2) The Robinson-Patman Act, with respect to the kinds of cost differentials required to support different prices in different markets;

(3) The Interstate Commerce Commission's Uniform System of Accounts—illustrated by reference to accounts prescribed for Class I and Class II Common and Contract Motor Carriers;

(4) Department of Labor legislation, including: (a) the Labor-Management Reporting and Disclosure Act (LMRDA), amended in 1965, affecting union members, employers, labor relations consultants, surety companies; (b) the Welfare and Pension Plans Disclosure Act, amended 1962, outlining the responsibilities of plan administrators, and requiring plan descriptions and annual reports; and, (c) the Employee Retirement Income Security Act of 1974, containing broad new provisions for the private pension system, with respect to eligibility, vesting, funding, and additional reporting requirements;

(5) The Federal Reserve System's Regulations (X, G, T, and U) covering many aspects of Securities Credit Transactions; and,

(6) The Cost Accounting Standards Board requirements, established by Congress to introduce uniformity in reporting in defense contract accounting.

Reference is made frequently in other chapters to the above topics, particularly the Securities and Exchange Regulations, which are discussed here. In addition, other areas of regulatory accounting are discussed elsewhere to complement the subject matter being considered; for example, tax accounting is given the significance of specialized treatment in Chapters 23 and 24. The impact of the Securities and Exchange legislation on reporting standards in the United States was discussed in preceding sections where applicable. A detailed analysis of pertinent provisions of Securities and Exchange Legislation follows, representing perhaps the most applicable phase of governmental regulation to accountants after that of tax legislation.

The Securities Exchange Act of 1933

Known as a *disclosure statute,* the Securities Exchange Act of 1933 contained requirements for full and accurate disclosure of all pertinent information relating to a registrant's securities, financial position, and earnings. The philosophy expressed in the Act was that the seller (not the buyer) must beware—the public was to be protected, not the issuer or the underwriter of the securities.

In the enforcement of the 1933 Act, the Commission strives to prevent fraudulent practices in the sale of securities, but does not guarantee the investor against loss. A registration statement and prospectus must be furnished the buyer of a registered security. Financial statements are also included among the documents furnished the investor.

A registration statement to which the Commission objects must be corrected by means of an appropriate amendment. If the latter does not cure the deficiency, the Commission may exercise a stop-order or refusal, which prevents the registration statement from becoming effective and the securities from being sold.

In addition, the 1933 Act provides for the civil liability of the issuer or underwriter and experts if materially false or inadequate responses are found. The law also imposes criminal penalties for fraudulent acts and practices in the sale of securities in interstate commerce, whether the securities are registered or not. The 1933 Act is concerned primarily with the *distribution* of securities, rather than with the *trading* of the securities, which is under the jurisdiction of the Act of 1934.[1]

Power of Commission to Determine Accepted Accounting Practice

The 1933 Act contains broad powers of the Commission to make, amend, or rescind any rules and regulations that may be necessary to carry out the provisions of the law. The Commission is authorized to define accounting, technical, and trade terms used in the law. Power is given to prescribe the form in which required information shall be set forth and to determine the items to be shown in the financial statements.

The 1933 Act empowers the Commission to stipulate methods to be followed in the preparation of accounts, the appraisal or valuation of the assets and liabilities, and the determination of depreciation and depletion. With reference to the preparation of consolidated financial statements, the Act conveys authority to prescribe the methods to be followed in the preparation of consolidated financial statements of companies controlling, or controlled by the issuer, or under common control with the issuer.[2]

The Securities Exchange Act of 1934

The Securities and Exchange Commission was created by the Securities Exchange Act of 1934. The Commission's functions include the administration of a number of acts, and the regulation of the sale of corporate securities to the public and the trading of securities. In addition, the 1934 Act empowers the Commission to prescribe the form in which the information required shall be set forth and to determine the items or details to be shown in the financial statements. Financial statements are included in the prospectuses and annual reports filed with the Commission. The Commission has sweeping authority to require the application of certain accounting principles, but has not exercised such authority fully or issued detailed rules on such accounting methods.[3]

The philosophy of the 1934 Act is the same as that of the 1933 Act—to protect the public, not the issuer, nor brokers, nor dealers. Provision is made for the filing of an application for registration by any company desiring to have its securities registered and listed for trading on a national securities exchange.

The Holding Company Act of 1935

Under the Holding Company Act of 1935, registered holding companies and their subsidiaries were required to keep such accounts and records as the Commission might deem appropriate to be in the public interest.

The Commission approved two uniform systems of accounts under the Act of 1935: one for public utility holding companies and one for mutual service companies and subsidiary service companies. This action suggests that the Commission is not opposed to the exercise of its authority as far as the introduction of uniformity is concerned, when the facts so warrant.

Investment Company Act of 1940

The provisions of the Investment Company Act of 1940 stipulate that registered investment companies must maintain such accounts and documents as constitute the basis for the financial statements required to be filed with the Commission.

Authority is given the Commission to issue rules and regulations providing for a reasonable degree of uniformity in the accounting policies and principles to be followed by registered investment companies. Such uniformity applies to the maintenance of accounting records and the preparation of financial statements.

Again, the Acts of 1935 and 1940 indicate that the Commission has long had authority to prescribe rules and procedures which have as their objective the introduction of meaningful uniformity into the accounts and the financial statements prepared from such accounts.

Regulation S-X

Acting under the authority of the various acts outlined above, the Commission released Regulation S-X in 1940. Although amended several times since that date, this Regulation is the principal accounting provision of the Commission. Its scope includes the form and content of most financial statements required to be filed under the Securities Acts of 1933 and 1934, the Public Utility Holding Act of 1935, and the Investment Company Act of 1940.

In addition to Regulation S-X, the media used by the Commission to make its views on accounting known are its decided cases. These create a sort of Securities and Exchange Commission common law of accounting. Also important are the published opinions of the Commission's Chief Accountant. Serving in that capacity, Andrew Barr replied as follows to a question concerning the Commission's policy on consolidation practices of United States parent corporations with foreign subsidiaries:

> Our requirements for consolidated statements are contained in Article 4 of Regulation S-X, our basic accounting regulation. In general, we expect United States companies, in reports they are required to file with the SEC, to apply U.S. accounting standards to their foreign subsidiaries whether they are included in consolidation or reported on separately. Exceptions to this policy would have to be considered on an individual basis. You will note in Rule 4-02 (c) some special considerations that must be taken into account in the determination of whether foreign subsidiaries should be consolidated.[4]

Accounting Series Releases

Notices of new and amending rules and regulations of the Securities and Exchange Commission are given in so-called *Accounting Series Releases.* The first release in the series appeared in 1937. Only 158 releases have been made through July of 1974[5] apparently because of the Commission's policy of encouraging the accounting profession to originate accounting and auditing pronouncements.

When the Commission finds it desirable to issue an opinion with respect to major accounting and auditing questions or administrative policy with respect to financial statements, copies of the proposed opinion are furnished to professional accounting organizations for suggestions.

Accounting Series Release No. 4 was issued by the Commission in 1938 with reference to the preparation of financial statements. A statement of the Commission's policy was included with respect to the acceptance or rejection of accounting principles and financial statements embodying such principles. Financial statements filed with the Commission pursuant to the regulations of the 1933 or 1934 Acts will be presumed to be misleading or inaccurate if based upon accounting principles for which there is no "substantial authoritative support."[6]

In Release No. 4, it was made clear that if the differences involved are material no accompanying disclosures contained in the certificate of the accountant or in footnotes would cure the defect. If a difference of opinion develops between the Commission and the registrant as to which of several principles should be followed—all having substantial authoritative support—disclosure will be accepted in lieu of correction of the statements.

The "substantial authoritative support," cited above, has not been interpreted or elaborated upon by the Commission. L.H. Rappaport indicated that such support includes the pronouncements of the American Institute of Certified Public Accountants, the American Accounting Association, and the uniform systems of accounts of federal and state regulatory authorities in the fields of communication, transportation, and public utilities.[7]

Management's Responsibility for Statements Filed with the Commission

Corporate management's responsibility for the contents and presentation of financial statements was stressed in Accounting Series Release No. 62, issued in 1947.[8] Reference is made in the release to the accuracy of information filed with the Commission and distributed to investors. Management does not discharge its obligations by the employment of independent public accountants in the eyes of the Commission. The accountants' certificates are required, not as a substitute for management's accounting of its stewardship, but as a check upon that accounting.

Policy Regarding the Development of Accounting Principles

A series of accounting releases has been issued by the Commission generally endorsing the accounting principles accepted by the accounting profession, pronounced in Accounting Research and Terminology Bulletins, Accounting Principles Board Opinions and statements of the Financial Accounting Standards Board of the American Institute of Certified Public Accountants.

The Commission is in a position to be more persuasive with corporate management than any independent auditor and to insist on compliance with generally accepted accounting principles in the preparation of financial statements. One of the chief difficulties encountered by the Commission results from the inclusion in registration statements of financial statements prepared on a tax basis, but certified by public accountants as being in conformity with generally accepted principles of accounting.[9]

Policy on Consolidation of Operating Results of Foreign Subsidiaries

With respect to the consolidation of foreign subsidiaries, the Commission accepts that presentation that most clearly exhibits the entity's financial condition. The criterion of consolidation is the degree of integration of foreign and domestic operations. There is a presumption in favor of consolidation.[10]

SEC Reporting Requirements

Publicly-held companies are required to file the following reports with the SEC for compliance by that commission with its regulatory responsibilities and for review by interested investors:

(1) 10-K, the annual report certified by an independent accountant;
(2) Form 10-Q, an interim, unaudited financial statement, filed quarterly, reflecting adjustments and allocations required by management to present a complete picture; and,
(3) Form 8-K, a monthly report, required only when certain specified events occur, such as the acquisition of a subsidiary or an investment of comparable significance for purposes of expansion.[11]

An innovative feature of Form 8-K is the requirement that management report the engagement of a new independent auditor through a supplemental letter to the Form 8-K. In addition, any material disagreement with the former auditor within the preceding 18 months must be disclosed and that auditor's comment on the controversy attached. In this manner, both the SEC and interested investors are alerted to give the statements particular analysis with respect to the issue causing the disagreement.[12]

Other areas of regulatory accounting, while significant to large segments of the economy do not have the impact on accounting principles and disclosure that the SEC regulations exert. Accordingly, briefer coverage is afforded such topics, discussed below, beginning with regulations prohibiting price discrimination.

Relevant Provisions of the Robinson-Patman Act

Price discrimination between competing customers is prohibited under the Robinson-Patman Act. Flexible pricing policies must be based on differences in the costs of serving particular markets. By definition, "costs" in this context mean full or absorption costing, as well as distribution costs including marketing, warehousing, and freight out. However, in most cases the issues at stake in the enforcement of the Robinson-Patman Act have been those of lessening, competition and price-cutting in particular markets.[13]

To invoke the Act it must usually be proven that discrimination between customers was practiced with respect to:

(1) Price differences;
(2) Discounts;
(3) Delivery service;
(4) Allowances for services;
(5) Advertising appropriations;
(6) Brokerage or commissions; and
(7) Consignment policies.

Thus, the Act makes allowances for cost differences in serving customers but requires definite justification for price differentials granted.[14]

The Interstate Commerce Commission's Uniform System of Accounts

Uniformity in recording accounting transactions and in financial disclosure is required by regulatory commissions responsible for the operations of utilities, including interstate carriers. The Interstate Commerce Commission's prescribed system of accounts, effective January 1, 1974, is used to highlight certain differences between regulatory accounting and that used in industry in general.

The classification of carriers for purposes of accounting and reporting under Interstate Commerce Regulations includes three classes:[15]

(a) Class I carriers having average annual gross operating revenues of $3 million or more from total property motor carrier operations;
(b) Class II carriers having average annual gross operating revenues of

$500,000 but less than $3 million from property carrier operations; and,

(c) Class III carriers with average annual gross operating revenues of
less than $500,000 from property motor operations.

The above classifications are determined from the annual gross
operating revenues of each carrier for the past three calendar years. Any
carrier may elect the accounting methods of a group higher than the one
in which it falls on the basis of its gross operating revenues and is required
to advise the Commission promptly of such action.

Nature of Prescribed Records

The purpose of the uniform accounting system is stated as that of
obtaining greater simplification and coordination of accounting without
resulting in an adverse effect upon the public. The accounts of carriers
subject to the jurisdiction of the Interstate Commerce Commission are to
contain the data necessary to meet the financial and cost informational
needs of motor carrier management, the Commission, and other interested
persons such as tariff associations.[16]

Modifications to the uniform accounting system in 1974 were made
to meet the requirements of both the Commission and carrier management. Each carrier was to benefit from a better knowledge of its costs,
resulting in responsibility accounting, and improved cost control and
profit-planning.[17] The chart of accounts now provides for the accumulation of expenses, doing so first by natural cost classification and secondly,
by activity. One result may be a meaningful separation of fixed and
variable expenses. In addition, better separation of major cost centers
permits the use of responsibility accounting. Advantages of the new
system are held to include greater simplification in transaction classification, as well as greater management efficiency through increased availability of accurate data. Meaningful comparisons with other carriers are
facilitated which should be important to the carriers as well as to the
regulatory Commission.

Prior to the effective date of January 1, 1974, the newly revised
system of accounts was modified by additions in the form of separate
classifications of revenues and expenses for: carriers of household goods;
the interperiod tax allocation method of accounting for income taxes;
and, the equity method of accounting for certain long-term investments in
common stock.[18] The Interstate Commerce Commission published an

order that contained changes, effective January 1, 1975, to correct certain inconsistencies noted subsequent to the adoption of the newly revised system of accounts.[19]

In Figure 10-1, a control account is designated for each expense according to natural classification and a total of nine different activities are given sub-accounts within the control account. These activities may

CLASS I AND CLASS II MOTOR CARRIERS, CHART OF ACCOUNTS

MATRIX OF OPERATING EXPENSES FOR INSTRUCTION 27 AND 28A CARRIERS—Continued

Natural classification	Control	Line-haul	Pickup and delivery	Billing and collecting	Platform	Terminal	Mainte-nance	Traffic and sales	Insurance and safety	General and administrative
	0	1	2	3	4	5	6	7	8	9
410 Salaries—Officers and Supervisory Personnel	4100									
1 Officers	4110	4111	4112	4113	4114	4115	4116	4117	4118	4119
2 Terminal, Department, and Division Managers	4120	4121	4122	4123	4124	4125	4126	4127	4128	4129
3 Supervisory and Administrative Personnel	4130	4131	4132	4133	4134	4135	4136	4137	4138	4139
420 Salaries and Wages	4200									
1 Clerical and Administrative	4210	4211	4212	4213	4214	4215	4216	4217	4218	4219
2 Drivers and Helpers	4220	4221	4222							
3 Cargo Handlers	4230				4234					
4 Vehicle Repair and Service	4240	4241	4242		4244	4245	4246	4247	4248	4249
5 Owner-operator drivers	4250	4251	4252							
9 Other Labor	4290	4291	4292	4293	4294	4295	4296	4297	4298	4299
430 Miscellaneous Paid Time Off	4300	4301	4302	4303	4304	4305	4306	4307	4308	4309
1 Clerical and Administrative	4310	4311	4312	4313	4314	4315	4316	4317	4318	4319
2 Drivers and Helpers	4320	4321	4322							
3 Cargo Handlers	4330				4334					
4 Vehicle Repair and Service	4340	4341	4342				4346			
5 Owner-operator Drivers	4350	4351	4352							
9 Other Labor	4390	4391	4392	4393	4394	4395	4396	4397	4398	4399
440 Other Fringes	4400	4401	4402	4403	4404	4405	4406	4407	4408	4409
1 Federal Payroll Taxes	4410	4411	4412	4413	4414	4415	4416	4417	4418	4419
2 State Payroll Taxes	4420	4421	4422	4423	4424	4425	4426	4427	4428	4429
3 Workmen's Compensation	4430	4431	4432	4433	4434	4435	4436	4437	4438	4439
4 Group Insurance	4440	4441	4442	4443	4444	4445	4446	4447	4448	4449
5 Pension and Retirement Plans	4450	4451	4452	4453	4454	4455	4456	4457	4458	4459
6 Health, Welfare, and Pensions	4460	4461	4462	4463	4464	4465	4466	4467	4468	4469
9 Other Fringes	4490	4491	4492	4493	4494	4495	4496	4497	4498	4499
450 Operating Supplies and Expenses	4500									
1 Fuel for Motor Vehicles	4510	4511	4512			4515	4516			
2 Oil, Lubricants, and Coolants for Motor Vehicles	4520	4521	4522			4525	4526			
3 Vehicle Parts	4530	4531	4532			4535	4536	4537	4538	4539
4 Vehicle Maintenance/Outside Vendors	4540	4541	4542			4545	4546	4547	4548	4549
5 Tires and Tubes	4550	4551	4552			4555	4556	4557	4558	4559
9 Other Operating Supplies and Expenses	4590	4591	4592		4594	4595	4596			

Figure 10-1

Source: Uniform System of Accounts for Class I and Class II Common and Contract Motor Carriers of Property, Title 49-Transportation, Rules and Regulations Chapter X—Interstate Commerce Commission, No. 32155 (Sub-No. 2 and No. 3, reprinted in the FEDERAL REGISTER, Vol. 39, No. 211, October 31, 1974, p. 38539.

Interstate Commerce Commission Reports

From the system of accounts effective prior to January 1, 1974 to the system of accounts effective January 1, 1974			
System of accounts effective prior to Jan. 1, 1974		System of accounts effective Jan. 1, 1974	
Account Title	No.	No.	Account Title
Administrative and General			
Salaries; general officers	4611	4119	Salaries - officers - general and administrative
		4129	Salaries - department & division managers - general and administrative
Salaries; revenue accounting	4612	4213	Salaries and wages - clerical and administration - billing & collecting
		4313	Miscellaneous paid time off - clerical & administrative - billing and collecting
		4653	Outside Fees - billing & collecting
Salaries; other general office employees	4613	4139	Salaries - supervisory and administrative personnel - general & administrative
Purchasing & store expenses	4675	4219	Salaries and wages - clerical and administrative - general and administrative
Other general expenses	4680	4299	Salaries and wages - other labor - general and administrative
		4319	Miscellaneous paid time off - clerical and administrative - general and administrative
		4399	Miscellaneous paid time off - other labor - general and administrative
		4699	Other general supplies and expenses - general and administrative

From the system of accounts effective prior to January 1, 1974 to the system of accounts effective January 1, 1974			
System of accounts effective prior to Jan. 1, 1974		System of accounts effective Jan. 1, 1974	
Account Title	No.	No.	Account Title
Expenses of general officers	4621	4249	Salaries & wages - vehicle repair & service - general general & administrative
		4539	Vehicle parts - general & administrative
Expenses of general office employees	4622	4549	Vehicle maintenance by outside vendors - general & administrative
		4559	Tires and tubes - general & administrative
		4669	Officers' & supervisory personnel expenses - general & administrative
		4679	Other employees' expenses - general & administrative
		4729	Vehicle license & registration fees - ownership (Federal) - general & administrative
		4739	Vehicle license & registration fees - usage (Federal) - general & administrative
		4779	Vehicle license & registration fees - ownership (state and other) - general & administrative
		4789	Vehicle license & registration fees - usage (state & other) -general & administrative
Other general office expenses	4623	4619	Office supplies - general & administrative
		5129	Utilities expenses - general & administrative
		5529	Office equipment & rents- general & administrative
Law expenses	4630	5939	Professional services - debit - general & administrative

Figure 10-2

Source: Uniform System of Accounts, Interstate Commerce Commission, (49 CFR. 1207) No. 32155 (Sub—No. 2) April 1973, pp. 316-7.

reflect responsibilities by departments or cost centers. Data resulting from the new system is expected to be more reliable for rate-making purposes and to facilitate better regulation of the industry as directed in the national transportation policy declared by Congress.[20] Also, the operating expenses shown in Figure 10-1 indicate that the matrix of expenses proposed may facilitate the use of computer applications and may also be adaptable to the use of manual subledgers.

Although the chart of accounts permits a standardized management reporting system, strict adherence is not mandatory. The carrier is encouraged by the structure of the accounts to use the detailed activities in such a way as to develop a system fully responsive to that carrier's specific needs.[21]

Figure 10-2 shows the expansion of the uniform system from that existing before the 1974 revisions. For example, expenses of general office employees (account 4622) have been expanded into nine different accounts (4539 through 4789) to provide the flexibility and detail now desired by carrier management.

The new chart of accounts is expected to facilitate financial reporting in accordance with generally accepted accounting principles for the benefit of stockholders while at the same time providing the Commission the type of regulatory information it requires. Carrier management is not forgotten—responsibility accounting is encouraged by the increased flexibility and account expansion indicated in Figure 10-2.

Labor Department Legislation

The Labor-Management Reporting and Disclosure Act (LMRDA) was enacted in 1959 and amended in 1965. It provides for the reporting of certain financial and administrative practices of labor unions. The Act's overall purposes are to prevent abuses by labor unions, provide standards with respect to the election of officers and accomplish other objectives described in seven different titles, discussed below.

The first of these is called the bill of rights, setting forth certain basic rights which Congress believed should be guaranteed to union members by federal law. Enforcement responsibilities were assigned to the Secretary of Labor. Titles II through VI deal with the kinds of reports required by labor unions, the officers, members, labor relations consultants, and trusteeships with respect to elections and safeguards thought necessary. The last title (VII) contains amendments introduced through the Taft Hartley Act (1947) to the labor management relations act with respect to matters administered by the National Labor Relations Board, an independent federal agency not a part of the Department of Labor.

Reporting Requirements Under LMRDA

The Labor Organization Annual Report (Fm. LM-2) must be filed by each union. The administration of the union's affairs is the subject of Items 8 through 12. Items to be reported in this audit of union management include: the acquisition of goods or property other than by purchase; disposition of union property by means other than sale; the reduction or liquidation of liabilities without disbursement of cash and the holding of cash in bank accounts under names other than that of the union.

Information as to changes in union management during the reporting period and the financial activities of union officers are also disclosed (Items 35 through 70). The modified balance sheet required calls for the assets and liabilities of the organization at both the beginning and end of the period and employs a balancing factor called "Net Assets" (Item 34).

Supporting schedules require the reporting of sensitive items, such as loans to officers, employees or members of the union; the purposes and amounts of such loans; and the balances remaining at the end of the period. Details of investments made in marketable securities and other securities by officers, as well as loans obtained, gifts and grants awarded, and the sale of union assets must be explained in schedules provided on pages 3 and 4.

Separate annual report forms are provided for unions with annual receipts of $30,000 or more and those with less than that amount on Form LM-3 (Revised 11/69). An information report, described below, must accompany each union's annual report.

Labor Organization Information Report

Also useful in the Labor Department's administrative audit of union management is form LM-1. (Revised 11/69). All unions engaged in an industry affecting commerce must file this information report under section 201(a) of the Labor-Management Reporting and Disclosure Act. Data required includes the names and titles of officers and fees assessed to the membership. Copies of the union's constitution and by-laws must be attached, along with a detailed statement as to qualifications for, and restrictions on, membership in the union.

Authorizations required for the disbursement of the union's funds, for the calling of strikes, and for the audit of financial transactions must also be disclosed by the union. Both the annual report and information return must be filed within 90 days of the close of the union's fiscal year.

As suggested by its title, the Department of Labor, Office of Labor-Management and Welfare Pension Reports, receives the above reports, as well as those required under the Welfare and Pension Plans Disclosure Act which are discussed next.

The Welfare and Pension Plans Disclosure Act

Under the Act, plant administrators are required to report on two different types of coverage: (1) "employee welfare benefit" referring to medical, surgical, hospital care and benefits in the event of sickness, accident, death or unemployment; and (2) "employee pension benefit" relating to the purchase of annuity contracts, profit-sharing plans, pensions and other benefits upon retirement.

The present disclosure form (D-1, Revised April 1971) is required for both plans, that is, welfare and pension benefits. A description of the plan with all amendments or modifications must be made available by the administrator at the principal office, along with the latest annual report (D-2, Revised 1971). Upon written request the administrator must deliver to a participant or beneficiary a copy of the plan description and a summary of the latest annual report.

The information report asks for the type of plan; groups covered under the plan (salaried, hourly or other); identification of the administrator and industry being reported on; whether the plan is mentioned in a collective bargaining agreement; and functions performed by the administrator. The kinds of benefits provided must be disclosed, along with the designated insurance carriers, trusts, or self-insured plans, and unfunded sources, such as the general assets of the employer or union.

Annual Report—Employee Welfare or Pension Benefit Plan

As amended by Public Law 87-420, the Welfare and Pension Plans Disclosure Act prescribes that the Annual Report be filed if participation in the plan numbers 100 or more employees at any time during the reporting year. If less than 100, a short form (D-1A) is filed.

Each plan requires a separate form filed by the administrator designated in the plan or under a collective bargaining agreement, clothed with ultimate control or management of monies received or contributed. If no such person is designated in the plan, the individual responsible for the duties of the administrator must file the annual report.

All plans covered under the Act must be reported in Part I and attested to by the administrator's signature where indicated. The completion of Parts I and II (for completely unfunded plans) gives all data required for plans providing benefits solely from the general assets of the employer, union, or other organization. Part III must be filled out by administrators of plans providing benefits through insurance carriers, and Part IV applies to plans involving a trust or separately maintained fund.

The delegation of signature authority must be evidenced in writing except where this is apparent from the form of the organization, such as a partnership, that the signatory has authority to act as agent for the group covered under the plan. To so indicate, a copy of the partnership minutes in which such authority was delegated should be attached to the annual report.

The Employee Retirement Income Security Act of 1974

The past three decades have witnessed a period of unparalled growth in the private pension system in the United States, from coverage of four million individuals in 1940 to about thirty-five million in December, 1974.[22] The latter involves assets of private, noninsured pension funds of over $150 billion, underscoring the need for improved standards and controls applicable to pension plan operations.[23] To facilitate such control, the Employee Retirement Income Security Act of 1974 greatly increased the disclosure and financial reporting standards for employee benefit plans. An excerpt of section 103 of the Act is shown in Figure 10-3 with respect to the annual reports pertaining to every employee benefit plan which must now be filed with the Secretary of Labor.

Included in the annual report must be audited financial statements indicating specific transactions of the plan as well as its assets and liabilities, identification of those covered under the plan as well as those providing such services, and a detailed actuarial statement and expression of opinion as to the extent of the plan's actual provision of the benefits it describes.

The accounting and actuarial professions find themselves mutually involved in meeting the requirements of this legislation, because of the required audited financial statements and the content of the accompanying actuarial statement. Government agencies, private plan administrators and pension fund trustees also find themselves with specific responsibilities under the new Act to insure that the financial security of over thirty-five million employees is protected during their retirement years.[24]

The next type of regulatory legislation discussed has reference to responsibilities assumed by the Board of Governors of the Federal Reserve System.

The Employee Retirement Income Security Act of 1974

(Excerpts from Section 103—Annual Reports)
(Printed in The Journal of Accountancy, December
1974, pp. 63-66).

The Employee Retirement Income Security Act of 1974 (excerpts of section 103—"annual reports")

a(1) (A) An annual report shall be published with respect to every employee benefit plan to which this part applies. Such report shall be filed with the Secretary in accordance with section 104(a), and shall be made available and furnished to participants in accordance with section 104(b).

(B) The annual report shall include the information described in subsections (b) and (c) and where applicable subsections (d) and (e) and shall also include—

(i) a financial statement and opinion, as required by paragraph (3) of this subsection, and

(ii) an actuarial statement and opinion, as required by paragraph (4) of this subsection.

(2) If some or all of the information necessary to enable the administrator to comply with the requirements of this title is maintained by—

(A) an insurance carrier or other organization which provides some or all of the benefits under the plan, or holds assets of the plan in a separate account,

(B) a bank or similar institution which holds some or all of the assets of the plan in a common or collective trust or a separate trust, or custodial account, or

(C) a plan sponsor as defined in section 3(16)(B),

such carrier, organization, bank, institution, or plan sponsor shall transmit and certify the accuracy of such information to the administrator within 120 days after the end of the plan year (or such other date as may be prescribed under regulations of the Secretary).

(3)(A) Except as provided in subparagraph (C), the administrator of an employee benefit plan shall engage, on behalf of all plan participants, an independent qualified public accountant, who shall conduct such an examination of any financial statements of the plan, and of other books and records of the plan, as the accountant may deem necessary to enable the accountant to form an opinion as to whether the financial statements and schedules required to be included in

Figure 10-3

the annual report by subsection (b) of this section are presented fairly in conformity with generally accepted accounting principles applied on a basis consistent with that of the preceding year. Such examination shall be conducted in accordance with generally accepted auditing standards, and shall involve such tests of the books and records of the plan as are considered necessary by the independent qualified public accountant. The independent qualified public accountant shall also offer his opinion as to whether the separate schedules specified in subsection (b)(3) of this section and the summary material required under section 104(b)(3) present fairly, and in all material respects the information contained therein when considered in conjunction with the financial statements taken as a whole. The opinion by the independent qualified public accountant shall be made a part of the annual report. In a case where a plan is not required to file an annual report, the requirements of this paragraph shall not apply. In a case where by reason of section 104(a) (2) a plan is required only to file a simplified annual report, the Secretary may waive the requirements of this paragraph.

(B) In offering his opinion under this section the accountant may rely on the correctness of any actuarial matter certified to by an enrolled actuary, if he so states his reliance.

(4)(A) The administrator of an employee pension benefit plan subject to the reporting requirement of subsection (d) of this section shall engage, on behalf of all plan participants, an enrolled actuary who shall be responsible for the preparation of the materials comprising the actuarial statement required under

subsection (d) of this section. In a case where a plan is not required to file an annual report, the requirement of this paragraph shall not apply, and, in a case where by reason of section 104(a)(2), a plan is required only to file a simplified report, the Secretary may waive the requirement of this paragraph.

(B) The enrolled actuary shall utilize such assumptions and techniques as are necessary to enable him to form an opinion as to whether the contents of the matters reported under subsection (d) of this section—

(i) are in the aggregate reasonably related to the experience of the plan and to reasonable expectations; and

(ii) represent his best estimate of anticipated experience under the plan.

The opinion by the enrolled actuary shall be made with respect to, and shall be made a part of, each annual report.

b An annual report under this section shall include a financial statement containing the following information:

(2) With respect to an employee pension benefit plan: a statement of assets and liabilities, and a statement of changes in net assets available for plan benefits which shall include details of revenues and expenses and other changes aggregated by general source and application. In the notes to financial statements, disclosures concerning the following items shall be considered by the accountant: a description of the plan including any significant changes in the plan made during the period and the impact of such changes on benefits; the funding policy (including policy with respect to prior service cost), and any changes in such

Figure 10-3 *(continued)*

policies during the year; a description of any significant changes in plan benefits made during the period; a description of material lease commitments, other commitments, and contingent liabilities; a description of agreements and transactions with persons known to be parties in interest; a general description of priorities upon termination of the plan; information concerning whether or not a tax ruling or determination letter has been obtained; and any other matters necessary to fully and fairly present the financial statements of such pension plan.

d With respect to an employee benefit plan (other than (A) a profit sharing, savings, or other plan, which is an individual account plan, (B) a plan described in section 301(b), or (C) a plan described both in section 4021(b) and in paragraph (1), (2), (3), (4), (5), (6), or (7) of section 301 (a)) an annual report under this section for a plan year shall include a complete actuarial statement applicable to the plan year which shall include the following:

(1) The date of the plan year, and the date of the actuarial valuation applicable to the plan year for which the report is filed.

(2) The date and amount of the contribution (or contributions) received by the plan for the plan year for which the report is filed and contributions for prior plan years not previously reported.

(3) The following information applicable to the plan year for which the report is filed: the normal costs, the accrued liabilities, an identification of benefits not included in the calculation; a statement of the other facts and actuarial assumptions and methods used to deter-

mine costs, and a justification for any change in actuarial assumptions or cost methods; and the minimum contribution required under section 302.

(4) The number of participants and beneficiaries, both retired and nonretired, covered by the plan.

(5) The current value of the assets accumulated in the plan, and the present value of the assets of the plan used by the actuary in any computation of the amount of contributions to the plan required under section 302 and a statement explaining the basis of such valuation of present value of assets.

(6) The present value of all of the plan's liabilities for nonforfeitable pension benefits allocated by the termination priority categories as set forth in section 4044 of this Act, and the actuarial assumptions used in these computations. The Secretary shall establish regulations defining (for purposes of this section) "termination priority categories" and acceptable methods, including approximate methods, for allocating the plan's liabilities to such termination priority categories.

(7) A certification of the contribution necessary to reduce the accumulated funding deficiency to zero.

(8) A statement by the enrolled actuary—

(A) that to the best of his knowledge the report is complete and accurate, and

(B) the requirements of section 302(c)(3) (relating to reasonable actuarial assumptions and methods) have been complied with.

(9) A copy of the opinion required by subsection (a)(4).

Figure 10-3 (continued)

(10) Such other information regarding the plan as the Secretary may by regulation require.

(11) Such other information as may be necessary to fully and fairly disclose the actuarial position of the plan.

Such actuary shall make an actuarial valuation of the plan for every third plan year, unless he determines that a more frequent valuation is necessary to support his opinion under subsection (a)(4) of this section.

Figure 10-3 *(continued)*

Securities Credit Transactions—Federal Reserve System Regulations

The scope of this discussion permits coverage of only a few, typical Federal Reserve Regulations. Known as "X," "G," "T," and "U," these were issued by the Board of Governors of the Federal Reserve System for the control of margin requirements on securities credit transactions. Titles, dates of issue, amendments, and exhibit numbers where typical reports are illustrated follow:

Regulation X, "Rules governing borrowers who obtain securities credit," effective November, 1971, amended May, 1973, referring to the maximum loan value of margin securities.

Regulation G, "Securities credit by persons other than banks, brokers, or dealers," effective May 30, 1971, amended May 23, 1973.

Regulation T, "Credit by brokers and dealers," effective May 15, 1970, amended May 23, 1973.

Regulation U, "Credit by banks for the purpose of purchasing or for carrying margin stocks," effective July 10, 1971, amended June 16, 1973.

Regulation X was issued by the Board of Governors as Part 224 of the Code of Federal Regulations, Title 12, in conjunction with the Securities Exchange Act of 1934, as amended. It applies to persons who obtain credit from *outside* the United States to purchase securities of companies registered *in* the United States. The purpose of the regulation is to control the injection of credit into the United States' stock market in circumvention of the provisions of the Board's margin regulations. The loan of funds by borrowers, who falsely certify the purpose of a loan is prohibited if the intent is to willfully and intentionally evade the provisions of Regulation X and use such funds to purchase securities.

Regulation G indicates that false or dishonest statements in the process of recording the amount, title, and purpose of credit collateralized by securities are punishable by fine or imprisonment.

Under Regulation G, a statement of purpose is required for an extension of credit secured by margin securities. Federal Reserve Form G-3 illustrates the form to be executed by persons other than banks, brokers, or dealers, who extend $50,000 or more in credit or have a total of $100,000 or more outstanding at any time during the calendar quarter. Such loans must be secured directly or indirectly by collateral which includes any margin securities, not subject to Regulation T or U. Grantors must register within 30 days after the close of the quarter with the Federal Reserve Bank in their district, filing Form G-1.

Regulation T applies to credit by brokers and dealers and includes every member of a national securities exchange. Under F.R. Fm. T-4, a statement of purpose is required for an extension of credit based on a margin security, other than an exempt security.

Concluding this brief illustration of securities credit control by the Federal Reserve System Regulations, it is noted that F.R. Fm. U-1 is required by bank officers with respect to stock secured credit under Regulation U. To extend credit, secured directly or indirectly by any stock, the bank must obtain and retain this statement in its records for at least three years. It must be executed by both customer and lender, the latter being a duly authorized officer of the bank.

The last type of regulatory legislation discussed is one of the most recent. It applies to cost accounting standards for the defense contractors accepting federal contracts.

Legislation Creating the Cost Accounting Standards Board

The role of standards in both cost accounting for defense contractors and in connection with general accounting principles has been of great interest, leading to the development of boards for both, composed of the most qualified accountants obtainable.

The 23-member professional staff of the Cost Accounting Standards Board is an agent of the Congress. Under Public Law 91-379, the Board was directed to "promulgate cost-accounting standards designed to achieve uniformity and consistency in the cost-accounting principles followed by defense contractors and subcontractors under Federal contracts."

Various sources of input (library research, field visits, committee liaisons, questionnaire responses, and Board guidances) are available to the staff in the exhaustive process of evaluating solutions to problems and proposing possible cost-accounting standards.

As a condition of contracting with the federal government, contractors are required under the law cited above "to disclose in writing their cost-accounting principles, including methods of distinguishing direct costs from indirect costs and the basis used for allocating indirect costs."[25] Among other purposes such legislation may further encourage the development of *information systems and standards* of performance such as described in Chapter 15.

An illustration of the use of standard costs for direct materials and direct labor is included in Figure 10-4. The data furnished is to provide criteria to contractors that may be useful in improving their cost measurement and assignment techniques. An important objective of the standard cost requirements is to facilitate the pricing, administration, and settlement of all contracts negotiated, both prime and subcontract, for national defense procurements in excess of $100,000. It is required by law that such standards be incorporated into the contractor's books of account (see Figure 10-4) and related standard cost variances accounted for at the level of the production unit. In addition, the method used to dispose of variances must be indicated in writing and consistently followed.[26]

New regulatory legislation will undoubtedly continue to emerge, be amended, or repealed. Such developments simply attest to the continuing close relationship of accounting and legal considerations at many governmental levels and the wisdom of having a working knowledge of business law and relevant legislation by today's practicing accountants.

Excerpts from Cost Accounting Standard

PART 407—USE OF STANDARD COSTS FOR DIRECT
MATERIAL AND DIRECT LABOR

§ 407.10 General applicability.

This Standard shall be used by defense contractors and subcontractors under Federal contracts entered into after the effective date hereof and by all relevant Federal agencies in estimating, accumulating, and reporting costs in connection with the pricing, administration, and settlement of all negotiated prime contract and subcontract national defense procurements with the United States in excess of $100,000, other than contracts or subcontracts where the price negotiated is based on: (a) Established catalog or market prices of commercial items sold in substantial quantities to the general public, or (b) prices set by law or regulation.

Figure 10-4

§ 407.20 Purpose.

(a) The purpose of this Cost Accounting Standard is to provide criteria under which standard costs may be used for estimating, accumulating, and reporting costs of direct material and direct labor; and to provide criteria relating to the establishment of standards, accumulation of standard costs, and accumulation and disposition of variances from standard costs. Consistent application of these criteria where standard costs are in use will improve cost measurement and cost assignment.

(b) This Cost Accounting Standard is not intended to cover the use of pre-established measures solely for estimating.

§ 407.30 Definitions.

(a) The following definitions of terms which are prominent in this Cost Accounting Standard are reprinted from Part 400 of this chapter for convenience. Other terms which are used in this Cost Accounting Standard are defined in Part 400 of this chapter have the meanings ascribed to them in that part unless the text demands a different definition or the definition is modified in paragraph (b) of this section.

(1) Labor cost at standard. A pre-established measure of the labor element of cost, computed by multiplying labor-rate standard by labor-time standard.

(2) Labor-rate standard. A pre-established measure, expressed in monetary terms, of the price of labor.

(3) Labor-time standard. A pre-established measure, expressed in temporal terms, of the quantity of labor.

(4) Material cost at standard. A pre-established measure of the material element of cost, computed by multiplying material-price standard by material-quantity standard.

(5) Material-price standard. A pre-established measure, expressed in monetary terms, of the price of material.

(6) Material-quantity standard. A pre-established measure, expressed in physical terms, of the quantity of material.

(7) Production unit. A grouping of activities which either uses homogeneous inputs of direct material and direct labor or yields homogeneous outputs such that the costs or statistics related to these homogeneous inputs or outputs are appropriate as bases for allocating variances.

(8) Standard cost. Any cost computed with the use of pre-established measures.

Figure 10-4 *(continued)*

(9) Variance. The difference between a pre-established measure and an actual measure.

(b) The following modifications of definitions set forth in Part 400 of this chapter are applicable to this Cost Accounting Standard:

(1) Actual cost. An amount determined on the basis of cost incurred.

§ 407.40   Fundamental requirement.

Standard costs may be used for estimating, accumulating, and reporting costs of direct material and direct labor only when all of the following criteria are met:

(a) Standard costs are entered into the books of account;

(b) Standard costs and related variances are appropriately accounted for at the level of the production unit; and

(c) Practices with respect to the setting and revising of standards, use of standard costs, and disposition of variances are stated in writing and are consistently followed.

§ 407.50   Techniques for application. (Excerpts only)

(a)(1) A contractor's written statement of practices with respect to standards shall include the bases and criteria (such as engineering studies, experience, or other supporting data) used in setting and revising standards; the period during which standards are to remain effective; the level (such as ideal or realistic) at which material-quantity standards and labor-time standards are set; and conditions (such as those expected to prevail at the beginning of a period) which material-price standards and labor-rate standards are designed to reflect.

(2) Where only either the material price or material quantity is set at standard, with the other component stated at actual, the result of the multiplication shall be treated as material cost at standard. Similarly, where only either the labor rate or labor time is set at standard, with the other component stated at actual, the result of the multiplication shall be treated as labor cost at standard.

(3) A labor-rate standard may be set to cover a category of direct labor only if the functions performed within that category are not materially disparate and the employees involved are interchangeable with respect to the functions performed.

(b)(1) Material-price standards may be used and their related variances may be recognized either at the time purchases of material are entered into

Figure 10-4 *(continued)*

the books of account or at the time material cost is allocated to production units.

(2) Where material-price standards are used and related variances are recognized at the time purchases of material are entered into the books of account, they shall be accumulated separately by homogeneous groupings of material. Examples of homogeneous groupings of material are:

(3) Where material-price variances are recognized at the time purchases of material are entered into the books of account, variances of each homogeneous grouping of material shall be allocated (except as provided in paragraph (b)(4) of this section), at least annually, to items in purchased-items inventory and to production units receiving items from that homogeneous grouping of material, in accordance with either one of the following practices, which shall be consistently followed:

(i) Items in purchased-items inventory of a homogeneous grouping of material are adjusted from standard cost to actual cost; the balance of the material-price variance, after reflecting these adjustments, shall be allocated to production units on the basis of the total of standard cost of material received from that homogeneous grouping of material by each of the production units; or

(ii) Items, at standard cost, in purchased-items inventory of a homogeneous grouping of material, are treated, collectively, as a production unit; the material-price variance shall be allocated to production units on the basis of standard cost of material received from that homogeneous grouping of material by each of the production units.

(4) Where material-price variances are recognized at the time purchases of material are entered into the books of account, variances of each homogeneous grouping of material which are insignificant may be included in appropriate indirect cost pools for allocation to applicable cost objectives.

(c) Labor-cost variances shall be recognized at the time labor cost is introduced into production units. Labor-rate variances and labor-time variances may be combined into one labor-cost variance account. A separate labor-cost variance shall be accumulated for each production unit.

(d) A contractor's established practice with respect to the disposition of variances accumulated by production unit shall be in accordance with one of the following paragraphs:

(1) Variances are allocated to cost objectives (including ending in-process inventory) at least annually. Where a variance related to material is allocated, the allocation shall be on the basis of the material cost at standard, or, where outputs are homogeneous, on the basis of units of output. Similarly, where a variance related to labor is allocated, the

Figure 10-4 *(continued)*

allocation shall be on the basis of the labor cost at standard or labor hours at standard, or, where outputs are homogeneous, on the basis of units of output; or

(2) Variances which are immaterial may be included in appropriate indirect cost pools for allocation to applicable cost objectives.

Figure 10-4 *(continued)*

REFERENCES

[1]Louis H. Rappaport. *SEC Accounting Practice and Procedure,* Third Edition Copyright (c) 1972, The Ronald Press Company, New York.

[2]*Ibid.*

[3]American Institute of Certified Public Accountants, "Professional Accounting in 25 Countries." American Institute's Committee on International Relations. New York: 1965, p. 38.

[4]Andrew Barr, Chief Accountant, Securities and Exchange Commission, letter, dated August 15, 1965, Washington, D.C.

[5]Information obtained from the Securities and Exchange Commission, St. Louis Office, 8/19/74.

[6]Rappaport, *op. cit.*

[7]*Ibid.,* pp. 2-7.

[8]*Ibid.,* p. 2-8.

[9]*Ibid.,* p. 3-4.

[10]*Ibid.,* p. 15.

[11]Michael M. Boone, "Management Accountants and the Securities Laws," *Management Accounting,* May, 1973, p. 21.

[12]*Ibid.*

[13]H. Taggert, "Cost Justification" (Ann Arbor, Michigan, Bureau of Business Research, University of Michigan, 1959,) cited by Charles T. Horngren, *Accounting for Management Control* Prentice-Hall, p. 410.

[14]Adolph Matz, and Othel J. Curry, *Cost Accounting,* Fifth Edition, South-Western Publishing Co., 1972, pp. 627-628.

[15]Uniform System of Accounts for Class I and Class II Common and Contract Motor Carriers of Property (49 CFR. 1207) Interstate Commerce Commission, No. 32155 (Sub-No. 2), served April 24, 1973, p. 166.

[16]*Ibid.,* p. 140.

[17]*Ibid.,* p. 153.

[18]R.E. Hagen, Chief, Section of Accounting, Interstate Commerce Commission, Washington, D.C., February 21, 1975, pp. 1-2.

[19]*Ibid.*

[20]*Op. cit.,* Uniform System of Accounts, Interstate Commerce Commission, etc., p. 166.

[21]*Ibid.,* p. 145.

[22]"Auditing Single-Employer Pension Funds," Roy S. Good, *The Journal of Accountancy,* December 1974, p. 58.

[23]*Ibid.*

[24]*Ibid.,* p. 63.

[25]"Cost Accounting Standards Board: A Progress Report." *Management Accounting.* David H. Li, June 1973, p. 11.

[26]"The Cost Accounting Standards Board." Ernst & Ernst Financial Reporting Developments, June 1974, Retrieval No. 38178, p. 58.

11   **Job Order Costing**

Preceding this chapter, financial accounting has been illustrated as it is practiced and has been shown to be *externally-oriented,* culminating in the preparation of financial statements primarily for the benefit of investors and secondarily for operating management. In this chapter, and continuing through Chapter 15, cost accounting is illustrated as an *internally-oriented* tool of management.

Three key areas of cost accounting are: (1) cost determination, required primarily in inventory costing; (2) cost control, featuring the comparison of budgeted costs with actuals by cost centers and programs, resulting in shown variances from planned performance and thus stimulating corrective action by the appropriate level of management; and, (3) cost analysis, to assist in decision-making by answering the many "what if" types of managerial questions. Many of these are future-oriented, questioning for example: what will happen to profits if prices are increased or decreased, if product lines are added or deleted, or *if* fixed assets or entire plants are acquired?

Job Order Costs

Figure 11-1 shows the relationship of general-ledger accounts and factory-ledger accounts. The operations of many widely dispersed factories, each doing its own factory-ledger accounting, will be controlled usually through one common account, namely the general-ledger control account in corporate headquarters.

225

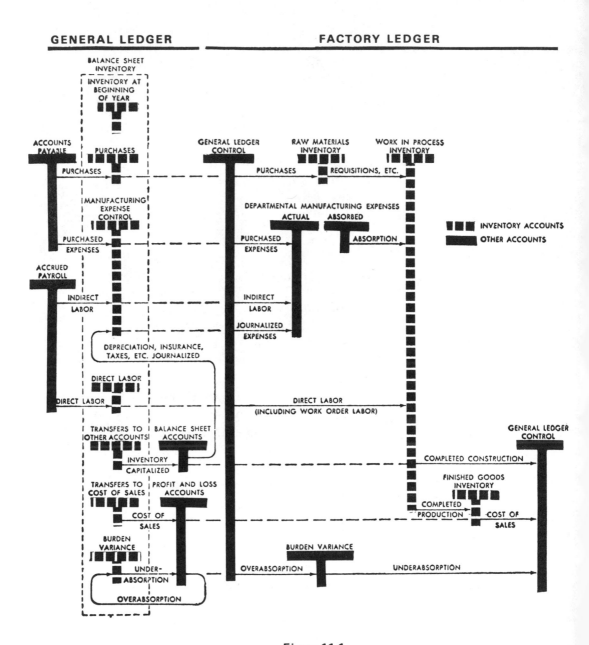

Figure 11-1

Source: W. J. Plaides, "The Accounting Flow Chart," *The Journal of Accountancy,* © 1965 by the American Institute of Certified Public Accountants, Inc. July 1965, p. 53.

Figure 11-1 illustrates the involvement of corporate headquarters in accounting for the *procurement* of raw materials for factory usage, manufacturing supplies, services, other overhead items and direct labor. Shown balancing to the general-ledger control account for each factory are the factory accounts maintained at each plant. Receipts of raw materials inventories and their withdrawal to work-in-process (or jobs-in-process) are shown as recorded in the factory ledger. Departmental manufacturing expenses are shown accumulated in an account so labeled, representing the overhead control account at each factory. Immediately to the right is shown the "absorbed" or applied account whereby manufacturing overhead is credited and work-in-process (or jobs-in-process) debited. (Techniques described below for the absorption or distribution of overhead to jobs usually result in an over or under-absorption called "burden variance.") Also, payroll accounting is shown recorded in the home office's general-ledger accounts but the charges of direct labor to jobs-in-process are recorded in the factory ledger.

As a result of such balancing entries on general and factory ledgers, all costs can be matched with all income on the home office books in the preparation of the income statement—an *externally*-oriented report—and simultaneously each job-in-process can be costed at the manufacturing facility for *internal,* managerial control. Similarly, in the factory ledger are maintained all inventories—raw materials, in process, and finished goods—which, along with the "burden variance" and cost of sales of the period, are required by the general ledger accountant at the central office to complete the balance sheet and income statements.

Cost Determination

A cost-ledger sheet is usually set up for each order issued to the manufacturing staging area, as shown in Figure 11-2. All materials and parts requisitioned from inventory or purchased directly for a particular job are posted to that cost sheet. Direct labor costs and hours are posted on the cost sheet from time tickets or by computer as shown in Figure 11-3.

Automated direct labor reporting systems permit the insertion of a plastic punch card to a card reader, recording both the worker's attendance record for payroll computation, as well as the hours he spends on each job which is entered on that job's cost sheet. Direct labor hours worked on each job are recorded for desired periods—weekly, monthly, six-months, fiscal year-to-date or from the inception of the job.

"Overhead" is referred to in Figure 11-3 and shown receiving indirect labor hours and costs from the "Attendance and Labor Hour Reconciliation" block, as well as indirect material costs from the "Material Including Invoice Distribution" shown to the right.

Because of the difficulty of identifying how much indirect labor or other elements of overhead were actually used on each job, all such manufacturing costs are distributed (Figure 11-4) on the most applicable and available basis. Thus, direct labor *hours* is the basis used when manual labor is the predominant feature (Figure 11-5); direct labor *costs* may become the base for overhead distribution (Figure 11-6); or materials-used (Figure 11-7) may serve as a base. "Overhead pools," such as engineering, manufacturing, procurement, and general and administrative overhead, also are used commonly. Figure 11-8 illustrates the kinds of overhead costs usually relevant to the four "pools" named above.

An accumulation of six months of history of direct labor dollars, direct labor hours, or materials, is shown accumulated by jobs in the ledger sheets illustrated. Using the six months' accumulation in each cost ledger as a base (many firms use a full year), an overhead distribution "rate" is developed. The total overhead expense contemplated for that period in each pool is divided by the total volume for the same period, in labor hours, labor dollars, or material usage, to arrive at an overhead rate. It is then applied to each job in the next period as a basis for distributing manufacturing overhead in accordance with actual labor hours, etc., used on that job. The difference between this total overhead distribution during the accounting period and the actual manufacturing overhead represents the over or underabsorption or "burden variance," shown in Figure 11-1, which, in practice, is usually charged off to cost of sales of the period.

Figure 11-2, the job cost ledger, shows the total cost accumulation for each job, and related statistics. Labor hours and dollars, materials requisitioned to that job during the period, and allocated overhead are entered for the month, six-months, fiscal year-to-date and "cumulative from inception," which is important to contracts or jobs that take more than one year for completion. In addition, provision is made for the entry of "Accrued Earnings," cost of deliveries, and "in progress" totals for each job.

Companies have been observed to use as many as 35 different overhead distribution rates and, therefore, that many different pools of overhead. Often, however, four major overhead pools are used in job costing namely, engineering, manufacturing, procurement, and administrative pools, discussed next.

ACCOUNT	DESCRIPTION	MONTH		SIX MONTHS		FISCAL YEAR TO DATE	CUMULATIVE from INCEPTION
		CURRENT	Total Inc. Prior Period Adjustments	CURRENT	Total Inc. Prior Period Adjustments		
XXXX-XXX	LABOR HOURS						
-XXX	LABOR DOLLARS STRAIGHT TIME PREMIUM TOTAL						
-XXX -XXX -XXX -XXX	MATERIAL OVERHEAD DIRECT CHARGES OTHER CORPORATE EXPENSES						
-XXX	TOTAL COST						
-XXX -XXX -XXX	ACCRUED EARNINGS COST OF DELIVERES CONTRACTS IN PROGRESS						

Figure 11-2

COST ACCUMULATION SYSTEM

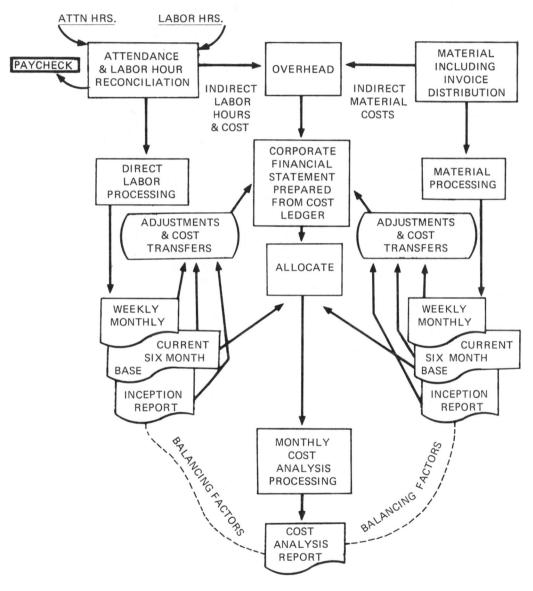

Figure 11-3

ACCOUNT	DESCRIPTION	MONTH		SIX MONTHS		FISCAL YEAR TO DATE	CUMULATIVE from INCEPTION
		CURRENT	TOTAL	CURRENT	TOTAL		
	OVERHEAD						
	DESIGN ENGINEERING						
	PRODUCT SUPPORT						
	AUTOMATION CENTER						
	TOOLING						
	PRODUCTION						
	QUALITY ASSURANCE						
	ELECTRONIC ENGINEERING						
	ELECTRONIC MANUFACTURING						
	ELECTRONIC SHIPPING						
	ELECTRONIC QUALITY ASSURANCE						
	GENERAL & ADMINISTRATIVE						
	TOTAL DIVISIONAL OVERHEAD						
	OTHER CORPORATE EXPENSE						
	DIRECT CHARGES						
	TRAVEL						
	DIRECT CHARGES						
	MO. TAX						
	PILOTS PAY						
	TOTAL DIRECT CHARGES						
	TOTAL OVERHEAD						

Figure 11-4

231

JOB COST LEDGER

CONTRACT XXXXXX

JOB NO. XXXX

DIRECT LABOR HOURS

31 AUGUST 19____

ACCOUNT	DESCRIPTION		MONTH			SIX MONTHS			CUMULATIVE from INCEPTION		
			REGULAR	OVERTIME	TOTAL	REGULAR	OVERTIME	TOTAL	REGULAR	OVERTIME	TOTAL
XXXX-XXX	DESIGN ENGINEERING	CURRENT									
		PRIOR									
		TOTAL									
-XXX	ELECTRONIC ENGINEERING	CURRENT									
		PRIOR									
		TOTAL									
-XXX	PRODUCT SUPPORT	CURRENT									
		PRIOR									
		TOTAL									
-XXX	AUTOMATION CENTER	CURRENT									
		PRIOR									
		TOTAL									
-XXX	TOOLING	CURRENT									
		PRIOR									
		TOTAL									
-XXX	PRODUCTION	CURRENT									
		PRIOR									
		TOTAL									
-XXX	QUALITY ASSURANCE	CURRENT									
		PRIOR									
		TOTAL									
-XXX	ELECTRONIC MFG.	CURRENT									
		PRIOR									
		TOTAL									
-XXX	ELECTRONIC QTY. ASSURANCE	CURRENT PRIOR									
		TOTAL									
-XXX	SHIPPING	CURRENT									
		PRIOR									
		TOTAL									

Figure 11-5

JOB COST LEDGER

DIRECT LABOR DOLLARS

CONTRACT XXXXXX

JOB NO.   XXXX

31 AUGUST 19 _____

ACCOUNT	DESCRIPTION		MONTH			SIX MONTHS			CUMULATIVE from INCEPTION		
			REGULAR	OVERTIME	TOTAL	REGULAR	OVERTIME	TOTAL	REGULAR	OVERTIME	TOTAL
XXXX-XXX	DESIGN ENGINEERING	CURRENT PRIOR TOTAL									
-XXX	ELECTRONIC ENGINEERING	CURRENT PRIOR TOTAL									
-XXX	PRODUCT SUPPORT	CURRENT PRIOR TOTAL									
-XXX	AUTOMATION CENTER	CURRENT PRIOR TOTAL									
-XXX	TOOLING	CURRENT PRIOR TOTAL									
-XXX	PRODUCTION	CURRENT PRIOR TOTAL									
-XXX	QUALITY ASSURANCE	CURRENT PRIOR TOTAL									
-XXX	ELECTRONIC MFG.	CURRENT PRIOR TOTAL									
-XXX	ELECTRONIC QTY. ASSURANCE	CURRENT PRIOR TOTAL									
-XXX	SHIPPING	CURRENT PRIOR TOTAL									

Figure 11-6

JOB COST LEDGER   CONTRACT XXXXXX

MATERIAL   JOB NO.   XXXX

31 August 19____

ACCOUNT	DESCRIPTION	MONTH			SIX MONTHS			FISCAL YEAR TO DATE	CUMULATIVE from INCEPTION
		CURRENT	Prior Period Adjustments	TOTAL	CURRENT	Prior Period Adjustments	TOTAL		
XXXX-XXX	USAGE								
-XXX	RAW, CLASS, 1,2 & 3								
-XXX	PAN STOCK								
-XXX	PURCHASED EQUIPMENT								
-XXX	CASTINGS, FORGINGS & EXTRUSIONS								
-XXX	MAJOR SUBCONTRACT								
-XXX	MINOR SUBCONTRACT								
	SUB TOTAL								
-XXX	INVENTORY								
-XXX	PURCHASED EQUIPMENT								
-XXX	RETURNED IN TRANSIT								
-XXX	SUB TOTAL								
-XXX	CASTINGS, FORGINGS & EXTRUSIONS								
-XXX	RETURNED IN TRANSIT								
-XXX	SUB TOTAL								
XXXX-XXX	TOTAL								

Figure 11-7

No.	Account Number Description	Title and Description	Eng.	Mfg.	Procure.	Admin.
xxxx	Indirect Labor	This account covers indirect labor costs, employees, including the time spent at meetings, first aid, severance pay (other than Lay-Off Benefits) and idle time resulting from power failures, etc. Such charges are reported for each department.	X	X		
xxxx	Processes	The purpose of this account is to cover the costs of testing new products or materials, as well as special tests for the development of techniques or materials which may facilitate design and production.	X	X		
xxxx	Studies	Costs recorded are for studies and development of experimental or advanced tools related to the improvement of manufacturing methods of fabrication, etc. Costs charged to this account are shown under the department performing the work to an approved Work Authorization.		X		
xxxx	Royalties	This account includes the expense of payments for the use of patents, royalties and licenses. Such costs are reflected under Vice President, Manufacturing Department.		X		
xxxx	Scrap Income	Included in this account is the *net* income or expense resulting from the accumulation, sorting and selling of scrap. Such charges are reflected in the departments performing the work of collecting the scrap and credits for the sale of such scrap are reflected in the Buildings Maintenance Department.				X
xxxx	Rearrangement	This account is charged with the cost of office and shop rearrangement including the installation of new telephones and the relocation of present telephones. Such costs are reflected under departments performing the work or to an approved Factory Order. Shut-down time utilized by employees for packing, crating, etc., is covered by a fiscal year Blanket Work Authorization. In addition, telephone company charges for rearrangement are distributed to appropriate departments.	X	X	X	X

Figure 11-8

The Use of Overhead "Pools"

In Figures 11-2 and 11-8, overhead is allocated to each job through the use of engineering, manufacturing, general and administrative, and procurement overhead pools. All indirect costs constituting overhead are assigned to one of these four pools (Figure 11-8) and a rate developed for the assessment of the total overhead of that pool to each job. For example, an engineering overhead rate is developed by dividing the six months' dollar total in the engineering pool by the total engineering man-hours accumulated within the same six months. Manufacturing overhead rates are developed similarly, using the running six-month total of manufacturing overhead, divided by the same period's total of manufacturing man-hours incurred in that period.

Procurement rates differ in their construction, being the result of dividing the six-month total overhead expense charged to this pool by the function served, that is, the total dollar cost of all *material purchases* for the same six month period. Using such six-month representative overhead accumulations, differences and fluctuations in production levels are ironed out, which can arise if a *monthly* rate is used. As far as general and administrative expenses are concerned, the total in this six-month pool is divided by the grand total of all other expenditures to develop a rate most nearly representative of the function that administration performs, that is, to serve all the administrative needs of engineering, manufacturing, procurement, and other divisional departments.

After all labor, material and overhead costs are assigned to jobs, the next event requires a subtotal for the purpose of balancing to the general-ledger control since *all* costs are now assigned to jobs. A trial balance is developed showing total costs incurred for the month being closed.

Earnings Determination by Jobs

Using the cost completion method, common with many manufacturing companies using job costing on long construction contracts, earnings are often measured by costs incurred to date, as suggested in Figure these are often measured by costs incurred to date, as suggested in Figure 11-2. Using dollar *costs* actually incurred for all material, labor and overhead on a given job from its inception, and comparing this total dollar figure with its original *planned* or estimated cost when the bid for the job was made, a percent of completion results that is applied against the total profits estimated for that job when bid to the customer, less any reserves thought necessary.

A manufacturing company might use the following approach in developing earnings by jobs (Figure 11-2).

An *accrued earnings account* might be used to accumulate the value of estimated earnings that were earned on undelivered items for the purpose of spreading the firm's earnings over all accounting periods during which the job is in process.

Charges will be made to the accrued earnings account to record earnings accrued for each job and a credit will be made to the appropriate sales account, depending upon the type of contract involved, that is, fixed price or incentive type.

Credits are made to accrued earnings under this approach when the product or end item involved is delivered and accepted by the customer, and accounts receivable is charged. Simultaneously, debits are made to accounts receivable—contract billings and credits to job-cost accounts, with the difference usually credited to a reserve account for modifications and contract settlements. The dollar amount is determined by formula— by applying the ratio of earnings to total cost by job to the delivery price. When the latter exceeds total cost, plus earnings, the excess is credited to the reserve account.

Accounts and entries involved in accumulating costs by jobs and recording estimated earnings with respect to undelivered products include the following:

Debit entries to job costs include those for direct labor, with distribution to jobs being made from payrolls; credit entries made to accrued liabilities—payroll and the appropriate employee payroll deductions accounts; charges for materials used, as well as subcontract costs and other direct charges, are made from receiving reports, suppliers' invoices and material requisitions, summarized in monthly journal entries and printouts showing the invoice distribution for the same period; a credit is made to accounts payable for inventory and other items procured; overhead distribution is summarized and journalized as debits to the appropriate jobs with the credit entry to allocation credit—overhead; credit entries to job cost accounts are for estimated costs plus earnings applicable to products delivered as summarized by journal entry.

This chapter illustrated practical techniques of cost determination through job-order cost accounting, collecting manufacturing costs by job work order for each customer's ordered services or each manufactured product, and the charging of both direct labor and material costs to jobs. "Pools" of overhead by types (engineering, manufacturing, procurement, and general administrative) were seen in the process of developing overhead rates for each pool, using a representative accumulation period (six months, for example), divided by the quantity of labor hours, labor dollars, or material usage of the same representative period to iron out month-to-month fluctuations in volume.

12 Process Cost Accounting

Process costing is the most practical means of cost accounting in a manufacturing operation involving mass production of like units, as opposed to production involving a relatively small volume of "made-to-order" items, described under Job Costing in the preceding chapter.

As the first step the production cycle in producing a continuous flow of similar items should be understood. In arriving at the actual production, or "equivalent units," produced for the period, the number of unfinished units on hand at the beginning and end of that period must be known as well as the total *actually* completed and transferred out of the department. *Equivalent units* of production include not only the units actually finished in a department but also the equivalent accomplished this period with respect to inventories in process.

In this chapter, three methods of process cost accounting are considered: (1) weighted average; (2) modified first-in, first-out; and (3) the standard cost technique. The first of these, the weighted average method, illustrated below, shows the tie-in of general ledger and factory ledger accounts, and the departmental cost of production report providing cost data for preparation of the income statement for the period.

239

Process Cost—Weighted Average Method

The sugar refining operation used as an illustration in this chapter[1] involves the functions of melting, filtering, boiling, and packing of granulated sugar and powdered sugar.

General and Factory Ledger "Tie-ins"

To control the factory ledger, usually maintained at remote plant locations, the home office may use conventional books of original entry such as the check and voucher register and a general journal. A factory ledger "contra" account may be used in these general ledger books as described below.

In the voucher register, the factory-ledger account is debited for all items purchased or expenses incurred for the factory and the usual accounts payable or other appropriate liability account is credited. The general ledger account, in turn, is credited in the Factory Journal (Figure 12-1) for all items received from the home office and the appropriate inventory account, i.e., raw materials or work-in-process—melting, filtering, boiling,—or overhead control account is charged.

The flow of materials within the factory starts with the transfer of raw sugar from raw materials inventory which account accordingly is credited and the first processing department receiving such raw sugar is debited, namely, "Work-in-Process—Melting". Other items carried and controlled under inventories, such as corn starch, used in Work-in-Process, packing powdered or packing supplies must be requisitioned also from the raw materials inventory account.

Direct labor used in each department is paid in this illustration by the home office where all aspects of payroll accounting are handled. The factory journal picks up the debit to the departments (work-in-process, melting, etc.) in which direct labor is incurred and shows the offsetting credit to the general ledger account. "Factory overhead control" is charged for all the indirect labor, indirect materials, and other manufacturing expenses, such as property taxes and depreciation.

Allocation is made through the "Actual Factory Overhead Distribution Sheets" (Figure 12-2) using the "step-down" method of spreading service department overhead to producing departments. The factory journal records "factory overhead applied" and the cost transfers between departments discussed in consideration of the Melting Department's "Production Cost Report," as illustrated in Figure 12-3.

FACTORY JOURNAL (*)
For the Month of _____

Date	Description	General Ledger Dr. (Cr.)	Materials Dr. (Cr.)	Work-in-Process Melting Dr. (Cr.)	Work-in-Process Filtering Dr. (Cr.)	Work-in-Process Boiling Dr. (Cr.)	Work-in-Process Packing Granulated Dr. (Cr.)	Work-in-Process Packing Powdered Dr. (Cr.)	Factory Overhead Control Dr. (Cr.)	Factory Overhead Applied Dr. (Cr.)	Finished Goods Dr. (Cr.)

Figure 12-1

ACTUAL FACTORY OVERHEAD DISTRIBUTION SHEET (*)

Month	Expense	Total	Melting	Filtering	Boiling	Packing Granulated	Packing Powdered	General Refinery Adm.	Heat Light & Power	Maintenance	Shipping & Warehousing
	Property Taxes	4,655.	1,443.	512.	978.	372.	140.	233.	233.	232.	512.
	Total	396,818.	19,479.	33,238.	12,712.	14,303.	6,164.	65,530.	80,364.	88,530.	76,498.
	General Refinery Adm.		7,282.	7,282.	7,281.	12,742.	1,820.	(65,530.)	7,281.	7,281.	14,561.
	Maintenance		11,976.	11,976.	11,976.	20,959.	2,994.		11,976.	(95,811.)	23,954.
	Heat, Light, and Power		24,905.	19,924.	34,867.	4,981.	997.		(99,621.)		13,947.
	Shipping to Selling Exp.	(128,960.)									(128,960.)
	Total Factory Overhead	267,858.	63,642.	72,420.	66,836.	52,985.	11,975.				
	Factory Overhead Applied to Producing Departments	242,463.	60,260.	71,137.	64,466.	30,347.	16,252.				
	Under or (Over) Applied Factory Overhead	25,395.	3,382.	1,283.	2,370.	22,638.	(4,277.)				

Figure 12-2

*Source: Adaptation and excerpts from Matz and McMichael, "The Mino Sugar Refining Company Practice Case",
(By permission of South-Western Publishing Co.)

MELTING DEPARTMENT
PRODUCTION COST REPORT(*)
For the Month Ending October 19XX—Weighted-Average Method

Quantities (CWT) (Lbs.)	(Step 1) Physical Flow	(Step 2) Equivalent Units — Materials	Conversion Costs (labor & O/H)	Equivalent Whole Unit
Work-in-process, beginning	65			
Units started	60,823			
To account for	60,888			
Units completed; (To Filtering)	60,640	60,640	60,640	
Work-in-process, end	60 (80%)**	60	48	
Lost in process	188	---	---	
Total accounted for	60,888	60,700	60,688	

Costs	Totals	Materials	Conversion Costs	Equivalent Whole Unit
Work-in-process, beginning	$ 4,093.	$ 3,978.	$ 115.	
Current costs—Materials	3,843,795.	3,843,795.	---	
" " —Labor	83,232.	---	83,232.	
" " —Overhead	60,260.	---	60,260.	
(Step 3) Total costs to account for	$3,991,380.	$3,847,773.	$143,607.	
Divide by equivalent units		÷ 60,700	÷ 60,688	
(Step 4) Cost (per CWT) per equivalent unit		$ 6.3390	$ .236	$ 6.575
(Step 5) Summary of costs				
Units Transferred	$3,987,080.			60,640 ($6.575)
Adj. Due To Rounding	384.			
Costs Transferred, Total	$3,987,464.			
Work-in-process (60)				
Materials	3,803.	60 (6.339)		
Conversion Costs	113.		48 (.236)	
Total cost of work in process	$ 3,916.			
Total costs accounted for	$3,991,380			

Figure 12-3

*Source: Format adapted from Horngren, Cost Accounting—A Managerial Emphasis, 3rd Edition, Prentice-Hall, Inc. 1972. Material adapted from Matz and McMichael, "The Mino Sugar Refining Company Practice Case," (by permission of South-Western Publishing Co.)

**Applies to Conversion effort only.

Basis for Overhead Distribution and Step-Down Costing

Various bases can be used in the distribution of specific overhead expense items to the producing departments, namely to Melting, Filtering, Boiling, Packing—Granulated, and Packing—Powdered. Service departments involved are: Administration, Heat, Light, Power, and Maintenance and Shipping. Many overheads are charged directly to the departments; others are prorated on a percentage basis to a number of departments. An example of prorated overhead is seen in the case of property taxes (Figure 12-2) spread on the basis of equipment in each department.

After this process is completed, "step-down" costing takes place. Figure 12-2 shows the distribution of the final total in the General Refinery Administration account as distributed to other departments. The basis frequently used for distribution is the number of personnel working in each department. The next departmental "pool" for distributed overhead is Maintenance, followed by Heat, Light, and Power. "Shipping and Warehousing" is not allocated to manufacturing—producing departments but picked up in the general ledger as a selling expense.

Such allocations of overhead through the step-down method, result in actual overhead cost accumulations for each producing department. This amount is compared with "Factory Overhead Applied" (also carried to each departmental cost report, discussed below) resulting in an "over or under" applied factory overhead for each department. The latter is totalled and carried to the income statement after "Cost of Sales."

Various bases can be used in applying factory overhead to producing departments, including machine hours, direct labor hours, or direct labor dollars, as discussed in greater length in Chapter 11. In this illustration, Figure 12-2 shows a distribution to the producing departments based on the direct labor dollars of each.

At the end of each accounting period, an entry is required in the factory journal to reflect the actual transfer of completed production from one department to the next. Thus, such costs from "Work-in-process—Melting" are carried to Filtering to Boiling to Packing—Granulated or Packing—Powdered, which is demonstrated in Figure 12-3, the Production Cost Report for the Melting Department, described next.

Cost of Production Reports Under Weighted Average Process Cost

In this illustration it is assumed that the Melting department transferred 60,640,000 pounds to the Filtering department, during this month; 60,000 pounds were in process at the month's end; and 188,168 pounds were lost in process of transfer to Filtering. Also, all necessary materials have been added to the ending work-in-process, but only 80% of the required labor and overhead have been incurred on these units.

On the Cost of Production report is shown the cost of the materials, labor, and factory overhead for the work done; the value of units transferred; and the value of the ending inventory.

The unit cost of materials used is computed by adding the cost of the materials in process at the beginning of the month to the cost of the materials put in process during the month. Since 188,168 pounds of sugar were lost during the month, such costs are allocated to the remaining good production.

The unit cost for labor and factory overhead is determined in the same way except that the equivalent production of the raw syrup in process at month's end is only 80% of the total raw syrup in process. The cost transfer to the next department, Filtering, is recorded in the factory journal.[2]

"Five Steps" Illustrated in Process Costing

The method of calculating the cost of production report for each manufacturing department is illustrated in the case of the Melting Department in Figure 12-3. The five basic steps in Process Cost Accounting are indicated as follows.[3] In Step 1, the *physical flow* is shown (per CWT) with respect to units started in production this period and those in process at the beginning of the period, representing the total quantity to be accounted for in this step. This total poundage *is* accounted for in Step 1, in the form of: the output transferred to the next department (raw syrup transferred to the Filtering Department); the ending inventory of raw syrup in process in the Melting Department; and the raw syrup lost in process. This accounts for the total number of pounds (60,888,168) concluding the objective of Step 1.

In Step 2, *equivalent units* of production are calculated. The physical flow in Step 1 is converted into equivalent units of production broken down between materials and conversion effort (labor and overhead) for the period. With respect to such conversion elements, the ending work-in-process inventory is shown as 80% complete. The next consideration applies to dollars.

Step 3 shows *total costs to account for*. Total labor, material and overhead dollars are shown which total will have to be accounted for in Step 5. Under the weighted average method of Process Costing, costs incurred in the previous period, represented in the beginning inventory, are added to all costs added in the current period.

Under Step 4, *costs per equivalent whole unit* are obtained. The number of equivalent units shown under 2 are divided into the total dollars costs determined in Step 3, segregated between material costs and conversion costs.

In Step 5, the *total costs are accounted for.* Under this caption are shown the units completed and transferred from the Melting Department to the next department, totalling 60,640,000 costed at a total unit cost of materials and conversion of $6.575 per CWT. Also shown is the ending work-in-process inventory, 60,000 units, as far as material costs are concerned, at the unit material cost of $6.339, and conversion costs, 60,000 units, 80% completed, or 48,000 equivalent units at the unit conversion cost of .236 (per CWT), to arrive at the total cost of the ending work-in-process inventory in Melting of $3,916. This along with all other departmental work-in-process inventories, will appear on the balance sheet as of the end of the period.

This costing process is repeated in the Filtering department to which Melting transfers 60,640,000 pounds at a cost of $3,987,464, after rounding off to the nearest dollar, and from Filtering to Boiling and Packing. In each case, the cost transferred to the next department is recorded in the factory journal as a credit to the department being relieved and a debit to the department receiving the transfer.

The last department in the process, Packing, is relieved for the cost of goods actually finished and sent to the Finished Goods Inventory. When goods are sold by the company, their cost is debited in the general ledger column of the factory journal and Finished Goods Inventory is credited.

In the general ledger the cost of goods sold is debited and the factory ledger credited. All costs incurred by the factory that are not manufacturing costs, such as the shipping and warehousing expense will be debited to selling expense control and credited to factory ledger. As a result, the general ledger trial balance will now contain all data needed for preparation of the balance sheet and income statement.

With respect to the factory ledger, the departmental Cost of Production report represents the major function. As demonstrated in the case of the Melting department, not only the total cost of production transferred to the next department, along with the valuation of ending inventories, but unit costs are computed serving cost control purposes in each department from month to month. However, these units costs will change if other methods are used, such as FIFO (first-in first-out) or standard. These procedures are discussed next.

Modified First-In, First-Out
(FIFO) Process Costing

A distinction between modified FIFO and the weighted average method of process costing is that FIFO is really a step in the direction of job order costing because it distinguishes *batches* whereas the weighted average method does not.[4] Under FIFO costs are carried over *separately* for units completed from beginning work-in-process, distinguished from units started and finished in the current month; the weighted average method does not distinguish between the two batches. Unit costs, therefore, differ for each batch (beginning inventory versus goods started in the same period) of the total goods transferred out during the month, with the result that the weighted average method involves fewer calculations and is far easier to use than FIFO.

Differences in results between FIFO and weighted average methods are usually insignificant, because industries using process costing usually involve mass production of a continuous nature. Therefore, beginning and ending inventory levels are not likely to change radically from month to month, nor are conversion costs per unit likely to fluctuate significantly over the same period whichever method is used.

This point is illustrated in Figure 12-4, which uses the same data as 12-3 but employs the modified FIFO procedure. Batches are carefully segregated in the calculation of 12-4 so that the beginning inventory costs (incurred in the previous period) are *not* mingled with the current period's costs, as is done under the average weighted method. But do these refinements result in significantly different costs per CWT per equivalent unit under FIFO as a result of all this effort? Figure 12-4 shows a cost of $6.3392 per CWT for material costs under FIFO as opposed to $6.339 under the average weighted method (Figure 12-3) and for conversion costs the cost for both methods is the same, .236 per CWT. Although arrived at differently, both show the cost of units transferred to the next department as $3,987,464 and the same ending inventory of $3,916.

Normal and Abnormal Spoilage Under FIFO

An additional refinement may be made under FIFO to isolate and, therefore, control the costs of spoilage or lost units between tolerated or normal spoilage and anything in excess of that accepted level of spoilage.

MELTING DEPARTMENT
PRODUCTION COST REPORT*

For the Month Ending October 19XX—Modified First-In, First-Out Method

		Equivalent Units	
Quantities (CWT) (Lbs.)	Physical Flow	Materials	Conversion Costs (labor & O/H)
Work-in-process, beginning	65 (2/5)**		
Units Started	60,823		
Units to Account for	60,888		
Units transferred to Filtering (60,640)			
From beginning inventory	65	----	39
From current production	60,575	60,575	60,575
Work-in-process, ending	60 (4/5)**	60	48
Lost in process	188	----	----
Units accounted for	60,888	60,635	60,662

Costs	Totals	Materials	Conversion Costs	Equivalent Whole Unit
Work-in-process, beginning	$ 4,093.	$ ----	----	
Current costs	3,987,287.	3,843,795.	$143,492.	
Total costs to account for	$3,991,380.	$3,843,795.	$143,492.	
Divide by equivalent units		÷ 60,635	÷ 60,662	
Cost per equivalent unit (CWT)		$ 6.3392	$ .236	$ 6.5752
Summary of costs:				
Units completed (60,640)				
From beginning inventory (65)	$ 4,093.			
Current costs added				
Materials	----		----	
Conversion costs	92.		39 ($.236)	
Total from beginning inventory	4,185.			
Started and completed (60,575)	3,982,927.			60,575 (6.5752)
Adjustment for rounding	352.			
Total costs transferred out	3,987,464.			
Work-in-process, end (60)				
Materials	$ 3,803.	$ 60 ($6.3392)		
Conversion costs	113.		48 ($.236)	
Total cost of work-in-process	3,916.			
Total costs accounted for	$3,991,380.			

Figure 12-4

*Source: Adapted from Matz and McMichael, "The Mino Sugar Refining Company Practice Case," (by permission of South-Western Publishing Co.) Format adapted from Horngren, *Cost Accounting—A Managerial Emphasis,* Prentice-Hall, Inc., p. 636.

**Applies to Conversion effort.

Figure 12-5 is prepared on the assumption that in the illustration developed in this chapter management has accepted .001 of good production (perhaps an industry standard) as a maximum for spoiled units inherent in present methods of manufacture.

In Figure 12-5 this tolerance level amounts to 61,000 (.001 of 60,640,000 units transferred out for the month). The excess over this normal spoilage, namely, 127,000 (of the 188,000 total lost units) is costed at $6.5548 representing both material and conversion costs based on the theory that the loss occurs at the end of the process in the Melting Department. Such abnormal spoilage is charged to the period in which it occurs as a debit to abnormal Spoilage and a credit to Work-in-Process— Melting. Normal spoilage is also costed but transferred out with the costs of good production to the next department. However, by isolating normal spoilage at any time, access can be made to the monthly cost reports for a given department to analyze normal spoilage and to determine whether the accepted tolerance level is really too high.

By relieving production of abnormal spoilage, a difference is noted in the transfer cost per CWT in Figure 12-5, where a $6.319 per CWT unit of material cost is shown, contrasted with $6.339 and $6.3392 in the case of the weighted average method (Figure 12-3) and FIFO (Figure 12-4), respectively.

In practice, the clerical burden of developing unit costs by batches as illustrated in Figures 12-4 and 12-5, has caused a rejection of FIFO by most process cost industries in favor of standard process costs described below.

Standard Costs in a Process Cost System

Figure 12-6 shows the use of standard costs for both material and conversion costs ($6.34 and $.24, respectively), thus eliminating the burdensome computations monthly of costs per equivalent unit because the standard cost *is* the cost per equivalent unit. These standards are usually developed over a representative period of operations under the same methods of production.

Advantages include the determination of monthly variances from standard for each department in addition to the benefit of the simplicity of computation. Thus, Figure 12-6 shows a favorable variance for October of $40,464 in materials and $2,097 in conversion costs, when the above standard unit costs are applied to the equivalent units developed under the first-in, first-out method. Variances can be broken into further refinements if detail is maintained and such refinements are acted on by management.

ADAPTATION OF MODIFIED FIRST-IN, FIRST-OUT METHOD (Fig. 12-4)
TO ISOLATE NORMAL AND ABNORMAL SPOILAGE*

MELTING DEPARTMENT

	Physical Flow	Equivalent Units Materials	Conversion Costs
Quantities (CWT) (Lbs.)			
Work-in-process, beginning	65 (2/5)		
Units started	60,823		
Units to account for	60,888		
Units Transferred to Filtering (60,640)			
From beginning inventory	65	----	39
From current production	60,575	60,575	60,575
Work-in-process, ending	60 (4/5)	60	48
Normal ** spoilage (.001 of good production) (60,640)	61	61	61
Abnormal ** spoilage (excess of total lost units (188) over accepted normal spoilage)	127	127	127
Units accounted for	60,888	60,823	60,850

Costs	Totals	Materials	Conversion Costs	Equivalent Whole Unit
Work-in-process, beginning	$ 4,093.	$ ----	$ ----	
Current costs	3,987,287.	3,843,795.	143,492.	
Total costs to account for	$3,991,380.			
Divide by (CWT) equivalent units		÷ 60,823	÷ 60,850	
Cost per equivalent unit		$ 6.319	$ .2358	$ 6.5548

Summary of Costs

Abnormal spoilage (127)	$ 8,325.			127 (6.5548)
Units completed (60,640)				
From beginning inventory (65)	$ 4,093.			
Current costs added	92.		39 (.2358)	
Total cost from beginning inventory before spoilage	4,185.			
Started and completed before spoilage (60,575) and $398. adj. for rounding	3,970,968.			60,575 ($6.5548)
Normal spoilage (61)	3,998.			61 ($5.5548)
Total Costs transferred out	3,979,151.			
Work-in-process, ending				
Materials	3,791.	60 (6.319)		
Conversion costs	113.		48 (.2358)	
Total cost of work-in-process	$ 3,904.			
Total costs accounted for	$3,991,380.			

Figure 12-5

*Format adapted from Horngren,*Cost Accounting—A Managerial Emphasis*, Prentice-Hall, Inc., pages 636-7. Material adapted from Matz and McMichael, "The Mino Sugar Refining Company Practice Case," (By permission of South-Western Publishing Co.)

**Assumption made that all material and conversion costs have been incurred before loss in units occurs; company policy provides that 001% of good output will be accepted as normal spoilage; units lost in excess of that percentage is charged to the period as abnormal spoilage, in amount shown.

MELTING DEPARTMENT
PRODUCTION COST REPORT*

For the Month Ending October 19XX—Standard Costs in a Process-Cost System

		Equivalent Units	
Quantities (CWT) (Lbs.)	Physical Flow	Materials	Conversion Costs (labor & O/H)
Work-in-process	65 (2/5)		
Units started	60,823		
Units to account for	60,888		
Units transferred to Filtering			
From beginning inventory	65	....	39
From current production	60,575	60,575	60,575
Work-in-process, end	60 (4/5)	60	48
Lost in process	188		
Units accounted for (Fig. 12-4)	60,888	60,635	60,662

Costs	Totals	Materials	Conversion Costs	Equivalent Whole Unit
Standard unit cost per CWT, (given) per equivalent units		$ 6.34	$ .24	$ 6.58
Equivalent units (above)		x 60,635.	x 60,662.	
Current standard costs	$3,989,848.	3,844,259.	145,589.	
Beginning inventory	4,093.			
Total to be accounted for	$3,993,941.			

Summary of costs				
Units completed (60,640)	$3,990,112.			60,640 (6.58)
Adjustment for rounding	(910)			
Work-in-process, end (60)				
Materials	$ 3,804.	60 (6.34)		
Conversion costs	115.		48 (.24)	
Total cost of work-in-process	3,919.			
Total costs accounted for	$3,993,941.			

Summary of variances for current performance:			
Current output in equivalent units		60,635.	60,662.
Current output at standard costs		3,884,259.	145,589.
Costs charged to Melting Department		3,843,795.	143,492.
Total variance (actual from standard)		($ 40,464.)	($ 2,097.)

Figure 12-6

Source: *Format adapted from Horngren, *Cost Accounting—A Managerial Emphasis.* Prentice-Hall, Inc., p. 637.

**Material adapted from Matz and McMichael, "The Mino Sugar Refining Company Practice Case," (By permission of South-Western Publishing Co.)

In this chapter, three methods of process costing have been demonstrated namely: the weighted average; first-in, first-out; and standard costing techniques. The need to reconcile the factory ledger on a continuing basis with a controlling account in the general ledger was illustrated in practice.

The outputs of the system, the production cost reports, were demonstrated in the case of one department resulting in unit costs for materials and conversion costs applied to equivalent units in both cases. The three different approaches demonstrated indicate that differences in unit costs between the weighted average and FIFO are not usually significant where a continuing, high volume of production is involved, although FIFO does give better control by isolating current costs. This is not the case under weighted average costing.

The advantages of standard costing, resulting in the elimination of detailed unit cost computations and replacement with engineered standards are twofold: (1) when used in comparison with actual costs for the period, it isolates material and conversion variances for corrective action by management; and (2) normal and abnormal spoilage can be determined monthly, as demonstrated, so that the period is charged with losses in excess of those considered normal by management and the latter included in the cost transfer to the next department.

REFERENCES

[1]Adapted from the Process Cost Practice Case, "The Mino Sugar Refining Company", by Adolph Matz and John H. McMichael, South-Western Publishing Company, 1967.

[2]*Ibid.,* pages 10 and 11.

[3]Charles T. Horngren, *Cost Accounting—A Managerial Emphasis,* Third Edition, Prentice-Hall, Inc. page 598.

[4]*Ibid.,* page 603.

13

Standard Cost Accounting

The use of standard material and conversion costs was demonstrated in Chapter 12 for industries using process costs such as chemical companies, sugar and starch refining, and many others. In this chapter procedures for using standards in the different accounts and isolating material, labor, and overhead variances under both job and process cost systems are outlined.

From large manufacturing companies to the operations of small contracting firms, the use of standard costs not only facilitates control over operations by inducing corrective action on variances from standard costs but is extremely helpful for bidding purposes.

Journal Entries Illustrating the Use of Standards in the Accounts

Illustrated in Figure 13-1 is the operation of a standard cost system. It indicates the standard cost for the construction of the company's end item "A" with respect to the number of raw material units required, the standard price of each, and the labor and overhead needed to convert such raw materials into the finished product, "A."

The flexible manufacturing overhead budget is shown at three levels of operations, that is, 90, 95, and 100% of operating capacity. This denominator level of volume is used with a numerator of estimated overhead for the period, to arrive at an applied overhead rate per direct labor hour worked on each job.

Illustration of a Standard Cost System: typical entries, isolation and analysis of variances.*

STANDARD COST SHEET—

END ITEM—BLACK BOX "A"

	Total
Materials—10 subassemblies x $15—standard price	$ 150
Labor—45 hours x $4—standard labor rate	180
Overhead—45 hours x $5—standard overhead rate	225
Total Standard Cost per Black Box "A"	$ 555

The manufacturing overhead budget is as follows:

	Operating Capacity		
	90%	95%	100%
Variable overhead	$180,000	$190,000	$200,000
Fixed overhead	200,000	200,000	200,000
Total overhead	$380,000	390,000	$400,000
Budgeted direct labor hours (Variable O/H rate 2.50)	72,000	76,000	80,000
Total Overhead Rate	$ 5.277	$ 5.131	$ 5.00

*Adapted from "A Standard Cost System in Operation", Carl L. Moore, and Robert K. Jaedicke, *Managerial Accounting,* 2nd Edition, (By permission of South-Western Publishing Company, 1967,) pp. 389-392.

Figure 13-1

The overhead rate chosen by management to be applied to all production is $5.00 per hour, based on a numerator of $400,000 total overhead anticipated and a denominator of 80,000 direct labor hours as the planned activity level for the year. In other words management plans to operate at 100% of plant capacity.

The following transactions are assumed for the year:

(1) Subassemblies purchased—18,000 at a unit cost of $16.00
(2) Subassemblies issued to the assembly department, $17,500.

(3) Gross payroll for the factory, $450,000; income taxes withheld, $91,000; social security taxes withheld, $19,500.

(4) Of the gross payroll in (3), factory labor was accounted for by 76,000 direct labor hours @ 4.15; indirect labor $130,000.

(5) Additional manufacturing overhead incurred or accrued during the period was:

Manufacturing supplies requisitioned	$130,000.
Insurance expense—Factory	5,000.
Depreciation expense—Factory and manufacturing equipment	60,000.
Other accrued manufacturing expense	40,000.

(6) Beginning inventories: Finished Goods "A", 300; ending inventory of "A"'s were 400. No beginning inventories of raw materials or work-in-process were on hand.

(7) During the year, 1700 finished products (A) were manufactured and 1600 were sold at $800 each.

Journal Entries

Recording Above in Summary Form

(1) SUBASSEMBLIES PURCHASED DURING THE YEAR:

MATERIALS INVENTORY	$ 270,000	
MATERIALS PRICE VARIANCE	18,000	
ACCOUNTS PAYABLE		288,000

    To charge inventory for the purchase
    of subassemblies as follows:
      STANDARD—18,000 UNITS x $15=$270,000
      ACTUAL—18,000 UNITS x $16=$288,000

(2) SUBASSEMBLIES ISSUED TO PRODUCTION DURING THE YEAR:

  (a) ON STANDARD MATERIAL REQUISITION (WHITE FORM)

WORK-IN-PROCESS INVENTORY	255,000	
MATERIALS INVENTORY		255,000

      To record materials used at standard:
        10 MATERIAL UNITS x 1700 END ITEMS "A" =
        17,000 STANDARD UNITS OF MATERIAL x $15=
        STANDARD UNIT COST OF $255,000

  (b) ON "EXCESS" MATERIAL REQUISITIONS (SAME FORM BUT IN RED)

MATERIALS QUANTITY VARIANCE	7,500	
MATERIALS INVENTORY		7,500

      To enter total of requisitions for:
        500 (17,500 ISSUED AGAINST 17,000
        STANDARD) REPRESENTING EXCESS SUB-
        ASSEMBLIES USED OVER STANDARD AT
        $15 STANDARD UNIT COST.

(3) TOTAL FACTORY PAYROLL FOR THE YEAR:
     FACTORY LABOR   450,000
       INCOME TAXES WITHHELD   91,000
       SOCIAL SECURITY TAXES WITHHELD   19,500
       WAGES PAYABLE   339,500
         To record the payment of all factory payrolls

(4) TOTAL FACTORY LABOR DISTRIBUTION
     (a) (ISOLATING THE LABOR PRICE VARIANCE):
          DIRECT LABOR   304,000
          INDIRECT LABOR   134,600
          LABOR RATE VARIANCE   11,400
            FACTORY LABOR   450,000
              To record labor distribution:
                ACTUAL DIRECT LABOR HOURS 76,000 x
                $4, (STANDARD HOURLY RATE) = $306,000
                PRICE VARIANCE: $.15 ($4.15 ACTUAL—
                $4 STANDARD) PER HOUR x 76,000 HOURS =
                $11,400.
     (b) (ISOLATING THE LABOR EFFICIENCY VARIANCE):
          WORK-IN-PROCESS INVENTORY   306,000
            EFFICIENCY VARIANCE   2,000
            DIRECT LABOR   304,000
              To charge work in process as follows:
                STANDARD HOURS PER END ITEM "A" 45
                x 1700 ITEM "A'"S = 76,000 STANDARD
                HOURS x $4 STANDARD RATE—$306,000
                FINISHED PRODUCT COST. ACTUAL HOURS
                WERE 500 LESS THAN STANDARD (76,000
                ACTUAL VERSUS 76,500 THE STANDARD
                REQUIREMENT FOR THE 1700 END ITEM
                "A" 'S PRODUCED) x $4—STANDARD COST =
                THE EFFICIENCY VARIANCE OF 500 HOURS
                x$4.00 STANDARD COST PER HOUR.

(5) OTHER MANUFACTURING OVERHEAD FOR THE YEAR (OTHER THAN IN-
     DIRECT LABOR):
     MANUFACTURING OVERHEAD . . . . $ 235,000
       SUPPLIES INVENTORY.   130,000
       UNEXPIRED INSURANCE   5,000
       ACCRUED EXPENSES PAYABLE   40,000
       ACCUMULATED DEPRECIATION   60,000
         To enter manufacturing overhead including
         accruals at end of year.

(6) MANUFACTURING OVERHEAD APPLIED DURING THE YEAR:
     WORK-IN-PROCESS INVENTORY   382,500
       APPLIED OVERHEAD   382,500

To charge jobs in process for:
    STANDARD HOURS REQUIRED FOR PRODUCTION
    OF 1700 END ITEM "A" 'S AT 45 PER UNIT =
    76,500 STANDARD HOURS x $5 RATE =
    $382,500 STANDARD OVERHEAD COST.

(7) FINISHED END ITEM A'S TRANSFERRED TO FINISHED GOODS INVEN-
    TORY:
    FINISHED GOODS INVENTORY   943,500
        WORK-IN-PROCESS INVENTORY   943,500
        TO TRANSFER 1700 A'S TO FINISHED INVENTORY
        AT A STANDARD COST OF $555 A PIECE.

(8) SALES AND COST OF SALES JOURNALIZED:
    ACCOUNTS RECEIVABLE (CASH)   1,280,000
        SALES   1,280,000
            RECORDING THE SALE OF 1600 A'S AT $800 EACH.
    COST OF GOODS SOLD   888,000
        FINISHED GOODS INVENTORY.   888,000
            THE STANDARD COST OF 1600 A'S SOLD IS CHARGED
            TO COST OF GOODS SOLD (1600 UNITS x $555 PER
            UNIT).

(9) CLOSING OF OVERHEAD CONTROL AND APPLIED OVERHEAD:
    APPLIED MANUFACTURING OVERHEAD.   382,500
    OVERHEAD VARIANCE   12,900
        MANUFACTURING OVERHEAD   369,600
            TO CLOSE ACTUAL AND APPLIED OVERHEAD
            ACCOUNTS. THE UNFAVORABLE VARIANCE IS
            RECORDED. (INDIRECT LABOR, $134,600 +
            OTHER MANUFACTURING OVERHEAD, $235,000 = $369,600.)

Input/Output Analysis of
Overhead Variance

CONTROLLABLE VARIANCE:
    SPENDING VARIANCE (INPUT-ORIENTED):
        ACTUAL OVERHEAD INCURRED $369,600
        FLEXIBLE BUDGET FOR 76,000 HOURS OF
        ACTUAL OPERATION*   390,000
        BUDGET VARIANCE (FAVORABLE) . . . .   ($ 20,400)
    EFFICIENCY VARIANCE (OUTPUT-ORIENTED):
        FLEXIBLE BUDGET FOR 76,000 HOURS OF
        OPERATION (ACTUAL).   390,000
        FLEXIBLE BUDGET FOR 76,500 STANDARD
        HOURS REQUIRED** (HOURS EARNED)   391,250
        EFFICIENCY VARIANCE (FAVORABLE) . . . .   (1,250)
    TOTAL CONTROLLABLE VARIANCE (FAVORABLE). . .   ($ 21,650)

CAPACITY VARIANCE: (output-oriented)
  FLEXIBLE BUDGET FOR 76,500 STANDARD HOURS
  REQUIRED TO PRODUCE 1700 FINISHED PRODUCT
  "A" 'S $391,250

  OVERHEAD APPLIED (76,500 STANDARD HOURS
  x THE $5 RATE) (BASED ON AN ANTICIPATED
  OUTPUT OF 1778 FINISHED PRODUCTS) (OR
  80,000 HOURS)   382,500

    CAPACITY VARIANCE (UNFAVORABLE)   8,750
TOTAL OVERHEAD VARIANCE (FAVORABLE) . . . .   ($ 12,900)

(10) FAVORABLE OVERHEAD VARIANCE CLOSED TO COST OF GOODS SOLD:
    MANUFACTURING OVERHEAD VARIANCE   12,900
      COST OF GOODS SOLD   12,900
        TO CLOSE OUT VARIANCE ACCOUNT FOR THE YEAR.

      *See manufacturing overhead budget.
      **Additional 500 hours x variable overhead rate of $2.50 is added to budget for 76,000 hours (see *
above.) No change occurs in fixed overhead over the relevant range of activity shown in the budget (through
80,000 hours).

The decision must be made at which level the company plans to operate. In this illustration the "denominator" level of activity selected is that of 100% of operating capacity or 80,000 budgeted labor hours, resulting in the use of a rate for applied overhead of $5.00 per hour.

The transactions for the accounting period are journalized for the purchase and use of materials, labor and overhead.

Material Price Variance

The price variance is the difference between the actual and standard costs of all raw materials purchased during the period. The invoice price is compared with the cost that the standard engineers have established for each raw material unit called out. An alternative procedure is to set up the material price variance on the quantity *used* during the period, rather than the total *purchased*.

In this illustration the total quantity of raw materials purchased during the year (rather than the quantity *used*) is the basis for development of the purchase price variance. The rationale behind this is that the purchasing agent should be charged with the responsibility of buying raw materials at the standard price for whatever quantity bought during the period, rather than the quantity actually *used*, thus giving him the benefit of buying at the best possible price break, and more faithfully reflecting efficiency in procurement.

Quantity Variance

Usage variance reflects the difference between the actual raw material quantities requisitioned out of the storeroom and the quantity that *should have been* used according to the standards engineers for the number of good end items inspected and transferred to finished goods inventory. One procedure for accomplishing this is to use a *standard* requisition form for the standard quantity of raw materials based on the output being made. If additional raw material units are needed because of inferior or ruined raw materials, the same form (in another color) is used. A requisition to get such extra or excess material usage is issued to the manufacturing staging area and in total these represent the material *usage* or quantity variance.

Labor Rate and Efficiency Variance

The liability for the month including total accruals of direct labor, less income taxes and social security taxes withheld, is set up and followed with an entry in which distribution is made to the appropriate accounts.

Labor rate or price variance is determined when direct labor is charged at standard for the total number of hours actually bought during the accounting period. In a second entry, the labor efficiency variance (comparable in nature to the material usage variance) is set up by debiting work-in-process inventory, based on the output of the period, that is, the total number of end products "A" actually manufactured.

When the number of standard hours per end item "A" is multiplied by the quantity of end items produced, the *allowed* number of hours is determined and multiplied by the standard rate per labor hour. The difference between this figure and the actual direct labor costs for the period is set up as the efficiency (or labor usage) variance.

Overhead Variance—Controllable and
Capacity Variances

In the next entry, actual manufacturing overhead for the period is set up, including indirect labor, indirect supplies, unexpired insurance, depreciation expense, and all other accrued manufacturing expenses. Applied manufacturing overhead is credited and work-in-process inventory is debited, based on the number of end items "A" produced during the period (1700). This amount is multiplied by the standard number of hours required for end item "A" (45) and the applied rate ($5.00) from the operating level selected by management, namely, 100% capacity. Total overhead of $400,000 as a numerator and a denominator activity level of 80,000 budgeted direct labor hours for a $5.00 overhead applied rate was selected, as described earlier, which multiplied by the number of standard hours earned (76,500) gives the applied overhead for the year of $382,500.

The result is that the end items completed were applied overhead at the selected $5.00 rate (based on 100% capacity of the factory or 80,000 standard hours), whereas only 95% capacity was attained (a rate of $5.13), accounting for the unfavorable capacity overhead variance of $8,500 (Figure 13-1), which is the responsibility of top management. Therefore, the production for the period has been undercharged as far as overhead goes in the amount of 13¢ for every hour billed.

The favorable manufacturing overhead variance difference of $12,900 is analyzed in the schedule concluding Figure 13-1. Of the many different approaches used in analyzing overhead, the one chosen in this illustration is limited to two major variances, namely, controllable (at the operating level) and capacity variance, for which top management is responsible. Operating supervision is charged with both the spending variance, that is, spending too much or too little for the actual hours purchased and with the efficiency variance.

The latter relates to output—using more or less than the standard number of hours for the quantity of good output of end item "A" actually produced. As noted, top management is charged with the capacity variance representing the difference of operating at something less than the 100% capacity, which level had been selected before the year's operations began in the determination of the applied overhead rate which should distribute the year's overhead equitably over all end item "A" 's produced.

The next entry shows finished goods being debited and work-in-process inventory being credited for the transfer of finished units "A" at the price of $800. Entries are then recorded showing sales and cost of goods sold at standard cost of $555 each.

The difference between actual and applied manufacturing overhead is closed to cost of sales. A credit to manufacturing overhead and a debit to applied manufacturing overhead closes these accounts.

Income Statements Under Standard Costing (Direct and Absorption Costing)

Figure 13-2 illustrates the income statement for the year, reflecting the journal entries described in this chapter. Both *direct costing* and *absorption costing* can be used under standard costing as illustrated.

Since direct costing, as a managerial or internal reporting tool, deducts *all* direct or variable costs from sales to arrive at *contribution margin*, the latter caption reflects the income or margin left to cover *all* fixed expense (treated as a period charge) and still make a contribution to net income. Inventories under direct costing are valued at variable cost only—no fixed overhead is included since it is shown in total as a period charge at the bottom of the statement.

Income Statement Presentation using standard costs—under both Direct and Absorption Costing *

INCOME STATEMENT

FOR PERIOD ENDING: _____

Direct Costing

Sales (1600 x $800)			$1,280,000.
Variable expenses:			
Beginning inventory (300 x $442.50)**	$ 132,750.		
Production (1700 x $442.50)	752,250.		
Available for sale	$ 885,000.		
Ending inventory (400 x $442.50)**	117,000.		
Standard variable cost of sales	$ 708,000.		
Variances from Standard:			
Materials price	$18,000.		
Materials quantity	7,500.		
Labor rate	11,400.		
Labor efficiency	(2,000.)		
Overhead-controllable	(21,650.)		
		13,250.	
Variable manufacturing, cost of sales			721,250.
Contribution margin			558,750.
Fixed Expenses:			
Manufacturing			200,000.
Net income			$ 358,750.

Figure 13-2

INCOME STATEMENT

FOR PERIOD ENDING: _____

Absorption Costing

Sales			$1,280,000.
Cost of sales:			
Beginning inventory (300 x $555)**		$ 166,500.	
Production (1700 x $555)		943,500.	
Available for sale		$1,110,000.	
Ending inventory		222,000.	
Standard Cost of Sales		$ 888,000.	
Variances from Standard:			
Materials price	$18,000.		
Materials quantity	7,500.		
Labor rate	11,400.		
Labor efficiency	(2,000.)		
Overhead-controllable	(21,650.)		
Overhead-capacity			
(fixed)	8,750.		
		$ 22,000.	$ 910,000.
Gross Margin			370,000.

*For analysis of "Direct versus absorption costing" in greater depth the reader is directed to Charles T. Horngren's *Accounting for Management Control,* Third Edition, Prentice-Hall, 1974, pp. 488-492.

**Fixed overhead of $112.50 per unit *excluded* from inventory under "Direct Costing" (included under "Absorption" or full costing).

Figure 13-2 *(continued)*

Absorption costing, also illustrated in Figure 13-2, follows the conventional format accepted in financial accounting for *external* reporting purposes and meets the needs of the investors and Securities and Exchange Commission. As to income presentation, absorption costing allocates fixed overhead to inventories and differs from direct costing primarily in this respect.

The American Institute of Certified Public Accountants has stated that the *exclusion* of fixed overheads from inventory does not constitute generally accepted accounting practice, and, therefore, absorption costing is required for investor-oriented reporting.

Both statements have their place—direct costing for managerial purposes in determining the contribution of each company, division, product-line, etc., to defray fixed costs and to contribute to income after all variable or out-of-pocket costs have been deducted from sales. The "break-even" point is facilitated under this approach. By dividing the unit contribution of each product after variable costs into the fixed overhead of the period, the break-even quantity is determined.

Since direct costing *excludes* all fixed overhead from inventories and absorption costing *includes* an appropriate portion of fixed overhead ($112.50) per unit in inventory, the net income figures reported under the two methods of costing will differ by the amount of the difference in inventory valuation. As noted in Figure 13-2, this amounts to $11,250. (100 unit increase in ending inventory over beginning) carried to the next period under absorption costing but absorbed as a "period" charge under direct costing.

The application of standard costing has become more popular in industries requiring process cost accounting than historical weighted-average or first-in, first-out methods. The basic reason is the simplicity and minimum of clerical computations in using standard costs. As a result, the extension of this procedure into smaller business operations, often considered job-cost oriented, has been encouraged. General contracting in the construction industry, for example, is a recent addition to the growing list of smaller-sized operations seeking to apply standard costing to their specific needs, primarily for planning, bidding, and control purposes. This application is seen in contractors' budget summaries, schedules of job estimating rates, and operating summaries, emphasizing variances between actual and standard performance as described in Chapter 14.

PART II

Computer Systems, Procedures, and Management Information Reporting

14 Systems and Programming Development – Using a Cost Versus Benefits Overlay

Importance of the Computer Justification Study

Each element of a computer installation's overall cost must be projected and related by management to the benefits to be derived from such an installation—the objectives that warrant the expenditure of the substantial sums represented in the hardware and software costs. Not only the original costs represented in the installation, but the on-going program costs also should be projected including all personnel required such as programmers, systems analysts, data base managers, electronic data processing executives, machine operators, coding clerks, keypunch operators and the like.

A project management approach is recommended when a firm is planning to install a computer. The firm develops guidelines as to what systems should be developed, how much should be budgeted for these systems, and how the efficiency and effectiveness of these systems will be evaluated.[1] (Project budgeting and management for a computer-based systems development is illustrated in Chapter 22, Part IV, under *Profit Planning*, where performance measurement is reported over the life of the project.)

---

[1] For information in-depth concerning mechanisms used to control resources allocated to the implementation of large computer systems, the reader is referred to Dearden and Nolan's article, "How to Control the Computer Resource," *Harvard Business Review,* November-December, 1973, pp. 68-78.

Figure 14-1 uses a milestone chart approach to relate each major phase of the installation of the computer to the schedule that was adopted for the entire installation project. Each phase of the installation, from planning-study approval to the final turnover of the program to the operating personnel is indicated in sequence. Figure 14-2 provides the basic framework for project control of the resources committed to the computer. In effect, the cost of the outputs of the system are matched with the benefits derived.

The basic question is: Are the applications running on the computer meeting the organization's goals established in the planning study and staying within the budget approved by management in that feasibility study? Only through monitoring the inputs and the processing in terms of the systems effort, the programming and machine operations, and the quality of the management reports and other applications, on a continuing basis can management control the efficiency and effectiveness of the total project as suggested in Figure 14-2.

Planning the Computer's Workload

The workload must be carefully projected and priorities must be assigned in order to determine the appropriate computer configuration or hardware as to capacity and quantity of input-output peripheral equipment. Figure 14-3 illustrates a listing of applications that are subject to approval and assignment of priorities based on a cost/benefits evaluation, preferably on a continuing basis, by a functional, senior-management steering committee. Each month's workload is estimated with respect to the elapsed time and central processing required for each application or project such as inventory control, production scheduling, and the major phases of the firm's financial information system as illustrated in Chapter 15.

Therefore input/output volume is projected, for example as in Figure 14-2, and additional characteristics are developed so that the proper computer configuration can be ordered. Items to be considered include:

(1) Predominant source language in which the majority of source code is programmed with respect to each application;
(2) Partition size or typical core requirement for the jobs identified by project or application;
(3) Project characteristic—whether the jobs are primarily oriented toward much processing by the central processing unit or are input-output oriented;

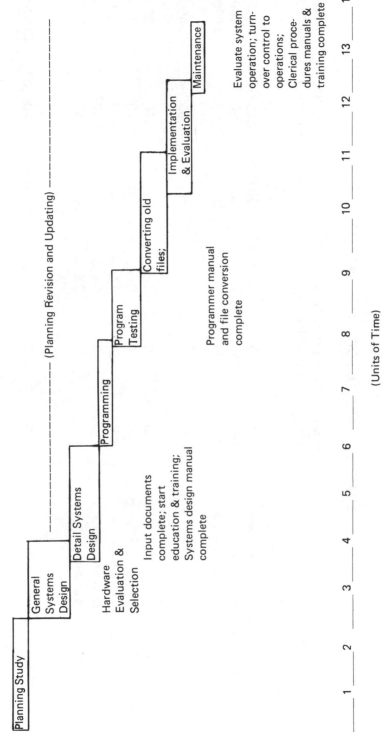

A MILESTONE APPROACH TO THE COMPUTER INSTALLATION

Board of Directors authorizes
planning study

Planning Study

General
Systems
Design

-------- (Planning Revision and Updating) --------

Detail Systems
Design

Hardware
Evaluation &
Selection

Programming

Input documents
complete; start
education & training;
Systems design manual
complete

Program
Testing

Converting old
files;

Implementation
& Evaluation

Maintenance

Programmer manual
and file conversion
complete

Evaluate system
operation; turn-
over control to
operations;
Clerical proce-
dures manuals &
training complete

1   2   3   4   5   6   7   8   9   10   11   12   13   14

(Units of Time)

Figure 14-1

269

WORKLOAD (ESTIMATED) FOR THE MONTH OF _____

Project or application	Elapsed Time, Hrs.	CPU Time, Hrs.	Tape/Disk I/O Count	Cards Read	Lines Printed	Number of Jobs
1. Cost Accumulation System	360	52	9.00×10^6	260×10^3	2.80×10^6	1,650
2. Data Base Development	150	15	5.0	60	.50	750
3. Payroll and direct labor processing	350	28	13.0	180	2.50	2,000
4. Inventory Accounting and production scheduling	85	7	3.0	85	.95	450
5. Marketing Intelligence System	85	10	2.4	165	.40	360
6. Financial Information System	25	4	0.5	90	.50	120
7. Test & Development	325	65	7.0	700	2.40	2,000
8. Special Requests-Management	115	15	3.0	175	1.80	500
9. Systems Programming Other	125	25	2.5	200	2.50	1,230
TOTALS	2,500	353	50.2×10^6	2875×10^3	17.20×10^6	13,87u

Figure 14-2

WORKLOAD CHARACTERISTICS

Project or application	Predominant Source Language	Partition Size (Typical)	Application Characteristic	Peripheral Requirements (Tapes/Disks)	Submission Frequency	Time Dependency	Job Source
1. Cost Accumulation System	FORTRAN	160K	I/O	2/3	Hourly	12 Hours	R
2. Data Base Development	PL/1	160K	I/O	1/4	Daily	4 Hours	L
3. Payroll and direct labor processing	COBOL	160K	I/O	1/3	Hourly	2 Hours	R
4. Inventory Accounting and production scheduling	COBOL	160K	I/O	2/3	Daily	24 Hours	R
5. Marketing Intelligence System	PL/1	160K	I/O	1/3	Daily	48 Hours	R
6. Financial Information System	COBOL	160K	I/O	1/3	Daily	24 Hours	R
7. Test & Development	All ASI-ST	160K	I/O	1/3	Hourly	4 Hours	L
8. Special Requests-Management	PL/1 COBOL	160K	Mixed	1/2	Hourly	4 Hours	L
9. Systems Programming Other	BAL	N/A	N/A	0/7	Hourly	2 Hours	L

Figure 14-3

(4) Peripheral requirements with respect to the typical number of tape-disk drives required to process a job of the type indicated on the existing system;

(5) Frequency—the number of times typical jobs are run, whether hourly, daily, weekly, monthly, etc.;

(6) Time requirements—hours within which jobs of the indicated type must be run by the computer; and,

(7) Job origin—the typical origin of input and the destination of print-out, local or remote, for the information involved including demands upon the system from remote terminals from out-lying plants or offices via teleprocessing.

The adequacy of the computer hardware selected can be checked with reference to the total workload predicted for the installation and spelled out in the specifications to prospective suppliers. (This is described in Chapter 22 under *Project Planning.*)

Systems and Design Effort—Control Techniques

The systems analyst's work may be viewed in sequential order by work items as in Figure 14-4. Provision is made on this form for the insertion with respect to each work item of estimated time projections in man-weeks. Preferably this is done after agreement between the systems analyst assigned to each project and the supervisor of the group.

As a result of this agreement the analyst then knows what is expected and will cooperate in meeting the schedule by bringing problems that might prevent meeting the target date to the attention of the supervisor. A project management control system is suggested to be used in conjunction with Figure 14-4. Figure 14-5 indicates the programs written for each system. The latter control form again projects the total estimated time required in man-weeks for each item of the program as well in total, and an agreed series of dates for start and stop with respect to each step in the program sequence. A job assignment control form (Figure 14-6) facilitates the costing of each project or assignments for the programs written.

By providing a projected cost for each job, the manager of the data processing facility furnishes the screening committee with a dollar value for the computer services that are involved in each project which is requested by a corporate department. By weighing such costs against the benefits of the project as understood by the screening committee, an allocation or rationing of expensive computer resources that best meets management's overall objectives as communicated to the committee may be undertaken.

Revolving Fund Structure

Figure 14-6 can also serve as a form for billing computer-using departments for all developmental costs of a project or system including: systems and programming personnel; travel costs involved in obtaining the requirements of outlying plants; consulting costs in such technical matters as teleprocessing and the use of package programs prepared by computer

SYSTEMS EFFORT

Work Item Sequence Number	Item Description	Total Est. Time Req'ed (Weeks)	Calendar Time Start	Stop
	Problem Definition and Review			
	Data Gathering—Personnel Interviews			
	Documentation of Present System (s)			
	General Design of Proposed System			
	New Design Documented—Submitted Approval			
	New Design Approved			
	Design Submitted to departments for Approval			
	Review Meetings with departments			
	Approval by Computer Committee			
	Detail System Design			
	Program Turnover			
	S.O.P.'s Written			
	Installation Plan Written			
	System Approved			
	TOTAL			

Figure 14-4

manufacturers; and, the running costs of such programs. The latter includes the preparation of data for input and processing on the computer involved. The cost of this should be communicated to, and understood by, departmental users. Such billings to the department that requested the job can become a charge anticipated in that department's budget. This justifies the computing center's operations through budgetary transfers in the nature of a revolving fund and relieves the computer center from deciding the worth of departmental projects. It also gives the manager of

PROGRAMMING EFFORT

Program Name _____

Program Description _____

_____

No. of Programs in project group: _____

Work Item Sequence Number	Item Description	Total Est. Time Req'ed (Weeks)	Calendar Time	
			Start	Stop
	Programs Logic Flow Chart			
	Program Documentation			
	Program Coding			
	Programs Keypunched			
	Programs Compiled			
	Program Test Data Preparation			
	Test Data Keypunched			
	Program Tested			
	Master Files Built			
	Program System Tested			
	Documentation Complete			
	TOTAL			

Figure 14-5

COST CONTROL BY COMPUTER PROJECTS/JOBS

Assignment Area
- ☐ Accounting
- ☐ Research
- ☐ Production management
- ☐ Other

Assignment Title: _____

Assignment Date: _____ Job Supervisor: _____

Personnel Assigned:

1. _____   4. _____
2. _____   5. _____
3. _____   6. _____

Job Assignment Description: _____

_____

_____

_____

Job Assignment Cost Analysis:

	Est. Hrs. Req'd.	Cost per Hr.	Total
Project Personnel Cost:			
Project Travel Cost:			
Outside Consulting Cost:			
Equipment Usage Reqm'ts. IBM			
Keypunch Verifier			
Other			

Estimated Total Cost

APPROVED: _____ DATE: _____

Figure 14-6

the using department the opportunity to know his data-processing costs and, if deemed excessive, to request permission to take the computing work elsewhere. This might mean to a service bureau or other resource. Such a request may not be unreasonable in companies where responsibility accounting is used to match all costs, including those of data processing, with the manager's budget and the latter's compensation and upward mobility in the organization based at least in part on this type of performance measurement.

Systems Description and Write-up Illustrated—Budgetary Control

An illustration of a systems effort is presented in (Figure 14-7) a sub-system entitled, "Cost Accumulation, Budget and Expenditure Master File Update." Under "System Description" the purpose of the system is indicated as that of 1) standardizing the procedures for preparing budgetary requests and, 2) incorporating such budgets to create meaningful management reports by departments or projects. Therefore, both budgetary and cost information must be stored for participating departments and later retrieved for printouts required by those departments.

To assist the programmer in working from the systems analyst's write-up and in understanding the system sufficiently to code it in the language selected, a dictionary of budgetary terms is provided routinely. Basic accounting terms may be foreign to the programmer but may be extremely important considerations for effective programming. Definitions of nominal and balance-sheet items contained in the firm's chart of accounts and procedures followed in maintaining such accounts as the use of the cash or accrual basis of accounting, can assist the programmer who has had no previous exposure to accounting.

Programs within this subsystem are required to update the Cost Accumulation Master File, produce error listings of invalid inputs, produce an audit trail through which all transactions can be traced by auditors and other interested parties, and to print out reports similiar to the one illustrated. A brief flowchart shows the program relationships involved in the processing and the output reports that result. In the descriptive narrative the name, number, purpose, inputs, output records and reports are identified. Each field of the output report is identified as to content and source, and such content is described headed, "Input-Output Description." To assist in keypunching, the card layouts are filled out for each activity, that is, add, delete, change, adjust, or print a record. The file master, usually on tape or disk, is shown on a prescribed layout form. The final result is the layout of the printouts tailored to the departmental user's needs.

The establishment of priorities with respect to the projects assigned computer time can be accomplished through the high-level screening committee mentioned earlier with representation from both user and development computer personnel, and with close communication with top management. Control forms described above can be of assistance to the committee in carefully choosing applications on a cost/benefit approach for new programs as well as in the review of those currently running. In this way, computer time and developmental expertise can be allocated to the projects considered most important by management. An example of such a project is the need for effective management information in the important functions of planning and controlling. Chapter 15 presents a typical information system developed to assist operating levels of management in meeting specific objectives approved by management, e.g., those described in the planning study conducted before the acquisition of a computer is justified in the eyes of management.

COST CONTROL AND BUDGET ADMINISTRATION

I. SYSTEM DESCRIPTION

This system is designed to standardize the procedures for preparing budgetary requests and to create meaningful management reports in the areas of budgetary control and cost reporting. The following will describe the Cost Control-Budget Administration system by subsystem:

A. Cost Accumulation, Budget and Expenditure Master File Update

The Cost Accumulation and Budget Expenditure Master File has been designed to accumulate and store budgetary and cost information by departments, cost centers, and accounts and to make available budgetary and cost control information at predetermined time intervals. The update subsystem will allow the following:

1. Delete a record.
2. Add a record.
3. Change a record.
4. Adjust a record.
5. Print a record.

Figure 14-7 *(includes pages 277 through page 290)*

Source: Adapted from "Cost Accounting—Its Role in a Hospital Information System," *Management Advisor,* Albert P. Ameiss and Warren A. Thompson, April, 1974, p. 33.

II. DICTIONARY OF BUDGETARY TERMS IN COMMON USAGE

The following definitions of major classes of expenditures guide in budget preparation and in the assignment of charges:

Operational Costs

Operation expenses include materials, supplies, and services used as the cost of sales to be matched against sales, arriving at gross profit on operations;

Capital improvement expenditures are those made for, and in connection with, the construction, renovation, or purchase of tangible assets of a permanent or fixed nature employed in operations with the expectation of existence for a period longer than one year or the operating cycle. Following are definitions of capital improvement accounting classes and examples of items that may be chargeable to them:

Land Acquisition

Purchase of Land

Professional Services and Advertising

Professional services performed in connection with capital improvement expenditures, such as legal, engineering, architectural or other services; surveys; advertisements for bids.

Land Improvement and Site Preparation

Improvement of land, including grading or drainage projects, bridging, damming, or impounding projects; fencing, landscaping or orchard projects; road or street construction or surfacing; labor and materials for such projects.

Building Construction

Construction of buildings; additions to existing structures; the initial installation or extension of service systems and other fixed equipment; excavation and construction of foundations; labor and materials for such projects.

Building Renovation—Major Repairs and Replacements

Renovation of existing structures such as a new roof, relocation of walls or floor modifications; renovation of service systems and other fixed equipment; labor and materials for such projects.

The definitions of capital improvement classes overlap to some degree the definitions of the operating expenditure classes. The following criteria are used in deciding whether expenditures should be budgeted as fixed assets or as current items:

If the expenditure is a major one in terms of the proposing department's spending experience and has a life of over one year it is a capital outlay.

Definitions of the bases of accounting used throughout the operation of the budgetary formulation, control and cost accounting systems are as follows:

CASH BASIS ACCOUNTING

Records expenses of the period only when paid and reports income only when cash is received.

ACCRUAL BASIS OF ACCOUNTING

Records expenses when incurred, regardless of date of payment and reflects income when earned regardless of date on which payment is received.

III. INTRODUCTORY NOTES OR COMMENTS PERTAINING TO STANDARD RULES TO BE FOLLOWED

Practical rules for distinguishing between the permanent (or balance sheet) accounts and temporary (or profit and loss) accounts within the chart of accounts are as follows:

Permanent Accounts:

Cost Center designation of the account must fall within the 600 series. In this case the total of the current year's activity is added to the beginning balance carried over from the previous year. If the account number is in the 600 series of cost centers, the account is not closed out at the end of the year.

Temporary Accounts:

All cost center accounts which do not fall within the 600 series are classified as nominal or temporary accounts which are closed out at the end of the year.

IV. SYSTEMS WRITE-UP

COST ACCUMULATION, BUDGET, AND EXPENDITURE MASTER FILE UPDATE

The programs included in the update of the above file can be segmented into the following steps:

1. Card to Tape Load and Data Check of the Master Update Activity Cards;

2. Sort of the Valid Loaded Update Activity Records;
3. Update of the Cost Accumulation, Budget, and Expenditure Master File;
4. Print of the Cost Accumulation, Budget, and Expenditure Master File;
5. Generation of report file for the preparation of the annual budgetary request;
6. Generation of report files—all other annual budgetary requests;
7. Generation of report file for the preparation of weekly, monthly, and annual budgetary control reports;
8. Generation of report file for the preparation of periodic cost reports;
9, 10, & 11. Print of the budgetary control, and cost reports, respectively.

COST ACCUMULATION, BUDGET, AND EXPENDITURE MASTER FILE UPDATE

PRINT OF THE COST ACCUMULATION, BUDGET, AND EXPENDITURE MASTER FILE LISTING

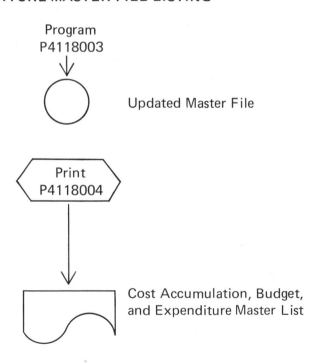

Program
P4118003

Updated Master File

Print
P4118004

Cost Accumulation, Budget, and Expenditure Master List

NAME

Cost Accumulation, Budget, and Expenditure Master File Listing.

NUMBER

P4118004

PURPOSE

The purpose of the report is to provide a listing of all master file accounts of each department and applicable descriptive information for all records on the Cost Accumulation, Budget, and Expenditure Master File.

INPUTS

    A.

        1. File Name: Updated Cost Accumulation, Budget, and Expenditure Master File.

        2. Sequence:
           Major   Department Code

        3. Exhibit Number of Master Record: 4

OUTPUT RECORDS

None

OUTPUT REPORT

    A. Cost Accumulation, Budget, and Expenditure Master File List (Exhibit Number 7)

      1. Data included in report:
      All accounts included in the Cost Accumulation, Budget, and Expenditure Master File.

      2. Report Content:

      (A) Headings:
      The page and column headings appear at the top of each page of the Cost Accumulation, Budget and Expenditure Master List.

      (B) Detail Line:

FIELD	DESCRIPTION
① Department Code	From the master record, designating the Department Identifying Number.
② Program Number	From the master record, designating the program or project number;
③ Cost Center	From the master record,

	designating the cost center or intermediate program, including balance sheet item designation.
④ Account Number	From the master record, designating the appropriate account code;
⑤ Effective Date	From the master record, indicating the date the account is to become or became authorized.

(C)   Report Totals:

| ⑥ | Total number of accounts in file. |

3. Sequence of Report: Sequential
                   Major   Department
4. Frequency of Report:
   Upon request.
5. Exhibit Number: 7

PROCESSING DESCRIPTION

The Updated Cost Accumulation, Budget and Expenditure Master File should be read into the print program, each master record formated according to the sample master file list presented in Exhibit Number 7 and the formated master record printed on the master list. On a control break the change in the first two digits of the code, the accumulated total of the number for each department should be printed in the format shown on the sample report, Exhibit Number 7. The page headings should appear at the top of each page of the report. All updated Cost Accumulation, Budget, and Expenditure Records should appear on the Master List.

DMD-DP-206

INPUT-OUTPUT DESCRIPTION

File Name: Cost Accumulation, Budget, and Expenditure Delete, Update Activity Card

Media: Card/Tape

Source of Data: _____

Processing Frequency: _____

Number: _____ Program _____

Disposition of Data: _____

Average Volume: _____

Maximum Volume: _____

A/N - Characteristic
A Alphabetic
N Numeric
A/N Alpha/Numeric
B Blank

Sign
S Signed
U Unsigned

Packing
X Blank   Packed   Unpacked

Blank
X Valid if Blank

Recognition
X Yes   Blank   No

Identification
X Yes   Blank   No

Source
A Activity
R Retained
G Program Generated
C Program Calculated

Item	Field Name	N/A	Length Tot	Dec	Last Pos.	Sign	Pack	Recog	Ident	Source	Blank	Validation/Source	Disp	Code	Error Message
1	Card Code	N	1	–	1							(Index: Sequential)			
2	Department Code	N	3	–	4			X							
3	Program Number	N	2	–	6				X						
4	Cost Center "	N	4	–	10										
5	Account "	N	5	–	15										

283

File Cost Accumulation, Budget, **Program**
Name and Expenditure – Add **Number** _____ **Media** Card/Tape
Activity Card or Record **Processing Frequency** _____
Source of Data _____ **Average Volume** _____
Disposition of Data _____ **Maximum Volume** _____

A/N - Characteristic
Alphabetic A
Numeric N
Alpha/Numeric A/N
Blank B

Sign
Signed S
Unsigned U

Packing Packed X Unpacked Blank

Blank X Valid if Blank

Recognition X Yes Blank No

Identification X Yes Blank No

Source
A Activity
R Retained
G Program Generated
C Program Calculated

Item	Field Name	A/N	Length Tot	Length Dec	Last Pos.	Sign	Pack	Recog	Ident	Source	Blank	Validation/Source	Disp	Code	Error Message
1	Card Code	N	1	–	1			X				(Index: Sequential)			
2	Department Code	N	3	–	4			X							
3	Program	N	2	–	6				X						
4	Cost Center	N	4	–	10										
5	Account Number	N	5	–	15										
6	Priority Number	N	2	–	17										
7	Asset(budget)code	N	3	–	20										
8	Description-Prog	A	25	–	45										
9	Description-Account	A	25	–	70										
10	Facility Title	A	25	–	95										
11	Asset(budget)item	A	25	–	120										

Cost Accumulation, Budget, Expenditure Status Request Program

File Name: Activity Card or Record
Media: Card/Tape Program Number: _____
Source of Data: _____ Processing Frequency: _____
Disposition of Data: _____ Average Volume: _____ Maximum Volume: _____

A/N - Characteristic
A Alphabetic
N Numeric
A/N Alpha/Numeric
B Blank

Sign
S Signed
U Unsigned

Packing
X Packed
Blank Unpacked

Blank
X Valid if Blank

Recognition
X Yes
Blank No

Identification
X Yes
Blank No

Source
A Activity
R Retained
G Program Generated
C Program Calculated

Item	Field Name	N/A	Length Tot	Length Dec	Last Pos.	Sign	Pack	Recog	Ident	Source	Blank	Validation/Source	Disp	Code	Message
1	Card Code	N	1	–	1										
2	Department Code	N	3	–	4			X							
3	Program Number	N	2	–	6				X						
4	Cost Center "	N	4	–	10										
5	Account Number	N	5	–	15										

285

File Name: Cost Accumulation, Budget and Expenditure Master Record
Program Number: _____ **Media:** Tape
Source of Data: _____ **Processing Frequency:** _____
Disposition of Data: _____ **Average Volume:** _____ **Maximum Volume:** _____

A/N - Characteristic
- A Alphabetic
- N Numeric
- A/N Alpha/Numeric
- B Blank

Sign
- S Signed
- U Unsigned

Packing
- X Packed
- Blank Unpacked

Blank
- X Valid if Blank

Recognition
- X Yes
- Blank No

Identification
- X Yes
- Blank No

Source
- A Activity
- R Retained
- G Program Generated
- C Program Calculated

Item	Field Name	A/N	Length Tot	Length Dec	Last Pos.	Sign	Pack	Recog	Ident	Source	Blank	Validation/Source	Error Disp	Error Code	Error Message
1	Department Code	N	3	–	3			X	X			From the update card	Code	2 –	– Field 2
2	Program Number	N	2	–	5							"	"	"	– Field 3
3	Cost Center "	N	4	–	9				X			"	"	"	– Field 4
4	Account Number	N	5	–	14							"	"	"	– Field 5
5	Priority Number	N	2	–	16							"	"	"	– Field 6
6	Asset (budget) code	N	3	–	19							"	"	"	– Field 7
7	Program Description	A	25	–	44							"	"	"	– Field 8
8	Account "	A	25	–	69							"	"	"	– Field 9
9	Facility Title	A	25	–	94							"	"	"	– Field 10
10	Asset (budget item description)	A	25	–	119							"	"	"	– Field 11

DATA PROCESSING DEPARTMENT
TAPE AND DISK LAYOUT*

DIVISION _____

COST ACCUMULATION BUDGET &
EXPENDITURE FILE MASTER

Delete | Dept | Program | Cost Center | Account No. | Facility No. | Asset No. | Description of Program | Description of Account

MASTER FILE (Cont.)

Asset Description | Expenditures 19X1-X2 | Expenditures 19X2-X3 | Expenditures Year (19X3 - 19X4) Annual | July | August | September | October

MASTER FILE (Cont.)

Expenditures Year (19X3 - 19X4) Current | January | February | March | April | May | June | July | August

MASTER FILE (Cont.)

Expenditures Year (19X4 - 19X5) | November | December | January | February | March | April | May | June

MASTER FILE (Cont.)

Budget (19X2-X3) | Budget (19X3-X4) | Budget Request Amount (Current) | Current Year's Budget (19X4-X5) | July | August | September | October | November

MASTER FILE (Cont.)

Current Year's Budget (December through June 19X5) | Effective Date M D Y | Update Date M D Y

*Source: "Cost Accounting-Its Role in a Hospital Information System" Ameiss and Thompson, *Management Adviser*, Mar. 1971, p. 35

287

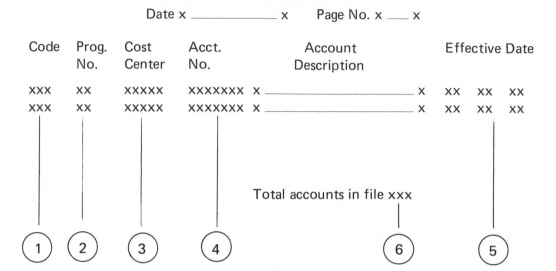

x_____x DEPARTMENT (Exhibit Number 7)

Cost Accumulation, Budget Expenditure, Master Account List

Date x _____ x   Page No. x ___ x

Code	Prog. No.	Cost Center	Acct. No.	Account Description	Effective Date
xxx	xx	xxxxx	xxxxxxx x _____ x		xx xx xx
xxx	xx	xxxxx	xxxxxxx x _____ x		xx xx xx

Total accounts in file xxx

① ② ③ ④ ⑥ ⑤

_____ DIVISION

COST ACCUMULATION AND ALLOCATION SYSTEM

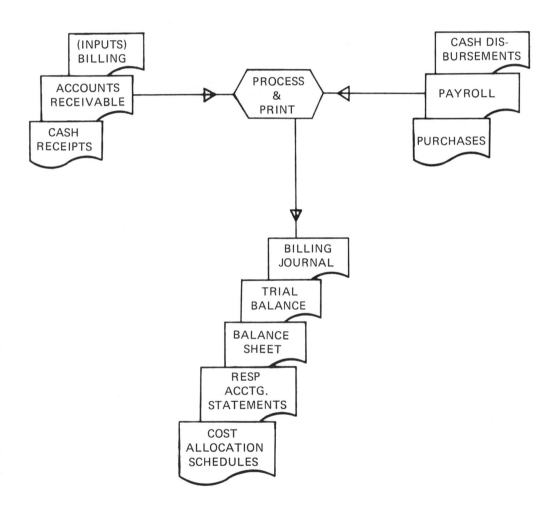

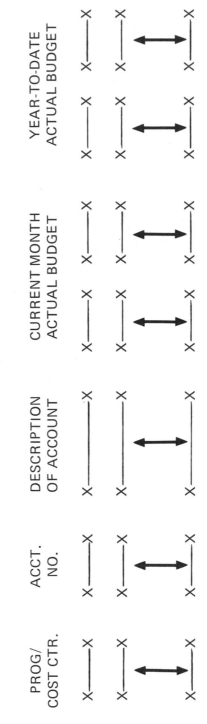

DIVISION
MANUFACTURING DEPARTMENT
EXPENDITURES FOR MONTH
BY PROGRAM/COST CENTER

PROG/ COST CTR.	ACCT. NO.	DESCRIPTION OF ACCOUNT	CURRENT MONTH ACTUAL BUDGET	YEAR-TO-DATE ACTUAL BUDGET

Source: Adapted from "Cost Accounting—Its Role in a Hospital Information System," *Management Advisor.* Ameiss and Thompson, April 1, 1974, p. 33.

290

15 Management Information Systems — Tools for Evaluation and Control

Although many definitions have been advanced for management information systems, simply defined, it is a system intended to serve management in its basic functions of organizing, planning, staffing, directing, and controlling. The requirements of such a system are detailed below and an operating system is illustrated for a manufacturing firm using job costs.

Management information systems may be broad in scope, serving many, if not all, departments or cost centers of a firm. Figure 15-1 illustrates a master information system with the following subsystems shown in the order of the data flow: (1) management planning; (2) sales order processing; (3) materials planning and control; (4) production scheduling and dispatching; and, involved in the operation of all these subsystems, (5) the financial control, from which financial data is prepared for external consumption and for internal purposes including the updating of management's planning efforts.

The financial control subsystem is examined in greater detail in Figure 15-2. Inputs from all systems are identified to such financial control subsystems and their processing is shown through the flow of transactions to the general ledger where budgetary and standard cost data is compared with actuals. Outputs are shown to contain internal reports including those relating to the status of the inventory and the identification of slow-moving and obsolete parts. Work-in-

General Data Flow in the MICRO SWITCH System

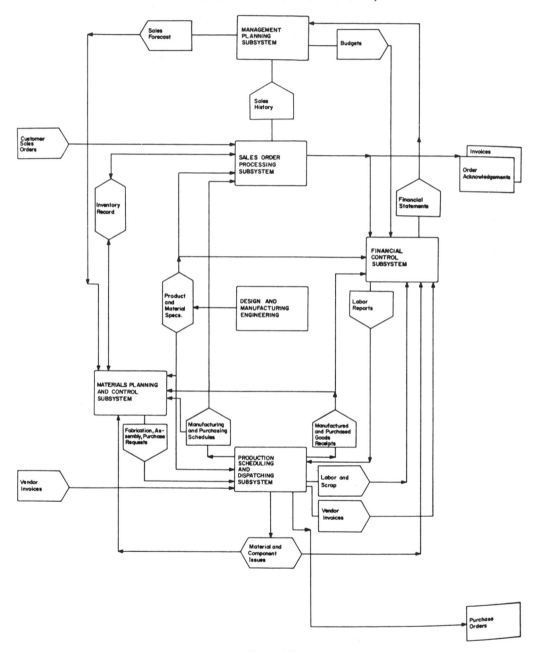

Figure 15-1

Source: "Integrated Management Information and Control System," *Application Reference Manual* Third Edition, Honeywell Inc., Wellesley Hills, Mass., 1967 p. 2-2.

Financial Control Subsystem

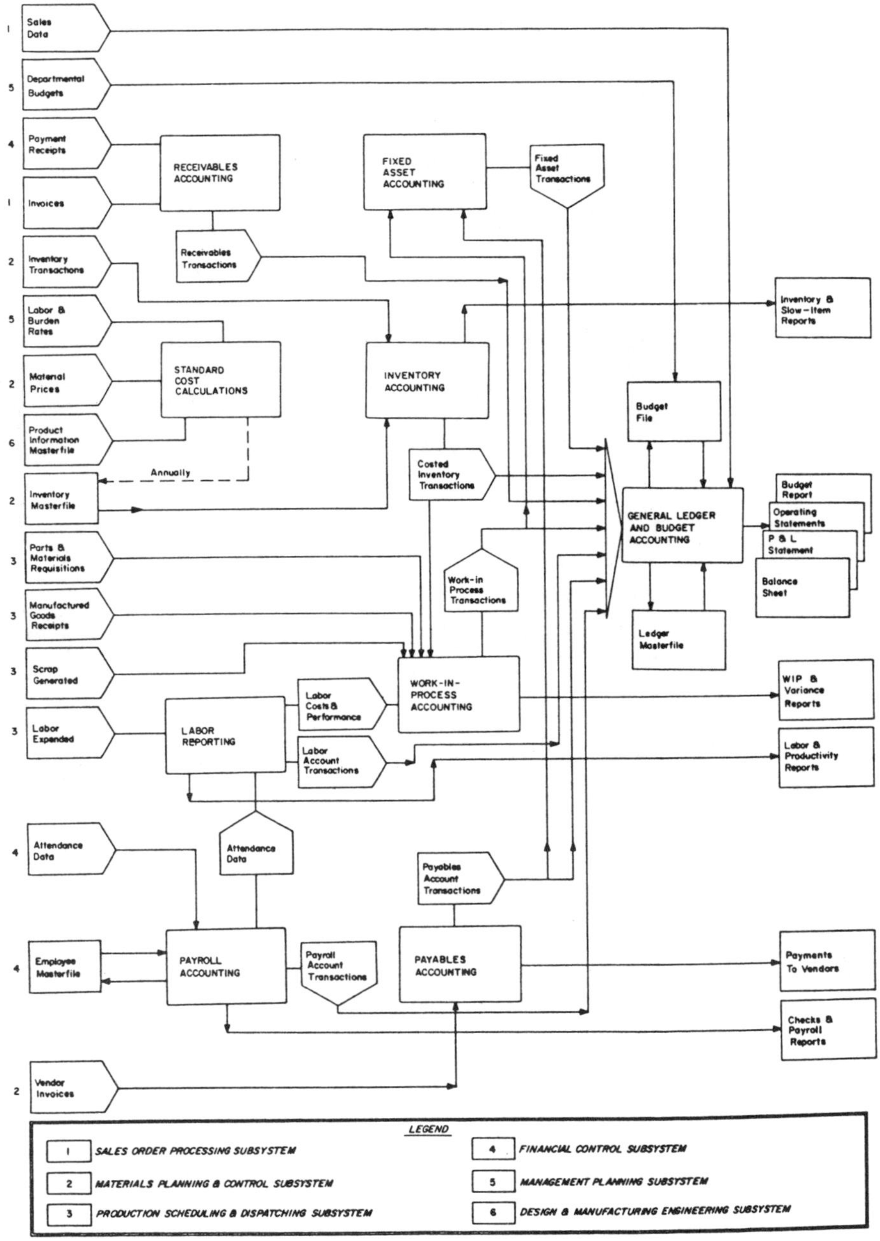

Figure 15-2

Source: "Integrated Management Information and Control System," *Application Reference Manual,* Third Edition, Honeywell Inc. Wellesley Hills, Mass., 1967, p. 6-2.

AN INSTRUMENT FOR MANAGEMENT EVALUATION

WITH RESPECT TO THE FUNCTIONS OF:

	ORGANIZING	PLANNING	STAFFING	DIRECTING	CONTROLLING
GOALS AND PURPOSES	Show lines of authority and assumption of responsibility by staff. Share responsibility of managers through delegation.	Predict future demands for service, e.g., by programs. Predict resource requirements to meet demands.	Acquire adequate staff. Maintain competent staff. Maintain satisfied staff.	Assign departmental responsibilities and program missions. Assign staff duties. Insure completion of tasks.	Assure execution of formal plans.
CRITERIA FOR GOAL ACHIEVEMENT	Existence of up-dated organization chart. Staff awareness of organizational structure. Number of personnel reporting to each manager.	Existence of formal plans, e.g., short-term operating budgets; performance standards; long-range capital expenditure budgets.	Number and duration of vacancies. Job competence. Level of staff morale and turnover rate.	Each manager's purview of his responsibilities and restrictions of delegated authority. Existence of updated position descriptions and operating procedures and job schedules. Tasks completed on time.	Extent to which operations coincide with plans, e.g., operating budgets and standards. Existence of comparative reporting system, e.g., by programs for all involved levels of supervision. Extent to which capital expenditures coincide with capital budgets.
METHODS FOR EVALUATION OF CRITERIA	Interview representative sample of employees. Interview all levels of supervision. Apply "Span of Control Principle."	Check all levels of supervision as to knowledge of existing formal plans.	Head count and check attendance records. Review employee efficiency ratings. Test morale and check for turnover.	Interview representative sample of employees. Interview all levels of supervision. Inspect schedules by tasks and compare with actual progress to date.	Compare last period's operating results with that period's budget and performance standards. Review operating reports published, as to content, distribution, promptness, and validity of measures of comparison employed.

Figure 15-3

Note: Adapted from "The Application of Internally Administered Management Audits to Hospital Programs and Cost Centers." A.P. Ameiss and Nicholas Kargas. *The National Public Accountant,* September 1974. p. 50-51.

process and variance reports, resulting from the incorporation of standard material, labor, and overhead costs are shown, as well as labor and productivity reports, and budget reports. Reports for external users, primarily the stockholders, include the operating statements, earnings statements, and the balance sheet.

Basic Management Systems Require Standards

As noted earlier, an effective information system facilitates management's performance and the exercise of the five basic managerial functions. Figure 15-3 highlights the role of timely, well-structured reports to management in the discharge of those functions. This instrument for evaluation presents the goals and purposes of each managerial function, the criteria suggested for determining whether such goals have been achieved, and methods for the evaluation of such criteria.

Organizing

In this function the hierarchy or structure of management is involved. Starting with the source of authority of the organization, (frequently the stockholders through the board of directors or its counterpart) the delegation of ultimate authority flows to the chief operating officer regardless of the title assumed, e.g. president, chairman of the board, executive officer, etc.

The chart shows the goals and purposes of organizing to include the sharing of management's responsibility with department heads or with the program managers reporting to them. While responsibility is assumed by such managers for all activities in their areas, this delegation of authority is simply that—it in no way relieves the delegator of the responsibility that he accepted in assuming the duties of his position. This ties in with the function of directing, which applies here to the assignment, instruction, and development of subordinates, discussed below.

Criteria for achieving the goals or purposes of organizing include the existence of a plan or chart of organization and an awareness of reporting levels on the part of all personnel. For effective organization, a delegation of authority must be made so that the number of personnel reporting to each manager does not exceed his capacity to direct these people efficiently.[1] Methods to evaluate such criteria may include interviews with

---

[1] For greater detail, see "The Application of Internally Administered Management Audits, etc." *Ibid.* p. 48.

a representative sample of managers and their subordinates at each level of the organization. Many criteria can be added to this, including the application of the *span of control* principle under which the number to be supervised at the highest level of management is relatively low (perhaps three to five), but broadens as lower levels are reached and the duties of the personnel become similar or, for other reasons, involve less direction from the supervisor.

Planning

This function is required at all levels of management but the amount usually varies directly with the level of management involved. The chief administrative officer, for example, devotes more time to planning than do his subordinates, who in turn will spend proportionally more of their time on directing and controlling.

The most formal plans of the firm are the by-laws adopted by the governing body. These plans should include a definition of the powers and duties of the board of directors, officers, committees, and chief administrative officer.

By-laws, rules, formal plans and control procedures are subject to approval by the board of directors. Provisions for effective participation by members of operating management are usually made so that policy can be developed to facilitate both short and long-term corporate planning and operations of an internal and external nature. Figure 15-3 shows the development of both short-term plans (usually of one-year duration, such as the operating budget) and long-term plans (capital acquisitions and construction requiring over one year) as the criteria for evaluating goal achievement.

Short-term planning or budgeting usually starts with a forecast of workload, that is, what products or services are to be offered in the coming year. (Chapter 21.) Following this, the human, physical, and financial resources are planned in the proper amount and scheduled for the amount time needed to meet the forecasted workload. Written policies or procedures for the control of the firm's cash, accounts receivable, inventories and other assets should be adopted and communicated to all levels of management.

In conducting a management audit, criteria to examine to see whether the stated goals of planning have been achieved by the firm include the determination that formal plans of the type described above *actually* exist and have been approved by the board of directors. After a review of such documents, discussions with executives at various levels of management would serve as a verification that such top-management plans are really operative. For example, the extent of communication to, and participation by, operating management in the preparation of the firm's master budget for the coming year would be indicated by the degree of importance line managers give it in their individual plans. This will reflect how important they think the budget is in their superior's mind. The budget's chances for serving as an effective instrument of planning and control depends upon its acceptance.

Staffing

Obtaining personnel with qualifications that match specific positions on the firm's organization chart is one of top management's greatest responsibilities. *Management has been defined as the art of accomplishing objectives through people.* As a result, the staffing function of management is a vital one as the organization grows or contracts.

Having recruited adequate and competent staff, the need remains to build a "back-up" through personnel development programs to insure continuity of the firm's operation. Personnel policies and practices should be reviewed periodically and the organization chart dated to indicate the most recent authorization of positions on each level. Position descriptions should be updated as necessary and incumbents or aspirants to such positions notified accordingly. Such manpower charts can become an important control instrument with respect to the additions, replacements or deletions authorized in the budget.

None of these should be made on the chart unless specifically indicated in the budget.

Complete personnel records should be kept for each employee and an established standard of content maintained for such files. If automated, personnel files can be built along the lines of a profile for each person showing a history of experience, by skills, and education, along with the results of periodic work performance evaluations, and physical and emotional checkups. The automated files can be used when there is a search for a person with certain experience or educational background. Promotions can be made from within to the greatest extent possible.

Goals of staffing include the acquisiton of adequate, competent and satisfied staff. Criteria to measure the achievement of these goals include the number and duration of vacancies, the level of morale and the amount of turnovers. A check of payroll and attendance records and reference to the organizational chart showing unfilled positions, will show vacancies— the stated criteria for insufficient staff. The criterion for the second goal of staffing, job competence, can be measured through employee efficiency ratings, along with updated position descriptions.

The third item shown under the goals and purposes of staffing is that of maintaining a *satisfied* staff. Criteria for this evaluation include the level or status of staff morale and the turnover rate and reasons for this and morale testing. By checking the turnovers through personnel and payroll records, employee morale can be evaluated.[2]

Directing

Closely allied to the function of staffing is the function of directing in which each supervisor exercises his responsibility of developing the individuals reporting to him.

Purposes of directing, shown in the chart, include clearly delegating authority and assigning duties. Awareness by the staff that they have such responsibilities represents proof or criteria that the delegation of authority has been accepted. This can be determined by interviewing a sample of such employees. Knowledge of total responsibilities, as well as restrictions, formalized in updated position descriptions, give the supervisor a proper purview of what *his* supervisors expect of him.[3]

Another goal of directing is to insure completion of tasks on time. The best criterion for checking this may come from supervisory and management personnel and the use of "milestone charts" as illustrated in the installation of a management information system at the end of this chapter. A comparison of the actual date each task was completed with the target date indicates whether the schedule is being observed or has been "slipped" and if it has slipped corrective action should be triggered.

Controlling

The functions of organization, planning, staffing, and directing are intended to facilitate but do not insure that management's objectives will be accomplished. What has been established is a blueprint that has to be followed in practice by operating managers. Controlling is the function whereby each level of management exercises the responsibility of taking

---

[2]*Ibid.*
[3]*Ibid.*

corrective action against deviations from planned performance. Controlling is a function of line supervision, acting on prompt and meaningful reports from the management information system to insure that management's goals, both financial and quantitative, are realized.

If the formal, budgetary plans of operation have been executed effectively, the goals of controlling have been met. Criteria to determine this include the extent to which operations of the period coincide with planned performance. Unfavorable variances of a manufacturing or distribution nature require corrective action at the appropriate level of the organization chart. The management information system must furnish prompt, meaningful information to show the extent to which budgeted performance has been achieved. One approach to this is responsibility accounting which furnishes department managers a comparative report of actual operations with budgeted performance.

A Management Information System Illustrated

Figure 15-4 illustrates the flow of information in a job cost environment for the purpose of meeting management's requirements in the form of reports shown at the bottom of the chart. The latter include "end item costs by responsibility groups," or departments within the Electronic Parts Division (EPD). This facilitates corporate top management's objective of establishing this division as a profit center, prior to spinning it off as a wholly-owned subsidiary. The division's costs must be identified to its end items and matched against its income which is derived primarily from the fabrication of electronic parts for corporate jobs authorized by an interdivisional work order. Other sources of income represented are sales of electronic parts to outside customers through sales orders, and reimbursement for factory orders, engineering study authorizations and other research and development efforts authorized by the corporation.

Because EPD's work on the corporation's jobs are to be accumulated with both the latter's and the division's jobs, a conversion and distribution table is used permitting the corporation to pick up EPD's actual material, labor, and overhead costs on corporate jobs. EPD not only accumulates such costs but, for internal purposes only, negotiates a price with the corporation based on estimates furnished from EPD operational departments in responding to a "Request for Estimate" from EPD's Contract Administration and Estimating Departments. The result is a series of estimates and milestone charts, coordinated into a budget and schedule

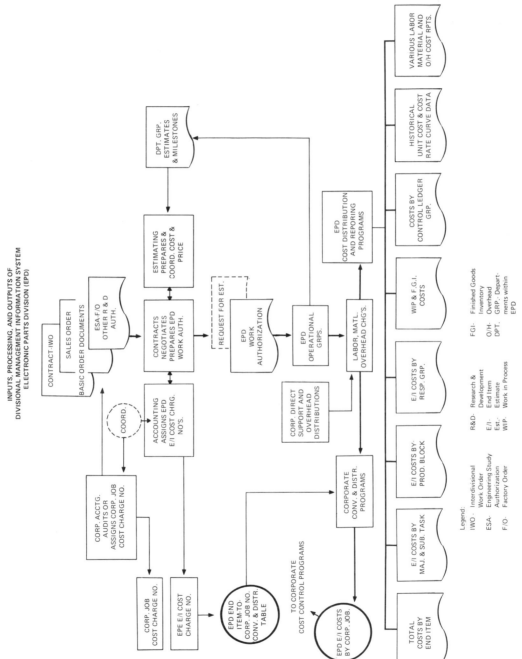

INPUTS, PROCESSING, AND OUTPUTS OF
DIVISIONAL MANAGEMENT INFORMATION SYSTEM
ELECTRONIC PARTS DIVISION (EPD)

Legend:

IWO - Interdivisional
Work Order
ESA- Engineering Study
Authorization
F/O- Factory Order

R&D- Research &
Development
E/I- End Item
Est.- Estimate
WIP- Work in Process

FGI- Finished Goods
Inventory
O/H- Overhead
DPT. GRP.- Depart-
ments within
EPD

Figure 15-4

for completion of all tasks on each EPD job. As a result, actual costs can be compared with budgeted performance by EPD's end items and responsible departments. In addition, EPD obtains the capability of determining earnings in accordance with the "percent of completion" method for products developed under contract while using the transactional approach to recognize income for items sold from finished goods inventory. In the latter case, the cost of sales will be charged based on the average unit cost of the end item sold.

Development Schedule

Figure 15-5 projects the number of man-weeks required for the installation of the cost accumulation system. Functions planned start with fact gathering (requiring 1.5 man-weeks of supervisory effort, 3 weeks of a senior analyst and 3.5 weeks of one analyst); problem definition; preliminary systems design; detail systems design; programming; forms design; procedures writing; conversion of files; and finally, implementation. The number of man-weeks for each function by each of the three types of effort is shown sequentially over the approximately 42 weeks required for the installation. By pricing the 88.5 man-weeks of EPD system effort, the cost can be budgeted and compared with actuals for control purposes as the installation progresses.

Chart of Accounts for Responsibility Accounting

Facilitating the installation of the system is the adoption of a chart of accounts shown in part in Figure 15-6. The first field identifies the division; the second, the location of the EPD facility; the third, the departmental group, Engineering, Manufacturing, etc.; and the fourth, the specific department such as "Manufacturing, Production," and "Manufacturing Controls" within the manufacturing group. Major task categories occupy the 6th position of the EPD charge number (Figure 15-7) permitting the printout of end-item costs, and major and sub-tasks as shown in Figure 15-4. The use of the charge number permits the isolation of end-item costs by production block for bidding purposes, unit costs and cost-rate curve data for both pricing and control purposes.

Examples of the operation of the EPD charge number and its conversion to the corporate cost accounts are suggested in Figure 15-8. Two documents from the corporation to EPD (Interdivisional Work Orders 066 and 764) illustrate the use of the new chart of accounts. Also

COST ACCUMULATION SYSTEM
DEVELOPMENT SCHEDULE

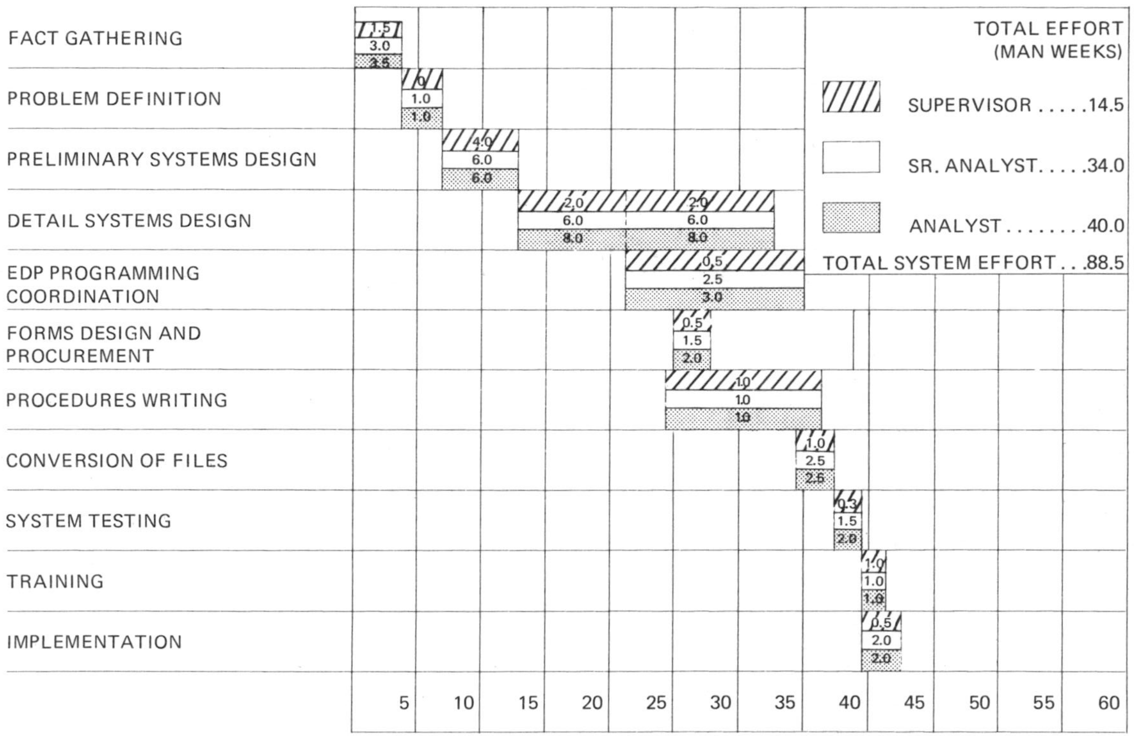

TOTAL EFFORT
(MAN WEEKS)

SUPERVISOR 14.5

SR. ANALYST. 34.0

ANALYST 40.0

TOTAL SYSTEM EFFORT . . .88.5

FACT GATHERING
1.5
3.0
3.5

PROBLEM DEFINITION
.5
1.0
1.0

PRELIMINARY SYSTEMS DESIGN
4.0
6.0
6.0

DETAIL SYSTEMS DESIGN
2.0
6.0
8.0
2.0
6.0
8.0

EDP PROGRAMMING COORDINATION
0.5
2.5
3.0

FORMS DESIGN AND PROCUREMENT
0.5
1.5
2.0

PROCEDURES WRITING
1.0
1.0
1.0
1.0

CONVERSION OF FILES
1.0
2.5
2.5

SYSTEM TESTING
0.5
1.5
2.0

TRAINING
1.0
1.0
1.0

IMPLEMENTATION
0.5
2.0
2.0

5   10   15   20   25   30   35   40   45   50   55   60

ASSUMPTION

SYSTEMS PERSONNEL
ANALYST   100%   AS
SR. ANALYST   80%   SHOWN
SUPERVISOR   35%   ABOVE

PROCEDURES PERSONNEL
ANALYST   100%
(FROM WEEK 24-36)

CORPORATE
PROGRAMMING PERSONNEL
PROGRAMMER 100% (FROM WEEK 21-39)
SR. PROGRAMMER 100% (FROM WEEK 25-39)

Figure 15-5

indicated is the translation to the corporate charge numbers for EPD effort on corporate jobs.

The interdivisional work orders (IWO 066 and IWO 764) indicate the items of effort to be accomplished by EPD by identifying the first column of the charge number as "L." The second field shows the end item, or product, which EPD is to deliver. Major task categories are referred to in the next column of the charge number, such as "A," Design and Development or "M," Manufacturing Engineering, Tooling and Production Test Equipment. Figure 15-7 identifies such major task categories on hardware contracts and describes the work to be charged to each. Further detail is given in the next field under sub-task, primarily for the purpose of bidding on future jobs. Under "Responsibility Group" reference is made to major corporate departments, such as Engineering (1), and Manufacturing (2).

Analyzing the Advantages of EPD's Management Information System

In this chapter the functions of management were identified and the impact of the management information system on such functions demonstrated. Planning, organizing, staffing, directing, and controlling are functions facilitated by the adoption of a chart of accounts as illustrated on pages 304 and 305. The various columns and fields of the charge number provide for cost accumulation by division, departmental groups, departments or programs within such homogenous groups, as well as by end items and major tasks within the production effort. As a result, responsibility accounting is accommodated as is profit-center profitability, demonstrated in the case of the Electronic Parts Division. Advantages accruing from such a management information system include the capability of corporate expansion and diversification by spinning off promising divisions as in the EPD example in this chapter. Such corporate expansion through internal growth may be superior to external means, such as business combinations during certain phases of the business cycle when a firm finds its stock prices depressed. This can make the timing of a stock exchange unattractive to the stockholders of the firm sought.

In addition, the exposure of the division's management to responsibility accounting and profit-center status simulates the competitive environment awaiting its spin-off and operation as a wholly-owned subsidiary. By providing a method of conversion and distribution of charges with the assistance of the computer, the corporation's accounts and cost control programs are not affected by divisional information system installations of

EPD RESPONSIBILITY NO.'S

Organization Titles

	RESP NO.			
	$M_A{}_J.$ $D_I{}_V$	$S_U{}_B.$ $D_I{}_V.$	$D_E{}_{P_T.}$ $G_{R_P.}$	$D_E{}_{P}{}_T.$
	A_N	A_N	N	N
General Manager	L	O	O	O
Manager, Administration	L	1	1	O
Manager, Contract Administration	L	1	1	1
Manager, Material	L	1	1	2
Controller	L	1	1	3
Personnel	L	1	1	4
Manager, Sales	L	1	2	O
Manager, Proposal Coordination	L	1	2	1
Manager, Program Coordination	L	1	2	2
Manager, Advertising Promotion	L	1	2	3
Manager, Corporate Interface Liaison	L	1	2	4
Field Sales Offices	L	1	2	5
Senior Sales Representative	L	1	2	6
Manager, Field Service Spare Parts	L	1	2	7
Manager, Manufacturing	L	1	3	O
Manager, Manufacturing Engineering	L	1	3	1
Superintendent, Production	L	1	3	2
Manager, Manufacturing Controls	L	1	3	3
Material Requirements and Stores	L	1	3	4
Manager, Advanced Manufacturing Research and Value Control	L	1	4	O
Manager, Value Control	L	1	4	1
Supervisor, Capital Assets and Facilities	L	1	4	2
Manager, Materials and Advance Process Engineering	L	1	4	3
Manager, Reliability and Quality Control	L	1	5	O
Manager, Quality Engineering	L	1	5	1
Manager, Reliability	L	1	5	2
Manager, Quality Control	L	1	5	3

↑
└─(1) identifies EPD

Figure 15-6

Manager, Research Advanced Systems and Planning	L	1	6	O
Manager, Research and Advanced Systems	L	1	6	1
Manager, Planning	L	1	6	2
Manager, Engineering	L	1	7	O
Manager, Guidance and Control	L	1	7	1
Manager, Space Communications	L	1	7	2
Manager, Aerospace Ground Equipment	L	1	7	3
Manager, Mechanical Engineering and Services	L	1	7	4
Manager, Design Compliance	L	1	7	5

Figure 15-6 *(continued)*

the type illustrated in this chapter. In addition, the corporation finds an excellent training technique for developing future managers and backup for present corporate executives by delegating authority to such divisional managers earlier in their careers than might be the case if such diversification or internal expansion were not attempted. The result can be an effective program of executive development in organizing, planning, staffing, directing, and controlling involving many of the kinds of decision-making required of senior corporate officers, assisted by a management information system tailored to meet the firm's most important objectives.

HARDWARE CONTRACTS

MAJOR TASK CATEGORIES

6th Position of EPD Cost Charge Number

A—DESIGN AND DEVELOPMENT—Electronic, electrical and mechanical design, bread board, experimental, and prototype (preproduction) model fabrication, and fabrication of other non-deliverable units other than developmental and service test models.

Figure 15-7

D—NON-DELIVERABLE UNIT(S)—DEVELOPMENTAL AND SERVICE TEST MODEL
Manufacturing, liaison, etc., required to produce the following:
a. Developmental Model-a model designed to meet performance requirements of the specification or established technical requirements for production equipment.
b. Service Test Model-a model to be used for test under service conditions for evaluation of suitability and conformance.

E—QUALIFICATION TESTING AND TEST REPORTING—Developmental and service model testing and test reporting effort.

G—MISCELLANEOUS OTHER TESTING—Miscellaneous testing not associated with Task E above e.g., reliability and other peculiar tests as specified in contract documents.

J—DRAWINGS AND DATA—Reproduction of drawings and preparation of data required by contract other than test reports prepared in conjunction with Tasks E and G above.

M—MANUFACTURING ENGINEERING, TOOLING AND PRODUCTION TEST EQUIP-MENT—Manufacturing fabrication and assembly planning, tooling design and fabrication, production test equipment design and fabrication.

P—MANUALS AND HANDBOOKS—Preparation and publication of fields operations and maintenance instruction manuals not otherwise provided for in Task J above.

S—REPAIR—Repair of items returned from the customer; includes manufacturing effort associated with the repair and special tools or test equipment which may be required.

T—TERMINATIONS—Labor, material and overhead associated with terminated or reduced contract requirement.

2—PRODUCTION—Manufacturing, direct inspection, sampling tests, and predelivery acceptance tests (PDA) required to produce deliverable equipment end items.

3—REWORK/MODIFICATION—Manufacturing, direct inspection, sampling tests, and predelivery acceptance tests (PDA) required to rework or modify end items returned from the customer or undelivered end items which must be reworked or modified due to an approved type change (customer approved design and scope change).

Figure 15-7 *(continued)*

EXAMPLE—EPD-TO-CORPORATE COST CHARGE DISTRIBUTION

IWO 066

EPD CHARGE NUMBER

Item		Div. Cde.	End Item	Maj. Task	Sub. Task	Resp. Grp.	Ultimate Corporate Charge
1.	Engineering Design and Development Cost Code 25-ZG-102	L	AB52	A	1-5	1	28-10-102
2.	Sets Design Approval Test Reports, incl. Testing Cost Code 25-XG-102	L	AB52	E	1	1	28-06-102
3.	1 PC. PN. XXXXXXX to be used in performance of item 2. Cost Code 25-XG-102	L	AB52	D	1	1	28-06-102
4.	Drawing and Data Cost Code 25-ZG-050	L	AB52	J	1	1	28-10-050
5.	Special Tooling and Test Equipment Cost Code 25-9C-102	L	AB52	M	A-B	2	28-23-102
6.	Production 7 Units Cost Code 2PC 25-KC-870 5PC 25-KG-870					2	22-07-870 28-07-870

IWO 764

Item		Div. Cde.	End Item	Maj. Task	Sub. Task	Resp. Grp.	Ultimate Corporate Charge
1.	Production 9 units Cost Code 2 PC 30-Y4-289 7 PC 30-Q4-199	L	AB52	2	1	2	34-08-289 34-07-199

*Production quantities are the basis for distribution from EPD to corporate job cost charge numbers.

Figure 15-8

PART III

Auditing Standards and Procedures

Chapter 16 enumerates the guidelines that influence and direct the work of the auditor—an area of increasing significance as more and more firms and individual practitioners are being held accountable for the scope and quality of their professional services. The profession's Rules of Conduct and related Interpretations are presented on pages 311-324 making them close at hand in this book as the practicing accountant wrestles with the problems of technical and promotional standards, operating practices, and the sensitive areas of relations with clients, the public, and fellow practitioners. The auditing standards guiding the quality of the independent auditor's work are presented and discussed on pages 324-329.

Chapter 17 presents and reviews some major aspects of the audit and deals with the day-to-day problems encountered in developing and refining audit procedures. It outlines the auditor's objectives in developing appropriate audit procedures for the examination of a client's financial statements. From there the discussion moves into the nature and timing of various procedures, a subject of vital importance for an efficient and alert examination. The chapter concludes with sections on the incorporation of statistical sampling techniques and the effect of the computer on audit procedures.

As companies become more complex and diverse in their operations, internal control is more important than ever before. Thus, Chapter 18 is devoted entirely to this important area. The role and responsibilities of the auditor for the system of internal control, always a controversial subject, is discussed on pages 350-352. The basic elements of internal control and the nature and extent of the auditor's study and review of the client's control procedures are outlined on pages 351-357. Finally, guidelines for summarizing findings and recommendations in an internal control report to the client and other interested parties are presented on pages 357-361.

Chapter 19 will be helpful especially to the auditor seeking guidelines on how to organize and develop audit workpapers. The chapter begins with a review of the all-important objectives and essential features of workpapers, then offers suggestions for their preparation. Included in this outline are illustrations of standard letters and other workpapers designed to reduce the time and effort spent by staff assistants in performing audit procedures. The chapter continues with a concise discussion on the classification and contents of the audit workpapers developed during the examination. The final section of the chapter offers suggestions on indexing and retention of workpapers.

Chapter 20 deals with the auditor's report. Suggested language for the standard short-form opinion is presented on page 380, followed by examples of variations in the opinion when special situations require the inclusion of a "middle" paragraph in addition to the usual "scope" and "opinion" paragraphs. The chapter also includes the reporting requirements for long-form reports and special reports for cash basis accounting systems, nonprofit organizations, and other engagements requiring reports in which the standard short-form report is not acceptable. A final section outlines the auditor's reporting responsibilities for subsequent events.

16   Professional Ethics and Auditing Standards

A client's trust and confidence are two essential ingredients to the acceptance of, and success in, any profession. Members of the public accounting profession, however, cannot be satisfied with this. They must have the confidence not only of their clients but also of investors, creditors, and other outside parties who rely upon their reports. These interested third parties usually are not acquainted personally with the individual practitioner or firm, so their acceptance of the audit report must be built upon respect for, and confidence in, the profession as a whole.

PROFESSIONAL ETHICS

The present high regard for the independent accountant in the financial community is evidence that, with a few exceptions, he has lived up to the respect and confidence accorded the profession. Certainly a significant factor in this has been the development of a Code of Professional Ethics under the leadership of the American Institute of Certified Public Accountants. Although the Code, which was issued as a supplement to the disciplinary clauses of the AICPA's By-Laws, is enforceable by the Institute only with respect to its membership, the principles involved are applicable to the profession generally. As the Institute continues to amend the Code with a view of the auditor's changing responsibilities and obligations, its Division of Professional Ethics has issued numbered Interpretations which serve to interpret and/or clarify certain of the rules and their application.

The Rules of Conduct

The Rules of Conduct consist of fifteen rules[1] of professional conduct. In summary, the individual practitioner is charged with an obligation to:

1. Exhibit independence in both thought and action.
2. Maintain strict confidence in regards to the affairs of his clients.
3. Continue to improve his professional skills and adhere to the generally accepted auditing standards in the performance of his services, and
4. Maintain the dignity and honor of the profession and its high standards of professional conduct.

The fifteen rules of professional conduct are divided into five major groups dealing with the most important aspects of the practitioner's responsibilities:

1. Independence, integrity, and objectivity (Rules 101 and 102).
2. Competence and technical standards (Rules 201 to 204).
3. Responsibilities to clients (Rules 301 and 302).
4. Responsibilities to colleagues (Rules 401 and 402).
5. Other responsibilities and practices (Rules 501 to 505).

Numbered Interpretations

The Rules of Conduct have been supplemented by twenty-five Interpretations[2] intended to help interpret and/or clarify certain aspects of the rules of professional conduct. The Rules and Interpretations, including a description of their subject matter, are outlined in the remaining paragraphs of this section. In order to relate the various Interpretations to the Rules, the Interpretations have been presented with the appropriate Rule to which they apply.

Independence, Integrity and Objectivity

RULE 101—INDEPENDENCE. A member or a firm of which he is a partner or shareholder shall not express an opinion on financial statements of an enterprise unless he and his firm are independent with respect to such enterprise. Independence will be considered to be impaired if, for example:

A. During the period of his professional engagement, or at the time of expressing his opinion, he or his firm

  1. Had or was committed to acquire any direct or material indirect financial interest in the enterprise; or

  2. Had any joint closely held business investment with the enterprise or any officer, director or principal stockholder thereof which was material in relation to his or his firm's net worth; or

  3. Had any loan to or from the enterprise or any officer, director or principal stockholder thereof. This latter proscription does not apply to the following loans from a financial institution when made under normal lending procedures, terms and requirements:

     (a) Loans obtained by a member or his firm which are not material in relation to the net worth of such borrower.

     (b) Home mortgages.

     (c) Other secured loans, except loans guaranteed by a member's firm which are otherwise unsecured.

B. During the period covered by the financial statements, during the period of the professional engagement or at the time of expressing an opinion, he or his firm

  1. Was connected with the enterprise as a promoter, underwriter or voting trustee, a director or officer or in any capacity equivalent to that of a member of management or of an employee; or

  2. Was a trustee of any trust or executor or administrator of any estate if such trust or estate had a direct or material indirect financial interest in the enterprise; or was a trustee for any pension or profit-sharing trust of the enterprise.

The above examples are not intended to be all-inclusive.

Interpretation 101-1—Directorships. Members are often asked to lend the prestige of their name as a director of a charitable, religious, civic or other similar type of nonprofit organization whose board is large and representative of the community's leadership. An auditor who permits his name to be used in this manner would not be considered lacking in independence under Rule 101 so long as he does not perform or give advice on management functions, and the board itself is sufficiently large that a third party would conclude that his membership was honorary.

Interpretation 101-2—Retired partners and firm independence. A retired partner having a relationship of a type specified in Rule 101 with a client of his former firm would not be considered as impairing the firm's independence with respect to the client provided that he is no longer active in the firm, that the fees received from such client do not have a material effect on his retirement benefits, and that he is not held out as being associated with his former partnership.

Interpretation 101-3—Accounting services. Members in public practice are sometimes asked to provide manual or automated bookkeeping or data processing services to clients who are of insufficient size to employ an adequate internal accounting staff. Computer systems design and programming assistance are also rendered by members either in conjunction with data processing services or as a separate engagement. Members who perform such services and who are engaged in the practice of public accounting are subject to the bylaws and Rules of Conduct.

On occasion members also rent "block time" on their computers to their clients but are not involved in the processing of transactions or maintaining the client's accounting records. In such cases the sale of block time constitutes a business rather than a professional relationship, and must be considered together with all other relationships between the member and his client to determine if their aggregate impact is such as to impair the member's independence.

When a member performs manual or automated bookkeeping services, concern may arise whether the performance of such services would impair his audit independence—that the performance of such basic accounting services would cause his audit to be lacking in a review of mechanical accuracy or that the accounting judgments made by him in recording transactions may somehow be less reliable than if made by him in connection with the subsequent audit.

Members are skilled in, and well-accustomed to, applying techniques to control mechanical accuracy, and the performance of the record-keeping function should have no effect on application of such techniques. With regard to accounting judgments, if third parties have confidence in a member's judgment in performing an audit, it is difficult to contend that they would have less confidence where the same judgment is applied in the process of preparing the underlying accounting records.

Nevertheless, a member performing accounting services for an audit client must meet the following requirements to retain the appearance that he is not virtually an employee and therefore lacking in independence in the eyes of a reasonable observer.

1. The CPA must not have any relationship or combination of relationships with the client or any conflict of interest which would impair his integrity and objectivity.

2. The client must accept the responsibility for the financial statements as his own. A small client may not have anyone in his employ to maintain accounting records and may rely on the CPA for this purpose. Nevertheless, the client must be sufficiently knowledgeable of the enterprise's activities and financial condition and the applicable accounting principles so that he can reasonably accept such responsibility, including, specifically, fairness of valuation and presentation and adequacy of disclosure. When necessary, the CPA must discuss accounting matters with the client to be sure that the client has the required degree of understanding.

3. The CPA must not assume the role of employee or of management conducting the operations of an enterprise. For example, the CPA shall not consummate transactions, have custody of assets or exercise authority on behalf of the client. The client must prepare the source documents on all transactions in sufficient detail to identify clearly the nature and amount of such transactions and maintain an accounting control over data processed by the CPA such as control totals and document counts. The CPA should not make changes in such basic data without the concurrence of the client.

4. The CPA, in making an examination of financial statements prepared from books and records which he has maintained completely or in part, must conform to generally accepted auditing standards. The fact that he has processed or maintained certain records does not eliminate the need to make sufficient audit tests.

When a client's securities become subject to regulation by the Securities and Exchange Commission or other federal or state regulatory body, responsibility for maintenance of the accounting records, including accounting classification decisions, must be assumed by accounting personnel employed by the client. The assumption of this responsibility must commence with the first fiscal year after which the client's securities qualify for such regulation.

RULE 102—INTEGRITY AND OBJECTIVITY. A member shall not knowingly misrepresent facts, and when engaged in the practice of public accounting, including the rendering of tax and management advisory services, shall not subordinate his judgment to others. In tax practice, a member may resolve doubt in favor of his client as long as there is reasonable support for his position.

Competence and Technical Standards

RULE 201—COMPETENCE. A member shall not undertake any engagement which he or his firm cannot reasonably expect to complete with professional competence.

Interpretation 201-1—Competence. A member who accepts a professional engagement implies that he has the necessary competence to complete the engagement according to professional standards, applying his knowledge and skill with reasonable care and diligence, but he does not assume a responsibility for infallibility of knowledge or judgment.

Competence in the practice of public accounting involves both the technical qualifications of the member and his staff and his ability to supervise and evaluate the quality of the work performed. Competence relates both to knowledge of the profession's standards, techniques and the technical subject matter involved, and to the capability to exercise sound judgment in applying such knowledge to each engagement.

The member may have the knowledge required to complete an engagement professionally before undertaking it. In many cases, however, additional research or consultation with others may be necessary during the course of the engagement. This does not ordinarily represent a lack of competence, but rather is a normal part of the professional conduct of an engagement.

However, if a CPA is unable to gain sufficient competence through these means, he should suggest, in fairness to his client and the public, the engagement of someone competent to perform the needed service, either independently or as an associate.

RULE 202—AUDITING STANDARDS. A member shall not permit his name to be associated with financial statements in such a manner as to imply that he is acting as an independent public accountant unless he has complied with the applicable generally accepted auditing standards promulgated by the Institute. Statements on Auditing Procedure issued by the Institute's committee on auditing procedure are, for purposes of this rule, considered to be interpretations of the generally accepted auditing standards, and departures from such statements must be justified by those who do not follow them.

RULE 203—ACCOUNTING PRINCIPLES. A member shall not express an opinion that financial statements are presented in conformity with generally accepted accounting principles if such statements contain any departure from an accounting principle promulgated by the body designated by Council to establish such principles which has a material effect on the statements taken as a whole, unless the member can demonstrate that due to unusual circumstances the financial statements would otherwise have been misleading. In such cases his report must describe the departure, the approximate effects thereof, if practicable, and the reasons why compliance with the principle would result in a misleading statement. *Interpretation 203-1—Departures from established accounting principles.* Rule 203 was adopted to require compliance with accounting principles promulgated by the body designated by Council to establish such principles. There is a strong presumption that adherence to officially established accounting principles would in nearly all instances result in financial statements that are not misleading.

However, in the establishment of accounting principles it is difficult to anticipate all of the circumstances to which such principles might be applied. The rule therefore recognizes that upon occasion there may be unusual circumstances where the literal application of pronouncements on accounting principles would have the effect of rendering financial statements misleading. In such cases, the proper accounting treatment is that which will render the financial statements not misleading.

The question of what constitutes unusual circumstances as referred to in Rule 203 is a matter of professional judgment involving the ability to support the position that adherence to a promulgated principle would be regarded generally by reasonable men as producing a misleading result.

RULE 204—FORECASTS. A member shall not permit his name to be used in conjunction with any forecast of future transactions in a manner which may lead to the belief that the member vouches for the achievability of the forecast.

Interpretation 204-1—Forecasts. Rule 204 does not prohibit a member from preparing, or assisting a client in the preparation of forecasts of the results of future transactions. When a member's name is associated with such forecasts, there shall be the presumption that such data may be used by parties other than the client. Therefore, full disclosure must be made of the sources of the information used and the major assumptions made in the preparation of the statements and analyses, the character of the work performed by the member, and the degree of the responsibility he is taking.

Responsibilities to Clients

RULE 301—CONFIDENTIAL CLIENT INFORMATION. A member shall not disclose any confidential information obtained in the course of a professional engagement except with the consent of the client.

This rule shall not be construed (a) to relieve a member of his obligation under Rules 202 and 203, (b) to affect in any way his compliance with a validly issued subpoena or summons enforceable by order of a court, (c) to prohibit review of a member's professional practices as a part of voluntary quality review under Institute authorization or (d) to preclude a member from responding to any inquiry made by the ethics division or Trial Board of the Institute, by a duly constituted investigative or disciplinary body of a state CPA society, or under state statutes.

Interpretation 301-1—Confidential information and technical standards. The prohibition against disclosure of confidential information obtained in the course of a professional engagement does not apply to disclosure of such information when required to properly discharge the member's responsibility according to the profession's standards.

RULE 302—CONTINGENT FEES. Professional services shall not be offered or rendered under an arrangement whereby no fee will be charged unless a specified finding or result is attained, or where the fee is otherwise contingent upon the findings or results of such services. However, a member's fees may vary depending, for example, on the complexity of the service rendered.

Fees are not regarded as being contingent if fixed by courts or other public authorities or, in tax matters, if determined based on the results of judicial proceedings or the findings of governmental agencies.

Responsibilities to Colleagues

RULE 401—ENCROACHMENT. A member shall not endeavor to provide a person or entity with a professional service which is currently provided by another public accountant except:

1. He may respond to a request for a proposal to render services and may furnish service to those who request it. However, if an audit client of another independent public accountant requests a member to provide professional advice on accounting or auditing matters in connection with an expression of opinion on financial statements, the member must first consult with the other accountant to ascertain that the member is aware of all the available relevant facts.
2. Where a member is required to express an opinion on combined or consolidated financial statements which include a subsidiary, branch or other component audited by another independent

public accountant, he may insist on auditing any such component which in his judgment is necessary to warrant the expression of his opinion.

A member who receives an engagement for services by referral from another public accountant shall not accept the client's request to extend his service beyond the specific engagement without first notifying the referring accountant, nor shall he seek to obtain any additional engagement from the client.

Interpretation 401-1—Relations with clients also served by other public accountants. The unsolicited sending to clients of firm literature or invitations to seminars which cover services that are currently being rendered to the client by another public accountant is considered a violation of Rule 401.

Interpretation 401-2—Reliance on work of others. Rule 401-2 makes clear that it is not improper for a member expressing his opinion on combined or consolidated financial statements to insist on auditing such components as in his judgment are necessary to warrant the expression of his opinion. However, the auditor's exercise of judgment in this regard is subject to review.

RULE 402—OFFERS OF EMPLOYMENT. A member in public practice shall not make a direct or indirect offer of employment to an employee of another public accountant on his own behalf or that of his client without first informing such accountant. This rule shall not apply if the employee of his own initiative or in response to a public advertisement applies for employment.

Other Responsibilities and Practices

RULE 501—ACTS DISCREDITABLE. A member shall not commit an act discreditable to the profession.

RULE 502—SOLICITATION AND ADVERTISING. A member shall not seek to obtain clients by solicitation. Advertising is a form of solicitation and is prohibited.

Interpretation 502-1—Announcements. Publication in a newspaper, magazine or similar medium of an announcement or what is technically known as a "card" is prohibited. Also prohibited is the issuance of a press release regarding firm mergers, opening of new offices, change of address or admission of new partners.

Announcements of such changes may be mailed to clients and individuals with whom professional contacts are maintained, such as lawyers and bankers. Such announcements should be dignified and should not refer to fields of specialization.

Interpretation 502-2—Office premises. Listing of the firm name in lobby directories of office buildings and on entrance doors solely for the purpose of enabling interested parties to locate an office is permissible. The listing should be in good taste and modest in size.

The indication of a specialty such as "income tax" in such listing constitutes advertising.

Interpretation 502-3—Directories: telephone, classified and trade association. A listing in a telephone, trade association, membership or other classified directory shall not:

1. Appear in a box or other form of display, or in a type or style which differentiates it from other listings in the same directory.
2. Appear in more than one place in the same classified directory.
3. Appear under a heading other than "Certified Public Accountant" or "Public Accountant" where the directory is classified by type of business occupation or service.
4. Be included in the yellow pages or business section of a telephone directory unless the member maintains a bona fide office in the geographic area covered. Determination of what constitutes an "area" shall be made by referring to the positions taken by state CPA societies in the light of local conditions.

Such listing may:

1. Include the firm name, partners' names, professional title (CPA), address and telephone number.
2. Be included under both the geographical and alphabetical section where the directory includes such sections.

Interpretation 502-4—Business stationery. A member's stationery should be in keeping with the dignity of the profession and not list any specialty.

The stationery may include the firm name, address and telephone number, names of partners, names of deceased partners and their years of service, names of professional staff when preceded by a line to separate them from the partners, and cities in which other offices and correspondents or associates are located. Membership in the Institute or state CPA society or associated group of CPA firms whose name does not indicate a specialty may also be shown. In the case of multi-office firms, it is suggested that the words "offices in other principal cities" (or other appropriate wording) be used instead of a full list of offices. Also, it is preferable to list only the names of partners resident in the office for which the stationery is used.

Interpretation 502-5—Business cards. Business cards may be used by partners, sole practitioners and staff members. They should be in good taste and should be limited to the name of the person presenting the card, his firm name, address and telephone number(s), the words "Certified Public Accountant(s)," or "CPA" and such words as "partner," "manager" or "consultant" but without any specialty designation.

Members not in the practice of public accounting may use the title "Certified Public Accountant" or "CPA" but shall not do so when engaged in sales promotion, selling or similar activities.

Interpretation 502-6—Help wanted advertisements. A member shall not include his name in help-wanted or situations-wanted display advertising on his own behalf or that of others in any publication. In display advertising, the use of a telephone number, address, or newspaper box number is permissible.

In classified advertisements other than display, the member's name should not appear in boldface type, capital letters or in any other manner which tends to distinguish the name from the body of the advertisement.

Interpretation 502-7—Firm publications. Newsletters, bulletins, house organs, recruiting brochures and other firm literature on accounting and related business subjects prepared and distributed by a firm for the information of its staff and clients serve a useful purpose. The distribution of such material outside the firm must be properly controlled and should be restricted to clients and individuals with whom professional contacts are maintained, such as lawyers and bankers. Copies may also be supplied to job applicants, to students considering employment interviews, to nonclients who specifically request them and to educational institutions.

If requests for multiple copies are received and granted, the member and his firm are responsible for any distribution by the party to whom they are issued.

Interpretation 502-8—Newsletters and publications prepared by others. A member shall not permit newsletters, tax booklets or similar publications to be imprinted with his firm's name if they have not been prepared by his firm.

Interpretation 502-9—Responsibility for publisher's promotional efforts. It is the responsibility of a member to see that the publisher or others who promote distribution of his writing, observe the boundaries of professional dignity and make no claims that are not truthful and in good taste. The promotion may indicate the author's background including, for example, his education, professional society affiliations and the name of his firm, the title of his position and principal activities therein. However, a general designation referring to any specialty, such as "tax expert" or "tax consultant" may not be used.

Interpretation 502-10—Statements and information to the public press. A member shall not directly or indirectly cultivate publicity which advertises his or his firm's professional attainments or services. He may respond factually when approached by the press for information concerning his firm, but he should not use press inquiries as a means of aggrandizing himself or his firm or of advertising professional attainments or services. When interviewed by a writer or reporter, he is charged with the knowledge that he cannot control the journalistic use of any information he may give and should notify the reporter of the limitations imposed by professional ethics.

Releases and statements made by members on subjects of public interest which may be reported by the news media, and publicity not initiated by a member such as that which may result from public service activities, are not considered advertising. However, press releases concerning internal matters in a member's firm are prohibited.

Interpretation 502-11—Participation in educational seminars. Participation by members in programs of educational seminars, either in person or through audio-visual techniques, on matters within the field of competence of CPAs is in the public interest and is to be encouraged. Such seminars should not be used as a means of soliciting clients. Therefore, certain restraints must be observed to avoid violation of the spirit of Rule 502 which prohibits solicitation and advertising. For example, a member or his firm should not:

1. Send announcements of a seminar to nonclients or invite them to attend. However, educators may be invited to attend to further their education.
2. Sponsor, or convey the impression that he is sponsoring, a seminar which will be attended by nonclients. However, a member or his firm may conduct educational seminars solely for clients and those serving his clients in a professional capacity, such as bankers and lawyers.

In addition, when a seminar is sponsored by others and attended by nonclients, a member or his firm should not:

1. Solicit the opportunity to appear on the program.
2. Permit the distribution of publicity relating to the member or his firm in connection with the seminar except as permitted under Interpretation 502-9.
3. Distribute firm literature which is not directly relevant to a subject being presented on the program by the member or persons connected with his firm.

Interpretation 502-12—Solicitation of former clients. Offers by a member to provide services after a client relationship has been clearly terminated, either by completion of a nonrecurring engagement or by direct action of the client, constitute a violation of Rule 502 prohibiting solicitation.

Interpretation 502-13—Soliciting work from other practitioners. Rule 502 does not prohibit a member in the practice of public accounting from informing other practitioners of his availability to provide them or their clients with professional services. Because advertising comes to the attention of the public, such offers to other practitioners must be made in letter form or by personal contact.

Interpretation 502-14—Fees and professional standards. The following statement is required to be published with the Code of Professional Ethics pursuant to the Final Judgment in the court decision referred to next:

> The former provision of the Code of Professional Ethics prohibiting competitive bidding, Rule 3.03, was declared null and void by the United States District Court for the District of Columbia in a consent judgment entered on July 6, 1972, in a civil antitrust suit brought by the United States against the American Institute. In consequence, no provision of the Code of Professional Ethics now prohibits the submission of price quotations for accounting services to persons seeking such services; and such submission of price quotations is not an unethical practice under any policy of the Institute. To avoid misunderstanding it is important to note that otherwise unethical conduct (e.g., advertising, solicitation, or substandard work) is subject to disciplinary sanctions regardless of whether or not such unethical conduct is preceded by, associated with, or followed by a submission of price quotations for accounting services. Members of the Institute should also be aware that neither the foregoing judgment nor any policy of the Institute affects the obligation of a certified public accountant to obey applicable laws, regulations or rules of any state or other governmental authority.

RULE 503—COMMISSIONS. A member shall not pay a commission to obtain a client, nor shall he accept a commission for a referral to a client of products or services of others. This rule shall not prohibit payments for the purchase of an accounting practice or retirement payments to individuals formerly engaged in the practice of public accounting or payments to their heirs or estates.

Interpretation 503-1—Fees in payment for services. Rule 503, which prohibits payment of a commission to obtain a client, was adopted to avoid a client's having to pay fees for which he did not receive commensurate services. However, payment of fees to a referring public accountant for professional services to the successor firm or to the client in connection with the engagement is not prohibited.

RULE 504—INCOMPATIBLE OCCUPATIONS. A member who is engaged in the practice of public accounting shall not concurrently engage in any business or occupation which impairs his objectivity in rendering professional services or serves as a feeder to his practice.

RULE 505—FORM OF PRACTICE AND NAME. A member may practice public accounting, whether as an owner or employee, only in the form of a proprietorship, a partnership or a professional corporation whose characteristics conform to resolutions of Council. (See Code of Professional Ethics, Appendix B, page 28.)

A member shall not practice under a firm name which includes any fictitious name, indicates specialization or is misleading as to the type of organization (proprietorship, partnership or corporation). However, names of one or more past partners or shareholders may be included in the firm name of a successor partnership or corporation. Also, a partner surviving the death or withdrawal of all other partners may continue to practice under the partnership name for up to two years after becoming a sole practitioner.

A firm may not designate itself as "Members of the American Institute of Certified Public Accountants" unless all of its partners or shareholders are members of the Institute.

Interpretation 505-1—Investment in commercial accounting corporation. A member in the practice of public accounting may have a financial interest in a commercial corporation which performs for the public services of a type performed by public accountants and whose characteristics do not conform to resolutions of Council, provided such interest is not material to the corporation's net worth, and the member's interest in and relation to the corporation is solely that of an investor.

GENERALLY ACCEPTED AUDITING STANDARDS

The preceding section on the Rules of Conduct and the numbered Interpretations outlined the professional ethics governing the practice of public accounting by the independent auditor. Generally accepted auditing standards outline the concepts governing the quality of the services performed by the auditor in rendering an opinion on a client's financial statements. The auditor's report to investors, creditors, and other interested parties states that:

> ... Our examination was made in accordance with generally accepted auditing standards, and accordingly included such tests of the accounting records and such other auditing procedures as we considered necessary in the circumstances.[3]

The quality of the auditor's examination is judged on the basis of both auditing standards and auditing procedures. Auditing standards differ from auditing procedures in that the *standards are measures of the quality* of, and the objectives to be attained by, the procedures undertaken, whereas the *procedures are specific acts to be performed* in an examination. The auditing standards are listed and briefly discussed in the remainder of this chapter; auditing procedures are discussed in Chapter 17.

General Standards

1. The examination is to be performed by a person or persons having adequate technical training and proficiency as an auditor.
2. In all matters relating to the assignment, an independence in mental attitude is to be maintained by the auditor or auditors.
3. Due professional care is to be exercised in the performance of the examination and preparation of the report.[4]

The general standards are personal in nature, and are concerned with the qualifications of the independent auditor and the quality of his work. The auditor's opinion provides reasonable assurance to outside interested parties that a fair presentation of relevant information has been made in the client's financial statements. When the auditor conducts an examination and renders an opinion, he holds himself out as an expert proficient in both accounting practices and auditing procedures. The development of this proficiency begins, of course, with the auditor's formal education. He maintains and develops his expertise through continuous reading and study of pronouncements on accounting principles and auditing procedures as they are developed by authoritative bodies, and the accumulation of audit judgment obtained through experience.

The second standard recognizes that in order to instill and maintain public trust and confidence, the auditor must be independent in both fact and appearance. Being independent means not only being intellectually honest and being recognized as independent, but also being free from any obligation to a client.

The third standard requires that the independent auditor perform his work with due professional care. "Due care" describes what the auditor does and how well he does it. A paragraph appearing in *Cooley on Torts* best summarizes the intent of this standard:

> Every man who offers his service to another and is employed assumes the duty to exercise in the employment such skill as he possesses with reasonable care and diligence. In all these employments where peculiar skill is prerequisite, if one offers his service, he is understood as holding himself out to the public as possessing the degree of skill commonly possessed by others in the same employment, and, if his pretentions are unfounded, he commits a species of fraud upon every man who employs him in reliance upon his public profession. But no man, whether skilled or unskilled, undertakes that the task he assumes shall be performed successfully, and without fault or error. He undertakes for good faith and integrity, but not for infallibility, and he is liable to his employer for negligence, bad faith, or dishonesty, but not for losses consequent upon pure errors of judgment.[5]

Standards of Field Work

1. The work is to be adequately planned and assistants, if any, are to be properly supervised.
2. There is to be a proper study and evaluation of the existing internal control as a basis for reliance thereon and for the determination of the resultant extent of the tests to which auditing procedures are to be restricted.
3. Sufficient competent evidential matter is to be obtained through inspection, observation, inquiries, and confirmations to afford a reasonable basis for an opinion regarding the financial statements under examination.[6]

The first standard recognizes that timely appointment of the auditor is advantageous not only to the auditor but also to the client. Early appointment permits the auditor to carefully plan the timing of his interim work, such as the examination of the client's records and procedures and the all-important observation of the taking of physical inventories and the confirmation of receivables, and to determine the audit procedures to be undertaken after the balance sheet date. Allowing the auditor sufficient time to plan and conduct his examination will also save the client additional fees and avoid costly delays or interruptions in his normal business operations. More importantly from the client's standpoint, the inability of the auditor to perform a timely and adequate examination because of delay in beginning the audit work may affect the type of opinion the auditor may render on the financial statements. The nature and timing of several aspects of the examination are outlined in Chapter 17.

The second standard, concerning the proper study and evaluation of the client's system of internal control, is discussed in more detail in Chapter 18.

The third standard requires that the basis for the auditor's opinion on the financial statements of a client rests upon his accumulation and evaluation of sufficient competent evidential matter supporting the information presented in the statements. How much constitutes a sufficient amount of evidence depends upon the circumstances involved. As a general rule, there should be a reasonable relationship between the cost of obtaining the evidence versus the usefulness of the information obtained. To be competent, evidence should be valid and relevant. Validity of evidential matter depends so heavily upon the circumstances under which it is obtained that generalizations cannot be made about the various types of evidence. The subject of audit evidence is discussed more fully in Chapter 19. To conclude the discussion of this standard, it is enough to state that what is sufficient, competent evidential matter represents an exercise of the auditor's judgment. However, the auditor must be thorough in his search for, and examination of, evidence; it would not be acceptable to express an opinion merely on the grounds that nothing came to his attention to cause him to question the presentations made in the financial statements.

Standards of Reporting

1. The report shall state whether the financial statements are presented in accordance with generally accepted accounting principles.
2. The report shall state whether such principles have been consistently observed in the current period in relation to the preceding period.
3. Informative disclosures in the financial statements are to be regarded as reasonably adequate unless otherwise stated in the report.
4. The report shall either contain an expression of opinion regarding the financial statement, taken as a whole, or an assertion to the effect that

an opinion cannot be expressed. When an overall opinion cannot be expressed, the reasons therefore should be stated. In all cases where an auditor's name is associated with financial statements, the report should contain a clear-cut indication of the character of the auditor's examination. If any, and the degree of responsibility he is taking.[7]

The first standard requires the auditor to express an opinion as to whether or not the financial statements are presented in conformity with accounting principles and practices, including the client's method of applying them. Of course, generally accepted accounting principles are constantly changing, not only as a result of pronouncements issued by the American Institute of Certified Public Accountants and other authoritative bodies but also as a result of becoming acceptable through common business usage. This standard assumes the auditor will be aware of such changes and will take them into consideration in expressing his opinion.

The second standard requires the auditor to state whether or not the accounting principles have been consistently applied in the period under review in relation to the preceding period. The objective of the consistency standard is: (1) to give assurance that the comparability of the statements between accounting periods has not been materially affected by changes in the accounting principles or in their application, and (2) to require a statement as to the nature of their effects if material changes have affected the comparability of the statements.

The third standard states that fairness in financial statement presentations is based not only upon consistently applied, generally accepted accounting principles but also upon the adequacy of disclosures involving certain material matters. These matters include the form, arrangement, and content of the statements; the footnotes accompanying the statements and the nature and extent of the detailed information provided. What constitutes a matter requiring disclosure calls for the exercise of the auditor's judgment, taking into consideration the circumstances and facts he is aware of at that time. In this respect, careful consideration must be given to the disclosure of confidential information the auditor receives that achieves the status of priviledged communication. Without such confidence the auditor would at times have difficulty in obtaining information necessary for him to express an opinion. If such information does not require disclosure for the financial statement not to be misleading, the auditor need not require that such disclosures be made in the statements.

The objective of the fourth standard is to avoid misunderstanding as to the degree of responsibility the independent auditor is assuming whenever his name is associated with a client's financial statements. The independent auditor usually issues an unqualified opinion, or short form report. However, there may be occasions when the auditor may be required to express a qualified, an adverse or disclaimer of opinion. The subject of audit reports is discussed more fully in Chapter 20.

REFERENCES

1. *Code of Professional Ethics.* Copyright © 1972 by the American Institute of Certified Public Accountants, Inc., pp. 20-25.

2. *Ibid.,* pp. 32-43.

3. *Statement on Auditing Standards No. 1.* Copyright © 1973 by the American Institute of Certified Public Accountants, Inc., Section 511.04.

4. *Ibid.,* Section 150-02.

5. *Ibid.,* Section 230-03.

6. *Ibid.,* Section 150.02.

7. *Ibid.*

17   Audit Procedures

The independent auditor examines a client's financial statements for the purpose of determining their fairness. His opinion as to the fairness with which the statements present the financial position, the results of operations and changes in financial position, is based on the results of various audit procedures.

Audit procedures are specific acts performed during the auditor's examination to test the reliability of various types of evidence, and thus determine the reasonableness of the statement presentations. A proper examination should include not only generally recognized audit procedures as prescribed by the American Institute of CPAs and other authoritative bodies but also any additional audit procedures that, while not generally recognized, may be necessary in light of the circumstances of a particular engagement.

In determining appropriate audit procedures, the auditor should keep the following objectives in mind:

1. To obtain information about the client's background, policies, and procedures as a basis for an efficient and alert examination.
2. To study and evaluate the client's system of internal control to determine the reliability of the evidence underlying the financial statement presentations.
3. To determine the genuineness of the transactions underlying account balances.

4. To ascertain that account balances are fairly stated and properly classified on the financial statements, and supported by adequate disclosure of significant information when necessary.
5. To ascertain that the financial statements are presented in accordance with generally accepted accounting principles.
6. To ascertain that these accounting principles have been applied on the basis consistent with the preceding period.
7. To detect major fraud or other irregularities, although the examination is not necessarily designed to achieve this objective.

PRELIMINARY PLANNING

In planning his examination, the auditor is guided by the first standard of field work:

> The work is to be adequately planned and assistants, if any, are to be properly supervised.[1]

Prior to and during the early stages of his examination the auditor should deal with the following matters: (1) discussion with the client about the engagement; (2) staff arrangements; and, (3) those preparatory procedures necessary for an efficient and alert examination.

The Client

Matters to be discussed with the client depend to a great extent on the nature of the client's business, the type of examination to be performed, and whether it is a new or a continuing engagement. The following items are not necessarily all inclusive, but are merely indicative of some of the points to be covered.

Fees

Since the fee is usually in the mind of the client, the auditor should frankly discuss this matter, but without creating the impression that his primary interest is in the earning of a fee.

Reason for the Audit

It is always important for the auditor to determine early in the planning stages the reason the client requests the audit. This is particularly true

---

1. *Statement on Auditing Standards No. 1.* Copyright © 1973 by the American Institute of Certified Public Accountants, Inc., Section 150.02.

in a new audit, but it should be kept in mind that even a recurring engagement may involve varying audit requirements during the year as well as from one year to the next.

Type of Report

The auditor should determine whether the client desires the usual short-form report or a long-form report. In the latter instance, he should determine the specific type of information required to meet the client's needs.

Meaning of the Report

This subject is particularly important in new audit engagements. If the client has not received previously a report from an independent auditor, the meaning of the various types of audit reports (i.e., unqualified, qualified, etc.) should be reviewed and explained.

Required and Special Auditing Procedures

The auditor should outline and explain those audit procedures required as generally accepted procedures and any special procedures that he may consider necessary in the circumstances.

Cooperation of Client's Staff

The auditor should emphasize the desirability and importance of obtaining the cooperation of the client's staff, particularly in view of the close time schedule under which he works. The client should make sure that the books and records are kept current and will be ready for immediate examination. The trial balance should also be ready by the time the auditor is ready to begin his work. Many working papers can be prepared by the client's staff, thereby not only reducing the cost of the audit but also freeing the auditor from routine work.

Many CPA firms submit an "engagement letter" outlining the above matters to the client for his review and approval. The specific matters listed and the format of the letter vary among firms, but a typical engagement letter is shown in Figure 17-1.

Staff Arrangements

Prior to the beginning of the engagement, the auditor should determine his staff requirements. This involves not only consideration as to the

(Name and Address of
appropriate executive
or committee)

Dear _____ :

This letter is written to confirm our understanding as to the extent of our examination of your company's financial statements for the year ending _____ .

Our examination will be performed in accordance with generally accepted auditing standards and will include all procedures considered necessary in order to be able to express an opinion on the fairness of the financial statements. The examination will include:

1. A study and evaluation of the system of internal control.
2. Such tests of the accounting records and other evidence as we consider necessary, based on our study and evaluation of the system of internal control.
3. Our examination will include the observation of your physical inventory count on _____ and the circularization of accounts receivable as of a date to be determined by us.
4. Preparation of a short-form report.

If our examination reveals certain deficiencies in the system of internal control, we shall also submit a letter outlining these deficiencies and recommendations for correction for your consideration.

In order that we may perform our examination as efficiently as possible, it is understood that your employees will provide us with a year-end trial balance by _____ and also certain audit working papers which we will discuss with the appropriate members of your staff in the next few days. Our examination will be completed and our report submitted to you by _____ .

Our fees for this examination will be based on the time spent by various members of our staff at their regular rates, plus travel and related expenses.

Sincerely yours,

Accepted by _____
Date _____

Figure 17-1:
Format for Engagement Letter

number of staff assistants needed but also their availability throughout the engagement. The auditor in charge of the audit must be selected, staff assistants must be assigned, and proper arrangements should be made for adequate supervision of their activities throughout the engagement.

Preparatory Procedures

At the beginning of the audit engagement and during the early stages of the examination, the auditor should determine the nature, extent, and timing of those audit procedures—normal or special—necessary in order to formulate an opinion as to the fairness of the financial statements. Several matters should be reviewed in his preparatory planning of the audit.

Prior Years' Audit Workpapers and Tax Returns

The auditor should review the audit workpapers and tax returns from previous audits for such information as problem areas requiring special handling, suggestions for modification of certain procedures for the current examination, and other background information for the audit.

Company Policies and Procedures

The auditor should obtain or update information concerning the client's products, operations, organizational structure, and personnel. This information should be obtained from the client, and be maintained in a permanent file for use in subsequent engagements.

Financial Records and Reports

The auditor should make a preliminary review of the client's financial records and reports to help determine his needs, and to uncover any special problems that may arise during the audit.

Internal Control

The auditor should study and evaluate the client's system of internal control to help determine the scope of the examination. This area is discussed in more detail in Chapter 18.

Audit Programs

After completing his preliminary review of the matters outlined in the preceding paragraphs, the auditor can develop an appropriate plan for the audit. The audit program outlines the objectives, nature, timing, and other matters concerning the audit procedures necessary to conduct the examination. Although audit programs vary in form and content because of differing client requirements, all programs reflect a broad basic pattern of approaches and techniques necessary for an adequate examination.

An outline listing basic audit procedures is shown in Figure 17-2. A more detailed discussion of audit programs is the subject of the next section.

Audit Area	Audit Considerations
1. Internal Control	Review and evaluate the system of internal control over a particular accounting activity.
2. Company Policies and Procedures	Determine and evaluate company policy and practices involved in a particular accounting activity.
3. Review of the General Ledger	a. Substantiate opening balance(s) and compare end-of-period statement balance(s) with general ledger balance(s). b. Check mathematical accuracy of footings, crossfootings, etc. and scan account(s) activity for unusual posting sources, amounts, and activity. c. If applicable, obtain schedule of material activity in a particular account(s).
4. Review of Subsidiary Ledgers	a. Obtain schedule(s) and compare balance(s) to controlling account(s) and subsidiary ledger balance(s). b. Check mathematical accuracy of footings, crossfootings, etc. and scan account(s) activity for unusual posting sources, amounts, and activity. c. For test period or selected sample, trace postings to source(s) of original entries.

Figure 17-2
Outline for Basic Audit Program
(To be developed for each balance sheet caption)

5. Examination of internal evidence	For test period or selected sample, vouch entries to appropriate source documentation.
6. Accumulation of external evidence	a. Obtain, whenever practical, external evidence via confirmations, counts, inspection and/or observation, and inquiries of management. b. Compare evidence with accounting records and workpapers, and satisfactorily reconcile significant differences.
7. Cut-off examination	Review transactions for period before and after the balance sheet date for appropriate cut-off of account(s) activity.
8. Generally accepted accounting principles and statement presentation.	a. Determine that generally accepted accounting principles have been followed on a basis consistent with prior periods. b. Determine adequacy of statement presentation and necessity for statement and/or footnote disclosure(s) regarding significant transactions or events.
9. Overall evaluation	Conduct overall evaluation of accuracy and reasonableness of financial statements via appropriate statement ratios and percentages and comparison tests with prior years' financial statements.
10. Post Balance Sheet Review	Review records, minutes of meetings, etc. to determine necessity for disclosure of subsequent events.

Figure 17-2 *(continued)*

THE AUDIT PROGRAM

An audit program is a standard, detailed outline of audit procedures to be performed in the verification of each material item on the financial statements.

Detailed preprinted audit instructions in the audit program provide assurance that certain essential steps are not overlooked. However, since the conditions and problems encountered vary with each audit engagement, it may be necessary for the auditor in charge of the examination to determine what procedures might appropriately be deleted and what procedures may have to be expanded. The audit program for a particular engagement is determined primarily by the strength or weakness of the client's system of internal control. Weak internal control systems obviously would require more extensive audit work than would be necessary for an organization with strong internal control. (The study and evaluation of internal control is the subject of Chapter 18.) Also, the great variety of accounting methods and special problems peculiar to each organization require that the audit program be tailored to suit the circumstances encountered in a specific engagement.

As each step in the audit program is completed, the auditor who performed the work should place his initials and the date opposite the step. This information not only establishes the responsibility for the work performed but also enables the auditor in charge of the engagement to determine the progress of the examination.

Interim Procedures

Certain steps in the audit program may be performed prior to the balance-sheet date, commonly called the *interim period,* and certain procedures may, or can only, be performed after that date. A substantial part of the auditor's examination and the bulk of the audit procedures can be undertaken during the interim period, although the amount or type of work done depends on such factors as the objectives of each phase of the examination, the accounts being reviewed, the availability of client's staff, the auditor's staffing situation in connection with scheduling interim and year-end work, and the year-end pressures on the auditor to complete the examination and issue his report. Generally, the following areas of the examination may be completed during the interim period:

1. Review of the company's policies and procedures.
2. Review of the system of internal control.
3. Detailed test work on appropriate accounts for test periods of time or selected samples, and
4. Preparatory planning for work to be done after the balance-sheet date (such as preparing workpapers to be completed by client personnel, appropriate confirmations, etc.).

Year-End Audit Procedures

The year-end work performed by the auditor should not be considered as merely "cleaning up" interim work. Several areas of audit procedure must be performed at this time because they can be completed only at year-end. For example, the following up and reconciling of matters uncovered during the interim work; the cut-off examination; the year-end account balances that require confirmation, count, or inspection; the calculation of overall operating ratios and percentages; and the final review of accounting principles and statement presentation cannot be performed during the interim phase of the examination. The precise division of audit procedures between interim and year-end requires the auditor to exercise professional judgment, relying on his past experience with the client.

STATISTICAL SAMPLING

Statistical vs. Judgmental Sampling

Sampling, whether judgmental or statistical, is the process of selecting a sample from a group of items (called the population) and examining the characteristics of the sample to reach conclusions about the characteristics of the population as a whole. The basic assumption is that the characteristics of the sample will be representative of the population.

Statistical sampling involves the same general process as judgmental sampling techniques, but is superior in two respects. There is always the risk that, regardless of the techniques used, the sample may not be representative of the population, and incorrect conclusions may be assumed concerning the population. Statistical sampling techniques allow the auditor to quantitatively measure the probability that his conclusions regarding the population are valid, and thereby be aware of the degree of risk he is assuming in accepting the sample results. Judgmental sampling methods do not provide for this measurement of risk.

Although the risk of assuming incorrect conclusions about the population can be reduced by increasing the sample size, audit procedures become more costly and time-consuming as a greater portion of the population is examined. A key factor in utilizing sampling effectively is the balance between the risk of error in interpreting the characteristics of the sample and the cost of increasing the sample size. Because there is no opportunity in judgmental sampling to measure the degree of risk of error in the sample, larger and more costly samples may be drawn by the auditor without any significant reduction in the risk of formulating incorrect conclusions regarding the population.

Using Statistical Sampling

In any discussion of the value of statistical sampling techniques, it is important to recognize that they are only useful for helping the auditor select items from a population to be sampled, and evaluating the results in statistical terms. They do not affect the scope of the examination or diminish the exercise of judgment by the auditor in conducting the examination and formulating his opinion on the financial statements. Indeed, the very decision as to the appropriateness of statistical sampling techniques in conducting the examination requires the exercise of the auditor's professional judgment.

The utilization of statistical sampling techniques requires the auditor to:

1. Determine the objectives of the examination (review of internal control or test of transactions),
2. Determine the sample size to be selected,
3. Determine the sampling method and select the sample, and
4. Interpret the results of the examination of the sample items.

The Sample Size

The most important decision the auditor must make in applying statistical sampling is determining the size of the sample to be examined. Too small a sample will result almost certainly in incorrect conclusions concerning the population; too large a sample is costly and time-consuming without measurably increasing the auditor's confidence that he achieved an accurate picture of the population being evaluated.

The size of the sample is dependent upon the precision and level of confidence desired by the auditor and his estimate of the occurrence (or error) rate. Only in rare instances will the characteristics of the sample items be representative exactly of the characteristics of the population. In determining precision and the confidence level, the auditor attempts to measure the degree in which the sample is representative of the population. *Precision* is the range, set by + or - limits from the sample results, within which the true characteristics of the population being evaluated are likely to lie. The *level of confidence* is the percentage of the time the sample results can be expected to represent the characteristics of the population within a specified range of precision. The *occurrence rate* is the frequency in which specified characteristics occur in the sample being examined. Since the auditor is looking for adherence to certain prescribed managerial policies and procedures as he makes his examination, the occurrence rate is usually viewed in terms of how frequently the sample indicates that the characteristics *do not* conform to the appropriate policies and procedures.

The determination of the degree of precision, the level of confidence, and estimated occurrence rate require the exercise of judgment by the auditor. Such factors as prior experience on the audit, the quality of the system of internal control, the objective of the tests, and the significance of the items being examined have a bearing on this decision. The size of the sample can then be determined by reference to appropriate sampling tables found in most auditing and/or statistics text books.

Selecting the Sample

Four methods for selecting the sample may be used by the auditor: (1) random selection; (2) systematic selection; (3) stratified selection; and (4) cluster selection. The essential requirement in all of these methods is that each item in a population must have the same chance of being selected for examination as every other item. The random selection method has achieved the widest acceptance for normal audit situations. Systematic selection is also useful, but must be used with more care. Stratified selection is especially appropriate when the population contains items of varying dollar amounts or frequency of occurrence. Cluster selection usually necessitates the assistance of an expert in statistical sampling because of the special requirements necessary to correctly apply this method.

Random Selection

The simplest method of selecting items to be tested is through the use of random digit tables. These tables are available in most auditing and/or statistics textbooks, and can be adapted easily to the needs of the auditor in the selection of the sample. In some cases where a large number of items must be selected, the auditor may use special computer programs that provide any length list of random numbers appropriate for the size of a particular population.

Systematic Selection

Systematic selection from a population involves drawing every nth item from the group. For example, if a sample of 10 items is to be drawn from a population of 1,000, every 100th item would be selected. To avoid drawing a nonrandom sample the auditor should make sure first that the items in the population are in random order. If certain items of the population are not arranged in random order, the population should first be stratified into appropriate segments, each of which should be in random order, before systematic selection is applied to each segment.

Stratified Selection

Stratified selection is not in itself a method for drawing samples, but is used to arrange the population into various segments of importance before utilizing other sample selection techniques. The auditor usually is concerned with the materiality as well as the type of items selected for examination. Thus, if a population is composed of items that vary in dollar amounts or that represent different types of transactions, the auditor may decide to first stratify the population, then select his sample. For example, in reviewing accounts receivable, the auditor may decide to examine all accounts over a certain dollar amount, and then utilize random selection or systematic selection in selecting accounts below that amount.

Cluster Selection

Frequently the auditor will encounter a population that may be broken down conveniently into sub-groups; each of these sub-groups may be defined as a cluster. For example, if 1,000 accounts receivable ledger cards are kept in 10 trays, each tray would be considered a cluster of items to be examined. Each cluster must be treated as a single item under this selection method. This method appears simple, compared with the other methods already discussed. However, if the clusters contain a large number of items, the evaluation becomes a formidable task because of statistical requirements that must be met in treating each cluster as a sample item to be examined.

Interpreting the Sample Results

Four methods of interpreting sample results have gained recognition by the profession: (1) acceptance sampling; (2) estimation sampling for attributes; (3) discovery sampling; and, (4) estimation sampling for variables. The auditor should evaluate any exceptions to prescribed procedures with the following questions in mind: (1) Do these exceptions represent a lack of important internal controls? (2) Do they represent a circumvention of prescribed managerial policies and procedures? and, (3) Do they represent evidence of fraudulent intent?

Acceptance Sampling

Acceptance sampling involves a decision to accept or reject an entire population. This method may be of limited value to the auditor because the only alternatives to the decision to reject a population may be a 100 percent examination of the population or a qualified opinion on the financial statements. Netiher of these alternatives is likely to be practical in most audit examinations, and this method has declined in popularity as more practical methods have been developed.

Estimation Sampling for Attributes

Estimation sampling for attributes (or frequency sampling) enables the auditor to determine, within predetermined limits of precision and confidence, the frequency of certain characteristics within a population. Generally, the auditor will use this method in evaluating exceptions to prescribed procedures because the application of this method produces results expressed in terms of the number of exceptions found in relation to the number of items examined. The auditor can then make a decision to accept or reject a population based on the number of exceptions observed compared to the number of exceptions he would consider acceptable.

Discovery Sampling

Discovery sampling is a modification of acceptance sampling. The purpose of this method is to detect at least one exception of a certain type, assuming the exception occurs within the population with at least a predetermined occurrence rate. Usually the auditor attempts to determine an occurrence rate as a result of sampling, but in discovery sampling situations he may consider only one exception to be more important to his examination. Thus when this exception, such as the discovery of some form of fraud, is critical, even one occurrence is intolerable. The auditor may then decide to abandon sampling procedures and begin a 100 percent examination of the population.

After you complete each statistical sampling application, complete this form and send it to the
National Personnel Office.

Office Name _____   Office Number _____

Client _____   Period Ended _____

Sample designed by _____   Approved by _____

Have sample designer and reviewer attended a nationally-presented Ernst & Ernst statistical
sampling course? (0 both; 1 designer only; 2 reviewer only; 3 neither have) ⊔

Business Code ⊔⊔
1. Agriculture, Forestry   6. Manufacturing   11. Transportation, Warehousing
   and Fisheries   7. Insurance   and Utilities
2. Brokerage Houses   8. Universities   12. Natural Resources
3. Construction   9. Retailers   13. Wholesaling
4. Hospitals   10. Service   14. Financial Institutions
5. Municipalities   15. (Other) _____

Audit Area ⊔⊔
1. Cash Receipts   6. Confirmation   11. Price Test
2. Cash Disbursements   7. Receivable Aging   12. LIFO Index
3. Outstanding Checks   8. Test Counting   13. Accounts Payable
4. Sales   9. Perpetual Inventory Records 14. (Other) _____
5. Payroll   10. Obsolescence Review   _____

Briefly describe the audit objective:

_____

_____

When was test performed? (0 interim; 1 final) . . . . ⊔

Population size ⊔
1.   0 -   499   4. 3,000 - 4,999   7. 25,000 - 49,999
2.   500 -   999   5. 5,000 - 9,999   8. 50,000 - 99,999
3. 1,000 - 2,999   6. 10,000 - 24,999   9. 100,000 and over

Is this an Auditronic 16 application: (0 yes; 1 no). If yes, and a variable estimation application, ⊔
attach copy of frequency distribution run (Code 1012), preliminary evaluation of selected sample
(Code 1014) and sample result analysis projections (Code 1015).

Statistical technique selected ⊔
1. Attribute   3. Difference   5. Ratio   7. Stop and Go
2. Cluster   4. Discovery   6. Simple Extension

Method of sample selection ⊔
1. Random   3. Single Start Systematic   5. Other (describe on reverse side)
2. Random Systematic   4. Multiple Start Systematic   6. Auditronic 16 (Code 1014)

Number of strata . . . . ⊔⊔

Total sample size (Indicate source of table or method of determination. Show calculation, ⊔⊔⊔⊔
if appropriate).

Precision and Reliability as originally contemplated:
Precision
Attribute--upper precision limit percentage . . . . ⊔⊔

Variable--precision (in thousands of dollars) . . . .⊔⊔⊔⊔
       --precision as a percentage of total estimated dollars . . . . ⊔⊔
Reliability or confidence level (as a percentage) . . . . ⊔⊔

Precision and Reliability Achieved:
Precision
Attribute--upper precision limit percentage . . . . ⊔⊔

Variable--precision (in thousands of dollars) . . . .⊔⊔⊔⊔
       --precision as a percentage of total dollars . . . . ⊔⊔

Reliability or confidence level (as a percentage) . . . . ⊔⊔

Did book value fall within precision interval? (0 yes; 1 no; 2 not applicable) . . . . ⊔

Do you plan to use sampling next year in this area? (0 yes; 1 no) . . . . ⊔

Technical review by M.C.S.? (0 yes; 1 no) . . . . ⊔

Comments
Explain any unique aspects or difficulties encountered--nonresponse problem, bad addresses, counting
difficulties, cutoff procedures, sample bias, evaluation difficulties, etc. (Use reverse side).

                                        Signature of Preparer _____

Form P-59   Date _____
(Revised 12/70)

Figure 17-3

Source: Ernst & Ernst

Estimation Sampling for Variables

Estimation sampling for variables (or dollar value estimation) enables the auditor to estimate the dollar amount of exceptions uncovered in his examination. This method is designed to estimate the average dollar value of items in a population, within predetermined limits of precision and confidence, by determining the average dollar value of the sample. (The method can be modified to provide total dollar values if desired.) However, considerable proficiency in statistics is required in applying this method. Reference should be made to statistics textbooks for detailed explanations regarding this procedure.

Many CPA firms have designed work sheets outlining the points discussed briefly in this section. These work sheets not only serve as a guide for the auditor in considering the applicability of statistical sampling techniques in his examination but also provide a checklist of the requirements to implement the sampling plan. An example of a statistical sampling plan and specifications work sheet is shown in Figure 17-3.

ELECTRONIC DATA PROCESSING SYSTEMS

The growth of use of electronic data processing (EDP) in business has had the greatest impact on the public accounting profession than perhaps any other event in its history. As more and more clients maintain their financial records on EDP systems, the auditor finds it necessary to consider and to utilize computers in performing many of his audit procedures. This section highlights some of the more significant ways audit procedures are affected by EDP.

Internal Control

By far the greatest effect on audit procedures has been in the area of internal control. In the traditional system of internal control, no single employee has complete responsibility for a transaction. The work of one employee is checked by the work of another, who handles different aspects of the same transaction. This separation of duties is designed not only to provide reasonable assurance as to the accuracy and validity of the financial statements but also to protect the client against losses due to carelessness or fraud. With the conversion to EDP systems, however, the work formerly performed by several employees is performed by a single computer.

Despite the integration of several functions into one EDP system, the importance of internal control is not diminished. Separation of duties and clearly defined responsibilities are still essential elements in spite of the loss of familiar departmental boundaries. The traditional control concepts must be supplemented with controls built into the computer hardware and written into computer programs.

The auditor may use several techniques to study and evaluate the internal control of an EDP system. The more commonly employed approaches include:

1. Specially designed internal control questionnaires, or analyses of clients' flow charts,
2. Utilization of test decks, and
3. Duplicate or generalized computer audit programs.

Questionnaires and Flow Charts

The auditor obtains answers to the questionnaire by making inquires of appropriate personnel, personal observations, and inspecting various records and documents. The questionnaire approach is best suited for a review of organizational and operating controls affecting data input and output. However, it may be of limited value in determining the effectiveness of the program controls, because the auditor may not always detect situations in which program controls would not be adequate in preventing errors or other irregularities.

The flow chart approach may be more useful in the study and evaluation of internal controls than a questionnaire. Most EDP departments have systems and program flow charts available on their computer applications; these flow charts may be used by the auditor in his investigation as a supplement to, or in place of, the questionnaire.

Test Decks

In auditing manual accounting systems the auditor traces selected transactions through the records from source document to final disposition. In the audit of an EDP system a comparable approach usually involves the utilization of test decks. The auditor may use his own decks or those developed by the client's programmers (provided in the latter situation he assures himself that the tests are valid). The test decks should contain all types of transactions and exceptions or errors, such as missing transactions, erroneous transactions, illogical transactions, out-of-balance batches, and out-of-sequence controls. After running the test decks the auditor should evaluate the exceptions or errors discovered and plan his subsequent procedures accordingly.

Duplicate of Generalized Audit Programs

As an alternative to the test deck approach, the auditor may supervise the processing of data using duplicate programs over which he maintains control. He then compares his results to that generated by the client's program.

Many CPA firms have developed generalized computer audit programs that not only test the reliability of the client's program but also perform various auditing functions. These audit programs are designed to perform processing functions essentially equivalent to that of the client's program. They use the same data as the client's program, simulate the client's processing of the data and, ideally, should produce the same results. The generalized audit program compares the simulated output to the client's records and prepares a list of discrepancies that are checked by the auditor.

Other Audit Considerations

The independent auditor may have to adjust his audit procedures because the client utilizes an on-line, real-time EDP system on his premises, utilizes a computer service center, or utilizes a computer on a time-sharing arrangement.

When an on-line, real-time system is in use, the auditor is faced with several problems requiring modifications in his audit procedures; problems such as the lack of source documents to support input to the computer, the lack of conventional printouts of financial records, and a considerable reduction in the volume of hard copy normally included in an audit trail. In a system of this type there must be a greater degree of reliance upon the computer for internal control. Input and output discrepancies are detected primarily through appropriate program controls. These controls should be sufficient to prevent manipulation of the system as a whole since the lack of periodic hard copy reduces the opportunity for the verification of output.

Computer service centers strengthen internal control over deliberate manipulation of a company's financial records because personnel involved in processing the client's data do not have access to the company's assets. In addition, because the center processes input in small batches, it provides periodic hard copy to the client, thus providing the auditor with an adequate audit trail for evaluating the processing performed by the center. Even though the data processing performed for the client may be relatively simple, the operations of the center may be quite complex. Therefore the auditor usually just evaluates the reliability of the data processing by examining the output, and possibly utilizes test decks to check the center's program. An evaluation of the internal control of the center itself is usually neither practical or necessary.

Time-sharing systems consist of a large central computer used by a large number of independent clients at distant locations. Each client has access to the central computer through his own terminal. The client's files are maintained at the central facility, and access to these files and the use of the computer requires an identification code number assigned to each user. The center should maintain appropriate controls to prevent unauthorized use of a client's programs, loss or destruction of his data files, or alteration of his programs; thus the internal controls most important to the auditor under time-sharing arrangements should be the client's controls over input data and program controls. Usually periodic hard copy output is generated by the client's terminal, so an adequate audit trail will be available to evaluate the reliability of the data processing. As in the case of computer service centers, it is usually not feasible or necessary for the auditor to test or evaluate the internal control for the central computer center itself.

18   Internal Control

Internal control is defined as

> ... the plan of organization and all of the coordinate methods and measures adopted within a business to safeguard its assets, check the accuracy and reliability of its accounting data, promote operational efficiency, and encourage adherence to prescribed managerial policies ...[1]

The definition is broader than the usual interpretation associated with the term. It describes a concept of internal control going beyond just the activities of the accounting or finance department and includes such nonaccounting matters as budgetary controls, various types of statistical analyses, employee training programs, and even the activities of an internal audit staff, if one exists within an organization.

The four basic elements considered essential in a satisfactory system of internal control are:

1. A plan of organization which provides appropriate segregation of functional responsibility.
2. A system of authorization and record procedures adequate to provide reasonable accounting control over assets, liabilities, revenues, and expenses.
3. Sound practices to be followed in performance of duties and functions of each of the organizational departments, and
4. A degree of quality of personnel commensurate with responsibilities.[2]

THE AUDITOR'S RESPONSIBILITY FOR
THE SYSTEM OF INTERNAL CONTROL

Management, the internal auditing department, if any, and the independent auditor all share the responsibility for the system of internal control. The latter's responsibility is clearly stated in the second standard of field work:

> There is to be a proper study and evaluation of the existing internal control as a basis for reliance thereon and for the determination of the resultant extent of the tests to which auditing procedures are to be restricted.[3]

The definition of internal control and the essential elements of the system recognize both accounting and nonaccounting controls. However, the independent auditor generally assumes responsibility only for those controls of an accounting nature. The AICPA's Committee on Auditing Procedure clarified this distinction by separating the elements of an internal control system into two broad categories:

> *Administrative control* includes, but is not limited to, the plan of organization and the procedures and records that are concerned with the decision processes leading to management's authorization of transactions . . .
> *Accounting control* comprises the plan of organization and the procedures and records that are concerned with the safeguarding of assets and the reliability of financial records and consequently are designed to provide reasonable assurance that:
> a. Transactions are executed in accordance with management's general or specific authorization.
> b. Transactions are recorded as necessary (1) to permit preparation of financial statements in conformity with generally accepted accounting principles or any other criteria applicable to such statements and (2) to maintain accountability for assets.
> c. Access to assets is permitted only in accordance with management's authorization.
> d. The recorded accountability for assets is compared with the existing assets at reasonable intervals and appropriate action is taken with respect to any differences.[4]

Having made this distinction, the Committee concluded that the independent auditor should be concerned only with the accounting controls, since these controls are directly and significantly related to the reliability of the financial records and statements. Administrative controls, on the other hand, are usually indirectly related to the records and therefore would not necessarily require evaluation. Of course, if the auditor believes that certain administrative controls have some bearing on the reliability of the records, he should use his judgment as to the need for extending his examination to include them.

THE AUDITOR'S REVIEW OF THE SYSTEM OF INTERNAL CONTROL

Purpose

The independent auditor's study and evaluation of the system of internal control should enable him:

1. To determine the client's policies and procedures as a starting point for an efficient and alert examination. (The review of the system of internal control may indicate areas that are questionable or susceptible to fraud and require more careful and intensive examination.)
2. To determine the quantitative and qualitative scope of the examination. (Audit procedures involve tests of transactions. If the tests do not reveal significant errors or irregularities it is assumed that transactions not examined are as free from errors or irregularities as the transactions tested. The better the system of internal control the greater the reliability of the evidence examined by the auditor. A poor system of internal control, on the other hand, would require the auditor to accumulate and evaluate a greater variety of evidence.)
3. To determine whether certain audit procedures should be performed at interim dates or after the balance sheet date.
4. To gain assurance as to the over-all accuracy of the financial statements when he formulates his opinion.
5. To provide an additional service to the client by preparing a special letter or report identifying those areas of the system of internal control that require strengthening, and recommending corrective action.

When possible, the auditor's review of the system of internal control should be conducted as a separate phase of the audit, preferably before or at the beginning of the interim work. This would facilitate greatly his determination of the nature, extent, and timing of his audit procedures in order to achieve the objectives of his review as listed in the preceding paragraph. It is not anticipated that the auditor will be able to conduct an in-depth review of all the control procedures during any single audit, so the review is usually arranged so as to provide for a complete review over a period of several years. However, the review of those controls that relate directly to the financial records should be conducted each year.

Procedures

The study and evaluation of the client's system of internal control by the auditor is performed in two distinct phases: (1) a review of the control procedures; and, (2) various tests to determine adherence to prescribed procedures by the client's employees.

The Auditor's Review

In the first phase the auditor accumulates information about the client's policies and the procedures underlying the system. This information is usually obtained through personal observation, discussion with appropriate personnel, and reference to various documents and reports. Typical sources of information for the latter would include:

1. Organization charts, indicating lines of authority.
2. Job description manuals or write-ups, detailing the scope of activities and responsibilities delegated to various job classifications.
3. Charts, or texts of account, describing the purpose and content of each account.
4. Procedures manual, describing approved practices to be followed in all areas of operation.
5. Examination of accounting records and supporting forms and documents underlying the recording of transactions.
6. Questionnaires and other working papers concerning the review of the system of internal control conducted in prior audit examinations.

The traditional approach to this part of the review is the completion of an internal control questionnaire. The questionnaire consists of a series of questions covering such areas as general operations, cash receipts and disbursements, payables, payroll, etc. and is designed to highlight weaknesses in the system. All questionnaires require a "yes" or "no" answer, but vary in any additional information to be recorded. Space may be provided to indicate: how the information is obtained (inquiry, observation, or test), whether the weakness, if any, is considered significant, and in some cases, a detailed description or write-up of the weakness so it may be included in the internal control report to the client. Several features have contributed to the popularity of this form of evaluation of the system of internal control. The questionnaire serves as a check list of major areas to be covered and prevents most oversights. The "yes" or "no" type answers emphasize the strong and weak points in control procedures. Because the auditor who prepares the responses places his initials on the appropriate line, responsibility for the review is established. Finally, because of the close relationship between the review of internal control and the development of the audit program, the inquiries serve to clarify the objectives of the applicable audit procedures.

Many auditors, however, have expressed dissatisfaction with the questionnaire approach to reviewing internal controls. There is often a tendency by assistants to record unsubstantiated answers. Deficiencies could exist that are not specifically covered in the questionnaire, and therefore could be overlooked. Also, the questionnaire presents difficulties in providing an overall view of the organizational structure and flow of operations of the organization, and difficulties arise in appraising the overall adequacy of control procedures. The questionnaire has been supplemented, and in some instances replaced, by two other forms of evaluation—internal control write-ups and flow charts.

An internal control write-up is a written description of the flow of transactions, records maintained and the activities and responsibilities of the employees performing the work. After preparing this written description of the control procedures in a particular area, the auditor may summarize his appraisal as strong, adequate, or weak and revise his audit procedures if necessary. An example of an internal control write-up is shown in Figure 18-1.

A flow chart is a symbolic representation of an area of internal control. The flow chart should enable the auditor to evaluate at a glance the effectiveness of certain controls, and eliminate the detailed study required for written descriptions for the interpretation of lengthy questionnaires. An example of a systems flow chart is shown in Figure 18-2.

Bennington Co., Inc.
Cash Receipts Procedures
December 31, 1974

Lorraine Martin is cashier, cash receipts journal bookkeeper, and petty cash custodian. She picks up all mail at Bennington's post office box each workday morning. All cash receipts are received by mail in the form of current-dated checks, and are for trade accounts receivable remittances only. No securities or notes receivable are ever handled by Bennington Co., Inc.

Miss Martin gives the mail to Helen Ellis, the head bookkeeper, who opens all mail and distributes it as required. Customer's checks are given to Miss Martin at the adjacent desk, who immediately prepares bank deposit slips in duplicate and enters the remittances in the cash receipts journal. Miss Martin mails each day's deposit intact, daily, direct to First National Bank. The bank returns the validated duplicate deposit slips by mail, and Mrs. Ellis files them in chronological sequence. Mrs. Ellis posts the accounts receivable subsidiary ledger from the cash receipts journal. No other Bennington employee ever reviews or controls the bank deposits prepared by Miss Martin.

Any Bennington customer checks charged back by First National Bank are given by Mrs. Ellis to William Dale, controller, who follows up and redeposits the checks when appropriate. Mr. Dale also makes periodic reviews of the cash receipts journal for the propriety of sales discounts taken by customers.

Mrs. Ellis forwards monthly First National Bank statements and paid checks received in the mail to Mr. Dale. As part of his monthly bank reconciliation procedures, Mr. Dale compares dates and amounts of deposits recorded in the bank statement with the dates and amounts of entries in the cash receipts journal.

Miss Martin, Mrs. Ellis, and Mr. Dale are all bonded.

Figure 18-1:
Internal Control Write-up

Source: Walter B. Meigs, E. John Larsen, and Robert F. Meigs, *Principles of Auditing,* Fifth Edition (Homewood, Ill.: Richard D. Irwin, 1973), p. 144.

Internal Control Systems Flowchart

Bennington Co., Inc.
Cash Receipts Systems Flowchart
December 31, 19XX

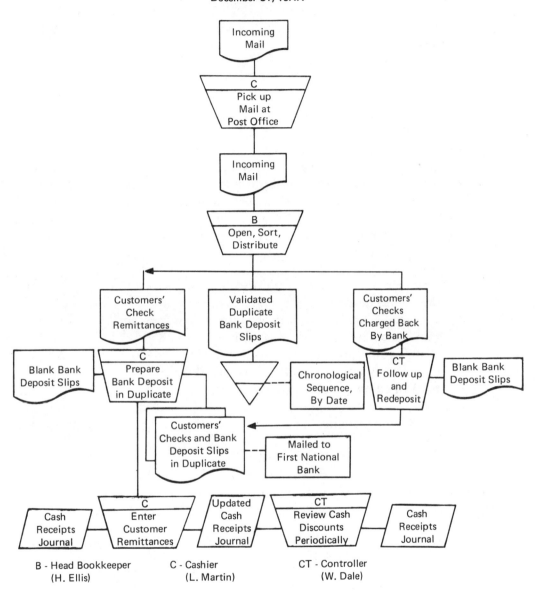

Figure 18-2

Source: Walter B. Meigs, E. John Larsen, and Robert F. Meigs, *Principles of Auditing,*
Fifth Edition (Homewood, Ill.: Richard D. Irwin, 1973), p. 146.

The Auditor's Tests

In the second phase of evaluation, the auditor conducts tests of transactions to provide reasonable assurance that prescribed control procedures are being carried out. However, the auditor should first decide whether such tests should be performed *before* continuing his examination of the system of internal control. Tests of transactions are necessary if the auditor is going to use the results of these tests to determine the nature, timing, and extent of substantial tests of other transactions or accounts. If the control procedures are not going to be relied upon for this purpose, or if the effort necessary to ascertain the reliability of the procedures exceeds the advantage achieved by such reliance, the tests would not be necessary. The assumption in the next paragraphs is that the auditor decides to perform tests to determine the reliability of control procedures.

The following guidelines suggest the logical approach for performing the appropriate audit tests:

1. Consider the nature of any errors, omissions, or other irregularities that could occur within the area being examined.
2. Consider what control procedures would normally prevent or reveal such errors, omissions, or irregularities.
3. Compare the procedures considered in #2 with the client's system of internal control and determine if they are being properly performed by the client's employees.
4. Evaluate any weakness uncovered and determine its effect on the nature, timing, and extent of other audit procedures to be performed.

The nature of the control procedures and the supporting evidence will influence the nature and timing of the auditor's tests. In this respect, the Committee on Auditing Procedure made the following statements:

> Some aspects of accounting control require procedures that are not necessarily required for the execution of transactions ... Tests of such procedures require inspection of the related documents to obtain evidence in the form of signatures, initials, audit stamps, and the like, to indicate whether and by whom they were performed and to permit an evaluation of the propriety of their performance.
> ... Independent auditors often make such tests during interim work. When this has been done, application of such tests throughout the

remaining period may not be necessary. Factors to be considered in this respect include (a) the results of the tests during the interim period, (b) responses to inquiries concerning the remaining period, (c) the length of the remaining period, (d) the nature and amount of the transactions or balances involved, (e) evidence of compliance within the remaining period that may be obtained from substantive tests performed by the independent auditor or from tests performed by internal auditors, and (f) other matters the auditor considers relevant in the circumstances.

Other aspects of accounting control require a segregation of duties so that certain procedures are performed independently . . . The performance of these procedures is largely self-evident from the operation of the business or the existence of its essential records; consequently, tests of determining whether they were performed by persons having no incompatible functions . . . Since such procedures frequently leave no audit trail of documentary evidence as to who performed them, tests of compliance in these situations necessarily are limited to inquiries of different personnel and observation of office personnel and routines to corroborate the information obtained during the initial review of the system.

As to accounting control procedures that depend primarily on segregation of duties and leave no audit trail, the inquiries . . . should relate to the entire period under audit, but the observations described therein ordinarily may be confined to the periods during which the auditor is present on the client's premises in conducting other phases of his audit.[5]

THE AUDITOR'S REPORT ON THE SYSTEM OF INTERNAL CONTROL

When serious deficiencies in the system of internal control are revealed, the auditor should prepare a letter or report outlining the weaknesses and making suggestions for overcoming them. Since the study and evaluation of the system is part of the auditor's work that is performed before the balance sheet date, the letter or report should precede the auditor's report and opinion by several weeks. When he issues such an internal control letter or report, he not only renders an additional service to the client but also may reduce his liability in the event that serious defalcations are later uncovered.

Usefulness of the Report

Traditionally the letter or report has been issued to management, which bears the ultimate responsibility for internal control. Often, it is directed to the client's Board of Directors or to an Audit Committee within the Board.

In recent years other groups outside the client's organization have become more interested in the independent auditor's report on internal control. Regulatory agencies, for example, may be interested because of the report's relevance for regulatory purposes or for the agency's examination function. A client or principle auditor may retain several CPA firms to audit various divisions or branches; those firms would also be interested in the auditor's report. In some cases management and/or a regulatory agency may consider the report useful to the general public. Because of this increased interest by such diverse groups, the AICPA's Committee on Auditing Procedure issued *Statement on Auditing Procedure No. 49,* "Reports on Internal Control," now section 640 in *Statement on Auditing Standards No. 1.* The objective of the Statement was to improve the understanding of the internal control report by the various recipients and to offer recommendations regarding the introductory language of such reports.

The Committee felt that there would be no problem of the client's management, regulatory agencies, or other CPAs misunderstanding the nature and meaning of the report on internal control. It assumed that these groups were comprised of individuals whose training, experience, and knowledge of the organization's affairs would provide a sound basis for understanding the auditor's study and evaluation of the system of internal control.

However, in contrast to these groups, the usefulness of the auditor's report to the general public raised some questions. To begin with, because of the technical and complex nature of a system of internal control, it is doubtful that members of this group would have the background necessary to understand the significance of the report. Also, the groups discussed in the preceding paragraph are directly concerned with the organization, and are in a position to take direct action based on such reports. Members of the general public are not generally in a position to take appropriate action. Finally, there is the question of the relevance of the auditor's report to the general public's evaluation of the performance of the organization. The auditor's report does not lend any additional credibility to his report on audited financial statements. And very little benefit, if any, accrues to the general public if the auditor's report is associated with interim or unaudited statements; not only because his report covers an earlier period but also because of the limited value of the statements themselves. The Committee concluded that whether internal control reports should be made available to the general public was a decision to be made by the client and/or a regulatory agency having jurisdiction in a particular case. Under no circumstances, however, should a report be issued to the general public in a document including unaudited statements.

Form for the Report

The Committee on Auditing Procedure indicated some preferences as to the format of the report issued by the independent auditor, depending upon whether the report is released in connection with the audit of the client's financial statements or as a result of special studies conducted for the client by the auditor.

Figure 18-3 shows the general introductory language suggested by the Committee for describing the objectives and limitations of a system of internal control, as well as the auditor's responsibility for, and evaluation of, the system. The introductory paragraphs are followed by a description of any material weaknesses relating to prescribed procedures or to compliance with them. Recommendations for improvements, if considered practical, or comments regarding corrective action taken, or in process by management, or the fact that no conclusion in that respect has been reached are included next.

In some cases the auditor may realize that although weaknesses in the system of internal control exist, corrective action by management is not practical under the circumstances. If the auditor decides to exclude references to these weaknesses in his report, the Committee recommended that the last sentence of the language suggested in Figure 18-3 be modified as follows:

> However, such study and evaluation disclosed the following conditions that we believe to be material weaknesses for which corrective action by management may be practicable in the circumstances.[6]

If there are no weaknesses in the system of internal control, the auditor may still use the suggested language in Figure 18-3, after revising the last sentence in the fourth paragraph.

Subsequent to the release of Statement No. 49, many regulatory agencies have begun or completed various publications outlining criteria for the evaluation of the system of internal control to aid them in their administrative responsibilities. In response to this development, the Committee on Auditing Procedure issued *Statement on Auditing*

Procedure No. 52: "Reports on Internal Control based on Criteria Established by Governmental Agencies," now section 641 in *Statement on Auditing Standards No. 1.* The purpose of Statement No. 52 was to supplement Statement No. 49 in regards to the special publications and reporting requirements being established by the agencies. The Committee's recommendations are summarized next.

—Because of the varying reporting criteria of the agencies involved, the auditor's report should clearly identify the matters covered by his study and indicate whether the study included tests of transactions for the control procedures covered in his examination.

—If the criteria established by the agencies are in questionnaire or other form that require objective answers, the auditor's report may express an overall conclusion regarding the adequacy of the control procedures reviewed, based on the required criteria, subject to any exceptions noted during the examination. In addition, the auditor should report any material weaknesses that come to his attention even though they are not included in the required criteria, describing these weaknesses in detail.

—Finally, when the auditor issues a report of this type, a statement should be included to indicate the purpose for which the report is being prepared, and should indicate that its use be limited only to the purposes for which it was intended.

We have examined the financial statements of ABC Company for the year ended December 31, 19____ , and have issued our report thereon dated February 23, 19____ . As a part of our examination, we reviewed and tested the Company's system of internal accounting control to the extent we considered necessary to evaluate the system as required by generally accepted auditing standards. Under these standards the purpose of such evaluation is to establish a basis for reliance thereon in determining the nature, timing, and extent of other auditing procedures that are necessary for expressing an opinion on the financial statements.

The objective of internal accounting control is to provide reasonable, but not absolute, assurance as to the safeguarding of assets against loss from unauthorized use or disposition, and the reliability of financial records for preparing financial statements and maintaining accountability for assets. The concept of reasonable assurance recognizes that the cost of a system of internal accounting control should not exceed the benefits derived and also recognizes that the evaluation of these factors necessarily requires estimates and judgments by management.

There are inherent limitations that should be recognized in considering the potential effectiveness of any system of internal accounting control. In the performance of most control procedures, errors can result from misunderstanding of instructions, mistakes of judgment, carelessness, or other personal factors. Control procedures whose effectiveness depends upon segregation of duties can be circumvented by collusion. Similarly, control procedures can be circumvented intentionally by management with respect either to the execution and recording of transactions or with respect to the estimates and judgments required in the preparation of financial statements. Further, projection of any evaluation of internal accounting control to future periods is subject to the risk that the procedures may become inadequate because of changes in conditions and that the degree of compliance with the procedures may deteriorate.

Our study and evaluation of the Company's system of internal accounting control for the year ended December 31, 19___ , which was made for the purpose set forth in the first paragraph above, would not necessarily disclose all weaknesses in the system. However, such study and evaluation disclosed the following conditions that we believe to be material weaknesses.

Figure 18-3:
Suggested Introductory Language for the Auditor's Report on Internal Control

Source: *Statement on Auditing Standards No. 1.* Copyright © 1973 by the American Institute of Certified Public Accountants, Inc., Section 640.12.

REFERENCES

1. *Statement on Auditing Standards No. 1.* Copyright © 1973 by the American Institute of Certified Public Accountants, Inc., Section 320.09.

2. *Internal Control: Elements of a Coordinated System and Its Importance to Management and the Independent Accountant.* Copyright © 1949 by the American Institute of Certified Public Accountants, Inc., p. 6.

3. *Statement on Auditing Standards No. 1.* Copyright © 1973 by the American Institute of Certified Public Accountants, Inc., Section 150.02.

4. *Ibid.,* Section 320.27-320.28.

5. *Ibid.,* Section 320.58-320.59, 320.61-320.63.

6. *Ibid.,* Section 640.13.

19   Audit Workpapers

The second standard of field work states that

> Sufficient competent evidential matter is to be obtained through inspection, observation, inquiries, and confirmations to afford a reasonable basis for an opinion regarding the financial statements under examination.[1]

In accumulating this evidence the auditor develops workpapers.

Workpapers are records of procedures followed, tests performed, information obtained, and conclusions reached during the auditor's examination. The principle objectives in developing workpapers include the following:

1. To provide guidelines for the organization and coordination of all phases of the examination.
2. To serve as a check list of evidence accumulated to substantiate account balances.
3. To provide a report of the work performed which can be used to review the overall adequacy of the examination.
4. To facilitate the preparation of the auditor's report.
5. To provide information regarding matters to be discussed with the client.
6. To provide information for the preparation and review of tax returns and governmental reports.

7. To provide evidence and information for subsequent audits, such as substantiation of opening balances in succeeding years, control and coordination over transactions and test periods examined in succeeding audits, and to serve as a guide to newly assigned assistants in performing various phases of the audit during the current examination.

ESSENTIAL FEATURES OF AUDIT WORKPAPERS

To show that he has conducted his examination in conformity with generally accepted auditing standards, the auditor must attach considerable importance to the development of workpapers. Generally, the workpapers should not only be complete, but free of nonessential information, but also appropriately organized and arranged for easy understanding and reference by others. The AICPA's Committee on Auditing Procedure suggested the following guidelines concerning the quantity, type, and content of working papers:

1. Data sufficient to demonstrate that the financial statements or other information upon which the auditor is reporting were in agreement with (or reconciled with) the client's records.
2. That the engagement had been planned, such as by use of work programs, and that the work of any assistants had been supervised and reviewed, indicating observance of the first standard of field work.
3. That the client's system of internal control had been reviewed and evaluated in determining the extent of the tests to which auditing procedures were restricted, indicating the observance of the second standard of field work.
4. The auditing procedures followed and testing performed in obtaining evidential matter, indicated observance of the third standard of field work. The record in these respects may take various forms, including memoranda, check lists, work programs and schedules, and would generally permit reasonable identification of the work done by the auditor.
5. How exceptions and unusual matters, if any, disclosed by the independent auditor's procedures were resolved or treated.
6. Appropriate commentaries prepared by the auditor indicating his conclusions concerning significant aspects of the engagement.[2]

GUIDELINES FOR PREPARING WORKPAPERS

The following guidelines reflect current professional practice in the development of audit workpapers:

1. A separate workpaper should be prepared for each topic, and only one side of the workpaper should be used.
2. Every workpaper should show the name of the client, the topic contained in the workpaper, and the audit date.
3. Every workpaper should show the name or initials of the auditor preparing it, the day it was prepared and the name or initials of the manager or partner reviewing it.
4. Every workpaper should indicate the source of the information presented and the nature of the work performed.
5. Every workpaper should be indexed to the lead schedule or to the working trial balance and brought together with other workpapers in a binder or file folder as soon as it is completed.
6. A separate workpaper containing questionable matters to be investigated should be developed as the audit proceeds. The matters listed should be reviewed and satisfactorily reconciled before the completion of the examination.

There are, of course, varying "formats" for preparing the workpapers developed during an examination. Usually a similar workpaper from the preceding audit is helpful; in some cases the form of the old workpaper may be copied without change, while in others some changes may be required. The auditor must consider the work to be shown, and develop a workpaper that clearly and most effectively presents the information and indicates the audit procedures performed.

CLASSIFICATION OF AUDIT WORKPAPERS

Permanent File

The auditor usually maintains two distinct sets of binders or files of workpapers during an examination: a permanent file and the current workpapers. The permanent file contains relatively unchanging information from prior audits that have a long-term value for subsequent examinations. Typical information maintained in the permanent file would include the following:

1. Extracts or copies of certificate of incorporation, charter amendments and by-laws.
2. Background information regarding the company, such as a brief history of the company, description of the business, location of branches or sales offices, if any, and lists of officers.

3. Extracts or copies of corporate minutes.
4. Extracts or copies of long-term contracts, leases, pension plans, and similar agreements.
5. Information regarding organization charts, job and procedures manuals, charts of account, and the system of internal control.
6. Summary, expanding schedules for such "permanent" accounts as fixed assets and depreciation, capital stock, and retained earnings.
7. Notations regarding periods selected for test examinations from year to year.
8. Continuing notes on the status of prior years' tax returns and summaries of revenue agents' examinations; also a description of differences between generally accepted and tax accounting principles applicable for the company.
9. Summary, comparative balance sheet and income statement amounts and operating ratios from preceding audits.

In addition to providing a convenient reference for matters used from year to year, eliminating the need to duplicate certain workpapers, the permanent file offers other advantages relevant to the examination. The file may serve as a check list of major items to be covered by the auditor-in-charge, and as a guide to familiarize new assistants with the nature and operations of the client. Also, reference to the contents of the permanent file may aid the manager or partner in his review of the overall adequacy of the examination.

Current Workpapers

The binders or files containing those workpapers developed during the current examination would include the following major items:

1. The audit programs, management and internal control questionnaires, and worksheets indicating reconciliation of questions raised during the audit and the review of the audit.*
2. The working trial balance.
3. Worksheets indicating suggested adjusting and reclassification journal entries.
4. A draft of the auditor's report, including the financial statements.
5. Letters of representations from the client and others.

---

*Audit programs were discussed in Chapter 17 and internal control questionnaires were reviewed in Chapter 18. Work sheets covering questions raised during the audit and the review were referred to in an earlier section of this chapter.

6. Worksheets showing supporting schedules and various computations and analyses developed in the course of accumulating evidence to substantiate account balances.

Working Trial Balance

The working trial balance is a work sheet containing columns for listing the balances of the accounts in the general ledger for the current and previous year, the auditor's adjustments and reclassification entries, and the final dollar amounts that will appear in the financial statements.

Adjusting and Reclassification Entries

During the course of an audit the auditor may uncover errors or omissions in the client's accounting records. To adjust these errors the auditor prepares appropriate journal entries for later discussion with the client. The auditor may also prepare reclassification journal entries for items which, although correctly recorded in the accounting records, require reclassification for fair presentation in the client's financial statements.

Letters of Representations

The auditor customarily obtains letters of representations from the client regarding receivables, inventories, fixed assets, liabilities, and other matters. The letters are addressed to the auditor, signed by the client, and contain statements regarding the correctness and authenticity of certain amounts shown on the financial statements, and any other matters for which the auditor requests such representation. The auditor may also obtain other letters from outside sources regarding certain matters relevant to the financial statements. For example, the auditor may write the attorney for the client and request a letter indicating what lawsuits, if any, the client may be engaged in currently, an indication as to the outcome of the suit, and the extent of claims for damages that may have to be settled in the event the client loses the lawsuit.

Other Workpapers

As the auditor verifies the individual items listed on the working trial balance he prepares a variety of working papers in substantiation of the accounts under examination. Some workpapers take the form of schedules, or listings of the details comprising the balance of an account. Other workpapers may present independent computations prepared by the auditor that are compared to the amount shown in the client's records. Still other workpapers present analyses of account balances. Finally, some workpapers may contain purely expository information, such as internal control write-ups, or take the form of letters and other documents.

While workpapers may take many different forms, some are very similar regardless of the nature of the client's operations, or problems encountered in the examinations. Thus, many CPA firms will provide preprinted or standard workpapers that can be utilized in any audit engagement. Standard workpapers not only reduce the amount of work necessary for assistants to prepare workpapers but also introduce an element of consistency in workpapers whenever possible. Figure 19-1 through Figure 19-4 show a representative sample of standard workpapers used by several CPA firms.

CONTENTS OF WORKPAPERS

Before the auditor can express an opinion on the client's financial statements he must accumulate sufficient competent evidence that the amounts shown on the financial statements are supported by the account balances in the general and subsidiary ledgers. In following the audit trail back through the records, he must determine that these balances correctly summarize all entries and that these entries reflect the proper interpretation of all transactions reported in various forms and documents. Sufficient evidential matter refers to the quantity of the evidence; competent evidential matter concerns the quality of the evidence in substantiating the presentations on the financial statements.

Sufficient Evidence

How much evidence is enough requires the exercise of the auditor's professional judgment. The following guidelines may prove useful in this respect:

1. The amount of evidence examined is dependent upon the quality of the system of internal control.
2. The evidence selected for examination should be representative of the types of transactions from which the items are drawn.
3. The evidence selected for examination should contain as many large transactions as possible so the auditor can substantiate most of the dollar amounts presented on the financial statements in as short a time as possible.
4. While cost should not be a determining factor, the examination of too much evidence adds little to the quality of the examination

ORIGINAL
To be retained by Bank

_____ 19____

Dear Sirs:

Your completion of the following report will be sincerely appreciated. IF THE ANSWER TO ANY ITEM IS "NONE", PLEASE SO STATE. Kindly mail it in the enclosed stamped, addressed envelope direct to the accountant named below.

Report from   Yours truly.

_____
(ACCOUNT NAME PER BANK RECORDS)

(Bank)_____   By_____
                                                        Authorized Signature

_____

_____

Bank customer should check here if confirmation of bank balances only (item 1) is desired. ☐

Ernst & Ernst
1200 Equitable Building
St. Louis, Missouri 63102

NOTE — If the space provided is inadequate, please enter totals hereon and attach a statement giving full details as called for by the columnar headings below.

Dear Sirs:

1. At the close of business on_____ 19____ our records showed the following balance(s) to the *credit* of the above named customer. In the event that we could readily ascertain whether there were any balances to the credit of the customer not designated in this request, the appropriate information is given below.

AMOUNT	ACCOUNT NAME	ACCOUNT NUMBER	SUBJECT TO WITH-DRAWAL BY CHECK?	INTEREST BEARING? GIVE RATE
$				

2. The customer was directly liable to us in respect of loans, acceptances, etc., at the close of business on that date in the total amount of $_____, as follows:

AMOUNT	DATE OF LOAN OR DISCOUNT	DUE DATE	INTEREST		DESCRIPTION OF LIABILITY, COLLATERAL, SECURITY INTERESTS, LIENS, ENDORSERS, ETC.
			RATE	PAID TO	
$					

3. The customer was contingently liable as endorser of notes discounted and/or as guarantor at the close of business on that date in the total amount of $_____, as below:

AMOUNT	NAME OF MAKER	DATE OF NOTE	DUE DATE	REMARKS
$				

4. Other direct or contingent liabilities, open letters of credit, and relative collateral, were

_____

_____

5. Security agreements under the Uniform Commercial Code or any other agreements providing for restrictions, not noted above, were as follows (if officially recorded, indicate date and office in which filed):

_____

_____

Yours truly, (Bank) _____

Date_____19____   By_____
A-4   Authorized Signature

Figure 19-1

Source: American Institute of Certified Public Accountants

369

CASH COUNT

COUNTED BY _____ DATE _____ TIME _____

CURRENCY

Twenties _____				
Tens _____				
Fives _____				
Twos _____				
Ones _____				

COIN (Silver)

Dollars _____				
Halves _____				
Quarters _____				
Dimes _____				
Nickels _____				
Cents _____				

WRAPPED COIN

Halves _____				
Quarters _____				
Dimes _____				
Nickels _____				
Cents _____				

Checks for Deposit	list attached	
Cash Items	" "	
Pay Roll Advances	" "	
Undistributed Disbursements	" "	
Bad Checks	" "	
Other	" "	
	TOTAL	

Received of representatives of Ernst & Ernst, Cash and Cash Items as hereon listed amounting to

($ _____) _____ DOLLARS

this being all cash or cash items in my possession for which I am accountable to _____

_____

_____	_____	_____
Place	Date	

Figure 19-2

Source: Ernst & Ernst

STANDARD CONFIRMATION INQUIRY
FOR LIFE INSURANCE POLICIES
Developed by
AMERICAN INSTITUTE OF CERTIFIED PUBLIC ACCOUNTANTS
LIFE OFFICE MANAGEMENT ASSOCIATION
MILLION DOLLAR ROUND TABLE

```
┌─────────────────────────┐
│      DUPLICATE          │
│  To be mailed to accountant │
└─────────────────────────┘
```

———————————19———

Dear Sirs:

Please furnish the information requested below in items 1 through 9 (and also in items 10 through 12 if any of those items are checked) for the policies identified on lines A, B and C. This information is requested as of the date indicated. IF THE ANSWER TO ANY ITEM IS "NONE," PLEASE SO STATE. The enclosed envelope is provided for the return of one copy of this form to the accountant named below.

(Ins. Co.)_____

_____

_____

(Name of owner as shown on policy contracts)

Information requested as of____ _____

Ernst & Ernst
1200 Equitable Building
St. Louis, Missouri 63102

Request authorized by

	Col. A	Col. B
A. Policy number		
B. Insured		
C. Beneficiaries as shown on policies (if verification requested in item 11) Col. A— Col. B—		
1. Face amount of basic policy	$	$
2. Values shown as of (insert date if other than date requested)		
3. Premiums, including prepaid premiums, are paid to (insert date)		
4. Policy surrender value (excluding dividends, additions and indebtedness adjustments)	$	$
5. Surrender value of all dividend credits, including accumulations and additions	$	$
6. Termination dividend currently available on surrender	$	$
7. Other surrender values available to policyowner — a. Prepaid premium value	$	$
b. Premium deposit funds	$	$
c. Other	$	$
8. Outstanding policy loans, excluding accrued interest	$	$
9. If any loans exist, complete either "a" or "b" a. Interest accrued on policy loans	$	$
b. 1.) Loan interest is paid to (enter date)		
2.) Interest rate is (enter rate)		

The accountant will indicate by a check (✔) which if any of items 10-12 are to be answered

☐ **10.** Is there an assignee of record? (enter Yes or No)		
☐ **11.** Is beneficiary of record as shown in item C above? (enter Yes or No*)	*	*
☐ **12.** Is the name of policyowner (subject to any assignment) as shown at the top of the form? (enter Yes or No)_____. If No, enter name of policyowner of record._____ _____		

*If answer to 11 is No, please give name of beneficiary or date of last beneficiary change._____

_____

Date _____By_____Title_____
                          For the insurance company addressed

A-6

Figure 19-3

Source: American Institute of Certified Public Accountants

APPROVED NAME   DATE

BY _____ ____

INVENTORY TEST COUNTS

E & E REPRESENTATIVE			NAME OF CLIENT					PAGE OF
PLANT OR WAREHOUSE			BUILDING	FLOOR	SECTION	DEPARTMENT		
DATE	TIME			STAGE OF COMPLETION. DESCRIPTION. CONDITION, ETC.				
	FROM	TO						
TAG NUMBER	PART NUMBER	UNIT	QUANTITY					
				1				
				2				
				3				
				4				
				5				
				6				
				7				
				8				
				9				
				10				
				11				
				12				
				13				
				14				
				15				
				16				
				17				
				18				
				19				
				20				
				21				
				22				
				23				
				24				
				25				
				26				
				27				

Figure 19-4

Source: Ernst & Ernst

but results in greater costs and time-consuming effort for the auditor.

(The size of the sample evidence and the alternative methods of selecting the sample items are discussed in Chapter 17.)

Competent Evidence

In exercising his judgment as to what constitutes competent evidence, the auditor usually considers its source:

1. Physical evidence.
2. Documentary evidence:
    a. Originating outside the organization and submitted directly to the auditor.
    b. Originating outside the organization but held by the client.
    c. Originating entirely within the organization.
3. The client's journals and ledgers.
4. The auditor's computations, comparisons, and ratios.

Physical Evidence

The auditor's actual inspection or count of certain items is the best evidence of physical existence. However, it should be noted that this type of examination is applicable only to certain assets listed on the financial statements, and still does not establish conclusively either the quality or ownership of these items. For example, observing the client's inventory merely substantiates its physical existence; the observation does not reveal its value or conclusively prove the client's ownership.

Documentary Evidence

The most important types of evidence examined by the auditor consist of documents. However, the worth of documentary evidence depends on its source.

Documentary evidence originating outside the organization and submitted directly to the auditor is the best source of evidence. Because it does not pass through the hands of the client, the information contained in the documents cannot be altered to conceal misrepresentations or fraud in the financial statements. Bank confirmations and accounts receivable confirmations are two examples of this type of evidence.

Evidence originating outside the organization but held by the client will represent the bulk of the externally generated documents examined by the auditor. In deciding how reliable this type of evidence may be, the auditor must consider whether the document is of a type that could easily be created or altered by someone within the organization. The auditor should be particularly wary of accepting as evidence any documents that have been altered in any way.

The degree of reliability placed on documents originating purely within the organization depends on the quality of the system of internal control. A strong system of internal control would allow the auditor to attribute a greater reliability to internally generated documents than a weak system.

Client's Journals and Ledgers

The dependability of the client's journals and ledgers is also determined by the quality of the internal controls covering their preparation.

Auditor's Computations, Comparisons, Ratios

The auditor's comparison of various asset, liability, revenue, and expense accounts with corresponding balances from the prior period is a simple but effective means of detecting significant changes that will require further investigation and/or reconciliation. In addition to comparing dollar amounts the auditor may also review the percentage relationships between items on the financial statements from year to year. Finally, the auditor may perform various independent computations to verify the accuracy of the client's records.

Evidence generally is not sufficient in itself as a means of substantiating amounts presented in the financial statements, but it may be useful in disclosing situations that require further investigation or corroboration from other forms of evidence. The auditor must continuously be cautious, alert, and questioning in accumulating the information necessary to enable him to express an opinion on the client's financial statements.

INDEXING AND RETENTION OF WORKPAPERS

As the workpapers are completed they should be indexed to supporting lead schedules or the working trial balance and inserted in a binder or file folder. The system of indexing the papers varies among CPA firms, but as mentioned earlier in this chapter, the purpose of indexing is solely to provide organization and easy reference to the workpapers. Figures 19-5 and 19-6 show indexing guides for both the permanent file and the current workpapers.

The workpapers are the property of the independent auditor, whether the workpapers were developed by the auditor or prepared by the client. The current workpapers should be stored in the firm's file room; the length of time the workpapers should be kept will vary depending on the needs of the auditor and state laws regarding retention of such records. For example, workpapers may be retained for a period of five years, while such bulky items as inventory observation work sheets and accounts receivable confirmations may be safely disposed of after three years.

The contents of the permanent file, on the other hand, are utilized from year to year by the auditor and his staff and therefore the decision affecting the retention of some workpapers and the removal of other depends upon the judgment of the auditor.

Index Reference	Workpapers Relating To
A	Charter and By-Laws
B	Internal Control Evaluation
C	Accounting Procedures
D	Contracts
E	Licensing Agreements
F	Leases
G	Depreciation Lapse Schedules
H	Loan Agreements
I	Compensation Contracts and Agreements
J	Pension and Profit Sharing Plans
K	Stock Option Plans
L	Analysis of Capital Stock, Paid-in Capital, and Retained Earnings
M	Computations of Retained Earnings Restrictions
N	Data Relating to Status of Income Taxes
O	Review of Minutes and Correspondence

Figure 19-5:
Indexing Guide for Permanent File Workpapers

Index Reference	Audit Workpapers
A-1	Statements and Audit Review Notes
A-2	Letters of Representation
A-3	Working Trial Balance
A-4	Adjustments
A-5	Reclassifications
A-6	Litigations
A-7	Contingencies
A-8	Purchase, Sales, and Other Committments
B-1	Internal Control Questionnaire
B-2	Audit Program
C	Cash
D	Marketable Securities
E	Notes and Accounts Receivable
F	Inventories
G	Investments and Other Assets
H	Fixed Assets
I	Prepaids, Intangibles, and Deferred Charges
J	Notes Payable
K	Accounts Payable and Accrued Expenses
L	Federal and State Income Taxes
M	Other Liabilities
N	Long-term Debt
O	Reserves
P	Capital Stock
Q	Retained Earnings
R	Sales
S	Purchases
T	Payroll
U-Z	Operations

Figure 19-6:
Indexing Guide for Current Audit Workpapers

REFERENCES

1. *Statement on Auditing Standards No. 1.* Copyright © 1973 by the American Institute of Certified Public Accountants, Inc., Section 150.02.

2. *Ibid.,* Section 338.05.

Considerable research has been conducted on the subject of audit reports, and much has been written in this area. Accordingly, this chapter does not attempt to cover the subject exhaustively, but merely outlines certain major aspects of the auditor's report. Reference should be made to such publications as the American Institute of Certified Public Accountants' *Statement on Auditing Standards No. 1,* and *Auditing Research Monograph No. 1* on the auditor's reporting obligation for more detailed discussions and examples.

The standards of reporting guide the auditor in preparing his opinion on a client's financial statements:

1. The report shall state whether the financial statements are presented in accordance with generally accepted accounting principles.
2. The report shall state whether such principles have been consistently observed in the current period in relation to the preceding period.
3. Informative disclosures in the financial statements are to be regarded as reasonably adequate unless otherwise stated in the report.
4. The report shall either contain an expression of opinion regarding the financial statements, taken as a whole, or an assertion to the effect that an opinion cannot be expressed. When an overall opinion

cannot be expressed, the reasons therefore should be stated. In all cases where an auditor's name is associated with financial statements, the report should contain a clear-cut indication of the character of the auditor's examination, if any, and the degree of responsibility he is taking.[1]

SHORT-FORM REPORTS

The short-form report is customarily issued in connection with the basic financial statements. The report usually consists of a *scope* paragraph that describes the scope of the auditor's examination, and an *opinion* paragraph that indicates the auditor's opinion on the fairness of the client's financial statements. The principle alternatives for short-form reports are:

1. Unqualified opinion
2. Qualified opinion
3. Adverse opinion
4. Disclaimer of opinion

Unqualified Opinion

The unqualified, or standard, short-form opinion generally used is as follows:

We have examined the consolidated balance sheets of _____ and its subsidiary companies as of_____and _____ and the related statements of consolidated earnings and retained earnings and changes in consolidated financial position for the years then ended. Our examination was made in accordance with generally accepted auditing standards, and accordingly included such tests of the accounting records and such other auditing procedures as we considered necessary in the circumstances.

In our opinion, the accompanying consolidated balance sheets and statements of consolidated earnings and retained earnings and changes in consolidated financial position present fairly the financial position of_____ and its subsidiary companies at _____and _____and the consolidated results of their operations and the changes in their financial position for the years then ended, in conformity with generally accepted accounting principles applied on a consistent basis.

Figure 20-1:
Standard Short-Form Report

The opinion reflects the most recent change in the standard short-form report—the inclusion of a reference to the statement of changes in financial position. The Accounting Principles Board in Opinion No. 19 required certain business entities to present a statement summarizing changes in financial position in addition to the traditional balance sheet and statements of income and retained earnings. The Committee on Auditing Procedure then issued *Statement on Auditing Procedure No. 50,* now section 511 in *Statement on Auditing Standards No. 1,* which revised the standard short-form report to include the statement of changes in financial position, and indicated the auditor's responsibilities on reporting on this statement.

An unqualified opinion may be expressed only when the auditor has formed his opinion on the basis of an examination made in conformity with generally accepted auditing standards, and when the financial statements (1) fairly present the financial position, results of operations, and changes in financial position of an entity in accordance with generally accepted accounting principles applied on a consistent basis and (2) include appropriate informative disclosures to make the statements not misleading.

Using the Work of Other Auditors

A modification in the wording of the standard short-form report may be necessary when the auditor shares the responsibility for an engagement with other auditors; that is, when other auditors perform an examination on subsidiaries, divisions, or branches of a client for the principal auditor. The effect on the report of the principal auditor is summarized below from *Statement on Auditing Procedure No. 45,* "Using the Work and Reports of Other Auditors," now section 543 in *Statement on Auditing Standards No. 1.*

If the principal auditor assumes responsibility for the work of the other auditor insofar as that work relates to the expression of his opinion, he need make no reference to the other's examination. The principal auditor would adopt this position when:

1. Part of the examination is made by another independent auditor which is an associated or correspondent firm and whose work is acceptable to the principal auditor based on his knowledge of the professional standards and competence of that firm; or
2. The other auditor was retained by the principal auditor and the work was performed under the principal auditor's guidance and control; or
3. The principal auditor, whether or not he selected the other auditor, nevertheless takes steps he considers necessary to satisfy himself as to

the other auditor's examination and accordingly is satisfied as to the reasonableness of the accounts for the purpose of inclusion in the financial statements on which he is expressing his opinion; or

4. The portion of the financial statements examined by the other auditor is not material to the financial statements covered by the principal auditor's opinion.[2]

On the other hand, if the principal auditor does not assume responsibility for the work of the other auditor, or he decides to make reference to the other auditor regardless of other considerations, the report should refer to the examination of the other auditor, clearly indicating the division of responsibility between himself and the other auditor, and show the magnitude of that portion of the financial statements that was examined by others.

The decision to make reference to the other auditor should not be interpreted as a qualification of the opinion, or be considered inferior to a report in which no reference is made. The report merely indicates the division of responsibility between auditors who performed the examinations on various components of the overall financial statements. The following illustrates the wording of a report where other auditors performed a portion of the examination.

We have examined the accompanying consolidated financial statements of _____ as of _____and _____ . Our examinations were made in accordance with generally accepted auditing standards and accordingly included such tests of the accounting records and such other auditing procedures as we considered necessary in the circumstances.

We did not examine the financial statements of _____, a consolidated subsidiary, which accounts for approximately 9% of the consolidated assets and revenues. These statements were examined by other independent accountants whose reports thereon have been furnished to us and our opinion expressed herein, insofar as it relates to the amounts included for _____ is based solely upon the reports of the other independent accountants.

In our opinion, based on our examinations, and the reports mentioned above of other independent accounts, the accompanying consolidated financial statements present fairly the

Figure 20-2
Short-Form Report—Reference to Other Auditors

financial position of _____ and its subsidiaries at _____ and _____, the results of their operations and changes in financial position for the years then ended in conformity with generally accepted accounting principles consistently applied.

Figure 20-2 *(continued)*

Whether or not the principal auditor decides to make reference to other auditors, he should make inquiries regarding their professional reputation and independence, and adopt appropriate measures to assure the coordination of his and the other auditor's work to achieve a proper examination affecting the overall financial statements. Section 543.10 suggests the following guidelines:

1. Make inquiries as to the professional reputation and standing of the other auditor to one or more of the following:
   a. The American Institute of Certified Public Accountants, the applicable state society of certified public accountants and/or the local chapter, or in the case of a foreign auditor, his corresponding professional organization.
   b. Other practitioners.
   c. Bankers and other credit grantors.
   d. Other appropriate sources.
2. Obtain a representation from the other auditor that he is independent under the requirements of the American Institute of Certified Public Accountants and, if appropriate, the requirements of the Securities and Exchange Commission.
3. Ascertain through communication with the other auditor:
   a. That he is aware that the financial statements of the component which he is to examine are to be included in the financial statements on which the principal auditor will report and that the other auditor's report thereon will be relied upon (and, where applicable, referred to) by the principal auditor.
   b. That he is familiar with accounting principles generally accepted in the United States and with the generally accepted auditing standards promulgated by the American Institute of Certified Public Accountants and will conduct his examination and will report in accordance therewith.
   c. That he has knowledge of the relevant financial reporting requirements for statements and schedules to be filed with regulatory agencies such as the Securities and Exchange Commission, if appropriate.
   d. That a review will be made of matters affecting elimination of

intercompany transactions and accounts and, if appropriate in the circumstances, the uniformity of accounting practices among the components included in the financial statements.

(Inquiries as to matters under 1, and 3b and c ordinarily would be unnecessary if the principal auditor already knows the professional reputation and standing of the other auditor and if the other auditor's primary place of practice is in the United States.)[3]

If the principal auditor decides *not* to make reference to the other auditors, section 543.12 suggests the following additional procedures also be considered:

1. Visit the other auditor and discuss the audit procedures followed and results thereof.
2. Review the audit programs of the other auditor. In some cases, it may be appropriate to issue instructions to the other auditor as to the scope of his audit work.
3. Review the working papers of the other auditor, including his evaluation of internal control and his conclusions as to other significant aspects of the engagement.[4]

Accounting Changes

Another modification in the wording of the standard short-form report is required when the auditor reports on a change in accounting principle effected by the client. A review of the Accounting Principles Board Opinion No. 20 concerning accounting changes is outlined in another section of this book. In regards to this section, the auditor must modify his report as to consistency in adherence to the first standard of reporting, and indicate the nature of the change in the report. It is assumed that the auditor concurs with the change unless he indicates his exception to the change in his opinion. However, to be more informative, it is suggested that the auditor indicate his concurrence explicity (unless the change is the correction of an error) in the opinion with the wording "with which we concur" or "which we approve." The wording of the report will vary, depending on the method of accounting for the effect of the change. Section 546 of *Statement on Auditing Standards No. 1* provides illustrations of suggested wording of the opinion paragraph of the report. A sample of a report on a change in accounting principle and the related note to the financial statements would be:

We have examined the consolidated balance sheets of _____ and subsidiaries as of _____ and _____ and the related statements of earnings, retained earnings, and changes in financial position for the years then ended. Our examination was made in accordance with generally accepted auditing standards and accordingly included such tests of the accounting records and such other auditing procedures as we considered necessary in the circumstances.

In our opinion, the aforementioned consolidated financial statements present fairly the financial position of _____ and subsidiaries at _____ and _____ and the results of their operations and changes in their financial position for the years then ended, in conformity with generally accepted accounting principles consistently applied during the period subsequent to the change, with which we concur, made as of _____, in the method of accounting for certain investments (see summary of significant accounting policies).

SUMMARY OF SIGNIFICANT ACCOUNTING POLICIES
INVESTMENT IN AFFILIATES

In accordance with Opinion No. 18 of the Accounting Principles Board, as of January 1, 19XX the company changed its method of accounting for investments in affiliates, owned more than 20% but not in excess of 50%, from the cost to the equity method. Under the equity method of accounting, investments are recorded at cost increased by the company's share of unremitted earnings since date of acquisition. Prior to _____, investments in affiliates which were 50%-owned were carried on the equity method, but investments less than 50%-owned were carried at cost. The effect of the change was to increase earnings before extraordinary item for _____ by $_____.

Figure 20-3:
Short-Form Report—Change in
Accounting Principle

Circumstances requiring the auditor to deviate from the standard short-form report are summarized as follows:

1. The scope of his examination is limited or affected:
    a. By restrictions imposed by the client,
    b. By other conditions which preclude the application of auditing

procedures considered necessary in the circumstances, or

   c. Because part of the examination has been made by other independent auditors (see preceding section.)

2. The financial statements are not presented in conformity with generally accepted accounting principles, which include adequate disclosure.
3. Accounting principles are not consistently applied.
4. Unusual uncertainties exist concerning future developments, the effects of which cannot be reasonably estimated or otherwise resolved satisfactorily.[5]

Qualified Opinion

When the auditor qualifies his opinion, he should clearly indicate the nature of his qualification, the reason therefore, and, if determinable, the effect this will have on the financial statements. The report may also refer the reader to a note to the financial statements to reveal the nature of the matter.

A qualified opinion usually takes one of two forms: *except for* type of opinion and *subject to* type of opinion. The *except for* opinion may, for example, indicate that the auditor is not in agreement with certain accounting principles applied by the client in preparing the financial statements, as shown next. In the note to the financial statements, the *reason* for the qualification, along with the *approximate amount* involved and its effect on the financial statements are shown.

We have examined the consolidated balance sheets of the _____ and its subsidiaries at _____ and _____ and the related consolidated statements of income, retained income and changes in financial position for the years then ended. Our examinations were made in accordance with generally accepted auditing standards and accordingly included such tests of the accounting records and such other auditing procedures as we considered necessary in the circumstances.

In our opinion, except that provision has not been made for the possible increase in income taxes of future periods as set forth in Note 2 to the financial statements, the accompanying statements examined by us present fairly the consolidated financial position of _____ and its subsidiaries at _____ and _____, the results of their operations and the changes in financial position for the years then

Figure 20-4:
Qualified Opinion—<u>Except for</u> Qualification

ended, in conformity with generally accepted accounting principles consistently applied.

Note 2. AMORTIZATION, ACCELERATED AND GUIDELINE DEPRECIATION: The Company and its subsidiaries maintain their books of account, and the accompanying statements have been prepared, in conformity with principles and methods of accounting prescribed or authorized by the Interstate Commerce Commission. These principles and methods do not require a provision for the income tax effect of the excess of tax amortization and depreciation over recorded depreciation as is necessary to conform with generally accepted accounting principles.

The supplementary income information shown below reflects the adjustments necessary to present net income in conformity with generally accepted accounting principles:

	(Year)	(Year)
Net income (in conformity with ICC principles) as set forth in the consolidated income statement	$	$
Adjustments to generally accepted accounting principles:		
Net income (as it would be stated in conformity with generally accepted accounting principles)	$	$
Earnings per share	$	$

The cumulative deferred effect on federal income taxes due to the abovementioned differences, computed at tax rates applicable to the individual years, not reflected in the accompanying balance sheet, amounted to $ _____ at _____.

Figure 20-4 *(continued)*

The *subject to* opinion is used when, for example, the outcome of certain litigation the client is involved in results in a qualified opinion by the auditor. An illustration of the wording of the opinion and the related note to the financial statements is:

We have examined the consolidated balance sheet of _____ and its subsidiaries as at _____ and the consolidated statements of income, retained earnings, contributed surplus and source and use of funds for the year then ended. Our examination of the financial statements of _____ and those subsidiaries of which we are the auditors included a general review of the accounting procedures and such tests of accounting records and other supporting evidence as we considered necessary in the circumstances. We have relied on the reports of the auditors who have examined the financial statements of the other subsidiaries.

In our opinion, subject to the final outcome of the litigation referred to in Note 12 these consolidated financial statements present fairly the financial position of the companies as at _____ and the results of their operations and the source and use of their funds for the year then ended, in accordance with generally accepted accounting principles applied on a basis consistent with that of the preceding year.

Note 12. Litigation:

(a) During _____ and _____ , _____, a subsidiary, was named in a number of class actions alleging violations of antitrust laws. These actions were brought in various jurisdictions and have been consolidated for pre-trial proceedings in the United States District Court for the District of _____ .

Legal counsel is unable to assess whether any of these actions have merit and _____,and counsel are unable to determine what damages, if any, may result from these actions.

(b) In _____, the company was named in a suit initiated by a former officer and director of a subsidiary company alleging breach of

Figure 20-5:
Qualified Opinion—Subject to Qualification

> contract. The plaintiff is seeking ordinary dam-
> ages of approximately $_____and punitive
> damages of $_____; Legal counsel is unable
> at this time to estimate the liability, if any,
> which may result from this action; however,
> counsel is of the opinion that punitive damages
> under the laws of the Commonwealth of
> _____are not normally recoverable.

Figure 20-5 *(continued)*

Adverse Opinion

The auditor must issue an adverse opinion when the financial statements clearly *do not* present fairly the client's financial position, results of operations, and changes in financial position. The exceptions to fair presentation must be *so* material that the auditor is not even justified in issuing a qualified opinion. The auditor should give the reason for the opinion in a middle paragraph to his report, for example:

> We have examined the consolidated balance sheet of _____ and its subsidiaries as at _____ and the consolidated statements of income, retained earnings, and source and use of funds for the year then ended. Our examination was made in accordance with generally accepted auditing standards, and accordingly included such tests of the accounting records and such other auditing procedures as we considered necessary in the circumstances.
>
> Although the proceeds of sales are collectible on the installment basis over a five-year period, revenue from such sales is recorded in full by the Company at time of sale. However, for income tax purposes, income is reported only as collections are received and no provision has been made for income taxes on install-ments to be collected in the future, as required by generally accepted accounting principles. If such provisions had been made, net income for _____and retained earnings as of _____, would have been reduced by approxi-mately $_____and $_____, respectively, and the balance sheet would have included a liability for deferred income taxes of approximately $_____.

Figure 20-6:
Adverse Opinion

Because of the materiality of the amounts of omitted income taxes as described in the preceding paragraph, we are of the opinion that the consolidated financial statements do not fairly present the financial position of the companies as at _____ and the results of their operations and the source and use of funds for the year then ended, in accordance with generally accepted accounting principles.

Figure 20-6 (continued)

Disclaimer of Opinion

A disclaimer of opinion is, in fact, no opinion at all. Several conditions may exist which require the auditor to disclaim an opinion:

1. The auditor may not be independent, and therefore cannot perform an examination in conformity with the first general standard of generally accepted auditing standards (see *Statement on Auditing Standards No. 1,* section 517, "Reporting When a Certified Public Accountant is Not Independent").
2. The auditor may not be able to conduct an examination in accordance with generally accepted auditing standards because of client-imposed restrictions (see *Statement on Auditing Standards No. 1,* section 541, "Restrictions Imposed by Client").
3. The auditor is unable to express an opinion on the financial statements because of material uncertainties dependent upon future developments or decisions beyond the client's control (see *Statement on Auditing Standards No. 1,* section 547, "Unusual Uncertainties as to the Effect of Future Developments on Certain Items").
4. The auditor has prepared the financial statements without conducting an examination in accordance with generally accepted auditing standards (see *Statement on Auditing Standards No. 1,* section 516, "Unaudited Financial Statements").

When the auditor disclaims an opinion he should also, as discussed in the issuance of qualified and adverse opinions, indicate the reason for the disclaimer in his report. The following example illustrates a disclaimer of opinion due to client-imposed restrictions in regards to the confirmation of accounts receivable and payable:

We have examined the consolidated balance sheet of _____ and its subsidiaries as at _____ and the consolidated statements of income, retained earnings, and source and use of funds for the year then ended. Our examination was made in accordance with generally accepted auditing standards, and accordingly included such tests of the accounting records and such other auditing procedures as we considered necessary in the circumstances, except as stated in the following paragraph.

In accordance with the terms of our engagement we did not request confirmation of balances as of _____ directly with the Company's customers and creditors.

Because the assets and liabilities to which the omitted auditing procedures relate enter materially into the determination of financial position, results of operations, and the source and use of funds, we do not express an opinion on the accompanying financial statements taken as a whole.

Figure 20-7:
Disclaimer of Opinion

LONG-FORM REPORTS

In addition to, or as a substitute for, the short-form report issued in connection with the financial statements, the auditor may be requested to prepare a long-form report.

Unlike the short-form report, no uniformity exists in the preparation of long-form reports. The report does contain the usual financial statements, but the additional information presented depends upon the specific needs of the client and/or interested outside parties. For example, the following detailed information may appear in the report:

1. Comparative summary of operations, showing percentage relationships as well as dollar amounts.
2. Detailed analyses of certain balance sheet and income statement accounts, such as receivables, fixed assets, long-term debt, and selling and administrative expenses.

If both a short-form and a long-form report are issued by the auditor, he should make sure that the long-form report does not contain any information which, if not referred to in the short-form report, might lead the reader to believe that the short-form report is misleading because material facts known to the auditor were not disclosed. Also, his comments concerning information presented in the long-form report should not lead the reader to assume that he is expressing exceptions or reservations as to the financial statement presentations, but only providing explanations regarding certain accounts.

If the auditor issues only a long-form report, the report should indicate the nature of his examination, if one was performed, and the responsibility he assumes for the information contained in the report. Since the language of the short-form report is generally modified, the auditor must clearly indicate his position regarding the detailed information in the long-form report. For example, the auditor may indicate that his examination was made primarily to express an opinion on the financial statements; the other information presented, although not considered necessary for a fair presentation in the statements, is included for the purpose of supplementary analysis, was subjected to appropriate audit procedures, and is stated fairly in all material respects in relation to the financial statements taken as a whole. On the other hand, if the auditor did not extend his procedures to include the other information presented in the report, he must state that it was not subjected to appropriate audit procedures and indicate the extent of any responsibility he assumes for this information.

SPECIAL REPORTS

The auditor is frequently requested to prepare special reports covering a variety of situations and purposes. An important and common characteristic of these reports is that the language of the short-form report is usually not applicable because: (1) there is no intent to present fairly financial position, results of operations, or changes in financial position, (2) the results of the report may be only to serve as a basis for managerial action; or (3) certain reporting standards may not fit the engagement.

Cash Basis Accounting Records

Financial statements prepared on a cash basis do not present fairly the financial position or results of operations of an entity because they are not prepared in accordance with generally accepted accounting principles.

In reporting on statements prepared substantially or entirely on a cash basis, disclosure must be made in the statements (or, if necessary, in the auditor's report) that the statements have been prepared on a cash basis. Also, the form of disclosure should indicate the general nature of those material items omitted (i.e., accounts receivable and accounts payable) and, where practical, the effect of such omissions on the financial statements. A sample report based on financial statements prepared on a cash basis is as follows:

We have examined the statement of cash receipts and disbursements of _____ for the year ended _____.
Our examination was made in accordance with generally accepted auditing standards, and accordingly included such tests of the accounting records and such other auditing procedures as we considered necessary in the circumstances.

In our opinion, the accompanying statement of cash receipts and disbursements summarizes fairly the cash transactions of _____
for the year ended _____.

Figure 20-8:
Special Report—Cash Basis Statements

Nonprofit Organizations

For many nonprofit organizations generally accepted accounting principles have not been defined clearly. In others (e.g., hospitals and educational institutions) commonly accepted accounting practices are not in conformity with generally accepted accounting principles.

The auditor preferably should report on the conformity of the entity's financial statements with generally accepted accounting principles; however, the report may indicate that the financial statements were prepared in accordance with established accounting practices applicable to a particular entity, and therefore fairly present the financial position and results of operations on that basis. In engagements where the auditor believes even commonly accepted accounting principles have not been clearly established, the language of his report should reflect the guidelines suggested in connection with cash basis accounting records discussed in the preceding section. The next opinion illustrates a report prepared for a charitable organization reporting on a cash basis:

> We have examined the statement of assets and liabilities arising from cash transactions of _____ as of _____ and the related statement of cash receipts and disbursements for the year then ended. Our examination was made in accordance with generally accepted auditing standards, and accordingly included such tests of the accounting records, and such other auditing procedures as we considered necessary in the circumstances.
>
> Because of the omission of accounts receivable and accounts payable, it is our opinion the accompanying statements do not present the financial position or results of operations of _____
>
> In our opinion, the accompanying statements of assets and liabilities and cash receipts and disbursements present fairly the assets and liabilities of _____ at _____ arising from cash transactions, and a summary of the cash transactions from the year then ended, on a basis consistent with that of the preceding year.

Figure 20-9:
Special Report—Nonprofit Organization

Reports Covering Incomplete
Financial Presentations

The auditor is asked sometimes to examine certain calculations or to review the impact of probable future transactions or events. Examples of such matters might include calculations of royalties, rentals, profit-sharing bonuses, and the conversion of convertible debt.

The report issued in these circumstances should state clearly what information is being presented, the basis on which it was prepared, and the auditor's opinion as to whether it is presented fairly on that basis. Of course, the auditor should also indicate the degree of responsibility he assumes in either preparing the report or in assisting the client in the preparation of the report, as illustrated in the next example concerning an examination performed to ascertain the fairness of gross sales reported by a client in connection with a lease agreement:

> We have examined the accounting records of_____ for the year ended _____ for the purpose of determining the amount of gross sales during _____as outlined in the agreement of _____covering the lease of property to _____by _____. Our examination was made in accordance with generally accepted auditing standards, and accordingly included such tests of the accounting records and such other auditing procedures as we considered necessary in the circumstances.
>
> In our opinion, the gross sales as outlined in the lease of _____ for the year ended _____ are fairly stated at $_____.

Figure 20-10:
Special Report—Incomplete Financial Presentation

Reports on Prescribed Report Forms

Statements prepared and filed on required forms designed by governmental agencies or regulatory bodies may require certain classifications or practices that in the auditor's opinion do not present fairly the financial position, results of operation, or changes in financial position of his client. In addition, the prescribed language of the auditor's report may call for conclusions that are not normally part of his functions or responsibilities as an independent auditor.

If the prescribed forms call for the auditor to express opinions which he believes he is not justified in making, he may either reword them or submit a separate report. Some forms can be brought into line with the auditor's functions or responsibilities simply by including additional captions or wording, while others may require complete revision. Usually a revised or separate report is accepted by the agencies or regulatory bodies with whom they are filed.

SUBSEQUENT EVENTS

The final section of this chapter concerns the matter of "subsequent events" uncovered by the auditor. While this subject could be integrated into the review of the various types of opinions presented earlier in the chapter, the importance in terms of the auditor's legal liability and his reporting obligation warrants a special section. The material reviewed in this section was originally discussed by the Committee on Auditing Procedures in *Statements on Auditing Procedures Nos. 41 and 47,* "Subsequent Discovery of Facts Existing at the Date of Auditor's Report" and "Subsequent Events," respectively, now sections 530, 560, and 561 in *Statement on Auditing Standards No. 1.* Filings under the Securities Act of 1933 are discussed in section 710.

Events Subsequent to the Balance Sheet Date But Prior to Issuance of the Statements and Auditor's Report

The period beyond the balance sheet date with which the auditor must be concerned in completing various phases of his examination is known as the *subsequent period.* This period extends to the date of the auditor's report, and its duration depends upon the practical requirements of each examination. As an audit approaches completion, the auditor is expected to concentrate more and more on resolving various auditing and reporting matters, and not to conduct a continuing review on those matters which he has already performed auditing procedures and obtained satisfaction. But certain procedures must be applied to transactions and events occurring after the balance sheet date specifically for the purpose of uncovering subsequent events that may affect the fairness of the financial statements. These procedures may include discussions with appropriate client personnel, review of corporate minutes and correspondence, review of interim financial statements, and examination of certain records.

Although the auditor's report ordinarily is issued in connection with historical statements that present the financial position, results of operation and changes in financial position for a period ended on a particular date, certain transactions or events that occur subsequent to the balance sheet date, but prior to the issuance of the financial statements and auditor's report, may require adjustments to, or disclosure in, the statements.

Events Requiring Adjustment

Some subsequent events provide additional evidence regarding conditions that existed at the balance sheet date, and affect estimates that are inherent in the preparation of the financial statements. For example, a substantial loss on an uncollectible account receivable may be revealed subsequent to the balance sheet date, but the situation nevertheless affects the fairness of the statements on that date. Subsequent events of this type require adjustments to the statements.

The date and type of report issued by the auditor is determined by the disposition of these types of events by the client. If the event occurs after the date of the auditor's report but prior to its issuance, the statements should be adjusted or the auditor should qualify his opinion. If the adjustment is made without disclosure, the auditor's report ordinarily should be dated as of the completion of the field work. On the other hand, if the adjustment and disclosure of the event is made, or no adjustment is made and a qualified opinion is given, the auditor may "dual date" the report—that is, date the report as of the completion of the field work with the exception of the date concerning the subsequent event uncovered. Or the auditor may date the report as of the date concerning the event. It should be kept in mind that the choice of methods available in dating the report will affect the auditor's responsibility for events occurring after the completion of the field work but prior to issuance of the report. Dual dating the report limits the auditor's responsibility for subsequent events to the specific event uncovered. Dating the report as of the later date extends his responsibility for subsequent events to that date.

Events Requiring Disclosure

Other subsequent events provide evidence in regards to conditions not existing as of the balance sheet date. For example, the client may have incurred a loss of fixed assets or inventories as a result of a fire, flood, or other natural catastrophe. The financial statements do not need to be adjusted for events of this type, but disclosure is usually required to prevent the statements from being misleading. The event may have such a substantial impact on the entity that the auditor may also wish to include a paragraph in his report to call the reader's attention to the event and its effect.

The dating and type of report necessitated by these types of events are the same as the guidelines discussed in connection with events requiring adjustments.

Events Subsequent to the Date of Auditor's Report that May Have Existed at the Date of the Report

Occasionally the auditor may become aware of information relating to financial statements on which he has issued a report that were not known to him at the date of the report, and that may have affected his report had he known the facts. The auditor should first conduct an investigation of the matter to determine if the information is reliable and did exist at the date of his report. If he then concludes that the report would have been affected had the information been known to him at the date of the report and had not been reflected in the financial statements, and if he believes there are persons relying upon, or likely to rely upon, the statements who would attach importance to the information, he should advise the client to make appropriate disclosure. Section 561.06 provides the following guidelines regarding disclosure:

1. If the effect on the financial statements or auditor's report of the subsequently discovered information can promptly be determined,

disclosure should consist of issuing, as soon as practicable, revised financial statements and auditor's report. The reasons for the revision usually should be described in a note to the financial statements and referred to in the auditor's report. Generally, only the most recently issued audited financial statements would need to be revised, even though the revision resulted from events that had occurred in prior years.

2. When issuance of financial statements accompanied by the auditor's report for a subsequent period is imminent, so that disclosure is not delayed, appropriate disclosure of the revision can be made in such statements instead of reissuing the earlier statements pursuant to subparagraph 1.

3. When the effect on the financial statements of the subsequently discovered information cannot be determined without a prolonged investigation, the issuance of revised financial statements and auditor's report would necessarily be delayed. In this circumstance, when it appears that the information will require a revision of the statements, appropriate disclosure would consist of notification by the client to persons who are known to be relying or who are likely to rely on the financial statements and the related report that they should not be relied upon, and that revised financial statements and auditor's report will be issued upon completion of an investigation. If applicable, the client should be advised to discuss with the Securities and Exchange Commission, stock exchanges, and appropriate regulatory agencies the disclosure to be made or other measures to be taken in the circumstances.[6]

If the client refuses to make the suggested disclosures, the auditor should notify the board of directors of such refusal and the fact that he will take the following steps, as appropriate, to prevent further reliance on his report:

1. Notification to the client that the auditor's report must no longer be associated with the financial statements.

2. Notification to regulatory agencies having jurisdiction over the client that the auditor's report should no longer be relied upon.

3. Notification to each person known to the auditor to be relying on the financial statements that his report should no longer be relied upon. In many instances, it will not be practicable for the auditor to give

appropriate individual notification to stockholders or investors at large, whose identities ordinarily are unknown to him; notification to a regulatory agency having jurisdiction over the client will usually be the only practicable way for the auditor to provide appropriate disclosure. Such notification should be accompanied by a request that the agency take whatever steps it may deem appropriate to accomplish the necessary disclosure. The Securities and Exchange Commission and the stock exchanges are appropriate agencies for this purpose as to corporations within their jurisdictions.[7]

The following guidelines govern the content of any disclosure made by the auditor in accordance with the steps just outlined to persons other than the client:

1. If the auditor has been able to make a satisfactory investigation of the information and has determined that the information is reliable:
   a. The disclosure should describe the effect the subsequently acquired information would have had on the auditor's report if it had been know to him at the date of his report and had not been reflected in the financial statements. The disclosure should include a description of the nature of the subsequently acquired information and of its effect on the financial statements.
   b. The information disclosed should be as precise and factual as possible and should not go beyond that which is reasonably necessary to accomplish the purpose mentioned in the preceding subparagraph a. Comments concerning the conduct or motives of any person should be avoided.
2. If the client has not cooperated and as a result the auditor is unable to conduct a satisfactory investigation of the information, his disclosure need not detail the specific information but can merely indicate that information has come to his attention which his client has not cooperated in attempting to substantiate and that, if the information is true, the auditor believes that his report must no longer be relied upon or be associated with the financial statements. No such disclosure should be made unless the auditor believes that the financial statements are likely to be misleading and that his report should not be relied on.[8]

REFERENCES

1. *Statement on Auditing Standard No. 1.* Copyright © 1973 by the American Institute of Certified Public Accountants, Inc., Section 150.02.

2. *Ibid.,* Section 543.05.

3. *Ibid.,* Section 543.10.

4. *Ibid.,* Section 543.12.

5. *Ibid.,* Section 540.01.

6. *Ibid.,* Section 561.06.

7. *Ibid.,* Section 561.08.

8. *Ibid.,* Section 561.09.

PART IV

Profit Planning

21 The Master Budget as a Control Instrument

The three phases of management's vital function of planning—short-term operating budgets (Chapter 21); working and capital budgets (Chapter 22); and, tax planning (Chapters 23 and 24)—are considered in Part IV.

Planning, although based on the most thorough deliberations of management, loses much of its potential value if not followed with prompt feedback from the operating levels of management. Comparison of planned performance with actual costs by department, program, or cost center highlights problem areas where corrective action is needed. Responsibility accounting is the description given to this exercise of comparison and control at each appropriate level of organizational structure. It is facilitated with a plan that is geared to the actual level of operations of the period. This is called flexible budgeting.

Modern business has turned increasingly to decentralization of operations because of significant increases in both size and complexity. Usually this move has been accompanied by centralization of administration, resulting in the need for improved communications between widely dispersed facilities. The advent of the computer and teleprocessing which connect corporate headquarters with multi-plan operations, provides the hardware for effective communications. But the software must be tailored to the real information requirements of all organizational levels.

Performance measurement through budgetary control is one of those needs. Through the process of data reduction, the great complexity of information from all operating levels is refined and summarized in a prompt, tailored manner. Top management then can coordinate all corporate activities toward its profit plans, both long and short term. These plans are carried out in responsibility accounting through the principle of *management by exception*, and the bulk of the control effort is exercised by the manager at the scene of operations—the manufacturing or distribution functions—to whom such specific authority has been delegated.

The functions of planning, organizing, staffing, directing, and controlling are all involved in the budgetary process. Performance measurement of the attainment of budgetary goals or objectives represents the heart of responsibility accounting. Those who participate in the measurement also have their performance measured. The use of standard costs for purposes of evaluation appears to be the keystone of effective management control as far as manufacturing functions are concerned. Such tools take away some of the mystery of managing and force managers to carefully think out and outline a plan prior to decision-making.[1] Another important benefit of standard costs used in conjunction with budgetary planning is manpower planning by adjusting personnel levels with a planned approach that is based on anticipated fluctuations in the volume of activity. Other benefits of using standard costs such as the justification of capital expenditures are discussed in Chapter 22.[2]

The Purpose and Preparation of the Operating Budget

The budgeting process is not a new concept. As indicated in Figure 21-2 "agricultural man" engaged in the same managerial functions in reaching his organization's objectives as does "modern man." Standards were set, the best growing area was selected and the land was properly prepared. If the yield was inadequate in comparison with the organization's objectives with particular respect to quantity, corrective action was taken by those to whom the authority for crops and land had been delegated.

Figure 21-2 supplements the planning process by supplying guidelines for reviewing objectives and for planning resources to support the forecasted volume of business. The availability of funds is projected in the working capital budget and the fixed assets that are required are planned in the capital expenditures budget. (Both of these are presented in Chapter 22.) In Figure 21-3, detailed steps in preparing the annual profit plan are shown starting with the sales budget with respect to volume,

THE BUDGETING PROCESS

Agricultural man	Modern man
1. Save seed and put it aside to grow next year. Set enough aside to take care of group.	1. Plan for profit or improvement, evaluate available resources, and draw on past experiences to determine availability of funds for future use.
2. Place seeds in container in dry place. Select area for growing in spring. Prepare land.	2. Organize for action—set up staff and statistics, and evaluate future opportunity. Prepare forms and procedures and establish a formal comprehensive budget plan for each activity and for the company as a whole.
3. Set seeds in ground, arrange to care for growing plants. Make persons assume responsibility for taking care of the growing assigned to them.	3. Administer actual performance; buy machines, establish flow of information, see that products and plans are operative. Establish responsibility of personnel for attaining objectives. (Pray for results.)
4. Harvest the grain and place in stores. Count stores to see if supply will meet food requirements of the tribe or group as planned.	4. Measure actual results to budget. Use accounting techniques to compare actual performance.
5. Increase planting area, save more seed, change planting area to plan for better yield, if needed, or for more members in the group when next year rolls around.	5. Correct and improve operating and financial practices for the next year. Institute cost reduction programs, reach for new product lines, discontinue marginal items, improve trading areas, etc.

Figure 21-1

Source: "The Budgeting Process" Paul A. May, *Management Accounting,* New York, January 1973, p. 20.

price, and discounts to be offered. Such sales forecasts usually represent a certain mix of products or product lines and a projected contribution margin for each. Models have been developed, as discussed in Chapter 8, to offer assistance to management in coping with such variables as the size of the market for each product line, the pricing strategy to be employed that is consistent with the elasticity of demand for the product involved, optional approaches to product distribution and many others.

Production schedules are prepared based on the sales forecast, and incorporate labor, material, and overhead costs using standard costs developed by the engineers as described in Chapter 13. In Figure 21-3 variable costs are accumulated, including distribution costs, and deducted from sales to show a gross return. Fixed or non-variable overhead is deducted, along with other items including estimated income taxes, to show operating income. The latter amount represents the targeted return on investment, or return on sales, constituting management's financial goals for the budget year, just as the sales forecast projects the operational or volume goals for the period.

Figure 21-1 points out the need to "organize for action" in planning for profit, including the preparation of forms and procedures representing a formal, comprehensive budget plan for each activity and the company as a whole. This approach is further illustrated in the "Budgetary Guidelines in a Job Cost Environment" (Figure 21-2). The firm's policies include the primary objectives of any large contractor such as insuring that costs are controlled and kept within "marketable limits as related to contract bidding." Responsibilities are spelled out—operating supervision controls manpower deployment subject to stipulated limitations; the Department of Budgets has the responsibility of coordinating and summarizing specific data into control groups by contract effort; and, overhead budgets are included. The results include rates for bidding purposes, consisting of hourly rates for direct manufacturing and engineering effort, and overhead rate percentages for the manufacturing, engineering, procurement, and general and administrative pools.

BUDGET GUIDELINES FOR A JOB COST FACTORY

PLANNED OBJECTIVES AND OPERATING POLICIES

A. The primary objective is to insure that future costs stay within planned limits—based on what the firm's markets will permit. Utilization of planned or budgeted performance for comparison with actuals for control purposes is also a major objective.

Figure 21-2

B. Quarterly budgets are prepared in line with anticipated production requirements and are flexible to the extent that monthly adjustments can be processed for jobs not previously included.

C. Anticipated requirements with respect to work force are budgeted only for attainable production in line with plant capacity.

D. Manpower needs are planned on the basis of total paid hours required, including overtime. Labor budgets include fringe benefits and overtime, considered controllable by operating supervision.

E. Budgeted equivalent personnel, defined as total hours, including overtime, divided by regular hours for one individual during the period, is compared to equivalent personnel based on actual hours worked to achieve manpower control.

F. Employment requisitions for budget approval will be used with a manpower factor, computed by dividing the latest four weeks of overtime by 160, adding the latest tabulated head count and comparing the resultant factored head count with the budget.

PROCEDURES

Ultimate responsibility for establishing quarterly budgets, including form and content, rests with the corporate controller.

Responsibility to determine manpower requirements rests with operating supervision, subject to the following limitations which require budget approval prior to initial action:

A. Reclassification of personnel between direct (on the clock personnel) and overhead (personnel not required to record hours worked on specific jobs.)

B. Transfer or loan of personnel between cost centers. If approved, loaned personnel will be charged to the benefitting department as to labor hours and dollars if the period exceeds three consecutive working days away from the individual's home department. Related fringe benefits remain in the home department.

C. All requisitions must be processed through the Personnel Department for the hire of all employees whether they represent replacements or new additions.

D. Personnel documents must be processed, including (1) job change, (2) employee release, (3) personnel review and (4) interdepartmental communications concerning the loan of employees. Transfers and job changes must be approved by the Personnel Department.

E. The Budgetary Control Department has the responsibility to obtain approved quarterly budgets by operating departments and sum-

Figure 21-2 (continued)

marize them by overhead pools, including engineering, manufacturing, procurement, and administration.

F. Quarterly budgets will be prepared by department heads and summarized by manpower effort and overhead accounts.

(1) Effort by jobs will be projected in the form of monthly direct charge hours and labor dollars allocated to each major product.

(a) Regular and overtime hours and dollars will be separated to permit the development of labor rates for bidding purposes.

(2) To prepare quarterly budgets for overhead, departmental summaries will show total direct charges along with all other indirect regular and overtime dollars and hours by overhead accounts. Each summary will be supported by a listing of personnel performing these hours including appropriate allowances for fringes.

(a) The Budgetary Control Department will furnish the monthly fringe factors.

G. The quarterly budget will be completed and in the hands of operating supervision prior to the start of the applicable quarter.

H. A preliminary budget printout, containing unapproved amounts, will precede the final approved quarterly budget and will be used in the approval process and for the computation of rates for bidding purposes.

For purposes of effective budgetary control, actual charges and hours worked, will be compared with those budgeted above in a monthly control report, prepared on a departmental basis.

DIRECT AND INDIRECT LABOR RATES USED

A. Direct Labor Rates:

Production and Engineering Departments—Direct labor hours will be multiplied by hourly rates resulting in direct labor dollars, exclusive of overtime premium.

Overtime premium in production and engineering departments will be calculated by multiplying direct labor dollars by a given percentage.

Quality Control Departments will use a percentage applied to production direct labor dollars.

B. Overhead Rates:

Production and Quality Control Departments will use a percentage, applied to all direct labor dollars (exclusive of overtime premium) to determine total allowable overhead dollars.

Costs of personnel engaged in bid and proposal effort will be included in Administrative Overhead.

Figure 21-2 *(continued)*

Engineering Departments will apply a percentage to all production direct labor dollars (exclusive of overtime premium) to determine total allowable overhead dollars, not including research and Bid and Proposal effort.

Procurement Departments will use a percentage, applied to direct material usage, including all raw materials and those in the hands of subcontractors.

Administrative Departments will use a percentage, applied to total direct material, direct labor (including overtime premium) and overhead dollars, including research and bid and proposal effort, for production, engineering and procurement overhead pools—resulting in administrative overhead, including patent allocation.

Figure 21-2 *(continued)*

STEPS IN PREPARING ANNUAL PROFIT PLAN

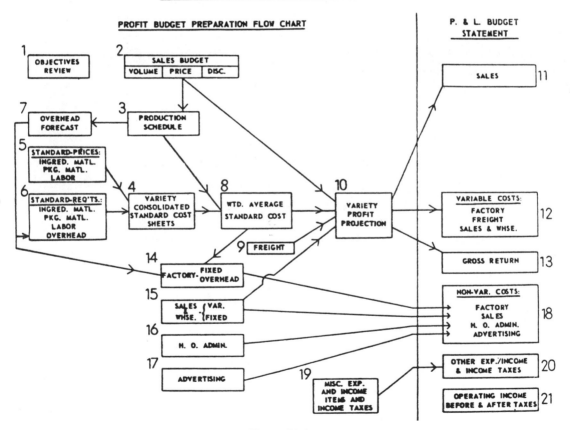

Figure 21-3

Source: *Responsibility Reporting,* Peat, Marwick, Mitchell & Co., 1961

To achieve the maximum in usefulness, budgetary or profit planning must be reinforced with timely reporting of actual operating results to make sure that planned performance is being realized and that the objectives agreed upon in the master budget are being met. Where such is not the case, corrective action by departmental managers is required. For this reason, responsibility statements serve a useful purpose—comparing each manager's actual costs for a given month or year with his budget (or standard if standard costing is employed) both in detail and in total.

Budgetary planning involves the acceptance of corporate objectives, usually starting with those involving sales volume, by-products, product lines, territories and corporate divisions. Using the contribution margin of each product and multiplying it by the targeted volume of all products represented in the sales mix for the year, it is possible to get a useful estimate of what is available for fixed overhead and for profit. Such projections have to be taken for what they are—simply estimates of most likely values as far as sales quantities, prices, costs, and profits are concerned for each product involved.[3] As a result, probabilistic profit budgets have been suggested. For example, in Figure 21-4, options are offered as far as volume is concerned, under the headings, "Pessimistic," "Most Likely," and "Optimistic," holding the sales price and unit costs constant under each of these three options.[4] This approach is somewhat comparable to the use of flexible budgets which apply to the determination of variable costs for each volume selected.

"Three-level" Probabilistic Budget Techniques

PROFIT BUDGET FOR YEAR ENDING JUNE 19XX

Sales (100,000 units @ $10)		$1,000,000
Variable costs		
Manufacturing ($5 per unit)	$500,000	
Marketing ($.50 per unit)	50,000	550,000
Marginal contribution		$ 450,000
Managed fixed costs		
Manufacturing	$ 20,000	
Marketing	10,000	
Administrative	40,000	70,000
Short-run margin		$ 380,000

Figure 21-4

Committed fixed costs		
Manufacturing	$180,000	
Marketing	40,000	
Administrative	60,000	280,000
Net income before tax		$ 100,000
Tax-50%		50,000
Net income after tax		$ 50,000

PROFIT BUDGET FOR YEAR ENDING JUNE 19XX

	Pessimistic	Most Likely	Optimistic
Sales ($10 per unit)	$800,000	$1,000,000	$1,100,000
Variable Costs			
Manufacturing	408,000	500,000	528,000
Marketing ($.50 per unit)	40,000	50,000	55,000
Marginal contribution	$352,000	$ 450,000	517,000
Managed fixed costs			
Manufacturing	10,000	20,000	30,000
Marketing	10,000	10,000	10,000
Administrative	25,000	40,000	40,000
Short-run margin	$307,000	$ 380,000	$ 437,000
Committed fixed costs			
Manufacturing	180,000	180,000	180,000
Marketing	40,000	40,000	40,000
Administrative	60,000	60,000	60,000
Net income before tax	$ 27,000	$ 100,000	$ 157,000
Tax-50%	13,500	50,000	78,500
Net income after tax	$ 13,500	$ 50,000	$ 78,500

[*]The data are based on optimistic, most likely, and pessimistic values for sales volume and variable costs being 110,000, 100,000, 80,000 and $4.80, $5.00, $5.10, respectively. Unit variable costs are assumed to vary inversely with volume. Committed costs and unit variable marketing cost are assumed to be certain; some managed costs are modified to reflect changing volume levels.

Figure 21-4 *(continued)*

Source: "Toward Probabilistic Profit Budgets," William L. Ferrara, and Jack C. Hayya, *Management Accounting,* New York, October 1970, p. 26.

Break-Even Analysis for Use in Sales Budgeting

By definition the break-even point stated in sales *dollars,* is that dollar total which covers all variable and fixed expenses but provides zero profit. Conversely, if stated in sales *volume,* the break-even sales volume is that number of *units* the sales value of which is equal to the total of all variable and fixed expenses.

Many costs are not completely variable or fixed in nature but are *mixed.* Maintenance expense, for example, may represent outlays for a full-time mechanic to keep the plant and machinery in operation eight hours a day, representing *fixed* expense. However, during the firm's busy season the machinery may be operated an extra four hours each day or an extra shift for several weeks or a month requiring the hiring of part-time maintenance people for such extra volume of production. The latter expense illustrates *variable* or direct maintenance expense, varying directly with volume. Such "mixed" expenses are usually more difficult to segregate between variable and fixed components than the above illustration suggests and require the use of techniques such as the mathematical method of least squares.

Cost behavior patterns (cost-volume-profit relationships) are analyzed through an application of simple regression analysis in the equation: Sales = Variable Expenses + Fixed Expenses + Net Income. The latter amount would be zero in the break-even sales determination illustrated below as follows:

(a) Assume: X = Quantity of end items to be sold to break-even (that is, cover all costs but provide no profit); a selling price of $1.00; variable costs of 60¢ and total fixed costs over the "relevant" ranges (that is, total fixed costs associated with the practical plant capacity now existing) of $800:

$$\underset{\substack{\text{(Break-even} \\ \text{sales volume)}}}{\$1.00\,X} \;=\; \underset{\substack{\text{(Variable} \\ \text{costs)}}}{.60\,X} \;+\; \underset{\substack{\text{(Fixed} \\ \text{costs)}}}{\$800} \;+\; \underset{\text{(Profit)}}{0}$$

Answer: 2000 units to be sold

Substituting this break-even sales quantity in the formula:

$$\underset{\substack{\$2{,}000 \\ \text{(Break-even sales)}}}{\$1\,(\,2000} \;=\; \underset{\substack{\$1{,}200 \\ \text{(Variable Costs)}}}{.60\,(2000)} \;+\; \underset{\substack{\$800 \\ \text{(Fixed Costs)}}}{\$800}$$

(b) Assume the use of the Contribution Margin approach to find X, break-even sales quantity, using the same values as in (a) above:

Unit Sales price ($1.00) less Variable Costs ($.60) = Contribution margin of .40 to fixed costs ($800) and profits (zero in break-even cases) =

$$\frac{\$800 \ (\text{Fixed costs over relevant range})}{.40 \qquad (\text{Unit contribution margin})} = 2000 \text{ units}$$

(c) Assume the break-even sales figure in *dollars* rather than *units* is desired in budgetary planning; using same values as above:

$$\text{B/E Sales Dollars (X)} = \frac{\text{Fixed Costs} + \text{Net Income (zero)}}{\text{Contribution Margin Rates} \left(\frac{.40}{(\$1.00)} \right)}$$

$$X = \frac{\$800}{40\%}$$

X = $2000 (the same break-even sales in dollars developed in (a) above)

The versatility of break-even techniques is seen in their use in answering management's "what if" questions in developing annual budgets.

Accepting the facts above that our break-even point is 2000 units at a sales price of $1.00, with fixed costs of $800, "what if" we: (1) wanted $1000 profit before taxes, or (2) lower the price to .80; purchase fixed assets in the amount of $4800 (assume straight line life of four years); and therefore increase depreciation and manufacturing overhead by $1,200? What would our new break-even point be for the year? In answer to question (1) the same equation used in (a) above would read:

$$\begin{array}{ccccccc}
\$1.00\ (X) & = & .60\ (X) & + & \$800 & + & \$1,000 \\
\text{Sales Volume} & = & \text{Variable} & + & \text{Fixed} & + & \text{Profit} \\
 & & \text{Costs} & & \text{Costs} & &
\end{array}$$

X = 4,500 units required to be sold to realize a profit of $1,000 before taxes.

In question (2), the new equation would read:

$$\begin{array}{cccc}
\$.80\ X & = & .60\ (X) & + & \$2,000 \\
(\text{New selling price} & = & (\text{Same unit vari-} & + & (\text{New fixed} \\
\text{X break-even quantity}) & & \text{able cost}) & & \text{cost})
\end{array}$$

The new break-even point in sales would be 10,000 units under these changed conditions.

A word of caution regarding the use of break-even analysis: It gives an approximate picture—not a completely precise one—because of the assumptions of linearity, and cost behavior on which based.

The Use of Standards in Flexible Budgeting

The budget is, in essence, an overall blueprint of anticipated revenues for the coming period, coupled with the costs of earning such revenues to meet planned profit objectives. Standards are introduced to implement the manufacturing cost budget in sufficient detail so that deviations from the manufacturing cost budget can be acted upon.

Not all such variances are the responsibility of *manufacturing* management. In the case of *price* variances of raw materials, the *Purchasing* Department is responsible for maintaining the budgeted standard. The responsibility of operating management includes correcting excessive *usage* of raw materials, labor, or variable overhead. Top management usually assumes responsibility for looking into excess capacity variances with respect to the incurrence of fixed overhead, such as depreciation on unused plant and equipment. Standards therefore serve as tools of implementation by which the budgeted goals are realized because action is taken on unfavorable variances from budgeted performance.

In addition to showing where corrective action is needed, standard costs allowed are based on actual production of finished goods for the period. This introduces flexibility into the system, and is therefore an extension of *flexible* budgeting based on volume produced as opposed to a static budget of a certain dollar total regardless of the volume level at which the department operated.

Example of a Budget for the Small Contractor

In the past, many contractors employing only a few personnel saw no beneficial results in what they considered sophisticated budgetary control procedures. Such refinements were thought to apply only to larger service or manufacturing operations.

But today's budgeting and accounting requirements are such that the small contractor needs such information for precisely the same reason that larger businesses do, namely, for intelligent bidding or for estimating and controlling costs to keep them in line with cost estimates contained in a bid for the job involved.

As an example, Figure 21-5A illustrates the budget summary for the preceding year for a paint contractor.[5] Figure 21-5B shows the details involved in computing job estimates. Estimating rates, or standards, have been developed with respect to productivity details by various types of painting, that is, brush, roller, and spray. The standards are based on the number of working hours per month, in order to provide flexible budgeting, and the number of square feet per hour which should be painted by each of these types of painting. Variable and fixed overhead are budgeted with respect to both manufacturing and distribution expense. The underlying assumption is that as square footage increases, a greater return on overhead, general administrative expense, and contribution to profit should be realized per hour.[6]

Labor rates per hour for each type of paint application are computed by multiplying the unit cost per thousand square feet by appropriate rates, namely, brush painting at 60 square feet per hour, roller at 200, and spray at 450, respectively.

Figure 21-5C illustrates a practical monthly operating summary in which actuals are compared with a budget based on man-hours permitting the contractor to see at a glance the current trend or milestone report and any imbalances with respect to the kinds of paint applications during that time period. Current trends are shown that may indicate how productivity in man-hours is holding up against what was expected in the budget.

Figure 21-5C also shows the usefulness of comparing overhead *actually distributed* or charged to the various jobs worked on during the month with the standard *allowed* overhead based on output. The result is a volume variance which often is the fault of top management for failing to bring in an adequate amount of business to operate at the budgeted level of activity determined at the beginning of the accounting period.

Therefore, the application of the same standard rates for charging overhead to various jobs as are used for estimating or bidding on new jobs results in an effective cost control mechanism for contractors regardless of operational size. Not only is a continuing validation of the rates available, but comparisons of actual expenditures to budgeted costs, actual hours to estimated hours, and actual materials to estimated materials give the contractor a very practical control *and* bidding tool.[7]

BUDGET SUMMARIES FOR 19XX*

Labor	No. of	Hours per:[1]		Rate	Amounts per:[2]	
Type	men	Week	Month	per hour	Week	Month
Brush	12	540	2,340	$4.50	$2,565.00	$11,115.00
Roller	6	270	1,170	4.55	1,296.75	5,619.25
Spray	6	270	1,170	4.65	1,325.25	5,742.75
Spray helper	6	270	1,170	4.40	1,254.00	5,434.00
Totals	30	1,350	5,850		$6,441.00	$27,911.00

Overhead	Budget per month @ 100%			Variable
Account	Total	Fixed	Variable	@ 85%
Salaries—office	$1,050.00	$1,050.00	$	$
FICA taxes	1,045.60	225.60	820.00	697.00
Unemployment benefit taxes	282.00	282.00		
Workmen's compensation insurance	360.00	90.00	270.00	229.50
Lights, heat, water	52.00	52.00		
Telephone	210.00	150.00	60.00	51.00
Office supplies and expense	100.00	60.00	40.00	34.00
Gas, oil—autos and trucks	1,000.00	250.00	750.00	637.50
Repairs and maintenance—buildings and equipment	450.00	100.00	350.00	297.50
Auto, truck repairs	450.00	100.00	350.00	297.50
Shop expense	320.00	120.00	200.00	170.00
Travel	75.00	50.00	25.00	21.25
Estimating expense	135.00	135.00		
Depreciation	510.00	510.00		
Building rental	200.00	200.00		
Equipment rental—office	30.00	30.00		
Taxes and licenses—general	70.00	70.00		
Insurance—general	270.00	270.00		
Sub-total—payroll related			1,090.00	926.50
Sub-total—other			1,775.00	1,508.75
Totals	$6,609.60	$3,744.60	$2,865.00	$2,435.25

Administrative	Budget per
Account	month
Salaries—officers	$2,100.00
Advertising	50.00
Dues and subscriptions	75.00
Travel and entertainment—officers	300.00
Legal and auditing	700.00
Donations	60.00
Bad debts	50.00
Penalties	40.00
Total	$3,375.00

Profit (pretax): $48,000.00 per year, or $4,000.00
   per month
1. Totals based on 45 hour week.
2. Amounts include overtime premium.

Figure 21-5A

*Source: "Standard Cost Accounting for Contractors." C.W. Walker *Management Accounting*
New York, July, 1972, pp.30-32.

SCHEDULE OF JOB ESTIMATING RATES*

Painting productivity details:

| Type | Hours per month | | Square feet per: | |
	@ 100%	@ 85%	Hour (net)	Month @ 85%
Brush	2,340	1,989.0	60	119,340
Roller	1,170	994.5	200	198,900
Spray	1,170	994.5	450	447,525
Total	4,680	3,978.0		765,765

Costs, expenses, and profit subject to operating variations

	Per month	Per MSF
Variable overhead—nonpayroll related—at 85%	$ 1,508.75	$ 1.97
Fixed overhead—at 100%	3,744.60	4.89
Administrative expenses—at 100%	3,375.00	4.41
Profit—pretax	4,000.00	5.22
Total (Excluding payroll related variable overhead)	$12,628.35	$16.49

Rates per hour:

| Labor | Brush | Roller | Spray |
	(60)	(200)	(450)
Dollars per month	$11,115.00	$5,619.25	$11,176.75
Hours per month @ 85%	1,989.0	994.5	994.5
Rates per hour	$ 5.58	5.65	11.24

Overhead:

	Brush	Roller	Spray
Variable—P/R related	$ .1402	$ .1402	$ .2804
Other	.1182	.3941	.8866
Sub-total	.2584	.5343	1.1670
Fixed	.2934	.9780	2.2005
Sub-total	.5518	1.5123	3.3675
General administrative	.2644	.8815	1.9833
Profit	.3134	1.0447	2.3506
Total overhead, etc.	1.1296	3.4385	7.7014
Total rate—all inclusive	$6.7116	$9.0888	$18.9400

Figure 21-5B

OPERATING SUMMARIES—FEBRUARY 19XX *

Time summary:
Week ended February 5, 19XX

	Brush	Roll	Spray	Helper	Actual wages	Standard overhead
		Actual hours				
Std overhead per hour all jobs	.5518	1.5123	3.3675	—		
Job #						
151	50	10	73	70		
189	84	93	110	112	$1,869.05	$ 557.40
193	63	86	41	41		
205	263	91	27	22		
Totals	460	280	251	245		

Activity summary:

	Brush	Roller	Spray	Total
		Actual hours		
Week ended:				
2-5	460	280	251	991
2-12	506	321	306	1,133
2-19	563	318	285	1,166
2-26	552	298	267	1,117
Totals	2,081	1,217	1,109	4,407
Normal budget at 100%	2,160	1,080	1,080	4,320

Overhead summary:

Type	Hours	Allowed Variable per hour	Amount	Standard Total per hour	Amount
Brush	2,081	$ .2584	$ 537.73	$ .5516	$1,147.88
Roller	1,217	.5343	650.24	1.5123	1,840.47
Spray	1,109	1.1670	1.294.20	3.3675	3,734.56
Totals	4,407		$2,482.17		$6,722.91[2]
Fixed overhead budget per month at 100%			3,744.60		
Total allowed			$6,226.77[1]		

Overhead variances:

Actual overhead	$6,523.88	
Allowed overhead	6,226.77[1]	
Spending Loss		$ 297.11
Standard overhead (charged to jobs)	6,722.91[2]	
Volume gain		(496.14)
Net gain		($ 199.03)

Figure 21-5C

1. Totals based on 45 hour week.
2. Amounts include overtime premium.

*Source: "Standard Cost Accounting for Contractors, "C.W. Walker, *Management Accounting*, New York, July, 1972, 0.32.

INCOME STATEMENT*
FOUR WEEKS ENDED FEBRUARY 19XX

Job income		$48,652.10
Cost of jobs billed		39,119.80
Gross profit at standard		$ 9,532.30
Overhead variances (favorable):		
Spending	$ 297.11	
Volume	(496.14)	
Total		(199.03)
Operating gain (loss)		$ 9,731.33
General adminstrative expense	$3,218.06	
Other (income) and deductions	(285.16)	
Total		2,932.90
Pretax Income (loss)		$ 6,798.43

Figure 21-5D

Ibid., p. 41.

Figure 21-5D further emphasizes the simplicity of this approach by condensing income statement essentials into a very brief but meaningful format. Other forms of presentation for effective budgetary control at all levels of the organizational structure are illustrated in Figures 21-6 and 21-7.

Reporting for Effective Budgetary Control

Someone has said that accountants and doctors of medicine have a common philosophy, namely, if therapy works, don't change it. The problem is that many *accounting* therapies—managerial reports and statements—are completely ineffective but are continued anyway.

For example, accounting reports may contain such a mass of figures that non-accounting, and even some accounting, executives simply will not take the time to go through them regardless of the information included. The same criticism applies to many computer printouts which are so voluminous that an additional analysis is needed to ferret out desired information from the mass of information received in the computer run and to summarize it into meaningful managerial reports.

Figure 21-6 illustrates *pro forma* responsibility reports that permit a division superintendent to see at a glance the expenditures of activities that are reported to him for the month, and year-to-date, and the budget variances in both cases. Using the principle of management by exception, the divisional manager can concentrate on the "bad actors"—those activities showing unfavorable variances from budget or standard for the period, and, more importantly for the year-to-date. The availability of the data that the division manager is checking, namely the expenditures of the Overhead Line Crews from that department's responsibility report is shown. The latter's manager, preparing an answer to his superior, obtains the details of labor and other components from the Function Ledger for the principal items, illustrated in this case by the operation, "Patrolling Lines."

For control reports for the first level of supervision, the use of standard costs permits a comparison with actual costs of a controllable nature, expressed in a format that the foreman can use. Favorable or unfavorable variances should be shown with respect to each item of expense for which the foreman is held responsible which usually means controllable items only and no overhead costs. Not only labor and material costs, but other sensitive factors can be included, such as rework, indirect labor and supplies. Comparison can be made to an earned standard, based on good units of output for the period.[8]

Budgetary Control at the Executive Level

Regardless of the importance that top management places on planning and the expertise used in such planning, these efforts can become so much lost motion if not accompanied by prompt feedback each operating period, showing the extent to which such plans or objectives were achieved. Figure 21-7 illustrates a model performance control report, prepared to be read at a glance, containing only those items that management wants. Emphasis on sales, sales deductions, variable costs, marginal contribution, and net-operating profit, along with favorable or unfavorable variances for each item is evident in this brief report. While this type of control report may take less than five minutes for the president to read, it focuses his attention on the bad actors—items with significant unfavorable variances from budgeted or planned performance—in the best tradition of management by exception.

Of primary concern to the systems man is the capture of the real requirements of the executive in developing the format of control reports. Frequently the method of conveying this information will take the form of charts and graphs. For example, a responsibility statement for the

Pro Forma Responsibility Reports*

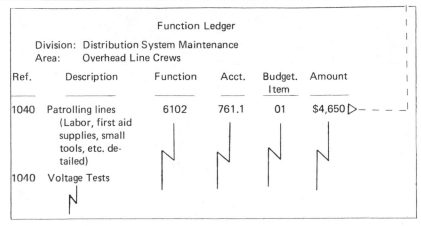

Figure 21-6

*Source: "Responsibility Reporting in Public Utilities" Raymond P. Foley, *Responsibility Reporting*, Peat Marwick, Mitchell & Co. 1961, p. 140.

president may be in chart form, using an organizational chart approach in which each department block shows a black or clear appearance based on a favorable or unfavorable variance from its budget with the amount of variance inserted therein. Again, attention naturally focuses on the departments that are showing poor performance.

PERFORMANCE CONTROL REPORT*

	Actual	Budget	Variance
Gross sales	$5,000	$4,800	$200F
Sales deductions	500	300	200U
Net sales	$4,500	$4,500	$ 0
Aggregate control value	$2,000	2,100	$100F
Manufacturing variance	11	0	11U
Other variable operating expenses	200	150	50U
Total variable cost	$2,211	$2,250	$39F
Marginal contribution	$2,289	$2,250	$39F
Manufacturing fixed costs	$1,000	$1,000	$ 0
Selling expenses	400	450	50F
Administrative expenses	500	450	50U
Miscellaneous expense and income	150	100	50U
Total fixed and miscellaneous	$2,050	$2,000	$50U
Net operating profit	$ 239	$ 250	$11U

F—Indicates Favorable Variance
U—Indicates Unfavorable Variance

Figure 21-7

*Source: "Budgetary Control in the Canvas Footwear Industry," Albert Wallace, Management Accounting, New York

REFERENCES

[1]"Performance Measurement Through Standard Costs and Budgetary Control", K.S. Axelson, *Responsibility Reporting,* Peat Marwick, Mitchell & Co., 1961 p. 48, reprinted from Management Controls, Feb. 1960, PMM & Co., p. 19.

[2]*Ibid.*

[3]"Toward Probabilistic Profit Budgets", William L. Ferrara and Jack C. Hayya, *Management Accounting,* October 1970, p. 24.

[4]"A New Way to Measure and Control Divisional Performance," R. Claden, *Management Services,* September- October, 1970, p. 23.

[5]"Standard Cost Accounting for Contractors," Charles W. Walker, *Management Accounting,* July 1972, p. 30.

[6]*Ibid.,* p. 30.

[7]*Ibid.,* p. 41.

[8]"Cost Reports and Analysis of Results," *Responsibility Reporting,* Peat Marwick, Mitchell & Co., 1961, *op. cit.,* p. 75.

22 Financial Planning Involving Working Capital, Long-Term Expenditures, and Program Budgeting

Introduction

In this chapter offshoots of the master budget are discussed that support the operating budget. These elements include resources of a short-term nature—cash and its equivalents—as well as capital expenditures required if the objectives of the operating budgets are to be achieved. Also included is a presentation of project or program budgeting and an evaluation with respect to contractor-type organizational structures where project management is superimposed on conventional line-staff relationships.

Cash or Working Capital Budgets

Projections of the sources and applications of cash and its equivalents, in support of the operating budget, constitute working capital budgets. For example, Figure 22-1 ilustrates a cash forecast by quarters, starting with beginning cash and equivalent balances, increased by cash receipts from all sources and decreased by disbursements of an operating and capital expenditure nature. Another approach is illustrated in Figure 22-2 which follows the format of the traditional statement of sources and applications of funds. Forecasts by quarters and cash sources are projected, starting with cash generated from operations and reduced by cash requirements for such periods, resulting in ending quarterly balances.

JONUS COMPANY
Cash Forecast
1st Quarter 1973

	January			February			March		
	Budget	Actual	(Over) under	Budget	Actual	(Over) under	Budget	Actual	(Over) under
1. Beginning balance									
Cash									
Marketable securities									
Total									
2. Cash receipts									
Collection on sales									
Sale of fixed assets									
Interest and dividend income									
Bank loans									
Sale of bonds or stocks									
Total									
3. Cash disbursements									
Payroll									
Material purchases									
Taxes									
Freight									
Operating expenses									
Advertising									
Pension Fund									
Insurance									
Dividends									
Interest expense									
Repayment of loans									
Capital expenditures									
Total									
4. Ending balance									
Cash									
Marketable securities									
Total									

Figure 22-1

THE CASE COMPANY
Cash Flow Forecast

	1st Quarter actual	2nd Quarter forecast	actual	3rd Quarter forecast	4th Quarter forecast
Cash Sources					
Net income					
Accrued income tax (ending balance)					
Depreciation					
Accounts receivable (beginning balance)					
Inventory (beginning balance)					
Note payable bank (ending balance)					
Prepaid expense (net — an increase in prepaid expense results in net outflow)					
Accrued liabilities (net — an increase in accrued liabilities increase cash flow)					
Total sources					
Cash Requirements					
Accounts receivable (ending balance)					
Inventory (ending balance)					
Notes payable (beginning balance)					
Income tax (payable — beginning balance)					
Debt payable — bonds (beginning balance)					
Total requirements					
Operating Cash					
Balance beginning					
Increase (decrease) period					
Balance end of period					

RULE OF THUMB

W. C. Asset		W. C. Liability	
Increase W. C. asset = Decrease in cash from operations	Decrease in W. C. asset = Increase in cash from operations	Decrease W. C. liability = Decrease in cash from operations	Increase in W. C. liability = Increase in cash from operations
Assets ↑ Cash Flow ↓	Assets ↑ Cash Flow ↓	W. C. Liability ↓ Cash Flow ↓	W. C. Liability ↑ Cash Flow ↑

Figure 22-2

Source: "Planning and Budgeting Cash," National Association of Accountants, New York, EDO-10, p. 16 (Jonus Company) and 17 (Case Company)

Capital Budgeting Considerations

"What if" questions are frequently the most important and difficult with respect to the capital expenditures budget. Relatively larger sums of money are involved over a longer period of years than is the case with the annual operating budget. Techniques described in Chapter 8 in the discussion of quantitative accounting are useful in answering management's questions as to the long-run advantages of acquiring new companies, or new assets over those presently owned. Among the methods used to measure the quality of an investment are the payback, return on book value, and discounted cash flow return on investments.

The Payback Method

Simplest of the three methods listed, the payback approach justifies an expenditure that can pay for itself from operating savings which it produces over a stipulated number of years. Although simple in execution, this method has serious limitations. For example, assume that capital expenditures are proposed, labeled Asset 1 and Asset 2, both of which will return savings in operations to pay for themselves in four years, approximately $15,000. Under the payback method either would be equally desirable, because they meet management's criterion of payback—four years. Yet Asset 1 may continue in operation for three more years, producing savings over that period. Asset 2 has gone to the scrap heap. In addition, no consideration has been given to the *time value* of money savings produced earlier in the economic life of Asset 1 than the slower accumulation of Asset 2.

The Rate of Return

Another technique used for the justification of capital expenditures is the rate of return resulting from the division of earnings by the sum of the assets producing those earnings. In such projections, a number of variations may be employed. For example, assets may be stated at gross values, or net after accumulated depreciation, and may include leased assets or be restricted to those to which title is presently held. The numerator may consist of earnings before income taxes or may represent net income after such taxes.

Regardless of the precise method selected, the rate of return suffers from the same limitations as the payback approach in that neither look at the time value of money. Two competing projects may be under consideration which are estimated to yield the same rate of return, yet one may produce early in the life of the project while the second's earnings may be spread evenly over its economic life. Under the rate of return method both projects would be rated equally, whereas under the discounted cash flow technique the first proposal would show a clear advantage.

Discounted Cash Flow Approach

It has been observed that the profitability of a business investment depends on two vital factors: (1) future net increases in cash inflows or net savings in cash outflows and (2) required investment.[1] Since a dollar in hand today is worth more than a dollar to be received (or spent) five years from today, it is apparent that the use of money has a cost attached to it, namely interest. The discounted cash flow method shows this time value of money and permits two main variations: (a) time-adjusted rate of return and (b) net present value.[2] The former has been defined as the discount rate that makes the present value of a project equal to the cost of the project and therefore satisfies one of the criteria for the asset's acquisition.[3] The net present value method assumes a definite minimum rate stipulated by management. Applying this rate to all expected future cash flows (using tables prepared for the purpose) results in their present value which is then compared with the amount of the proposed capital expenditure. If the present value equals or exceeds the capital outlay, the expenditure is justified.

As to timing capital expenditures, a period of sustained economic growth is usually accompanied by an increase in capital spending, but such corporate investment tends to occur late in the recovery from a recession, due perhaps to caution on the part of the investor as to the length of the recovery cycle.[4] As a result, capital spending typically follows a continued rise in labor costs, stimulating companies to appropriate funds for cost-cutting machinery and upgrading physical plants[5] with automated devices, including computers because of their labor-saving potential in both production and administrative applications.

Justification Procedures under the Discounted Cash Flow Technique

Where a computer program exists for the purpose of justification of capital expenditure, instructions in detail may be desirable for the guidance of foremen and managers in filling out the forms to be used in proposing long-term capital expenditures. Such instructions may be the subject of control procedures of the firm or simply may be listed on the reverse side of the computer input form from which 80-column cards will be punched and fed into the computer's reader.

Usually such instructions will state the purpose of the computer program indicating that tables of rates of return or cash flow values will be produced as an output of the discounted cash flow program. Such rates of return on investment can be compared with the firm's official or target rate before the expenditure will be approved. Another approach is to compare the total stream of cash flow values or savings and match it with the amount proposed for expenditure. If this stream over the normal expected economic life of the proposed asset exceeds the cash expenditure, the approving corporate official may have the justification under company policy to sanction the purchase.

Data required for such outputs includes an identification number and a brief description of the project. Actual cost, including working capital requirements when this information is known, maximum economic life estimate of the asset, effective tax rate with respect to federal, state and local income taxes and the estimate of savings or earnings which the proposed expenditure is expected to yield over its life are all required inputs to the program. More than one card is usually required to accommodate the above information as well as identify the manager desiring the project and his department. Depreciation, calculated according to the firm's policy, that is, straight-line or an accelerated method, will be checked appropriately on the input document and the estimated salvage value will also be required.

The output information from a discounted cash flow return on investment will usually contain identifying data as to date, project description, name and department of requestor, total investment proposed, maximum economic life and effective corporate income tax rate. In addition, the printout can show the annual earnings or savings amount, identify the method of depreciation used, and the salvage value of the asset. Calculations directed by the program will be reported showing the information desired by the approving corporate officer. The discounted cash flow return on the investment will be shown in earnings rates for each year of the asset's life, along with that year's depreciation, remaining salvage value, constant earnings amount, and the cash flow in terms of dollars, and rate. If the latter equals the firm's criterion rate for the number of years in the investment's economic life, the justification requirements have been met as far as this approach is concerned. Undoubtedly other criteria will have to be met, such as availability of the resources of financing required, but assuming that the input estimates are reasonable, the proposed project has met the test of adequate return on investment using the discounted cash flow technique.

Also included in this chapter is a brief discussion of the planning involved in facilities that use project or program management either on a stand-alone basis or superimposed on a typical line-staff organizational structure. Motivated by the desire to achieve optimum allocation of resources between competing projects or programs, the use of program budgeting and control has been found useful in achieving management by objectives as spelled out in annual budgets. Research organizations with constant competition by researchers for pet projects may find it possible to achieve balance between all programs funded by using the cost/benefits analysis and to control such projects using program management as described below.

Budgeting for Project Management

The unhappy Egyptian overseer who was forced, 5,000 years ago, to report to King Cheops that construction work on the Great Pyramid at Giza had fallen a year behind schedule had much in common with today's vice-president who recoils in dismay as he and the firm's chief executive discover that their new plant will be months late in delivering the production on which a major customer's contract depends.[6] The common thread between the two examples is poor management of a large, complex, one-time project or program, usually superimposed on the firm's existing functional, organizational structure. Whether it be the building of pyramids, the introduction of new products to the market, the opening of new plants, the installation of the new third-generation computer, a merger of two major corporations in a business combination, or the acceptance of a major contract from the government, new tools now exist for management to avert time and cost overruns on massive, complex projects.[7]

Organizational Considerations

Figure 22-3 shows an organizational structure in which the project manager operates in a staff capacity to the president or general manager who, in turn, retains line control. The project manager may wield great influence on the project under this arrangement but does not assume decision-making responsibility. In Figure 22-4 the project manager functions in a line capacity, reporting to the chief executive, and assumes responsibility for the detailed planning, budget projection, coordination, and ultimate outcome of the project.[8] Project management cuts across and often conflicts with the normal organization structure, requiring decisions and actions from a number of functional areas at once.[9] Therefore the main flow of information under project management is not vertical but lateral. Any attempt to obtain authority through functional, organizational, conventional channels may cripple the project by wrecking the time schedule.

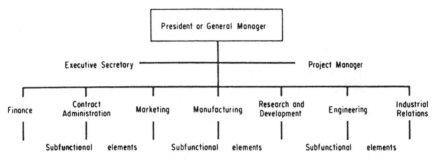

Functional organization with project manager in a staff capacity.

Figure 22-3

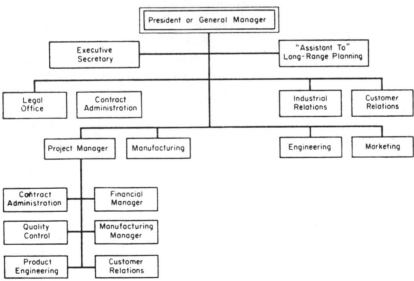

* *Functional organization with project manager in a line capacity. This organizational structure allows for vertical flow of functional authority and responsibility.*

Figure 22-4

Source: *Systems, Organizations, Analysis, Management: A Book of Readings.* David I. Cleland and William R. King, McGraw-Hill, p. 288.

Controls under project management must relate time to cost through network scheduling of the type shown in PERT (Program Evaluation and Review Technique) and the critical path method which calculates both normal and crash schedules for the project.[10] Project *cost* controls are required to reduce major project costs to manageable work packages as suggested in Figure 22-5. To determine when costs are exceeding budget, the project manager must have cost commitment reports at each decision stage. With a detailed cost printout and up-to-date information, the project manager is able to concentrate manpower on the trouble spots after the project is underway. Conventional cost reports including responsibility accounting statements are usually recurring, monthly comparisons of actual with budgeted costs. More dynamic budgetary control is required for projects where 20% of the project effort may account for at least 80% of the total project cost. As a result, a program may be required from which weekly or "whenever" printouts can be obtained for the guidance of the project manager in making quick decisions which may be necessary to prevent substantial overruns and to keep the project on target with its milestone chart.

Only if authority is delegated to the project manager which permits such quick response to budgetary control information by the cost packages shown in Figure 22-5, can he act with the dispatch needed and assume responsibility for the success of the project. An important by-product of project or program management is the opportunity offered for advancement and recognition for young personnel with executive potential but no opportunity to demonstrate this through conventional, functional organizational channels. By delegating project manager authority to such aspiring managers, as depicted in Figure 22-4, not only is the growth of the young executive accelerated, but an important back-up may be obtained for line officers nearing retirement or needed for assignment to newly acquired subsidiaries.

Accounting for Program Management

The organizational alternatives described in this chapter lend themselves to an accounting system that facilitates budgetary control to stay within their funding limits and at the same time permits the accumulation of costs by programs and accounts within programs. Figure 22-6 illustrates budgetary control under the mechanism of fund encumbrance. (See Chapter 2.)

Breakdown of Project Cost Responsibility
by Management Level*

Project Level	Responsibility			Management Level
Total Project	Develop, Manufacture, and Market a new line of equipment			Company President
Phases of the Project	Engineering	Manufacturing	Marketing	Division Director General Manager
Subphases	Tooling Capital	Facilities Capital	Launching & Start-Up	Division Director of Manufacturing
Work Packages	Enlarge Storage Area	Rearrange Final Assembly Line	Install New Paint Facilities	Plant Manager
Additional Detail Required at Local Levels	Purchase Conveyor System	Dig Pit and Pour Foundation	Strengthen Building Structure	Plant Facilities Manager, Plant Manager and others

Figure 22-5

*Source: "Making Project Management Work", John M. Stewart *(Systems, Organizations, Analysis, Management: A Book of Readings.* David J. Cleland and William R. King p. 301.) *Business Horizons,* Fall 1965.

    Cost accumulation by programs and the "step-down" allocation of service department costs to principal programs permits management to know the total cost of each project or program and to match the benefits of such programs against total costs. The result can be an improved allocation of scarce resources and funds wherever appropriations for specific projects are in order—in research programs, maintenance, capital expenditures programs or in new product development.

    The organizing, planning, directing, staffing, and controlling functions come into sharp focus in program management. The need for organizational changes to accommodate such programs or projects with responsible management was seen in the preceding pages. The need for responsibility accounting and its potential for performance evaluation become apparent in the discussion which follows.

PROGRAM/PROJECT MANAGEMENT

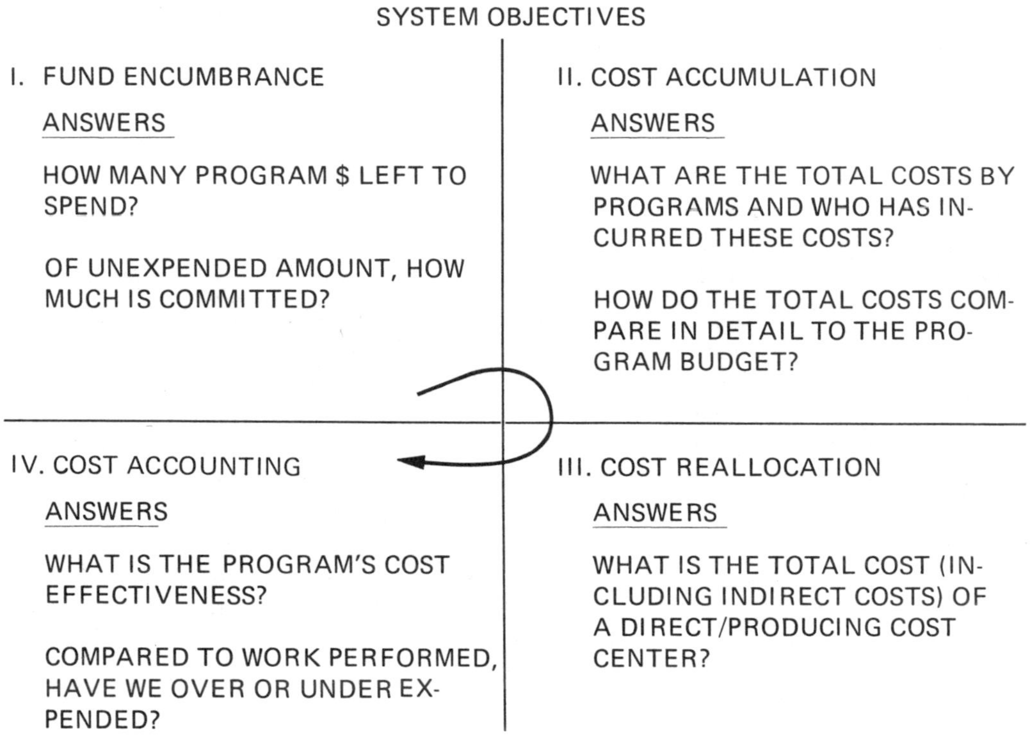

SYSTEM OBJECTIVES

I. FUND ENCUMBRANCE

ANSWERS

HOW MANY PROGRAM $ LEFT TO
SPEND?

OF UNEXPENDED AMOUNT, HOW
MUCH IS COMMITTED?

II. COST ACCUMULATION

ANSWERS

WHAT ARE THE TOTAL COSTS BY
PROGRAMS AND WHO HAS IN-
CURRED THESE COSTS?

HOW DO THE TOTAL COSTS COM-
PARE IN DETAIL TO THE PRO-
GRAM BUDGET?

IV. COST ACCOUNTING

ANSWERS

WHAT IS THE PROGRAM'S COST
EFFECTIVENESS?

COMPARED TO WORK PERFORMED,
HAVE WE OVER OR UNDER EX-
PENDED?

III. COST REALLOCATION

ANSWERS

WHAT IS THE TOTAL COST (IN-
CLUDING INDIRECT COSTS) OF
A DIRECT/PRODUCING COST
CENTER?

Figure 22-6

In this section, program management is discussed from the following viewpoints: (1) program budgeting, planning "Management by Objectives" (MBO) for each program and (2) program or project monitoring or evaluation as an extension of cost analysis with particular application to cost/benefit analysis. The overriding consideration is that of optimization as a continuous function in providing the best combination of the organization's resources to meet the objective of those selected programs to which such assets have been allocated in terms of performance, schedule and budgeted program cost.

Program Management

Program management has as its major objective the optimum allocation of scarce resources made available to that program. Program management starts with the planning stage—planning budgeting by programs to establish a base for a close analysis of each program based on its objectives through an effective management information system, presenting timely reporting of actual program costs, compared with its budget.

Project or program management is popular primarily in the defense industry and in government. In state operations, agencies are asked to identify programs, plan for the next year, justify budget requests in terms of program effect, and identify workload data as well as meaningful criteria to measure the performance or success of each program. This application of management by objectives permits each agency to coordinate its efforts to accomplish its goals and objectives through the development and execution of programs aided by timely, often computerized, reporting.

Role of the Financial Information
System in Program Management

The development of a Financial Information System to facilitate program management may incorporate a number of basic principles, as follows:

1. Basic fund accounting techniques, coupled with recognized *industrial* cost control procedures, may be used in the development of program evaluation reports shown; and,
2. The reporting system may be developed within the framework of a uniform chart of accounts, with emphasis on program management for major programs named. Provision is desirable for cost-center reporting within such programs.

Relationships Between Systems

A Financial Information System designed through a phased developmental approach incorporating four major segments: *Fund Encumbrance, Cost Accumulation by Programs, Cost Reallocation,* and *Cost Accounting by Programs,* is discussed next.

Fund Encumbrance—Phase 1

The objective of this system is to furnish an automated method of controlling the *funds* allocated to an organization, the initial yearly appropriations, and the quarterly allotments of such funds. Provisions may be incorporated to control up to any desired number of specific programs. The purpose of this system is to provide fund control over dollars encumbered, not to provide *cost* control by programs or cost centers, based upon workload as embodied in Program Management.

Cost Accumulation—Phase II

The major purpose of the cost accumulation system is the determination of actual costs for the period, by program, cost center or account number, for comparison with the budget so that corrective action can be taken by the responsible manager. However, these direct costs accumulated directly by program, cost center or expense account do not represent the *total* costs of such projects or programs. To arrive at such total costs, *indirect* or supporting costs are distributed on equitable bases from the service cost centers which serve the direct or producing cost centers. The process of distributing such indirect or service center costs (maintenance, sanitation, laboratory, etc.) may be accomplished through the cost reallocation program, described below.

Cost Reallocation—Phase III

Data processed in the Cost Accumulation System become direct inputs to the Cost Reallocation System in which appropriate bases are used for the proration of each service center's costs to direct centers, through a procedure called "Step-down" costing, culminating in true or full costs in each direct program.

Cost Accounting (Standard Costing)—Phase IV

After supporting costs and administrative costs have been allocated from service cost centers, to direct, productive programs, the latter show *total* costs for the period, compared with the budgeted costs for that program. A favorable or unfavorable variance from budget is calculated, which facilitates program management by the project director or his staff, encouraging corrective action to eliminate unfavorable variances in those direct programs, where actual, fully distributed costs, exceed the program budget established before the year began.

Evaluation

Program budgeting, with a clear definition of objectives of each program, may be the best method of allocating resources among competing demands. In determining whether or not progress is being made according to plan, an effective evaluation of the performance of each program is necessary. Performance standards that will meaningfully measure attainment of predetermined objectives and goals are required to insure optimization of resources by their allocation to the most desirable programs.

A program audit may be conducted involving a review of operations, according to specified audit procedures and standards, to evaluate progress and success or failure of programs by comparison with objectives stated in the program budget. Internal audit criteria that might be useful in evaluating an organization's programs would include: (1) Are funds being used to advance *programs* that will accomplish identifiable objectives according to (a) the written and oral representations of the organization under examination, and (b) the management's intent as reflected by prior budgets, current budget hearings, and perhaps public statements; and (2) Is the entire program *managed* and *operated* according to accepted standards?

While emphasis was placed on program planning in this chapter, dependence on the financial information system for evaluation and control was also stressed. The need for program managers to obtain prompt information on the operations under their control, measured against a yardstick in the form of a program budget, and audited regularly is essential.

Through the use of the systems described, program managers can be given information that permits them to do more than simply gain assurance that they haven't overspent their budget. Efficiency in the management of programs is enhanced through the use of information for controlling purposes at both the program level and sub-program level. Corrective action is thus encouraged permitting program managers to reach the objectives set under program budgeting. As a result of this interplay between program budgeting and program management, the quality of program management can be improved and the allocation of scarce resources optimized by achieving balance between performance, schedule, and total system cost.

REFERENCES

[1]*Accounting for Management Control—An Introduction,* Charles T. Horngren, Third Edition, Prentice-Hall, 1974, p. 421.

[2]*Ibid.*

[3]*Ibid.,* p. 422.

[4]"A Manager's Primer on Forecasting," Robert S. Sobek, the *Harvard Business Review,* May-June 1973, page 26.

[5]*Ibid.*

[6]"Making Project Management Work," John M. Stewart, Reading 29, *Systems, Organizations, Analysis, Management: A Book of Readings,* David I. Cleland and William R. King, p. 291.

[7]*Ibid.*

[8]*Ibid.* p. 295.

[9]*Ibid.*

[10]*Ibid.,* p. 300.

23

Effective Tax Planning and Management — Relevant Pronouncements

Any consideration of profit planning without considering the impact of income tax expense would be incomplete in today's business environment. It is beyond the scope of this book to do justice to all of the ramifications of corporate income tax that have an impact on present and future profits. However, an effort is made in this chapter to consider the methods and elections of reporting income, and the relevant pronouncements with respect to accounting for interperiod tax allocations, changes in accounting principles, temporary and permanent tax differences, undistributed earnings of subsidiaries, the investment tax credit, and proposed methods of corporate disclosure.

Application of such concepts in the reporting of tax expense and deferrals is the subject of Chapter 24. Current practice is reflected in corporate annual reports that suggest the impact of income tax expense and the importance of tax planning, communication, and management procedures.

Introduction—Tax Methods and Elections

Whatever method of accounting (essentially the procedures under which the timing of income and expense reporting are determined) is elected by a corporate taxpayer, it must give a clear reflection of net income, that is, income less the costs of earning that income. While this usually means the taxpayer will utilize either the cash or accrual method of accounting, some variations are possible, including hybrid methods as long as the clear reflection of income test is met.

In some circumstances, a corporate taxpayer may find it advantageous to use other methods for particular types of transactions. Thus, the installment sales method may be used for deferred payment transactions, or the percentage of completion or completed contract methods may be used for the reporting of income on long-term contracts. Generally, the taxpayer will select the method that provides the best tax result.

Cash Method of Accounting

Individual taxpayers in most cases find the use of the cash method of reporting income and expenses most advantageous. However, if the taxpayer is engaged in a trade or business where inventories are a material, income-producing item, the accrual method must be used even though the cash method is utilized for other transactions.

Under the cash method of accounting, income is taxed in the year received. Expenses of earning that income, and other allowable deductions, must be claimed in the year of payment. Prepaid income, such as rent or interest received in advance of the due date, and even though not actually earned, is generally included in gross income in the year of receipt. However, deductions are generally not allowable until the expenses are incurred even though the amounts are paid in advance.

Doctrine of Constructive Receipt

Under the cash method, income that is not actually received during the taxable year but which is available upon demand, such as interest on bank deposits, is nonetheless taxable under the doctrine of constructive receipt. Income, to be taxable under the provisions of this concept, must generally be subject to the unqualified demand of the taxpayer. In short, actual physical possession is not necessarily needed so long as the taxpayer has a legally exercisable power over the income. Thus, a check which is mailed and deposited in the taxpayer's mailbox on December 31 is includable in income in that year even though the check is not actually negotiated until the following year upon return of the taxpayer from an out-of-town trip.

Also, income received by another, as agent for the taxpayer, is taxable as though received by the taxpayer directly. For example, income and profits from investments held in a brokerage account are taxable in the year in which the income is received by the broker and do not depend upon the year in which the amounts are withdrawn by the taxpayer.

Taxpayers must also report income, even though not received directly, if such income provides an economic benefit. For example, income, such as salary, which is attached or garnished by a creditor is considered taxable to the employee because the amounts effectively produce the economic benefit to him by reducing an obligation to a creditor. Similarly, if an employer, by way of compensation for services, pays an expense of the employee, such as rent on his home or a vacation, the amount so paid by the employer is taxable to the employee on account of the economic benefit received.

Under the cash method, the taxpayer must also include the value of property received by way of income. Thus, if the employer compensates an employee by awarding him stock of the corporation (other than through particular types of stock option plans which receive special tax treatment), the employee is in receipt of income to the extent of the value of that stock.

Accrual Method of Accounting

Under the accrual method of accounting, income becomes taxable when earned, that is, when the taxpayer has the unconditional right to receive it. By the same token, expenses are deductible when the taxpayer has the unconditional obligation to pay.

Where an accrual basis taxpayer receives payment in advance, the income is generally taxable in the year of receipt even though not earned until the following year. There are, however, a few exceptions under which deferral of income, even though received in advance, is possible: (1) certain dues and subscriptions; (2) amounts received for rendering services that must be rendered by the end of the year following the year of receipt; and, (3) receipts on account of sales of property to be sold in the future.

Hybrid Methods of Accounting

In addition to the methods already described, a hybrid method of accounting is permitted if it clearly reflects income and is used consistently. In general, a hybrid method might involve the use of the cash method of accounting as the overall or basic method of accounting with certain items being treated under the accrual method, or vice versa.

However, it must be borne in mind that the Commissioner of Internal Revenue can prescribe a different method of accounting if the one used by the taxpayer does not clearly reflect income.

Net Worth Method

In the event that a taxpayer keeps no books of account while engaging in a business or otherwise earning income, or maintains such poor or incomplete records that there is no other way to establish his income, the Commissioner is empowered to use the net worth method.

Under this method, the taxpayer's net worth (assets less liabilities) as of the beginning of a particular year is compared to that which exists at the end of the taxable year. The increase, plus the estimated amount of living expenses during such period, is then treated as the taxpayer's income for the year unless he can establish that the increase was due to the receipt of cash or property under circumstances not constituting taxable income, such as gifts or inheritances. The net worth method is commonly used in fraud investigations where the taxpayer's records do not reflect the receipt of his total income.

Installment Sales Method

Under the installment method, the reporting of gain, but not loss, may be deferred in three types of payment transactions: (1) regular sales or dispositions of personal property (inventory) by dealers on an installment plan; (2) sales and other dispositions of real property (without regard to the amount of the selling price and whether or not the property is held as inventory by a dealer) if the payments received in the year of sale do not exceed 30% of the selling price; and (3) casual sales or other casual dispositions of personal property (but only if the property is not inventory and the selling price exceeds $1,000), assuming that the payments received in the year of sale do not exceed 30% of the selling price.

A dealer in personal property utilizing the installment method will report as ordinary income a portion of the total payments received in the taxable year from sales on an installment plan or a revolving credit plan (such payments being allocated to the year of the sale for which they apply). Ordinary income consists of payments received to the percent that the gross profit realized, or to be realized on the total sales on an installment plan or a revolving credit plan made during that year, bears to the total contract price of all sales made during that respective year.

In other words, in each year, the dealer will compute a profit ratio, determined as the ratio of gross profit to the total contract price of all installment sales made during the year. As payments are received in the years following, the payments will be allocated according to the year of the sale in which the payments are received. After such allocation, the profit ratio of each year will be applied to that year's allocated payments to determine the amount of income to be reported in the year that such payments are received.

In the case of the installment sales described in (2) and (3) above, payments in the year of sale may not exceed 30% of the selling price. Although it is not necessary for a taxpayer to receive any payment in the year of sale, it is essential that the taxpayer receive two or more payments of portions of the purchase price in two or more taxable years. Thus, it is not permissible for the taxpayer to negotiate a sale, without any payment in the *taxable* year of sale, with the total purchase price being totally paid within a subsequent taxable year.

If the taxpayer is eligible to calculate the gain on a sale or other disposition of real property, or on a casual sale or other casual disposition of personal property, under the installment method, the gain will be reportable over the period that the installment payments are actually received. The amount of gain reportable in each year will be determined by applying the gross profit percentage—that is, the ratio of the gross profit to contract price—to the amount of installment payments received in that year. The contract price is calculated as the selling price less any mortgage on the property assumed by the purchaser. The gross profit is determined by subtracting expenses of sale and the adjusted basis from the selling price.

Percentage of Completion and Completed Contract Method

In the case of long-term contracts, such as may be found in the construction industry, a taxpayer may use either the percentage of completion method or the completed contract method of accounting to report the profit earned from such contracts.

Under the *percentage of completion* method, that portion of the contract price is reported as income which corresponds to the percentage of the total contract completed during that taxable year. The percentage of completion can be determined on a physical basis, that is, the quantity or physical portion of the contract which is actually accomplished; or by comparing the actual costs incurred during the year with the total costs bid or anticipated on each contract. The costs incurred during the year are deducted from the percentage of the total contract price which is included in income.

Under the *completed contract* method, income from a long-term contract is reported, and all expenses properly allocable thereto deducted, in the year that the contract is completed and accepted.

Depreciation and other overhead costs must be allocated to specific jobs and unused inventories must be excluded as costs of the current taxable year. General and administrative selling expenses, not directly attributable to a long-term contract, are deductible only in the year paid or incurred, depending upon the method of accounting used—cash or accrual. Only contract costs can be included in the computations.

Emphasis on Corporate Tax Policy Disclosure

The tax accrual review process and financial statement presentation of income taxes is becoming increasingly important to the Securities and Exchange Commission, the investing public, and the accounting profession itself. With respect to financial statement disclosure, SEC Accounting Series Release No. 149 amended Regulation S-X to provide for improved disclosure of income tax expense.[1] However, the Commission's interest is not confined to financial statement disclosure. Permission to insert forecasts in filings with the Commission has been granted.

Securities Act Releases 5362 and 5276 indicate the Commission's position on the reporting of forecasts and budget projections in prospectuses.[2] Release 5362 describes forecasts by corporate management as "information of significant importance to investors" with the only mandatory requirement for such disclosures applying to projections made by the company to private parties. These must also be made available to the general investing public.[3]

The Commission also has endeavored to obtain financial disclosures that would provide answers as to why companies use alternative accounting and tax methods and what effect these alternatives have on earnings.[4]

APB Opinion No 11 contains a widely accepted proposal for disclosing the financial implications of a corporation's tax policy. Three major propositions are featured: (1) Income tax expense is considered as the net tax effect of all revenue and expense transactions; (2) Those tax effects that *temporarily* reduce current tax assessments are considered deferred credits rather than liabilities; and, (3) Financial disclosure is recommended that will present both the *current* tax assessment and temporary tax differences.[5]

earnings of subsidiaries, considered under APB Opinion No. 23, discussed below.

Undistributed Earnings of Subsidiaries— Provisions of APB Opinion No. 23

Separate income tax returns are frequently filed for a parent corporation and its subsidiaries, particularly in the case of foreign subsidiaries. As a result, it becomes possible for income taxes to be incurred by the parent upon receipt of its subsidiary's earnings through the payment of dividends. APB Opinion No. 23 assumes that undistributed earnings of subsidiaries will be transferred eventually to the parent company and so directs that the latter provide for such additional income. If the parent includes such earnings in the consolidated income statement, income tax expense should be set up on such amounts in that period. Taxes accrued may be determined by assuming that all income of the subsidiaries was received in the period in which earned and that the parent also received the benefit of all available tax-planning alternatives, tax credits and deductions.

However, the presumption of such constructive receipt by the parent may be overcome, and no additional tax provision will be required if sufficient evidence exists that the unremitted subsidiary earnings will be reinvested indefinitely or that such earnings will be remitted later to the parent in a tax-free liquidation. History of the parent's policy of reinvestment of subsidiarys' earnings and the existence of definite future programs are examples of the kind of evidence that may be required under APB No. 23. This substantiates the parent's intention of indefinite postponement of remittances from the subsidiary.

Illustrations in Chapter 24 show the kinds of footnotes being used on financial statements to support management's intent to reinvest indefinitely and therefore be relieved of the burden of providing income tax on such unremitted earnings.

Timing Differences—Investor's Share of Earnings of Investee Companies—APB Opinion No. 24

The tax effects of differences between taxable income and pre-tax accounting income, with respect to an investor's share of the earnings of investee companies accounted for under the equity method, have the characteristics of timing differences. Accordingly, the Accounting Principles Board concluded that such earnings would require interperiod tax allocation under the provisions of APB Opinion No. 11. A difference exists between the treatment accorded to subsidiary income under APB

Opinion No. 23 and that advocated for the *investee's* earnings. This difference hinges on the control exercised by a parent company that is not possessed by the investor.

Undistributed earnings that may be invested for indefinite periods under APB Opinion No. 23, subject to control by the parent company, and therefore are *not* taxed, do *not* find a counterpart in the case of the investee's earnings, under Opinion No. 24. Under the latter Opinion, income tax expense of the investor company must be increased to include taxes that would have been withheld if the undistributed earnings had been remitted as dividends. If the investor's equity in such earnings will, according to existing facts and evidence, be realized by ultimate disposition of the investment, the investor firm should accrue income taxes attributable to the timing difference at capital gains or other appropriate rates, recognizing all available deductions and credits.

Investment Tax Credit—APB Opinion No. 4

The Accounting Principles Board concluded in Opinion No. 4 that the deferral method of accounting for the investment credit promulgated in Opinion No. 2 was still the preferred approach but that the *flow through method* would also be acceptable. The latter procedure treats the tax credit as a reduction of federal income taxes of the year in which the credit arises.

In addition, paragraph 11 of APB Opinion No. 4 indicates the Board's emphasis that whichever method of accounting is elected for the investment credit, it is essential that full disclosure be made of the method followed and the amounts involved, when significant.

In Section 101(c) of the Revenue Act of 1971, "Accounting for Investment Credit in Certain Financial Reports and Reports to Federal Agencies," the intent of the Congress was described as that of restoring the investment tax credit and thus providing an incentive for modernization and growth of private industry. It was further stated that the taxpayer should disclose the method of accounting elected in all financial reporting.

Interim Financial Reporting—Provision for Income Taxes—APB Opinion No. 28

The purpose of APB Opinion No. 28 was stated as that of clarifying the application of accepted accounting principles to interim financial information and to the disclosure of summarized interim financial data of publicly traded companies.[9] Although guidelines are provided for the preparation of interim reports, including the determination of income tax expense rates, APB Opinion No. 28 does not *require* that such reports be issued. If management elects to report interim financial information, the guidelines in APB Opinion No. 28 are to be followed.

In estimating the effective tax rate to apply to interim income, the company is to use that which represents the best estimate for the *full* fiscal year. This rate should anticipate investment tax credits, foreign tax credits, percentage depletion, capital gains rates and all other available tax planning techniques. However, computation of the estimated full year effective tax rate should not include the effect of those items included in APB Opinion No. 30, such as disposal of a segment of a business or an extraordinary item. These are to be shown either separately or net of tax.[10]

Figure 23-4 illustrates the computations involved in planning or estimating the full year effective tax rate and applying it to the first quarter's pre-tax income. As noted in 23-4, APB Opinion No. 28 requires disclosure of the reasons for significant variations from the customary relationship between income tax expense and pre-tax accounting income, if not otherwise apparent in the statement.[11]

Although changes in accounting principles are usually reported as cumulative effect adjustments in the year of change, APB Opinion No. 28 calls for disclosure of the reasons for such changes and the resulting tax effects.

Securities and Exchange Commission Comments on Deficiences in Quarterly Reporting

In its Release No. 34-10547, the Securities and Exchange Commission directed attention to reporting problems and deficiencies being encountered by the SEC staff in reviewing Form 10-Q filings. One of the defects in such interim reporting documents related to the failure to disclose separately the deferred portion of the provision for income taxes. The Release noted that many of the substantive accounting problems relevant to Form 10-Q including the omission of the basis for restatement of prior periods, noted above[12], are discussed in APB Opinion No. 28.

Figure 23-5 reproduces Section A, "Summarized Financial Information" of Form 10-Q. Attention is requested to the instruction provided in footnote form to item 6, "Provision for taxes on income." Material provisions for deferred income taxes resulting from allocations are required to be disclosed and explained. In addition, the methods used in allocating the income tax effects of operating loss carry-backs, or other tax credits are also to be described.

Computation of estimated full year effective tax rate

Estimated pre-tax income before items below		$10,000,000
Less:		
State and local taxes	$750,000	
Dividend exclusion	50,000	
Percentage depletion	600,000	1,400,000
		8,600,000
Statutory federal income tax rate		48%
		4,128,000
Less:		
Investment tax credit	421,500	
Surtax exemption	6,500	428,000
Estimated federal income tax expense		3,700,000
Add state and local taxes (above)		750,000
Estimated full year effective income tax provision and rate		$ 4,450,000 or 44.5%[*]

Application of effective tax rate to first quarter

First quarter pre-tax income	$ 2,000,000
Estimated full year effective income tax rate	44.5%
Income tax provision—first quarter	$ 890,000

Figure 23-4

Source: Interim Financial Reporting, APB Opinion No. 28, Ernst & Ernst Financial Reporting Developments, April 1974, Retrieval No. 38165, p. 8.

---

[*]A footnote to the Opinion states that disclosure should be made of the reasons for significant variations in the customary relationship between income tax expense and pre-tax accounting income, if they are not otherwise apparent from the financial statements or from the nature of the entity's business (see APB Opinion No. 11, paragraph 63). In the above example a comment somewhat as follows would be appropriate: "The effective tax rate is less than the statutory rate principally because of the effect of percentage depletion and the investment tax credit."

A. SUMMARIZED FINANCIAL INFORMATION

Company or group of companies for which report is filed:

Profit and Loss Information   **For the**   **Months Ended:**

                                                   (Current Year)   (Preceding Year)

1. Gross sales less discounts, returns and allowances . . . . . $_____ $_____
2. Operating revenues . . . . $_____ $_____

   Instruction. If income is derived from both gross sales and operating revenues, captions 1 and 2 may be combined, provided the lesser amount is not more than 10 percent of the sum of the two captions.

3. Total of captions 1 and 2 . . . . $_____ $_____

   Instruction. If the total of gross sales and operating revenues includes excise taxes in an amount equal to 10 percent or more of such total, the amount of such excise taxes shall be stated separately.

4. Costs and expenses—
   (a) Cost of goods sold* . . . . $_____ $_____
   (b) Operating expenses* . . . . $_____ $_____
   (c) Selling, general and administrative expenses* . . . . . . $_____ $_____
   (d) Interest expense . . . . $_____ $_____
   (e) Other deductions, net* . . . . $_____ $_____

   Total costs and expenses . . . . $_____ $_____

5. Income (or loss) before taxes on income and extraordinary items $_____ $_____
6. Provision for taxes on income . . . . $_____ $_____

   Instruction. If the provision for taxes on income includes any material provisions for deferred income taxes resulting from allocations, they shall be disclosed and explained. The methods used (e.g., proportion of year expired, or estimated annual effective tax rate) in the allocation to the interim periods of the income tax effects of operating loss carry-backs, carry-forwards or other tax credits shall be described.

---

*Items marked with an asterisk may be combined or omitted.

7. Minority interest . . . . $_____ $_____
8. Income (loss) before extraordinary items . . . . $_____ $_____
9. Extraordinary items, less applicable income tax . . . . . . $_____ $_____

Figure 23-5

Instruction. State separately under this caption any material amounts of an unusual or non-recurring nature which qualify as extraordinary items included in the determination of net income or loss during the period covered by the report. The amount of income tax applicable shall be disclosed.

10. Net income (or loss) . . . . $_____ $_____
11. Earnings per share*
12. Dividends per share*

Figure 23-5 *(continued)*

Source: Form 10-Q, Section A. "Summarized Financial Information" Under Section 13 or 15(d) of the Securities Exchange Act of 1934.

Summary of Accounting Series Release No. 149—To Provide for Improved Disclosure of Income Tax Expense

The Securities and Exchange Commission adopted amendments to Rule 3-16(o) of Regulation S-X calling for improved disclosure of income expense in the filing of financial statements with the Commission.[13] Changes required include many of the reporting improvements discussed above, in connection with the provisions of Accounting Principles Board Opinions. Disclosure of the components of tax expense is to be expanded to include the reasons for timing differences between book and tax reporting that result in deferred income taxes. In addition, a reconciliation between the effective income tax rate indicated in the income statement filed with the Commission and the statutory Federal income tax rate is to be attached. Disclosure of deferred tax reversals is required only when the registrant expects that the cash outlay for income taxes in any of the succeeding three years will exceed substantially the income tax expense of those years.[14]

The stated purpose of Accounting Series Release No. 149 is to enable users of financial statements to understand better the basis for the registrant's tax accounting, and to understand why the firm is able to operate at a different level of tax expense than the statutory tax rate. In addition, readers should be able to distinguish more easily between one-time and continuing tax advantages enjoyed by a company and thus will be able to appraise the significance of changing effective tax rates. A final objective is that of providing financial planners with additional insights into the current and prospective cash drain associated with the payment of income taxes. Provisions of the amended rules relate to the presentation of Prepaid Expenses and Deferred Charges, Deferred Credits, and Income Tax Expense in the registrant's financial statements, as shown in Figure 23-6. In clarification of such rules, examples of disclosure and associated assumptions and computations (shown in Figure 23-7) were included in Accounting Series Release No. 149.

As noted earlier, the above coverage of the ramifications and effects of income taxes on corporate profit planning and financial management does little more than scratch the surface of this broad topic. But it is hoped that the exposure to the tax pronouncements in this chapter and their application in Chapter 24 will whet the appetite of the reader for more intensive investigation of this very important phase of accounting and its tax-planning significance.

Rule 3-16. General Notes to Financial Statements

(o) Income tax expense.—(1) Disclosure shall be made, in the income tax statement, including: (i) taxes currently payable; (ii) the net tax effects, as applicable, of (a) timing differences *(Indicate separately the amount of the estimated tax effect of each of the various types of timing differences, such as depreciation, research and development expense, warranty costs, etc. Types of timing differences that are individually less than 15 percent of the deferred tax amount in the income statement may be combined. If no individual type of difference is more than five percent of the amount computed by multiplying the income before tax by the applicable statutory Federal income tax rate and the aggregate amount of timing differences is less than five percent of such computed amount, disclosure of each of the separate types of timing differences may be omitted.)* and (b) operating losses; and (iii) the net deferred investment tax credits. Amounts applicable to *United States* Federal income taxes, *to foreign income taxes* and to other income taxes shall be stated separately for each *major* component, unless the amounts applicable to *foreign and* other income taxes do not exceed five percent of the total for the component.

(2) *If it is expected that the cash outlay for income taxes with respect to any of the succeeding three years will substantially exceed income tax expense for such year, that fact should be disclosed together with the approximate amount of the excess, the year (or years) of occurrence and the reasons therefor.*

(3) *Provide a reconciliation between the amount of reported total income tax expense and the amount computed by multiplying the income before tax by the applicable statutory Federal income tax rate,*

Figure 23-6

showing the estimated dollar amount of each of the underlying causes for the difference. If no individual reconciling item amounts to more than five percent of the amount computed by multiplying the income before tax by the applicable statutory Federal income tax rate, and the total difference to be reconciled is less than five percent of such computed amount, no reconciliation need be provided unless it would be significant in appraising the trend of earnings. Reconciling items that are individually less than five percent of the computed amount may be aggregated in the reconciliation. The reconciliation may be presented in percentages rather than in dollar amounts. Where the reporting person is a foreign entity, the income tax rate in that person's country of domicile should normally be used in making the above computation, but different rates should not be used for subsidiaries or other segments of a reporting entity. If the rate used by a reporting person is other than the United States Federal corporate income tax rate, the rate used and the basis for using such rate shall be disclosed.

Rule 5-02. Balance Sheets.

19. *Prepaid expenses and deferred charges.*—State separately any material items. Items properly classed as current may, however, be included under caption 8. *(See also Rule 3-16(o).)*

35. *Deferred credits.*—State separately amounts for (a) deferred income taxes, (b) deferred tax credits, and (c) material items of deferred income. The current portion of deferred income taxes shall be included under caption 26 (see Accounting Series Release No. 102). *(See also Rule 3-16(o).)*

Figure 23-6 *(continued)*

Source: Accounting Series Release No. 149, November 28, 1973.

III. Computational Guide

A.   Tax computations

      Book income before tax $15,000

          State income tax   (400)

Figure 23-7

Permanent differences:

Goodwill amortization	800	
Municipal bond income	(1,500)	
Foreign income, no domestic income tax	(2,400)	
Capital gain	(1,000)	(4,100)
		$10,500

Timing differences:

Excess depreciation	(1,250)
R & D deducted on tax return	(3,000)
Warranty cost not deductible until paid	1,400
Percentage of completion income	(2,000)
Taxable income (excl. cap. gain)	$ 5,650

Tax to be paid

Tax on ordinary income .48 x 5,650	$ 2,712
Plus capital gain tax .30 x 1,000	300
Less investment credit	(700)
Actual tax paid	$ 2,312

Tax expense per books

Tax expense on ordinary income .48 x 10,500	$ 5,040
Plus capital gain tax	300
Less investment credit	(700)
Tax expense—Federal	$ 4,640
Foreign tax	$ 780
State and local income tax	$ 400

B.   Facts affecting disclosure of net deferred income taxes.
Estimated Changes in Deferred Income Tax Accounts on Balance Sheets:

	19X4	19X5	19X6
Balance—beginning of year	$10,000	$11,000	$10,500
Additions for timing differences in each year /1/	3,000	1,500	500
Reversals of balances at beginning of each year	(2,000)	(2,000)	(4,500)
Balance—end of year	$11,000	$10,500	$ 6,500

Figure 23-7 (continued)

C.   Computations of disclosure limits per Rule 3-16(o)

Computed amount	15,000 x .48 = 7,200
5% of computed amount	.05 x 7,200 = 360
15% of deferred tax	.15 x 2,728 = 409

NOTE:

/1/ Includes effect of expected expenditures in each subsequent period which gives rise to additional tax deferrals.

Figure 23-7 *(continued)*

Source: ASR No. 149, November 28, 1973.

REFERENCES

[1]"Corporate Tax Review: The Auditor's Approach," Bruce M. Greenwald and Carl D. Harnick, *The Journal of Accountancy,* May 1974, p. 63.

[2]Alfred Rappaport, Public Reporting of Corporate Financial Forecasts, Center for Advanced Study in Accounting and Information Systems, Northwestern University, Commerce Clearing House, Inc., Chicago, Ill., p. 8.

[3]*Ibid.,* p. 89.

[4]"Disclosing Corporate Tax Policy," Larry Gene Pointer, *The Journal of Accountancy,* July 1973, p. 57.

[5]*Ibid.,* Pointer, p. 57.

[6]*Ibid.,* Pointer, p. 57.

[7]*Ibid.*

[8]*Ibid.,* Pointer, p. 58.

[9]Interim Financial Reporting, APB Opinion No. 28, Par 19.

[10]*Ibid.*

[11]Ernst & Ernst Financial Reporting Developments, April 1974, Retrieval No. 38165, p. 8.

[12]Securities Exchange Act Release No. 10547, 12/12/73, p. 3.

[13]Accounting Series Release No. 149, 1973 Securities and Exchange Commission, November 28, p. 1.

[14]*Ibid.*

24

Tax Accounting Management and Disclosure

Effective planning or budgeting requires some knowledge of the firm's financial history as a guide. Corporate tax planning is no exception. Opportunities for tax planning may start with a review of the proper tax treatment of transactions occurring during the tax year.[1] This look at history may be facilitated by a review of the year's audit workpapers for items of tax significance as is customarily done in many public accounting firms. Or it may be accomplished internally by the company's tax manager or controller, working with top management, including knowledgeable financial officers of all domestic and foreign subsidiaries. An example of a check list that's helpful in using last year's operations for future tax planning is shown in Figure 24-1.

On the theory that *audit* problems are frequently accompanied by *tax* problems, the tax planner may concentrate on the auditor's working papers which deal with significant problems, such as the purchase price allocation for a new acquisition.[2]

Objectives of the auditor's tax review include expressing an opinion on the adequacy of the tax liability shown on the client's balance sheet, and handling of such procedures as the balance sheet classification of current and deferred taxes,[3] or interperiod tax classification, as discussed in Chapter 23. Another auditor responsibility may be to advise corporate management on the adequacy of internal procedures in complying with relevant tax regulations and in taking advantage of all opportunities for tax reduction.[4]

SAMPLE TAX ACCRUAL QUESTIONNAIRE
XYZ COMPANY, INC.
YEAR ENDED

Subsidiary or division _____

Prepared by (audit
senior)   _____

Reviewed by (tax
reviewer)   _____

                         Workpaper
                         reference   Yes   No   N/A

1. Has the gross change method of interperiod allocation of income taxes been followed by the division?

2. Please attach a copy of schedule showing a summary of items having a special effect on the computation of the consolidated tax (Section 1231 or capital gains or losses, contributions, special deductions, foreign taxes).

3. Has the division changed its method of accounting with respect to any item of income or expense?

4. Has any potential tax liability which may arise from reallocation of deductions to foreign affiliates been considered (e.g., expenses incurred on behalf of a foreign affiliate or services performed for a foreign affiliate without proper reimbursement)? (Provide details.)

5. Are you satisfied that travel-entertainment expenditures are adequately substantiated in accordance with the requirements as to information and substantiation required by the Internal Revenue Code?

6. If the division or subsidiary has a branch office, plant, warehouse, property (including consignments) and employees or is doing business in any manner in a state, has an accrual been provided for all state and city income, franchise sales, property and employment taxes which are due for the current year?

7. Are there any amounts included in accounts payable and accruals which are of the nature of reserves and which may not be deductible for tax

Figure 24-1

purposes (contingencies, estimated losses, warranties, discounts, return allowances)?

8. Are there any items included in deferred charges (repairs, advertising, etc.) which may be claimed as deductions in the current return?

9a. Have deferred income and reserve accounts been examined to determine if they include income or deductions which should be reflected in the return?

9b. Are there any future income items whose realization or recognition could be accelerated or deferred, and are there any potential deductions which might properly be accelerated or deferred?

10. If the division or subsidiary made a "bargain sale" or a charitable contribution of appreciated property (including inventory), the workpapers should show all details.

11. Have there been any changes in depreciation methods, lives or capitalization policies during the year?

12. Have any devaluation gains or losses been recognized? If so, was this the result of an accrual or a completed transaction? Please describe the circumstances under which such gains or losses arose.

13a. Has unearned income such as rent, interest and similar items received in advance by the taxpayer under a claim of right been included in possible Schedule M items although it may have been treated as deferred income on the taxpayer's books?

13b. Has income received but deferred in a prior year been included in book income for the current year?

14. Has the division or subsidiary included as a tax preference item (1) allowable depreciation on real property in excess of straight-line depreciation and (2) net long-term capital gains?

15. Have there been any property dispositions which may result in investment credit or depreciation recapture?

16. Have stock issue expenses been identified and segregated, as well as expenses related to reorganizations and acquisitions which are capitalized items?

17. Have there been any writedowns on contracts due to losses anticipated upon the completion of the contract?

18. Have there been any sales of real or personal property that could qualify for the installment method? Has imputed interest under Section 483 been taken into account?

Figure 24-1 *(continued)*

19. Have all, if any, penalties or fines paid or accrued to a government for the violation of any law been reflected in the list of Schedule M items?

20. Indicate by workpaper reference items of income and expense reflected in U.S. operations which are attributable to foreign activities carried on by the domestic companies, and all foreign taxes paid or accrued.

Figure 24-1 *(continued)*

Source: "Corporate Tax Review: the Auditor's Approach," Bruce M. Greenwald and Carl D. Harnick, *The Journal of Accountancy,* Copyright © 1974, by the American Institute of Certified Public Accountants, Inc. May 1974, pp.68-70.

Need for Communications Between Public Accountant and Corporate Client for Effective Tax Planning

Although a review of the client's internal control procedures in the tax department may be beyond the scope of the usual balance sheet audit, communications between auditor and client, based on a checklist of questions such as those raised in Figure 24-1 may assure both that their mutual tax responsibilities are being met. In addition, the financial statements are still the basic responsibility of the company's management, notwithstanding the competence of the firm's auditors and their professional opinion on the compliance of such disclosure with generally accepted accounting principles. Identification of permanent and timing differences, the control of inter-company and intra-company tax reserves, and the inclusion of all contingent tax liabilities in the financial statements are representative of the many items of disclosure that require close communication between the auditor and his client.[5] This is particularly true in view of the increased attention being directed at the impact of tax accounting on reported corporate profits by the Securities and Exchange Commission, security analysts, and the investing public.

Need for Tax Planning Between Parent Corporation and Foreign Subsidiaries

In addition to the importance of close auditor-client cooperation for effective tax management of domestic operations, international companies may find it mandatory that the tax papers and receipts submitted by controlled foreign corporations be verified by someone not connected with their preparation.[6] It may be impossible for any tax manager to know all the tax laws confronting an American company operating in all states, subject to Federal, State and local taxing jurisdiction, much less those of other countries. However, the use of a checklist may again be helpful to the tax manager in order to take advantage of all possible legal tax benefits that are available in different countries and which should be included in the parent's overall tax planning.[7] Figure 24-2 illustrates the kinds of items that the parent corporation's financial officer may find important in discharging his tax accounting responsibilities. Included are tax projections from controllers of foreign subsidiaries and advice regarding major changes in the foreign country's tax legislation. In this way, overall corporate policy may be updated with respect to such things as future investments, cash flow, dividend remittances and minimum dividend distribution.[8]

Space limitations make it impossible in this section to consider pertinent Revenue Acts of various years or other tax regulations, such as those prescribing various tests to determine the amount of income of a controlled foreign corporation that is taxable to the parent. What is stressed is the availability of tools and techniques conducive to good tax management for domestic as well as international corporations.

Tax Accounting Techniques for Control and Planning Purposes

In order to be assured that income not subject to United States taxes will be properly reported to the parent and therefore exempted from taxation, most multinational companies have designed special information-gathering forms. These require detailed breakdowns of base company and non-base company income.[9] Such reporting instruments can be of assistance to multinational companies in profit planning, establishing short-term and long-term cash forecasts, and in preparing the sources and applications of funds' statements upon which expansion programs often depend.[10] Also useful are appropriate instruments and records for domestic corporations in complying with sound tax accounting pronouncements such as those described in Chapter 23.

CHECKLIST ITEMS FACILITATING TAX PLANNING WITH RESPECT TO AMERICAN-CONTROLLED FOREIGN CORPORATIONS*

1. Request tax projections from the respective controllers whereby the non tax-exempted items would be enumerated. Likewise timing differences due to accelerated depreciation, etc., should be shown.

Figure 24-2

2. Management should work out some minimum dividend distribution plan so that at year-end the group of companies can take advantage of any United States Tax concessions.

3. In a less developed country it might be preferable to operate through a less developed country corporation (LDCC) in order to qualify for a much lower effective United States tax rate.

4. Find avenues for bona fide reduction of the taxable profit (accelerated depreciation, inventory write-offs, etc.).

5. Check the local company's tax declarations.

6. Examine the local tax assessments and advise management of the non-deductibility of certain items so that corrective measures can be taken.

7. Verify that unjustified tax assessments are contested.

8. Verify that all relevant papers, tax returns, etc. and tax receipts (photocopies), are forwarded to the parent company in order to obtain foreign tax credits.

9. See that the American management is cognizant of major changes in local tax legislation so that corporate policy, as e.g., for future investments, cash flow, dividend remittances, minimum dividend distribution, etc., can be formed accordingly.

10. See to it that local personnel discharge their tax liabilities properly since in many countries the employer will be held responsible for the employees' personal tax liability.

11. See to it that value-added tax credits are fully taken up as advance payments as long as the tax is incurred within the group members. Related companies—but domiciled outside the EEC—can under certain conditions debit the value added tax to a related company which is domiciled in the respective country where the value added tax arose. The local company can then utilize this debit as an advance payment toward its own value added tax liability and thus grant a credit to the related non-resident company.

12. Check the variance if the effective tax rate of a CFC differs much from the official average rate. Perhaps some special investment benefits were deducted from the tax payments and no entries were made for the timing differences.

Figure 24-2 *(continued)*

*Source: "International Tax Managment," Ernst K. Briner, *Management Accounting,* New York, February 1973, p. 50.

Self-balancing record systems have been developed to accumulate data on both past and current interperiod tax adjustments in compliance with Accounting Principles Board Opinion No. 11.[11] This type of instrument can become a permanent office record of each corporate taxpayer's reconciliations of taxable book year-end earned surplus, and of all adjustments including those of revenue agents.[12] Figure 24-3 shows such a work sheet on which every entry that appears in the corporate income tax return's reconciliation schedule is shown, along with all adjustments shown in the revenue agent's report.[13] For a consolidated return, a workpaper file of this nature should be maintained for each member of the consolidated group with appropriate cross-references to the related companies.[14]

Illustration of Tax Practice in Application of Tax Accounting Principles and Pronouncements

Excerpts from annual corporate reports are contained in exhibits that follow in order to demonstrate the application in practice of many of the concepts embodied in the tax-oriented Accounting Principles Board Opinions discussed in Chapter 23.

Emphasis on Tax Policy Supporting Corporate Financial Statements

As suggested in Chapter 23, Accounting Principles Board Opinion No. 11 emphasized the importance of financial disclosure of income tax expense. In Paragraph 60 of the Opinion, reporting of the results of operations was to include the components of income tax expense for the period. These comprise taxes estimated to be payable, tax effects of timing differences, and tax effects of operating losses.[15] Such amounts were to be allocated to (a) income before extraordinary items and (b) extraordinary items. Separate presentations were recommended in the income statement, but, if combined, an explanatory footnote was to be included, giving the details of this allocation.[16]

Figure 24-4 illustrates clear disclosure in footnote form of the reasons for the differences in the company's effective tax rate of 37% in comparison with the United States corporate rate of 48%. Details of the underlying cause and their effect on the income tax provision are segregated in accordance with APB Opinion No. 11 between permanent and timing differences. The net effect of timing differences, operating loss

A Company
Schedule M Reconciliation
(In thousands of dollars)

Line No.		Balances 12/31/63	1964	1965	1966	1967	Form 1139	RAR 1964-1965	Balances 12/31/67	1968	Balances 12/31/68
1.	Taxable income	$150.0	$7.0	$15.1	$10.0	$ Loss	$(32.1)	$ -0-	$150.0	$5.0	$155.0
2.	Fixed assets										
	a. Tax over book depreciation	20.0	1.7	1.5	1.3	1.1			22.0	0.9	22.9
	b. Gain or (loss) on disposal					(3.6)		0.4			
	c. Repairs capitalized							(4.2)	(3.8)	0.5	(3.3)
3.	Unallowable reserves										
	a. Additions to	(19.0)	(10.0)	(10.0)	(1.0)	(1.0)			(28.0)	(1.0)	(27.0)
	b. Charges against		2.0	3.0	5.0	3.0				2.0	
4.	Expenses deferred on books		10.0	(2.0)	(2.0)	(2.0)			4.0	(2.0)	2.0
5.	Subtotal	$151.0	$10.7	$7.6	$13.3	$(2.5)	$(32.1)	$(3.8)	$144.2	$5.4	$149.6
6.	Carryovers and carrybacks										
	a. Ordinary loss carryover and carryback adjustments					(45.0)	32.1	3.8	(9.1)	9.1	-0-
	b. Capital loss		(0.5)	0.5	0.1				(1.0)	1.0	-0-
	c. Contribution		(0.2)	0.1							
7.	Writeup of building	13.0	(1.0)	(1.0)	(1.0)	(1.0)			9.0	(1.0)	8.0
8.	Nontaxable interest					(1.0)					
9.	Federal income tax					0.2				0.2	
10.	Permanent items summary	(80.0)	(4.5)	(3.7)	(6.2)				(94.2)	(0.9)	(94.9)
11.	Book income for year	$84.0	$4.5	$3.5	$6.2	$(49.3)	$ -0-	$ -0-	$	$13.8	$
12.	Earned surplus—beginning		64.0	66.5	68.0	72.2			48.9	22.9	62.7
13.	Adjustments to surplus										
	a. Sundry debits										
	b. Sundry credits										
	c. Dividends	(20.0)	(2.0)	(2.0)	(2.0)				(26.0)	(2.0)	(28.0)
14.	Earned surplus—ending	$64.0	$66.5	$68.0	$72.2	$22.9			$22.9	$34.7	$34.7
15. (B)	Federal tax paid	$70.2	$2.8	$7.0	$4.2	$ -0-	$(14.1)	$ -0-	$70.2	$0.8	$71.0
16. (B)	Investment credit			$0.3	$1.0	$1.0	$0.1	$0.3	$1.4	$0.6	$0.8
17. (B)	Foreign tax credit				$0.5	$0.5	$0.2	$	$0.7	$(0.7)	$ -0-

(A)

(A) Assumes any foreign tax credit or investment credit used in years 1964, 1965 or 1966 was carried back to applicable years and unrecovered portions are shown on bottom two lines of this column.

(B) Memo items.

Figure 24-3

sions deferred in prior years are being used to reduce subsequent provisions for income taxes which are higher because of tax depreciation or emergency facility amortization deductions having been claimed in such prior years on certain properties in Missouri, Illinois and Iowa. These treatments are in accordance with applicable regulatory commission policies.

INCOME TAXES

For income tax purposes, the Company and its utility subsidiaries compute depreciation using the most liberalized methods allowed by the Internal Revenue Service. Net depreciable property and plant used in this computation excludes costs (primarily the allowance for funds used during construction, taxes, pensions, and certain other items) which are charged to property and plant for financial statement purposes but are treated as expenses when incurred for income tax purposes.

The resulting reductions in income taxes are accounted for as deferred income taxes with respect to properties in Illinois and as reductions of current income taxes with respect to properties in Missouri and Iowa. Investment tax credits are treated in a similar manner. All other benefits from tax laws and regulations are accounted for, in the determination of earnings, as reductions of income taxes. These treatments are consistent with the rate-making policies of the respective state regulatory commissions.

UNBILLED REVENUE

The Company and its utility subsidiaries record on their books the estimated amount of accrued, but unbilled, revenue and also the accrued liability for the related taxes.

Figure 24-5 (continued)

Source: Union Electric Company, Annual Report 1973, Notes to Financial Statements, p. 18.

Income Taxes for the years ended September 30, 19X3 and 19X2 are summarized below (in millions):

	19X3	19X2
U.S.—current	$47.9	$35.4
Foreign—current	9.9	12.1
Deferred	5.8	5.6
State	5.6	4.4
	$69.2	$57.5

Figure 24-6

Investment tax credits applied as a reduction of income taxes amounted to $3.0 million in fiscal 19X3 and $2.5 million in 19X2. The provision for income taxes includes an amount sufficient to pay additional United States federal income taxes on unremitted foreign earnings except for certain tax exempt earnings, primarily in Puerto Rico, which are expected to be remitted in a tax-free liquidation.

The Internal Revenue Service has examined and cleared income tax returns of the Company through fiscal 19X1. Examinations for the fiscal years 19X2 through 19X0 have been completed and settled, except for certain matters relating principally to allocation of income and expenses between the Company and affiliated foreign companies. The income taxes liability account is considered adequate to provide for possible additional federal and state income taxes which might result from these and subsequent years' examinations.

These differences result primarily from excess tax depreciation, computed on accelerated bases, over book depreciation and, to a lesser extent, from estimated future federal income taxes on unremitted earnings of foreign subsidiaries.

Investment Tax Credits are accounted for by the flow-through method. Under this method, credits are taken as a reduction of the provision for income taxes in the year realized.

Deferred Income Taxes are recognized for the effect of timing differences between financial and tax reporting.

Figure 24-6 *(continued)*

Source: Ralston Purina Company Annual Report 1973, Summary of Accounting Policies, pp. 32 and 33.

Accrual of Income Taxes as a Timing Difference

Undistributed earnings of subsidiaries and corporate joint ventures included in consolidated earnings, were the subject of tax accrual under APB Opinion No. 23. Such accruals were to be accounted for as timing differences, unless evidence existed that such undistributed earnings would not be transferred to the investor.[17] Reasons for the absence of accrual of income tax expense for such earnings have been mentioned previously and include those intended for reinvestment or realization through a tax-free liquidation.

With respect to undistributed earnings of investees other than subsidiaries or joint ventures, included in consolidated earnings, APB Opinion No. 24 requires the accrual of income taxes and treatment as a timing difference as shown in Figure 24-7. Disclosure is made in a footnote to the effect that provision has been made for taxes on income attributable to the Company's share of undistributed earnings of investee companies in which the Company *cannot* control investment policies. For further clarification, the footnote explains tax treatment of subsidiaries, indicating that *no* provision is made for United States taxes on income on the Company's share of undistributed earnings of investee companies in which the Company *can* control or significantly influence investment policies. The reason given is that such earnings have been invested or are expected to be invested for the indefinite future.

Taxes on Income

Adequate provision is made annually for United States and foreign taxes on income. Such provision recognizes additional United States taxes on income attributable to the Company's share of undistributed earnings of investee companies in which the Company cannot control investment policies. No provision is made for United States taxes on income on the Company's share of undistributed earnings of investee companies in which the Company can control or significantly influence investment policies since such earnings have been invested or are expected to be invested for the indefinite future.

Investment tax credits are reflected as a reduction of the provision for income taxes in the year in which such credits are claimed.

(5) United States Taxes on Income

The Internal Revenue Service has examined the Company's income tax returns for the three years ended December 31, 19X8 and asserted certain adjustments thereto. The Company has agreed to a partial settlement of these adjustments and the resulting additional taxes have been paid. The remaining adjustment involves the Service's position that the Company should use an accounting practice which would increase the valuation of the Company's inventories, thereby increasing tax liabilities and earnings. The additional deficiency based on the remaining adjustment asserted by the Service, if sustained, would not exceed $375,000. However, legal counsel is of the opinion that meritorious defenses exist as to this adjustment and that additional taxes, if any, payable by the Company in final settlement will be substantially less than the asserted deficiency. Although the ultimate disposition of this matter is indeterminate at this time, management is of the opinion that any additional taxes which might become payable as a result of this controversy will not have a material adverse effect on the financial position or results of operations of the Company.

Figure 24-7

The Company's share of undistributed earnings of investee companies in which the Company can control or significantly influence investment policies on which deferred United States taxes on income have not been provided aggregated $9,425,000 and $8,160,000 at December 31, 19X2 and 19X1, respectively.

The investment credit, which amounted to approximately $425,000 and $80,000 in 19X2 and 19X1, has been reflected as a reduction of the provision for income taxes.

Figure 24-7 *(continued)*

Source: P.R. Mallory & Co. Inc., 1972 Annual Report, pp. 22, 23.

Deferred Credits—Income Taxes

Figure 24-8 explains the provision for the deferred income tax effects connected with transactions recorded in the company's accounts in a different tax period from that used for tax return reporting. Such accounting procedures allocate the income tax effects to the period in which the transactions are recorded so that the balance sheet shows the cumulative effect of net charges against earnings, deferring appropriate amounts to future periods.

Deferred Credits—Income Taxes

The financial statements reflect provision for the deferred income tax effects related to transactions recorded in the accounts in a period different from that in which these transactions are reported for income tax purposes. The principal deferred tax effects for which provision is made are those related to intangible drilling costs, exploratory expenditures, depreciation, and employee plans. This accounting policy allocates the income tax effects of transactions to the period in which such transactions are recorded for financial reporting purposes.

The deferred credits for income taxes shown in the balance sheet represent the cumulative effect of net charges against earnings to defer these income tax effects to appropriate future periods in the Company's financial statements.

No provision has been made for possible income taxes that might be payable if accumulated earnings of subsidiary companies were distributed, since the subsidiaries have reinvested these earnings. Similarly,

Figure 24-8

provision has not been made for possible income taxes that might be payable if the undistributed earnings of nonsubsidiary "corporate joint venture" companies accounted for on the equity method were distributed.

Figure 24-8 *(continued)*

Source: Texaco Inc. and Subsidiary Companies, Annual Report for 1972, p. 27.

Restatement of Financials Caused by Accounting Changes

A reclassification of current income taxes to long-term deferred taxes is explained in Figure 24-9. The financial statements reflected adjustments intended to change the timing of the Company's pension expense deduction for tax purposes—which difference will reverse over the 40 year period of funding the past service pension costs.

Changes in accounting principles are indicated in Figure 24-10, with respect to the recording of estimated income taxes that will become payable when certain undistributed earnings of foreign subsidiaries are distributed as dividends. The resultant reduction in earnings of both the current and prior year are reported in a footnote in compliance with Accounting Principles Board Opinion No. 23.

RAYBESTOS-MANHATTAN, INC. (DEC)

Notes to Consolidated Financial Statements

Note 1: Deferred Income Taxes—The 19X1 financial statements have been restated to reflect the reclassification of $1,474,230 from current income taxes to long-term deferred income taxes because of the Company's decision to change the timing of its pension expense deduction for tax purposes on its 19X1 consolidated tax return filed in 19X2. This timing difference will reverse over the 40 year period of funding the past service pension costs.

The deferred income taxes shown on the balance sheet at December 31, 19X2, as a current asset, of $2,577,144 result principally from the timing difference of the deductibility for tax purposes of expenses connected with the discontinuance of certain product lines. These timing differences will reverse in 19X3.

Figure 24-9

Source: Raybestos-Manhattan, Inc., Annual Report for 1972, reprinted from Accounting Trends & Techniques, American Institute of Certified Public Accountants, Inc., 1973, p. 27.

LIBBY, McNEILL & LIBBY (JUN)

Notes to Consolidated Financial Statements
Note E (in part): Income Taxes—

In accordance with Opinion No. 23 of Accounting Principles Board of the American Institute of Certified Public Accountants, the Company has recorded in the accounts estimated income taxes which will become payable when certain undistributed earnings of foreign subsidiaries are distributed as dividends. As a result of this change in accounting method, earnings retained in the business as of July 5, 19X0 have been reduced by $710,000 and net earnings as previously reported for the year ended July 3, 19X1 have been reduced by $116,000. The cumulative amount of undistributed foreign subsidiary earnings at July 1, 19X2 on which the Company has not recognized U.S. income taxes is $27,000,000. It is the intention of the Company to reinvest such undistributed earnings.

Figure 24-10

Source: Accounting Trends & Techniques, 1973, *Ibid.,* p.83.

Accounting Changes Required in Connection with Investments in Subsidiaries

Figure 24-11 illustrates a restatement of figures previously reported in the Company's annual report to provide for future income taxes on undistributed income in accordance with APB Opinion No. 24. Changes for prior years reflect investments in affiliates on the equity method of accounting. The adoption of the equity method for investments in associated companies (corporate joint ventures and 20% to 50% owned companies) required the restatement of financial statements as indicated in Figure 24-12.

ACCOUNTANTS' OPINION IS QUALIFIED AS TO CON-
SISTENCY FOR CHANGE TO PROVIDING DEFERRED
TAXES ON UNDISTRIBUTED EARNINGS OF
AFFILITATES

Celanese Corporation   12/31/X2   PMM   2823·

Accountants' Opinion, page 18:

Such principles, after restatement of the figures previously reported in the published annual reports (a) for years prior to 19X2 to reflect provision

Figure 24-11

for future income taxes on undistributed income of affiliates as required by Accounting Principles Board Opinion 24, and (b) for years prior to 19X2 to reflect investments in affiliates on the equity method of accounting, have been applied on a consistent basis.

Figure 24-11

Source: Haskins & Sells, Accounting Practices 1973, Illustrative Items of Current Interest from Published Annual Reports, Vol. 2, p. 619.

ACCOUNTANTS' OPINION INDICATES CONCURRENCE WITH ACCOUNTING CHANGE

Nation Steel Corporation   12/31/X2   E&E   3312

Accountants' Opinion, page 9:

. . . in conformity with generally accepted accounting principles applied on a consistent basis after restatement for the change, with which we concur, in the method of accounting for investments in associated companies as explained in Note B to the financial statements.

Note B, page 14:

Prior to 19X2, only investments in unconsolidated subsidiaries were accounted for by the equity method. In 19X2, pursuant to a recent opinion of the Accounting Principles Board, the Corporation adopted the equity method of accounting for investments in associated companies (corporate joint ventures and 20% to 50% owned companies). As a result of the change the 19X1 financial statements have been restated.

Figure 24-12

Source: *Ibid.*

A retroactive change to the equity method for non-consolidated subsidiaries is referred to in the Accountants' Opinion contained in Figure 24-13.

RETROACTIVE CHANGE TO EQUITY METHOD OF ACCOUNTING FOR NONCONSOLIDATED SUBSIDIARIES REFERRED TO IN ACCOUNTANTS' OPINION

Swift and Company   10/28/X2   AY   2011

Accountants' Opinion, page 42:

. . . in conformity with generally accepted accounting principles consistently applied during the period, except for the 19X2 change in the method of determining pension expense, and after restatement for the changes in methods of accounting for (1) inventories, (2) exploration and development costs incurred in the oil and gas operations, and (3) investments in

Figure 24-13

affiliated companies, all as described in the Financial Comments under the caption "Changes in Accounting." We concur with the above mentioned changes in accounting.

Figure 24-13 *(continued)*

Source: *Ibid.*

The need to restate financial statements of prior years is reported in footnote fashion in Figure 24-14 to give effect to a change from the former practice of providing federal income taxes on *all* undistributed earnings of subsidiaries outside the United States. The restatement provides taxes on only that portion of such earnings that will be distributed.

Note B, pages 22 and 23:

Prior to 19X2, federal income taxes were provided on the undistributed earnings of subsidiaries outside the United States. In 19X2, in conformity with Opinion No. 23 of the Accounting Principles Board, such provisions were adjusted to reflect only estimated taxes to be paid on earnings expected to be distributed. In addition, prior to 19X2 the company expensed as incurred the income taxes on unrealized profit which resulted from sales between affiliated companies and which was eliminated from the inventory accounts upon consolidation. In 19X2 such income taxes were recognized as timing differences.

Financial statements for the 19X1 have been restated to reflect these changes. The effect on income for 19X2 and on income as previously reported for the year 19X1 is as follows:

	Increase	
	19X2	19X1
Net income	$5,400,000	$4,350,000
Earnings per share	$.08	$.06

Figure 24-14

Source: *Ibid*, p. 809.

Improved Income Tax Disclosure in the Financial Statements

The Consolidated Statement of Income, shown in Figure 24-15, reports a "Credit for Federal income taxes (note 7)" under the caption,

"Expenses." In Figure 24-16 a footnote details the components of the provision for federal income taxes for the current year, in comparison with the previous year. In addition, the net credit applicable to the consolidated group is shown in detail, including the investment tax credits and deferred taxes for each year.

A slightly different approach is shown in the Statement of Consolidated Income and Retained Earnings in Figure 24-17, in which the provision for income taxes is split between current and deferred and the deferred item is described in a footnote (Figure 24-18). The Company's balance sheet makes reference to this footnote, following the item, "Deferred Credits—Income Taxes (Note 3)," as reproduced in Figure 24-19. In addition, the Statement of Changes in Consolidated Financial Position includes a "Provision for income taxes—deferred (Note 3)" as an item added back to net income in arriving at sources of income provided by operations. See Figure 24-20. The latter exhibit shows the composition of working capital of the Company to include, as an addition during the year, the item of "Estimated Income Taxes."

In compliance with urgent appeals from the Securities and Exchange Commission and other interested parties, annual reports are appearing with expanded explanatory material to support the financial statements. For example, Figure 24-21 indicates an effort to explain the Company's high effective tax rate in the financial review section of the annual report. Figure 24-22 explains what the Company describes as an "abnormally low effective tax rate," listing four reasons for this development.

Another company reports that "deferred taxes may never have to be paid" and supports this contention in Figure 24-23. A final exhibit (24-24) poses the question to its investors in the business review section of its annual report, "Why is St. Joe's effective corporate tax rate so low?" The reasons given include the effects of depletion on the Company's mineral resources.

A Look to the Future

Exhibits used in this chapter suggest the extent to which the Accounting Principles Board Opinions have had an impact on financial disclosure with respect to tax accounting. Such expanded coverage has not only been enlightening to readers in the financial community but should be of real value to management itself in its forecasting and financial planning efforts for future years. The use of the review techniques suggested in this chapter can afford management, as well as tax managers, the benefit of past years' experiences in planning the future. The objective "touching all bases" through the use of checklists, questionnaires, worksheets, and other tax accounting tools should be to achieve the ultimate test of good tax management—the minimization of the current year's tax liability through appropriate deferrals to, and the adoption of sound tax accounting policies for future years.

CONSOLIDATED STATEMENT OF INCOME

Year ended June 30, 19X3 with comparative figures for 19X2

Income:	19X3	19X2
Interest, fees and finance charges earned (note 3)	$22,514,868	$19,367,444
Interest and dividends on investment securities	7,119,533	5,431,439
Other income	1,289,250	1,124,436
	$30,923,651	$25,923,319
Equity in net income of industrial subsidiaries, less intercompany eliminations and adjustments and borrowing costs (net of income taxes) applicable to cash investments in such subsidiaries (note 4)	3,116,491	2,156,084
	34,040,142	28,079,403
Expenses:		
Salaries	6,557,938	6,139,540
Interest	15,387,603	12,487,540
Provision for doubtful accounts and loan losses	1,367,903	675,080
Credit for Federal income taxes (note 7)	(1,572,861)	(1,482,267)
Other	7,368,085	6,427,813
	29,108,668	24,247,706
Income before security gains and minority interests	4,931,474	3,831,697
Securities gains, less related Federal, state and local income taxes of $274,125 in 19X3 and $474,893 in 19X2	244,725	467,897
Income before minority interests	5,176,199	4,299,594
Minority interests in income of consolidated subsidiaries	271,491	297,625
Net income	$ 4,904,708	$ 4,001,969
Income per average common share (note 1h):		
Before securities gains, net	$ .95	$ .72
Net income	$1.00	$ .82
Income per average common share assuming full dilution (note 1h):		
Before securities gains, net	$ .84	$ .67
Net income	$ .87	$ .74

Figure 24-15

Source: Standard Prudential Company, Annual Report 1973, p. 8.

7) Federal Income Values:

The Company and its domestic subsidiaries, including the industrial subsidiaries, file a consolidated Federal income tax return. Consolidated

Figure 24-16

returns have been examined through June 30, 19X8. Subsidiaries accrue for income taxes as though they were filing separate returns and make periodic payments for such taxes to the parent company. The reduction in taxes in consolidation, arising, principally from deductible parent company interest charges, is credited to the parent.

The total provision for Federal income taxes for 19X3 and 19X2 by the Company and all of its domestic subsidiaries was allocated as follows:

Non-consolidated industrial subsidiaries	$ 3,925,921	$ 2,729,330
Consolidated group (credits):		
Borrowing costs applicable to cash invest-. . . .		
ment in industrial subsidiaries	(1,192,592)	(1,036,707)
Applicable to securities gains	220,013	426,780
Other (net credit)	(1,572,861)	(1,482,267)
	$ 1,380,481	$ 637,136

The net credit applicable to the consolidated group includes investment tax credits and deferred taxes as follows:

	19X3	19X2
Investment tax credit	($150,887)	($183,234)
Deferred taxes	354,912	136,049

Figure 24-16 *(continued)*

Source: Standard Prudential, *Ibid.*, p. 9.

STATEMENTS OF CONSOLIDATED INCOME AND RETAINED EARNINGS

For the years ended December 31, 19X2 and 19X1

Gross Income:	19X2	19X1
Sales and services	$8,692,991,000	$7,529,054,000
Equity in net income of nonsubsidiary companies, dividends, interest, and other income*	278,864,000	228,228,000
	$8,971,855,000	$7,757,282,000

Deductions:		
Costs and operating expenses*	$5,892,033,000	$4,845,317,000
Selling, general and administrative expenses	788,867,000	721,998,000
Dry hole costs	42,507,000	48,416,000
Depreciation, depletion, and amortization	426,872,000	392,768,000
Interest charges	107,810,000	83,964,000
Taxes other than income taxes**	254,260,000	229,059,000

Figure 24-17

Provision for income taxes—current	486,800,000	415,600,000
—deferred (Note 3)	69,492,000	103,543,000
Minority interest in net income	14,174,000	12,749,000
	$8,082,815,000	$6,853,414,000

Net Income	$ 889,040,000	$ 903,868,000
Net income per share (based on average number of		
shares outstanding)	$3.27	$3.32

Retained Earnings:

Balance at beginning of year	$4,497,126,000	$4,028,990,000
Add:		
Net income for the year	889,040,000	903,868,000
Deduct:		
Cash dividends—$1.66 per share in 19X2 and $1.60 in 19X1 . .	451,609,000	435,732,000
Balance at end of year	$4,934,557,000	$4,497,126,000

Figure 24-17 *(continued)*

*Restated, as described in description of significant accounting policies—investments and advances. In addition, motor fuel and other taxes collected from consumers and paid (or accrued) to governmental agencies in the United States and abroad amounted to $1,777,173,000 during 19X2 and $1,620,516,000 during 19X1.

Source: Texaco Inc. Annual Report, 1972, p. 23.

Note 3. Deferred Credits—Income Taxes

Texaco's accounting policy with respect to deferred income taxes is stated in the Description of Significant Accounting Policies.

The undistributed earnings of subsidiary companies, and of non-subsidiary "corporate joint venture" companies accounted for on the equity method, for which deferred income taxes have not been provided at December 31, 19X2, because of reinvestment of earnings by the companies involved, amounted to $608,182,000 and $487,613,000, respectively.

Figure 24-18

Liabilities and Stockholders' Equity	19X2	19X1
Current Liabilities:		
Notes payable and long-term debt due within one year	$ 742,985,000	$ 366,373,000
Accounts payable and accrued liabilities	1,129,149,000	976,470,000
Estimated income taxes	290,678,000	311,255,000
Total current liabilities	$ 2,162,812,000	$ 1,654,098,000
Long-Term Debt (Note 2)	$ 1,359,680,000	$ 1,289,614,000
Deferred Credits—Income Taxes (Note 3)	$ 1,171,388,000	$ 1,101,896,000
Reserves for Employe Plans (Note 4)	$ 70,969,000	$ 60,280,000
Minority Interest in Subsidiary Companies	$ 92,443,000	$ 82,364,000
Stockholders' Equity (Notes 2 and 4):		
Capital Stock—par value $6.25:		
Shares authorized—350,000,000		
Shares issued—274,285,270 in **19X2** and 274,285,268 in **19X1**,		
including treasury stock	$ 1,714,283,000	$ 1,714,283,000
Paid-in capital in excess of par value (Note 5)	597,904,000	597,364,000
Retained earnings	4,934,557,000	4,497,126,000
	$ 7,246,744,000	$ 6,808,773,000
Less—Capital stock held in treasury—2,266,297 shares in **19X2** and		
2,043,856 shares in **19X1**, at cost	71,862,000	63,733,000
Total stockholders' equity	$ 7,174,882,000	$ 6,745,040,000
Total	$12,032,174,000	$10,933,292,000

Figure 24-19

Source: Texaco Inc., Annual Report 1972, p. 30.

Consolidated Balance Sheet
As of December 31, **19X2** *and* **19X1**

	19X2	19X1
Assets		
Current Assets:		
Cash	$ 266,100,000	$ 290,730,000
Marketable securities and cash investments—at cost	283,619,000	213,639,000
Accounts and notes receivable, less allowance for doubtful accounts of		
$48,000,000 in **19X2** and **19X1**	1,745,486,000	1,540,083,000
Inventories:		
Crude oil, petroleum products, and other merchandise	763,061,000	719,868,000
Materials and supplies	60,694,000	56,062,000
Total current assets	$ 3,118,960,000	$ 2,820,382,000
Investments and Advances (Note 1)	$ 1,025,307,000	$ 844,404,000
Properties, Plant, and Equipment—at Cost:		
Producing	$ 6,734,826,000	$ 6,287,694,000
Manufacturing	2,268,263,000	2,087,230,000
Marketing	1,825,482,000	1,738,233,000
Marine	517,574,000	493,491,000
Pipe lines	387,476,000	369,028,000
Other	105,114,000	98,051,000
	$11,838,735,000	$11,073,727,000
Less—Depreciation, depletion, and amortization	3,990,022,000	3,850,780,000
Net properties, plant, and equipment	$ 7,848,713,000	$ 7,222,947,000
Deferred Charges	$ 39,194,000	$ 45,559,000
Total	$12,032,174,000	$10,933,292,000

Figure 24-19 *(continued)*

Source: Texaco Inc., Annual Report 1972, p. 29.

Statement of Changes in Consolidated Financial Position

For the years ended December 31, 19X2 and 19X1

Source:	19X2	19X1
Net income	$ 889,040,000	$ 903,868,000
Depreciation, depletion, and amortization	426,872,000	392,768,000
Provision for income taxes—deferred (Note 3)	69,492,000	103,543,000
Equity in undistributed earnings of nonsubsidiary companies (Note 1)	(80,869,000)	(121,471,000)
Minority interest in net income	14,174,000	12,749,000
Provided by operations	$1,318,709,000	$1,291,457,000
Properties, plant, and equipment retirements and sales	59,955,000	38,189,000
Additions to long-term debt (Note 2)	123,917,000	334,666,000
	$1,502,581,000	$1,664,312,000

Disposition		
Properties, plant, and equipment expenditures	$1,112,593,000	$1,047,185,000
Investments in nonsubsidiary companies	26,205,000	55,918,000
Total capital expenditures	$1,138,798,000	$1,103,103,000
Reductions in long-term debt (Note 2)	53,851,000	59,810,000
Purchases of treasury stock	9,066,000	4,000,000
Cash dividends paid to:		
The Company's stockholders	451,609,000	435,732,000
Minority stockholders of subsidiary companies	4,095,000	3,447,000
Other (net)	55,298,000	10,249,000
	$1,712,717,000	$1,616,341,000

Added to (or withdrawn from) working capital	$ (210,136,000)	$ 47,971,000
Working capital:		
At beginning of year	$1,166,284,000	$1,118,313,000
Additions (withdrawals) during year:		
Cash	(24,630,000)	54,982,000
Marketable securities and cash investments	69,980,000	(25,239,000)
Accounts and notes receivable, less allowance for doubtful accounts . . .	205,403,000	84,341,000
Inventories	47,825,000	83,172,000
Notes payable and long-term debt due within one year	(376,612,000)	24,202,000
Accounts payable and accrued liabilities	(152,679,000)	(190,729,000)
Estimated income taxes	20,577,000	17,242,000
	$ (210,136,000)	$ 47,971,000
At end of year	$ 956,148,000	$1,166,284,000

Figure 24-20

Source: Texaco Inc. and Subsidiary Companies Annual Report 1972, p. 31.

FINANCIAL REVIEW EXPLAINS HIGH EFFECTIVE TAX RATE

White Motor Corporation   12/31/X2   E&E   3711

Financial Review, page 11:

European Farm

The company continued to show losses in this sector. In 19X2, these losses were aggravated by the need to redesign the line of combines, to repair units sold in prior years and to absorb customers' interest costs on financed units which were not functioning. New operating management has resolved these problems and improvement can be expected in 19X3. Significantly, this operation is a foreign subsidiary. As such, its losses are not tax recoverable and fully penalize the reported net income of the corporation. For this reason, the reported income tax equal to 52.3 per cent of pre-tax corporate profit is the effective tax rate although it appears to be disproportionate. In February, 19X3, White decided to convert this operation into a branch of the North American operations which will result in tax recovery status for any future operating losses and enable the company to claim an investment tax recovery.

Figure 24-21

Source: Haskins & Sells, *op. cit.,* p. 785.

ABNORMALLY LOW EFFECTIVE TAX RATE

Uniroyal, Inc.   12/31/X2   H&S   3011

Notes, page 29:

The ratios between total Federal and foreign income taxes and income before taxes for the years 19X2 and 19X1 were influenced by investment credits; variations in income between countries having different tax rates; operating results in certain foreign countries which had little or no tax impact; and income tax at capital gains rates.

Figure 24-22

Source: *Ibid.,* p. 788.

Perhaps even more importantly, expanded tax disclosure and improved tax management techniques reflect the direction of corporate managerial thinking. The pressures from the financial community have resulted in recent years in an emphasis on financial planning including profit forecasting which is reflected in the financial statements and in expanded, explanatory footnotes, business reviews, and financial reviews in corporate annual reports. Such financial disclosure is in large part based on the vastly accelerated flow of accounting pronouncements of recent years, including those of the Accounting Principles Board, the Financial Accounting Standards Board and the Securities and Exchange Commission's Accounting Releases, as reported and discussed throughout this book.

COMMENT THAT DEFERRED TAXES MAY NEVER HAVE TO BE PAID

Seaboard Coast Line Industries, Inc.   12/31/X2   H&S   4011

Note 1, page 19:

Deferred taxes are provided in the financial statements to recognize the tax effect of significant timing differences, principally resulting from deductions (net) for depreciation and amortization of property for income tax purposes in excess of those recorded in the accounts. Accumulated tax effects resulting from recognizing these timing differences, which are shown in the accompanying consolidated balance sheet as deferred taxes, are not liabilities and in the normal course of business may never be paid because Industries believes that at its present rate of growth tax deferrals will continue to increase.

Figure 24-23

Source: *Ibid.,* p. 821.

ST.JOE MINERAL CORPORATION   12/31/X2   H&S   3332

Business Review, page 14:

Q. Why is St. Joe's effective corporate tax rate so low? A. It is at 32%, in the normal range for companies like St. Joe who deplete their natural resource assets. Also, CanDel pays no Canadian federal taxes because of a substantial carry-forward credit. However, it is worthy of note that St. Joe paid $15,932,341 in total taxes to federal, state, and local governments in 19X2—the federal income tax is only the most visible portion.

Figure 24-24

Source: *Ibid.,*p. 780.

A parting word of encouragement may be appropriate at this point. Many members of the accounting profession—both in public and private accounting—have felt pressures of "crisis" proportions as a result of the increased sophistication of financial critics, disclosures of court proceedings against public accountants and corporate executives for alleged misleading financial statements, and the attendant publicity, resulting from an increased interest on the part of the financial press. But a close look at the word "crisis" as depicted in the rich, picture language of the Orient shows that it is composed of two characters—danger and opportunity. The first of these may continue to haunt accountants for the rest of their professional lives. The second—opportunity—*should* continue to haunt and encourage the accounting profession to expand on the progress already experienced, and as illustrated here, to provide even greater service to the financial community. Such service appears to demand not only the kind of sound pronouncements on vital, timely accounting topics and problem areas that have been hammered out during the past decade, but also their close scrutiny, before acceptance, by practitioners in public and private accounting alike.

REFERENCES

[1]"Corporate Tax Review: the Auditor's Approach," Bruce M. Greenwald and Carl D. Harnick, *The Journal of Accountancy,* May 1974, p. 74.

[2]*Ibid.*

[3]*Ibid.,* p. 64.

[4]*Ibid.*

[5]*Ibid.,* pp. 64, 65.

[6]"International Tax Management," Ernst K. Briner, *Management Accounting,* February 1973, p. 47.

[7]*Ibid.,* p. 48.

[8]*Ibid.,* p. 50.

[9]*Ibid.,* p. 47.

[10]*Ibid.,* pp. 47, 48.

[11]"Accounting Records for Interperiod Tax Adjustments," Allen Finkenaur, *The Journal of Accountancy,* January 1970, p. 44.

[12]*Ibid.*

[13]*Ibid.*

[14]*Ibid.,* p. 48.

[15] Accounting Trends and Techniques, Annual Survey of Accounting Practices Followed in 600 Stockholders' Reports, Twenty-Seventh Edition 1973, p. 247.

[16]*Ibid.*

[17]*Ibid.,* p. 258.

INDEX